ROAD
WARRIORS

ROAD WARRIORS

DREAMS AND NIGHTMARES ALONG THE INFORMATION HIGHWAY

Daniel Burstein and David Kline

A DUTTON BOOK

DUTTON
Published by the Penguin Group
Penguin Books USA Inc., 375 Hudson Street,
New York, New York 10014, U.S.A.
Penguin Books Ltd, 27 Wrights Lane,
London W8 5TZ, England
Penguin Books Australia Ltd, Ringwood,
Victoria, Australia
Penguin Books Canada Ltd, 10 Alcorn Avenue,
Toronto, Ontario, Canada M4V 3B2
Penguin Books (N.Z.) Ltd, 182–190 Wairau Road,
Auckland 10, New Zealand

Penguin Books Ltd, Registered Offices:
Harmondsworth, Middlesex, England

First published by Dutton, an imprint of Dutton Signet,
a division of Penguin Books USA Inc.
Distributed in Canada by McClelland & Stewart Inc.

First Printing, November, 1995
10   9   8   7   6   5   4   3   2   1

 REGISTERED TRADEMARK—MARCA REGISTRADA

LIBRARY OF CONGRESS CATALOGING-IN-PUBLICATION DATA:

Burstein, Daniel.
    Road warriors : dreams and nightmares along the information highway/
Daniel Burstein and David Kline.
        p.   cm.
    Includes index.
    ISBN 0-525-93726-9
    1. Information superhighway—United States.   2. Telecommunication
policy—United States.   3. Telecommunication—United States.
I. Kline, David.   II. Title.
HE7572.U6B87   1995
004.6′7—dc20   95-32859
                                                                        CIP

Printed in the United States of America
Set in Bodoni Book

For David Daniel Burstein and Daniel Nathan Kline

who will come of age
in the twenty-first century
and find answers to the questions
we have left behind here

CONTENTS

ROAD
WARRIORS

INTRODUCTION

The Utopia Paradox

The future is an elusive beast. We hear its approaching footsteps, but just when it seems nearly upon us we discover that it's still quite some distance away. So we look back at the tracks it has laid through history, hoping to predict the shape and manner of its next appearance. But still it sneaks up on us in unexpected ways. It is a ghost, a specter wandering somewhere out in that distance between tomorrow's enormous possibilities and today's prosaic realities.

For those who wish to glimpse the future, navigating this netherland between potentiality and actuality has become more challenging than ever. Civilization now stands at one of those great historic junctures that arise only a few times in a millennium. The central organizing forces of society are being reshaped by powerful new technologies of light and silicon. But in what ways, and to what end?

To even begin to answer these questions is difficult, not least because the pace of technological advance in recent years has become so swift. It was only one decade ago, after all, that computers began to enter the lives of a statistically noticeable portion of the population. Now, seemingly overnight, computers have sneaked their way into nearly a third of American homes. CD-ROM encyclopedias didn't exist four years ago. Now they outsell printed versions by a mile. When our last president took office, cellular phones were used mainly by the rich. Today they are practically given away to middle-class consumers. Only yesterday we worried about how much violence our children watched on television. Now, in two-thirds of all households with kids, interactive video games show them how to rip the blood-soaked spines out of 3-D simulated bad guys.

But even more than their speed, it is the scope of today's technological changes that makes any definitive picture of the future elusive. The next few decades will witness profound alterations not only in the ways we live, work, entertain, and inform ourselves, but also in the strategies of businesses, the dynamics of the marketplace, the competition between companies and between countries, the process of wealth creation, and even the role of government. By whatever name we choose to call it—the Internet, multimedia, interactive TV, or the Information Highway—the Digital Revolution is going to transform the personal future of everyone reading this book.

Have you ever sent a wireless fax from the beach? Read a customized multimedia "newspaper" on a portable electronic tablet? Conducted remote "due diligence" on a proposed corporate acquisition from a plane 35,000 feet in the air and then beamed your report to the board of directors in advance of your arrival? Typed "cereal and diapers" into your Internet-linked computer and watched your printer spit out grocery coupons redeemable at the supermarket? Or shared family news, gossip and home videos via your interactive television with relatives across the country? Like the AT&T commercial says, "You will!" But of far greater significance than these new supergadgets and services will be the greatly expanded opportunities that will exist for meaningful work, for individual enrichment, and for personal communication.

But along with these new opportunities will come new challenges for which there exists no previous frame of reference. Companies in nearly all industries, for example, will have to contend with vastly speeded-up product cycles, splintered advertising targets, and a fragmented marketplace in which competitive advantage depends upon a rapid response to small shifts in consumer needs. In the social arena, the challenges will be equally unsettling. How, for example, do we act upon the will of the people when a cacophony of two hundred million electronically linked voices are heard and measured—instantly and endlessly—on any given issue? And for all the personal power to reach and communicate with others on a global basis offered by the Internet, are there not also dangers lurking in the shadows of this brave new world? Writes Lewis H. Lapham, editor of *Harper's:*

> [The Internet] invites each of us to construct a preferred reality, furnished with the objects of wish and dream. The commonwealth of shared meaning divides into remote worlds of our own invention, receding from one another literally at the speed of light. We need never see or talk to anybody with whom we don't agree.

Perhaps, but there is no escaping the impact of a technology that focuses all the contradictions of postmodern society for all to see. The Internet is a garden of eden of creativity, opportunity, and personal empowerment! No, it's a Pandora's box of narcissistic rant, obscenity, and avoidance of social responsibility! It's everything, apparently, except a floor wax or a dessert topping—how could such a powerful and illuminating mirror be anything else?

Heady stuff, to be sure, and it's no wonder that we look to the future with both excitement and anxiety. Most of us, after all, would feel hard pressed to say that we fully grasp the operating instructions for *this* world, let alone the next. But perhaps we may take some comfort in knowing that however exotic the landscape of tomorrow's world might become, the felt core of human existence—the urge for family in whatever form, the need for love and belonging, and the desire to live a significant and productive life—will remain as familiar as always.

While few would contest this point, some of the Digital Revolution's most articulate thinkers argue, in effect, that the world is a blank slate, and that digital bits and bytes are electronic chisels for sculpting an entirely new world order. The shopping mall is doomed, they say, because online commerce will create an electronic mall that meets all our needs. Books, with all their richness of feel and weight of narrative, will be superseded by multimedia "stories" that can be rewritten by the "user." Corporate structures will be split asunder by the centrifugal forces of decentralized computer networks and replaced by a panoply of "virtual" businesses continuously popping in and out of existence like bubbles in a boiling sea of change. And when all citizens are tied together in electronic communities, bureaucracy will give way to a democratic golden age in which government withers away, replaced by a kind of global Internet-ocracy.

Perhaps the most influential of the techno-idealists is the author George Gilder, whose fascinating and often unique insights into the impact of new digital technologies have gained wide currency in the business press. A fine writer with a gift for distilling complex technical issues into popular language, Gilder's infinite faith in technology's ability to reshape society overnight has thrust him into the spotlight as a leading voice in Newt Gingrich's inner sanctum of high-tech gurus and as a cheerleader for the rights of business interests unconstrained by government or society in any way.

"Over the *next decade*," writes Gilder (emphasis ours), "Hollywood and Wall Street will totter and diffuse to all points of the nation and the globe . . . TV will expire and transpire into a new cornucopia of choice and empowerment [and] video culture will transcend its current mass-media doldrums . . . the most deprived ghetto child in the most blighted project will gain educational opportunities exceeding those of today's suburban preppie."[1]

Leaving aside Gilder's impossibly optimistic timetable, his vision sounds almost plausible—until, that is, one looks at the actual effects of new technology in these areas. Rather than being shunted to the periphery of power by the Digital Revolution, an ever-adaptive Hollywood and Wall Street are in fact becoming more influential than ever as they step up their role in the funding and commercialization of new digital products and services. Mass-media television, rather than expiring of its own banality, is employing new technology to offer people a variety of additional means—from Court TV to CNN to network shows like *Hard Copy*—to share in such mass-culture phenomena as the O.J. Simpson trial. And as for Gilder's rosy estimate of the educational prospects of ghetto children, even with new technology these are becoming frighteningly dimmer with each passing day as the social cleavage in incomes, in access to new technology, and in the skills needed to use it grows ever wider.

What Gilder overlooks are the real dynamics of social and economic life. Centers of wealth and power may change over time, but the existence of such centers does not. They are as inbred in civilization (and for all their inequities, as vital to the creation of social wealth) as hierarchy is in animal species as a mechanism for transmitting their most successful genetic legacy to future generations. Greater diversity and choice at the grass roots is, indeed, being enabled by the decentralizing effects of digital technology. But this does not obviate the urge among people to create and share a common culture—the growing fragmentation of social life, in fact, only makes that urge more deeply felt. And while the Information Highway certainly offers our young the *possibility* of accessing vast libraries of learning, no amount of multimedia magic can put these possibilities into the hands of those who, because of class, racial, or economic barriers, are simply unable to pay for or use it.

Gilder-style utopianism has even infected the bottom-line-driven world of business and finance (never mind Gilder's dire outlook for Wall Street itself). All sorts of hyperbolic nonsense has been promulgated in recent years about the near-term profit potential of interactive TV, CD-ROMs, and more recently, the Internet. As one breathless brochure promoting a $695-per-person seminar for business executives put it, the Internet is "a multitrillion-dollar industry . . . an electronic global community . . . and the biggest new market opportunity in history."

Eventually, of course, this may be true. But so far, few are making major profits selling products or services via the Internet. Nor are they likely to do so, so long as (among many other reasons) the people who actually do most of the shopping in our society—mainstream consumers and women—comprise barely 15 percent of the Internet's users. (And as for the Internet's "global community," one must at least be cautious about the vitality and consequence of any community in which women play such a marginal role.)

The point, of course, is not to discount the enormous promise that digital technology offers society, but rather to put that promise in context. One can be very bullish on the Digital Revolution's prospects over the long term, as we are, without losing sight of the fact that sound business plans still depend upon an accurate assessment of current market conditions, demographics, and revenue flows as well as upon marketing strategies that take account of the evolutionary pace at which new markets actually develop.

Ironically, in failing to examine new technology in context, Gilder's utopianism bears a striking resemblance to the darkly *dystopian* vision of such observers as the author and academic Neal Postman. Gilder ignores America's growing social dysfunction and imagines the Digital Revolution automatically sparking a cultural renaissance and a rebirth of town hall democracy via cyberspace. But Postman represents the opposite extreme. He dismisses America's deep democratic traditions and predicts the consolidation of a totalitarian "technopoly" that spews out trivialized mass culture over hundreds of TV channels and lynches thoughtful public discourse through the promotion of "electronic mob rule."

Dispite their divergent notions of the future, Gilder and Postman actually share common ground in an age-old philosophical debate: does base determine superstructure and existence precede essence . . . or vice versa? In assigning a priori power to technology, both men greatly underestimate the extent to which tomorrow's possibilities are shaped upon the anvil of today's social and economic realities.

The truth is that technological change comes to the world only *on the world's terms*, constrained within the limits of human nature and our political economy. To be sure, like a child in the womb, new technologies reshape—slowly, imperceptibly at first, and often in sometimes surprising ways—the lives of all around them. But to truly glimpse the shape and direction of technological change, one must appreciate the myriad ways in which economic cycles, financial markets, the exigencies of industrial competition, the regulatory mood in Washington, the political climate in the heartland, and trends in social taste and consumer spending all affect the prospects for the commercialization of new technologies and their long-term social uses and economic effects. This is *REAL WORLD FUTURISM,* and it is the approach and methodology we have tried to use in our exploration of the Digital Revolution.

One of the most striking features of this debate over possible futures is the extent to which it has become a part of the broader national discourse. Some 2,500 articles about the Internet alone now appear *each month* in American newspapers. Thousands more discuss multimedia and CD-ROMs, interactive TV, the coming changes in the telecommunications industry, and the likely effects of digital technology upon jobs, communities, education, health care, and the like. Politicians wax prophetic about it, educators pontificate about it, comedians joke about it on late-night TV.

Perhaps one reason for the enormous visibility of all things digital is that, unlike the inventors of the spinning jenny or the steam engine 230 years ago, the architects of today's technology revolution already command public attention. They give interviews to the press, appear on TV and radio, and debate their visions of the future at high-profile conferences. They are part of the power structure that runs the media, Wall Street, Hollywood, and Silicon Valley. And because they hold many of the levers of power, wealth, and prestige in society, their soap-operatic battles with each other—the long takeover fight for Paramount studios being a case in point—offer the juicy, gossipy thrills of a *Dallas* or *Dynasty* with all the high-stakes futuristic consequence of Mel Gibson's *Road Warrior*.

Indeed, ours is the first epochal technological shift in human history to be observed, as they say, in real time. In effect, the Digital Revolution has become self-aware.

One of the most prominent forces in this uniquely self-conscious process—and, significantly, one that speaks to both the avant-garde cyber underground as well as to the top echelons of corporate America—has been *Wired* magazine, which the *London Observer* calls "the most important magazine in the world today." Since its inception in 1993, *Wired* has attempted to provide the meaning and context so often missing in the developing maelstrom of technological change.

In a manifesto announcing *Wired*'s premiere issue, editor and publisher Louis Rossetto declared that "the Digital Revolution is whipping through our lives like a Bengali typhoon," bringing with it "social changes so profound their only parallel is probably the discovery of fire."[2] And the mission of the magazine, said Rossetto, would be to write "about the most powerful people on the planet today—the Digital Generation. These are people who not only foresaw how the merger of computers, telecommunications, and the media is transforming life at the cusp of the millennium, they are making it happen."

Wired's sometimes breathless prose was criticized, of course, by those who are less than enthusiastic about the significance of the Digital Revolution. Yet it's important to note that this magazine was trying to shout an essential truth above the rising cacophony of megadeals and techno-hype: the Digital Revolution is not fundamentally about this or that company's bottom line, or this or that new high-tech supergadget. Rather, when viewed over the course of its long-term trajectory, it is about the wholesale reordering of the genetic makeup of our economies, political systems, social structures, and cultures.

It may be stretching the metaphor, of course, to say that the Digital Revolution's *only* parallel is the discovery of fire. A more appropriate and, indeed, more informative parallel is to the Industrial Revolution. Fire, after all, was a single technology, whereas the Industrial Revolution represented the same sort of convergence of multiple technologies and economic shifts that we are seeing today. Fire, dramatic as it was, undoubtedly took a long time to diffuse through early human cultures, whereas the Industrial Revolution, at least in Britain and the United States, spread at a remarkably swift pace, changing people's lives dramatically in the space of a couple of generations.

As poetry, however, *Wired*'s fire metaphor is rather elegant and attractive. It captures the ubiquitousness, the portability, and the variety of uses of digital technology. It suggests the sense of awe we feel at the wondrous new supergadgets and communications media being unleashed in society. And it underscores the relationship between new technology and human development by suggesting that, just as fire altered human experience untold millennia ago, so, too, will the virtual fire of bits and bandwidth that has now begun to sweep across the globe transform us once again.

When the Digital Revolution has largely completed its transformative task—say, 50 years from now—it will have touched, influenced, and altered many of our most basic institutions and patterns of social life. In doing so, it will generate its own unique values, economic and social relationships, political institutions, belief systems, ideas, truths, biases, and dogmas.

In this, the Digital Revolution suggests an additional parallel: that of the nineteenth-century American frontier. Like the Old West, today's digital frontier also has its dangers, its fierce struggles for power and for control of resources, and its bitter conflicts of values. And like the Old West, the digital frontier has nourished a culture of zealous individualism and entrepreneurialism. It has its gold rushes (Wall Street), its uncharted lands (the Internet), its territories newly opened to farmers and homesteaders (the World Wide Web), a pony express (electronic mail), plenty of outlaws (hackers) but nary a sheriff (security), and its few settled towns (e.g., America Online and Prodigy) where decent folk can enjoy some of the comforts of civilization. One can even find ruthless and greedy railroad barons (Microsoft) running roughshod over those who get in the way.

Although still only embryonic, the new values, belief systems, and social relations nurtured by the Digital Revolution have already begun their long, epochal competition with those that have shaped our world until now. This is particularly true in the United States and other developed countries, where the sun has been steadily setting on the industrial era and rising on the Information Age for some time now. But it is also true to some degree in parts of the world where the ancient agrarian and feudal orders still prevail. Indeed, the answer to whether the big emerging markets of the world— China, Southeast Asia, Mexico, Latin America—can successfully emerge from the confines of their traditional pasts into the twenty-first century lies in large part in the twin issues of how they use new digital technologies and to what degree they are able to adapt their political and social systems harmoniously to the exigencies of the emerging Information Age.

"The medium, or process, of our time—electric technology—is reshaping and restructuring patterns of social interdependence and every aspect of our personal life," observed the father of modern media theory, Marshall McLuhan. "It is forcing us to reconsider and reevaluate practically every thought, every action, and every institution formerly taken for granted. Everything is changing—you, your family, your education, your neighborhood, your job, your government, your relation to 'the others.' And they are changing dramatically."[3]

It is interesting to note that McLuhan made this statement in 1967. Back then, he had already documented and analyzed the swirl of economic, social, political, and personal change wrought by the breakdown of the Gutenberg order of printed media and the rise of television and electronic media. Indeed, it is already almost 40 years since Daniel Bell began to speak of a "postindustrial" economy and society. It is a quarter of a century since Alvin and Heidi Toffler first diagnosed modern society as speeding up, fragmenting, decentralizing, and demassifying into a state of "future shock." Anyone who read their books or heard them lecture in the 1970s would have already understood that a "third wave" of historical development was rolling in, rich in information and technology, and that it was colliding with, challenging, and preparing to overthrow the assumptions of "first wave" feudal-agrarian societies and "second wave" industrial–mass production societies.

From the pronouncements of Peter Drucker to those of Kenichi

Ohmae and John Naisbitt, from the arcane analyses in the pages of the *Harvard Business Review* to the journalistic fast food of *USA Today*, no thinking person living through the 1970s and 1980s could possibly have missed the idea that information technology was shaping a new economic order and defining a new historic era. The shift from brawn to brainpower, from manufacturing to services, from mainframe to microprocessor, and from big, smokestack-belching heavy industries vertically integrated under hierarchical management structures to the lighter, cleaner, more decentralized technology industries horizontally networked into matrices of "virtual" organizations—all these shifts and their impacts on the economy and social life have been copiously commented on and analyzed from many quarters.

What, then, is so revolutionary about the Digital Revolution? What is new and different from the patterns and processes of change that have already been established over the past quarter-century or so?

One way to look at these questions is to say that the Digital Revolution represents the next stage of an already ongoing Information Revolution. It is the next evolution of an already-begun Information Age, the Second Coming of high-tech, the high tide of the Third Wave that has been crashing against the shores of society for some time. It's a bit like the second half of the TV game show *Jeopardy*, where "everything doubles and the scores could really change."

It is easy nowadays to generalize in broad brush strokes about the development of human societies. We speak, for example, of the Industrial Age as if it were all one period of time. But consider, for a moment, the rich variety of experience contained within the two centuries of "industrialism" that followed the development of the steam engine by James Watt in 1769 and the invention that same year of the spinning jenny by Richard Arkwright. The Industrial Revolution that these technologies inspired may have taken off relatively quickly—first in Britain, and shortly thereafter spreading to Europe, North America, Australia, and eventually Japan and other parts of the world. But the process of Industrial Age formation was not a single or homogenized one. One mini-revolution followed another: the cotton mills of the eighteenth and early nineteenth centuries. The golden age of railroads in the late nineteenth century. The birth of electricity and the introduction of the telephone in the early twentieth century. Henry Ford and mass production. The age of automobiles and aviation, television, rocketry, nuclear power, post–World War II economic growth, and the rise of the modern American corporation and Organization Man.

Each of these mini-revolutions had its corollary in the political arena. The violent erosion of feudalism and the birth of constitutional monarchy in Europe. The American Revolution of 1776 and the emergence of popular democratic institutions. The French Revolution and the Paris Commune. The destruction of slavery in the United States and the integration of the agrarian South into a continent-wide industrial economy and political system. The age of the robber barons. The rise of industrial labor unions. The socialist revolutions early this century—and their later decline as these proved unable to compete with capitalism.

In the long view of economic and social history, all of these periods are closely interconnected. Economically, they shared certain premises about the need for mass production and mass scale, about the value of centralization and formal hierarchy in industrial organization, about the role of raw materials and factory labor as key inputs in manufacturing, and about manufacturing itself as the principal means of wealth creation. Obviously, Ford's River Rouge plant in mid-twentieth-century America—where "raw steel came in one end and automobiles rolled off the line at the other"—is a world apart from that of Eli Whitney tooling around with a machine for ginning cotton 150 years earlier. Yet in a historical sense, they are but two successive stages—one primitive, one more advanced—of the same industrial system.

Even the early generation of computers—particularly the quintessential mainframes of the 1950s and 1960s—are best thought of as part of the Industrial Age, although clearly they also signaled the beginning of society's exit path from industrialism to the Information Age. Despite the computer's centrality to the Information Age, its original architectures and uses actually represented the zenith of industrial organization. Indeed, IBM was the sine qua non of advanced industrial companies—highly centralized and standardized (from dress code to software specifications), hierarchical and vertically integrated in its management structure, zealously close-systemed and proprietary, and religiously devoted to the idea that bigger is better.

Within this diverse span we can now call the Industrial Age, there were certain periods when quantum leaps took place in technological development and wealth creation. The rise of the railroads, for example, allowed the early advances of the Industrial Revolution to diffuse rapidly and broadly across geographic boundaries, altering patterns of development and generating vast new fortunes in the process. The United States, although it declared its independence from Britain at the very moment the Industrial Revolution was first unfolding, did not become a modern, cohesive, continent-wide marketplace—and the world's most dynamic economy—until the railroad age.

This same sort of *evolutionary* revolution is happening today. Whatever you choose to call this new age—postindustrialism, postmodernism, or the Information Age—it has already been with us for some time. But if one had to fix a point in time when the Information Age really took off (in the way that historians argue that the Industrial Revolution began with Watt's invention of the steam engine), then the moment to pick is probably the birth of the microprocessor in 1971. Only now, however, with the Digital Revolution of the 1990s, can the Information Age realize its fullest, widest, and most dynamic promise.

In some ways, the process is akin to that which occurs in a human embryo. At first the nascent brain is a mere quantity of rapidly dividing cells. But at a certain stage this quantitative process yields a qualitatively new result—consciousness. So it is with technology. Quantitative improvements in microprocessor power and communications capacity have now reached critical mass and are erupting into qualitative technological, social, and economic change.

To understand how great these quantitative improvements in microprocessors have been, consider those little greeting cards that play a prerecorded "Happy Birthday" message when opened. Each contains more computer processing power than existed in the entire world before 1950. Your home video camcorder wields more processing power than an IBM 360, the wonder machine that launched the mainframe age. Today's $100 video game machines use a higher-performance processor than that which powered a 1976 Cray supercomputer, which cost millions of dollars and was available in its day only to the most elite physicists.[4]

Measured by value, an average late-model automobile now contains far more electronic circuitry and onboard computer power than steel; there are almost three times as many computer chips as spark plugs in most cars. Hidden inside the electronic devices of the average American home—from microwave ovens to washing machines to TVs, VCRs, set-top boxes, and desktop computers—are over one hundred embedded controller chips today, a number that experts anticipate will double by the end of the decade.[5]

With current technology already able to produce a thumbnail-sized "brain" inside a computer that can operate at a *hundred million instructions per second*, we can now begin to speak meaningfully about the futuristic devices and applications that computer scientists have heretofore only dreamed of. This power, for example, makes it possible to process the enormous volume of digital bits coming down a video-on-demand system, direct them to the right places, and also send back up and across the system the instructions, desires, and ideas of the consumer. It sets the stage for all the other functions we have heard so much about, from "telemedicine" to "distance learning," from powerful virtual reality simulations to intelligent software agents moving through vast webs of data at the speed of light, doing our shopping and making our travel reservations.

Quantities of technological development are creating qualitatively different realities for the world we live in. It is not just that we can do more of what we used to do more easily or faster, we can now start to do *qualitatively different things*. And the "we" who can participate in these new activities is changing as well. Indeed, one of the most significant of the qualitative changes now occurring is that the digitized intelligence previously available only to the richest and most powerful of society is rapidly coming down the pipeline to much wider sectors of the population.

From the imaginings of Jules Verne to the cartoon wonders of the Jetsons, the visions of science fiction are starting to become practical realities. We stand on the threshold of a world where highly intelligent, enormously powerful, and easily usable devices will proliferate. These will be handheld computers, smart TVs, video-telephones, and other hybrids of today's technology, to be sure. But they will also be entirely new devices—smart-wallet cards controlling worldwide links into electronic money systems, smart cars traveling intelligent highways, exciting new home entertainment systems, and much more.

But it must be remembered: while digital technology may function at the speed of light, its full impact upon social and economic life will only be felt over time. This truth, however, has unfortunately often been ignored by much of the popular press in their efforts to chronicle and explain the process of technological change.

To wit, a *Time* magazine report on April 12, 1993:

> The brave new world that futurists have been predicting for decades is not years away *but months* [emphasis added]. By this time next year, vast new video services will be available, at a price, to millions of Americans in all fifty states.

And another *Time* report, this time on May 23, 1994:

> The faith behind [interactive TV] is being sorely tested. It is here that the rhetoric about the info highway comes face to face with the realities of engineering.

What a difference a year makes! Although *Time* didn't specify exactly *whose* rhetoric had come face-to-face with reality, it is clear that the "vast new video services" *Time* thought were only months away in the spring of 1993 are still years away even now—at least in terms of reaching the vast majority of citizens in all fifty states. Had the magazine spent more time studying the history of invention, it might have understood that new technologies—even the most revolutionary ones—generally filter into society only through a fitful, uneven, and painstakingly slow evolutionary process.

Consider, for example, the lowly zipper, one of the first technologies we learn to master as children and among the most ubiquitous machines of everyday life. First patented in 1893 by Whitcomb L. Judson, a Chicago inventor, the Clasp Locker was notoriously unreliable and expensive—which explains, no doubt, why apparently only the U.S. Post Office was foolish enough to buy any of the early devices (for use in mailbags). But Judson and his financial backers kept the faith, and after much trial and error, a design very much like the modern one was patented in 1917 by his assistant, Gideon Sundback. There followed 20 more years of only marginal commercial success when the zipper was hawked as a novelty item by traveling salesmen—the Veg-O-Matic of the early twentieth century, the historian Robert Friedel calls it. But in the 1930s, 40 years after its first invention, the zipper finally achieved success. A whole confluence of factors—declining costs of production, new tradition-bucking trends in fashion, and a shift by zipper producers from retail promotion to trade marketing aimed at clothing manufacturers—finally pushed the device into general use. In 1936, only 6 percent of summer suits had zippers; in 1938 the proportion was 20 percent and rising rapidly. By 1940, a survey of Princeton students revealed that nearly 90 percent wore zippered clothing.

Notes historian Robert Friedel: "This little machine clamps its myriad teeth around the most compelling issues of technology, capitalism, and entrepreneurial endurance."[6]

What's more, new technologies often find unexpected uses and bring with them unintended consequences—hence the old warning that those who gaze at crystal balls may wind up eating ground glass. Who, for example, would have guessed that an automated spreadsheet software program, Lotus 1-2-3, would be the principal catalyst for the explosive growth of a nearly $100 billion personal computer industry? Likewise, did anyone predict that X-rated movies would be chiefly responsible for driving the consumer adoption curve that ultimately led to the mass proliferation of VCRs into 80 percent of American homes?

The list goes on and on. As the Stanford economist Nathan Rosenberg has observed, the steam engine was invented specifically to pump water from flooded mines; no one foresaw how it would enable railroad transportation and fuel industrial growth throughout the whole of the nineteenth century. Likewise, Marconi never envisioned radio as a broadcasting medium at all, but expected it would instead be used only when wired communication was impossible, as in ship-to-ship communication. In 1949, IBM thought worldwide demand for the computer could be satisfied by at most 15 computers. And in the 1960s, lawyers at Bell Laboratories almost failed to patent the newly invented laser, believing that this new technology, which underlies today's fiber optics, had no possible relevance to the telephone.[7]

This law of unintended consequences can even assume a terrible and tragic power, as in Rwanda. The 1994 ritual slaughter there of half a million Tutsi men, women, and children by their Hutu countrymen shocked the world. How, people in the West wondered, was such a holocaust possible?

Learned African scholars and area specialists, of course, spoke of the persistence of ancient tribal passions and the legacy of underdevelopment and colonialism. All true, to be sure, but the additional influence of modern technology was hardly mentioned in this context. We refer not to the technologies of modern warfare, such as assault rifles or tanks or strategic bombing, for the Hutus took to their bloody task with the oldest killing implements known to our species: clubs and sharpened sticks. Rather, we are speaking of the modern technology of radio.

In ages past, tribal wars tended to be self-limiting owing to the finite psychological and geographic reach of those doing the killing. In Rwanda, however, radio enabled this latest carnage to achieve a scale previously unknown. It carried the Hutu leaders' slanders about the Tutsis to millions throughout the country. And in every village and hamlet, neighbor began hacking neighbor to death.

Thus, the device Marconi originally invented as an aid in ship-to-ship communication—and which eventually served as a mass broadcast medium uniting whole peoples—was in this case used as an instrument of mass destruction.

All of which brings us to a most crucial aspect of this discussion: the question of conscious choice—especially the choices made by whole societies. Machines do not make history, after all, men and women do. And since we are not merely passive witnesses to the enormous changes cascading down upon us, how should we as citizens attempt to direct the trajectory of the Digital Revolution? Who will benefit, who may suffer? And how can we affect the process in a way that benefits the whole of society?

Unfortunately, there has been far too little discussion of the deeper citizenship issues that stir like fault pressures beneath the bedrock surface of the emerging Information Highway. This has been evident ever since the first big coming-out party for digital technology took place at the Beverly Hilton Hotel in Los Angeles in 1993. The Digital World Conference featured a parade of glitterati from half a dozen different industries, who all showed up in a fever of excitement. Besides John Sculley (then of Apple) and Bob Carberry (then of IBM), Craig McCaw (then of McCaw Cellular before it was acquired by AT&T) made an appearance, as did Brian Roberts of Comcast Cable, Illinois Bell Chairman Richard Brown, and a host of Hollywood celebs including the directors John Badham, James Cameron, and Martha Coolidge. It was quite the interactive lovefest.

There was plenty of high-minded talk, of course, about the social promise of this new technology. Everyone seemed to agree that interactive television could change all our lives, transforming us from slumbering couch potatoes into bright-eyed, eager explorers of wondrous new worlds of information, education, and entertainment. It was further agreed that such technology could help solve long-festering social ills. High-speed networks could enhance public services, improve health care, and rejuvenate the American economy. And consumer demand for multimedia products could help create millions of new Information Age jobs.

Vague talk of more jobs, better health care, and other possible social benefits of the Digital Revolution quickly gave way, however, to the real issue on everyone's minds: money. As the official program guide put it: "It's hard to recall a technology in recent history that's sparked as much excitement and raw greed as interactive television . . . a wildly lucrative business opportunity." Indeed, the sweaty scent of money wafted throughout the hotel as an orgy of corporate matchmaking and wanton market-swapping took place in private suites. Meanwhile, in the main conference room, a procession of corporate suitors took the stage, and in their speeches, swooned unabashedly over the ripening young technology's luscious new markets and heaving revenues.

Finally Mitch Kapor, the founder and former chief of Lotus software (and now with the public interest group Electronic Frontier Foundation) took the stage. Wearing his usual Hawaiian shirt, the 45-year-old maverick mogul did what he does best—he made the suit-and-tie guys nervous.

"We are not just consumers," he declared. "We are also citizens." With all this talk about markets and profits in the new digital world order, he said, perhaps it's time to start thinking about what *kind* of world we want it to be!

Talk about a party pooper! One could almost hear one thousand frozen smiles cracking in the audience. Some people tittered nervously. A few rolled their eyes and muttered under their breath that anyone who made a half-billion-dollar personal fortune from software was in no position to lecture others about putting people ahead of profits. But Kapor's point was well taken. For all the industry seminars and all the media coverage, there has been far too little discussion of the implications of attempting to weave new technologies into an old and badly frayed social fabric.

This is hardly surprising when you think about it. In America, the prevailing cultural view of technology is that it is some sort of autonomous, mythic force beyond the reach of human control—and devoid of political, economic, and ideological influences. Indeed, technology is viewed as something akin to the weather or God's will.

In part, this magical belief reflects humanity's age-old dream— that technology might one day liberate us from the burdens and constraints of nature and enable us to achieve our full self-determination as socially mature beings. Indeed, as the historian of technology John Michael Staudenmaier, a professor at the University of Detroit and author of *Technology's Storytellers*, has pointed out, this apolitical view of technology is promoted at every turn.

Describing a ride through the General Motors "World of Motion" exhibit at Walt Disney's EPCOT Center, viewed by 20 million people annually, Staudenmaier writes:

> [The exhibit] teaches the history of transportation technologies. But it treats earlier technologies and earlier human beings as inept. You're invited to laugh at the past. Then, somewhere around 1920, you begin to hear serious background music with a serious voice telling of the engineering experts who gradually solved the problems of transportation through automotive technologies. Finally, as your moving chair rounds the bend from the present to tomorrow, you enter a world of high gloss and pinpoint lighting. The implicit message [is that] the future holds near-perfect promise for us all.[8]

There is no hint at EPCOT (nor in much of today's public discourse about interactive media) that the design and use of new technology necessarily entails contests over political power. Yet in regard to the last superhighways built in America (the ones made of asphalt not electrons), they most certainly did.

"Why did the highway engineers who designed the U.S. interstate system in the fifties and sixties run the system through major cities rather than only up to their outer circumference?" Staudenmaier asks. "Who decided that those freeways were more important, as civic assets, than the neighborhoods they sliced through?"[9]

And how, we might add, did their decisions reflect the goals, the influence, and the anti-mass-transit bias of the automobile, trucking, and oil industries?

The design, construction, and operation of the new Info Highway will also entail contests over political power. Indeed, some of these conflicts are already out in the open.

Who, if anyone, should control the content that will run along the Highway? How can service be made as affordable as possible for all Americans? How should regulatory laws be changed to allow for the corporate concentration necessary to fund the Highway's enormous cost, while at the same time stimulating greater competition—with all its social and economic benefits—in communications and media markets?

Far more troublesome issues, however, lie below the surface, embedded in the political and economic structure of our society. For no matter what the promise of the Digital Revolution to revitalize society—and the potential here is enormous—the reality is that this promise rests upon the precarious edifice of an America that has become dangerously fractured and increasingly dysfunctional.

Everywhere around us we see a society that is no longer working. Deep structural flaws in our economy have turned the promise of continuously rising living standards into little more than the faded memory of those over 40. Our public education system stands at the brink of collapse, too organizationally and financially bankrupt to meet the challenges of the late twentieth, let alone the twenty-first century. And literally tens of millions of people are in effect disenfranchised, confined to inner-city warrens and cut off from any realistic hope of playing a meaningful and productive role in society.

And in the face of it all, our national political system stands trembling in its impotence, seemingly unable to effect any genuine and fundamental change or even to slow the downward-spiraling doom loop in which our society appears to be caught.

To be sure, it has become fashionable for politicians to dress up their proposed solutions to these social problems in high-tech clothes. But when Al Gore suggests piping the Internet into our decayed and violence-ridden schools—or when Newt Gingrich talks of giving tax credits to the poor so they can buy laptop computers—their lame attempts at cyberspeak reflect an artificiality of analysis and an archaic approach to problem solving that is deeply disconnected from both the challenges posed by this new technology and the realities of daily life.

Until fairly recently, of course, daily life in our system worked well. Born of machine-age technology, industrial capitalism drew tens of millions of rural folk into the new factories and cities of nineteenth- and twentieth-century America, and created the richest and most productive society on earth. This system had its inequities, its tyrannies, and its bloodshed, as all systems do. But for the first time in history, democracy, literacy, and public health were extended to the masses, who enjoyed the greatest advance in living standards and quality of life ever seen on the planet.

Now the Industrial Age is at its end, sputtering in ever-worsening paroxysms of chaos and uncertainty as if in protest against the coming of the new Information Age. Spurred by the decentralizing and globalizing effects of computer and communications technologies, mass society is exploding into a universe of custom cultures, and the gravitational pull of large central institutions is fragmenting into the mini-orbital fields of special interests and local allegiances.

Indeed, a massive power shift from the center to the periphery is occurring everywhere. Organization Man has become a consultant, thanks to technology resources once available only to the largest enterprises. And top-down corporate hierarchies are flattening into horizontal, decentralized networks of self-governing work teams. But this flattening process is also crushing and marginalizing millions of once-productive citizens. Whole strata of blue-collar and white-collar workers are being "downsized" into oblivion, their work now performed more efficiently by networked information systems or farmed out to cheap-labor production centers in new global markets overseas.

This is the crumbling landscape upon which the coming Information Highway is being built, and all the wondrous new technology in the world won't automatically heal the dysfunction all around us or guarantee Information Age jobs to the millions already scratching a bare existence along society's margins. Indeed, while digital technology will offer new opportunities for collective renewal, it will also add new and more troubling dimensions to America's grievous social dilemmas in the twenty-first century.

What does the future look like? For some—the affluent, the mobile, the educated—it promises a wonderland of new choices and new opportunities in work and leisure. But for others—the unskilled, the underclass, the unnecessary—it may offer only banishment to a new, techno-coated Dark Ages. No society can possibly sustain such a stark dissonance of parallel futures for long.

Which future, then, will it be?

Will the Information Highway serve only to widen the distance between Watts and Beverly Hills?

Will tomorrow's information haves end up barricading themselves inside their virtual communities against the rage and frustration of tens of millions of marginalized, unemployable information have-nots?

Or will we leaven our high-tech visions of tomorrow with some "Smart Tech" policies today—policies that can help fashion a new American Dream and a new global vision for the twenty-first century? Can we find the political will needed to confront our complex and deeply entrenched social problems—from the paralysis of our institutions to the structural inertia in our economic life—and develop creative new policies that use this new technology to help kick-start a broad-based social and economic resurgence for the nation as a whole?

Prophecy is always a dangerous business, as even Karl Marx might ruefully concede were he alive today. Examining the impact of new technology, he once wrote: "The hand-mill gives you society with the feudal lord; the steam-mill, society with the industrial capitalist."[10]

A rather oversimplified view, to be sure, but it does suggest an interesting question: what society will the Information Highway give us?

No one yet knows the answer. We can point to the broadening possibilities for citizen empowerment born of new technology, and offer a perspective for overcoming the lethargy of our public institutions in integrating those possibilities into a new social compact. We can speak of the new dynamics of wealth creation—especially in the United States, where the most advanced technological experience, business development, and marketplace are now concentrated—and illuminate the strategies and tactics necessary to ensure a company its place in today's fast-evolving competitive environment. And as writer-observers, participant-advisors, and consultants to some of the leading companies in the technology and media fields, we can even dig deep into the critical challenges and opportunities facing businesses in today's emerging digital industries and show who is most likely to succeed or fail and why.

But while we can hopefully clarify the direction of technological change, neither we nor anyone else can predict its ultimate destination. Like weathermen, the best we can do is interpret developing storm patterns and suggest ways to secure the high ground as the tides of change approach.

Even in this uncertain hour, however, one thing is clear: our future will not be decided by the high-tech gizmos of tomorrow, but by the flesh-and-blood men and women of today now engaged in an epochal quest whose outcome no one can predict. In their efforts one can find greed and the lust for power and perhaps all the other deadly sins. But one can also discover creativity and vision and a sometimes courageous intelligence about the deeper meaning and implications of their work.

It is precisely this sort of courageous intelligence that will be needed in the years ahead as the whirlwinds of change come sweeping down upon us.

PART ONE

Where the Roads Connect

■ 1 ■

The Fog of War

Even after all these years, Leanne Clement still remembers the strange blend of anxiety and excitement she felt when the new I-5 interstate was extended through her little town of Cottage Grove, Oregon. She and her sister Karen would lie awake in their bedroom at night, in this working-class lumber town two hours south of Portland, listening for the sound of the occasional car as it sped down the new freeway and faded off into the darkness, on its way toward some exotic and unknowable destination.

"I couldn't imagine where all these people were going," Leanne recalls, "but I thought it was probably someplace exciting. It really had an effect on me. Every time a car drove by—going who knows where—I felt like I was being left behind."

The year was 1956, and America's new interstate highway system had already begun to draw together once-isolated little communities like Cottage Grove into orbit around a new, more integrated American universe. The automobile had by then already become the gravitational center of national life. It ruled U.S. employment patterns, dominated the nation's political ideology—"What's good for General Motors is good for the country," as they used to say—and had sprouted a whole galaxy of suburbs, gas stations, motels, insurance companies, and fast-food drive-in lifestyles that would soon alter the motion and trajectory of American life.

Forty years have passed, and Leanne Clement no longer feels left behind. From her cubicle office in California's Silicon Valley—that sprawling ferment of industrial parks, research labs, and bedroom communities stretching like one vast suburban technopolis between San Francisco and San Jose—she now has a bird's-eye view of the complex movements of money, technology, and politics that have already begun to shape the direction of social traffic in the next millennium.

"I get to go everywhere now," she smiles, with a hint of the old small-town wonder in her eyes. And indeed, as research and information manager for General Magic, a small technology company developing communications software for a new generation of handheld consumer products called personal communicators, Leanne travels daily upon the Internet, using her computer to hunt down news and information that may prove critical to the company's success. Responding to a request from David Lefler, the company's zealous head of user testing, Leanne zipped around the electronic ether looking for research on gender-difference factors in product design. In an electronic library in New Jersey, she found a study on redesigning computer touch-screen buttons so that women with fingernails could effectively use them. And for General Magic CEO Marc Porat, who was about to meet with a European high-tech executive, she located data on the firm's market strength that proved valuable to Porat's negotiating strategy, thanks to a database published in Ohio. All this, of course, without ever leaving her desk. Porat calls her his info goddess.

To some people, perhaps, cruising along the Information Highway—even if you're burning rubber in the passing lane to meet the boss's deadline—might not at first seem like very exciting work. But as Mel Gibson's character might have said in the movie *Road Warrior*, it's not the job—it's the stakes. And working for General Magic has given Leanne Clement a ringside seat at an epic technology race that has all the heart-stopping lure of a multi*trillion* dollar Grand Prix and the wicked thrill of a crash-and-burn corporate demolition derby. The little girl from Cottage Grove, it seems, has become a road warrior in what is likely to become the greatest global economic contest in the history of the world.

"It's not for the faint of heart, I tell you," laughs Magic CEO Porat, clearly relishing the fact that his little firm is playing with the big boys in a contest involving thousands of companies, billions in investment, and trillions in potential revenues. The former head of development for Apple Computer's Advanced Technology Group before launching General Magic in 1990, Marc Porat at 48 still has the hip, youthful good looks that seem to adhere to so many California baby boomers, despite the egregious lifestyle sins that so often litter their pasts. Dark-haired and favoring dark slacks and dark silk shirts, he also has that articulate charm and look-you-in-the-eye sincerity of someone who clearly knows how to work the tables. Unlike most smooth-talking types, however, Porat often has something important to say and has thought about it deeply before he says it.

Much has happened to Porat's company since he was first interviewed in early 1993 at the firm's former offices in Mountain View, California (its headquarters are now in nearby Sunnyvale.) After several years' effort by employees working 80-hour weeks, and many delays, the company finally released its software in 1994 first to Sony and then to Motorola, who began selling competing personal communicators using the software. And then on February 10, 1995, Magic offered 5.5 million shares of its stock to the public in what became one of the most dizzying (and instructive) roller-coaster rides in the history of public offerings.

Within minutes of the opening, Magic shares soared to $32, more than double their $14 offering price. Clearly driving the stock surge was investors' desire to capitalize on the corporate craze to commercialize cyberspace. General Magic, with technology that promised to make buying and selling products and services on the Internet easier and with a blue-ribbon slate of world-class corporate backers, seemed like a pure play—at least as a concept.

"Everyone is hot on the Information Highway," explained Richard Shaffer, publisher of *Technologic Computerletter*, an industry newsletter. "[General Magic] is one of the few small companies you can own a piece of."[1]

But apparently many shareholders had second thoughts about what it was, exactly, that they had bought. Within two weeks, Magic's share price was back down to $16 and within two months it had fallen as low as $12 as investors finally began to read the company prospectus—especially the part noting that the firm had posted only

$2.5 million in revenues in 1994 while racking up a cumulative loss of $53.1 million, with no profits expected until 1997.

"There are no earnings here. It's all on the come," conceded Jon Hickman, a portfolio manager at Wells Fargo Investment Management who bought shares at $14 and then quickly "flipped" them for a tidy profit on opening day.[2]

Such wild gyrations in investor mood are hardly unusual when it comes to technology and media companies. Alternating between euphoria and cynicism, Wall Street and the press have found it extremely difficult to embrace simultaneously both the long-term revolutionary prospects of new digital businesses and the slow, evolutionary, step-by-step efforts needed for these businesses to realize those prospects in their bottom lines. Will General Magic eventually be a good business and an important player in the Information Highway of tomorrow? Time will tell, but much to his credit, Marc Porat himself has always emphasized General Magic's *long-term* outlook for success.

"Personal communicators are going to take a good ten years to become a real mass-market business," he noted during that first interview back in 1993. "And it'll maybe take 25 years—a generation or more—before our vision of any-time, any-place communications and information access is a reality for most of the population."

Sitting in a small conference room next to his office, Porat's real-world view of his company's future seemed a bit at odds with the sign on the door identifying this as the Yoda Room—a suggestion, perhaps, that something of *Star Wars*–like proportion was happening here. But then again, it only reinforced the duality of technology change: visions that soar above the clouds of tomorrow's possibilities coexist with the realities of slogging through the mud of day-to-day business. If commerce is the engine driving change—and a new technology must be saleable in some way or it will never see the light of day—then vision is the steering wheel.

"Our starting point is you, the human being," Porat explained. "Until now, people have had to fit themselves around this impenetrable computer technology, and most of us couldn't." (One study not long ago found that even 55 percent of *computer company* executives couldn't operate a computer.)[3] "So we tried instead to create a technology that fits around people. We asked ourselves, what do people actually do in their lives? One, we *communicate*, we maintain relationships. Two, we need to *remember* and manage our daily tasks and personal agendas. And three, we need to *know*. We need easy, convenient ways of finding out things—whether it's movie listings and flight times or more specialized information needed to get our jobs done. We call this approach Whole Person Thinking."

Whole person thinking . . . is this man from California or what? Porat seems to read the interviewer's thoughts. "Fruits and nuts, right? I know, I know . . . it sounds like fruits and nuts. But, hey, we've got the best technologists on the planet here working on it. And we've got the most powerful, no-bullshit companies in the world supporting us."

Indeed, playing the Oppenheimer to a kind of private-sector Manhattan Project, Porat has assembled one of the most outstanding multidisciplinary technology teams of recent history—a group one writer called "the interface ninjas of our time . . . definitely the A team."[4] Chief Scientist Bill Atkinson and Software Wizard (that's really his title) Andy Hertzfeld were the lead designers on the Apple Macintosh, the first computer that could be operated by pointing-and-clicking on visual icons instead of having to type the arcane command language typical of computers at the time (i.e., point to the "trash can" rather than type DEL FILENAME.EXT to delete a file). Other key Magicians, as they are called, include Susan Kare, the artist who designed the Macintosh icons, and two legends in the field of networked communications and electronic messaging, Jim White and Rich Miller. Rounding out the team is Marketing Vice President Joanna Hoffman, another former Macintosh guru and a physicist, engineer, archeologist, and linguist—not to mention one of the few women in top management in Silicon Valley. Around this baby-boomer talent core Porat has built a 160-person team of twenty-something artists, writers, engineers, and communications experts—some with little or no experience in computing but with "exceptional minds," as Porat puts it. Their goal, quite simply, is to reinvent mass communication, redefine commerce, and reorder the balance of power between humans and computers.

Not a small task, to be sure. But it's clear that Magic's new Telescript communications language does signal a breakthrough in both the theory and practice of electronic communication. What sets Telescript apart is its use of "intelligent agents"—smart, self-adjusting software programs—that can enable even the technologically illiterate to venture into the Tower of Babel of the world's burgeoning communications networks to locate information or perform tasks like booking airline tickets, paying bills, or shopping in electronic bazaars. With these agents doing the grunt work in the user's place, Telescript should, at least in theory, enable even a complete neophyte to "express his wishes and desires," as Porat puts it, without having to know anything at all about computers or networks or the rigid protocols and command procedures common to both.

The user guides and launches these agents through a human-machine interface called Magic Cap, the company's second invention. Magic Cap is an intuitive visual operating environment that recreates the metaphor of the town square on the surface of a computer screen. A tap on the "department store" image on the street, for example, takes you inside the building for an electronic shopping spree (credit cards automatically billed). A tap on the image of the "postcard" in the office allows you to write a message and have it automatically sent to the recipient of your choice by the most appropriate of several means—fax, electronic mail, cellular, or other wireless communication.

Though initially deployed in handheld communicators, General Magic aims to implant Telescript and Magic Cap in a whole range of devices, including PCs, next-generation screen phones, and the most ubiquitous appliance in the American home—television. Simply surfing through the expected multiplicity of channels on tomorrow's televisions could take up to an hour, hence the need for "navigators" that filter in or out whole classes of programs (like soap operas or Westerns). Magic's technology will do more than just filter, however. It will look for patterns in the programs you watch, and adjust its programming menu to your viewing habits and desires accordingly.

"You may tell everyone that you watch *Masterpiece Theatre*," Porat jokes. "But Magic TV will figure out that what you really like to watch is *Masturbate Theater*." A cute pun, but it illustrates his point. Instead of dealing with 500-channel bulimia, viewers who use Magic's technology will create one "channel"—their own custom channel. Other companies are also exploring ways to simplify interactive TV use, including Lexicus Motorola, which has developed a pen-and-tablet interface enabling users to simply write in *John Wayne* to call up a list of John Wayne movies rather than having to scroll through an endless series of menus. Whatever approach is ultimately adopted most widely, it is clear that intelligent agents and easy-to-use navigational tools will play an important role in spurring broad public acceptance of interactive TV and other complex systems.

Most intriguing of all, perhaps, is the notion that Magic's agent technology may also resurrect the ancient economic form of the bazaar, only in cyberspace. It's no accident that Magic Cap is the first software interface to use the town square shopping metaphor. Porat believes electronic commerce will be the biggest consumer application of new interactive technologies. One problem with the embryonic current electronic shopping systems to date is that online time is money—users are billed for the time spent browsing on the network in addition to any purchases they make. But smart agents can go off by themselves on user-instructed shopping errands without the user having to remain online. The agent enters one "store," and then another and another, until it finds what its owner wants. Agents also have the potential to reduce the seller-advantaged nature of retailing today, creating a multidimensional marketplace that enhances the choice and bargaining power of individual consumers. Why limit oneself to the Macy's jewelry collection, for instance, when one can send an agent to search out the offerings of a variety of vendors, both large retailers and freelance, mom-and-pop designers? The agent will sort through the various selections and prices until it locates an item that meets your pre-set requirements. Then, too, agent-enabled commerce could enable consumers for the first time to send into the electronic ether their own individual RFPs (Request for Proposals), creating in the process the sort of competitive bidding by vendors of products and services that large corporations have long enjoyed.

It sounds intriguing, to be sure. But all of Porat's brilliant technology and two dollars still wouldn't get him cup of cappuccino were it not for the unusual alliance of 15 (often competing) world-class companies backing General Magic's efforts. Five of the world's largest communications companies—AT&T, Northern Telecom, Nippon Telephone and Telegraph (NTT), Cable and Wireless (serving the United Kingdom, Europe, and Hong Kong), and Motorola—as well as six of the biggest competing consumer electronics companies—Sony, Matsushita, Okidata, Mitsubishi, Sanyo, and Philips— have all lent their financial and marketing support to Porat's group. In theory at least, so has Apple Computer, though after the flop of

Apple's own handheld device, a clunker called Newton, it must surely regret ever letting the General Magic design team go. With such an unruly brood of industry behemoths in his stable, Porat's talent for working the tables doubtless comes in quite handy.

"Conflict of interest is always in the air," he admits. "These companies cooperate in helping us develop the right hardware and software elements of our technology. But you can see their minds working, planning for the next phase. Because when they start selling their own Magic-based devices, they're going to compete like hell."

He pauses a moment to let the listener know that what he says next will be important. "Actually, I welcome the conflict. It's good for us because the art of making this alliance work really lies in creating a constant state of dynamic tension. It's like the Stealth Bomber, which is basically in a constant state of crashing. The only reason the Stealth flies at all is because there are 15 computers on board constantly adjusting its flight. And it's precisely this instability that is the secret of the Stealth's high-performance maneuverability. That's how it is with our alliance. We're not 'aerodynamically' stable, and we're not designed to be. Harmony leads to complacency. But properly managed, dynamic tension produces growth and innovation."

If General Magic's technology does take off and become widely deployed in networks, consumer devices, and personal communicators, it'll be against formidable opposition—in particular, billionaire Bill Gates's Microsoft Corporation, the most powerful computer company in the world. Few are those, indeed, who have developed an innovative technology and managed not to be either bought or crushed by the Microsoft behemoth, and Porat is not unaware of the dangers that lie ahead. "We've put ourselves in a blocking move against Microsoft, market for market," he says, his voice quieter now. "I can feel their avionics on my skin. They've locked in, you know, and I can feel it."

He pauses a moment, almost shudders. "It's a very physical sensation. They're going to try and squash us!"

Welcome to the Digital Revolution, a curious revolution if ever there was one. Its target is not the levers of political or economic power but rather the dials on your television and buttons on your PC. Its weapons aren't guns or street protests but cutthroat commerce and high-risk finance. It promises not deliverance from oppression, but rather entry into a high-tech utopia so advanced it will make the gee-whiz gadgetry of the Jetsons seem more like the simple stone tools of the Flintstones. And ironically, while aiming simply to empower the individual with hybrid "tele-computers" that deliver a host of new information and entertainment services, the Digital Revolution will actually do more to alter the shape of government, the economy, and the American way of life than even the most radical social activists have imagined in their wildest dreams.

We've heard such talk before. At the dawn of the personal computer era, we were promised the knowledge of the universe sitting atop our desks, and at home, wondrous new worlds of discovery and learning for our children. Nearly two decades later we're still trying to decipher all those stupefying computer manuals, and at home, our kids are even more firmly super-glued to the TV thanks to witless video games like Mortal Kombat and Crash and Burn. Meanwhile, most Americans still can't program their VCRs or even stop them from blinking 12:00 . . . 12:00 . . . 12:00 . . .

But the Second Coming of high tech will be different. Although new gizmos such as personal communicators will appear, for the most part new technologies will reshape the ordinary appliances of daily life—especially the TV and the telephone—and infuse these with all the power and intelligence of computers. The computer itself will evolve into more of a communications device than a stand-alone data processor. And you'll no more need to master the inner workings of these telecomputers than you need to fathom what's going on under the hood of your car. You just step on the gas—or press the button on your clicker—and go.

High-tech, low-maintenance.

Three parallel developments make this *applianc-izing* of technology possible. In the first, the size and cost of immensely powerful computer microprocessors are collapsing. According to Moore's Law (named after chipmaker Intel's chairman, Gordon Moore), computers roughly double in power every 18 months at the same time that their cost is reduced by half. Indeed, computer processors have now become small and cheap enough to fit inside common household appliances, TVs, and telephones and serve as their tiny brains.

More important, owing to the vast explosion of communications bandwidth, it has now become possible to cheaply and speedily transmit vast streams of voice, images, and data. "It's all a question now of access, of communicating all the information we have," notes Paul Saffo, a research fellow at the Institute for the Future in Menlo Park, California. "The 1980s were shaped by the microprocessor. But the nineties are being shaped by the cheap communications laser, shooting pulses of light down a fiber-optic line. By the end of this decade, a computer sitting on a desk, unconnected to other computers or networks, will be like a phone not plugged into a wall jack. It'll be a paperweight, that's all."

But the most significant development of all is the fact that the world is going digital. The words in our books, the pictures on our TVs, and the voices in our phones are being converted from the printed type, light waves, and sound waves first utilized by Johannes Gutenberg, Alexander Graham Bell, and Thomas Edison into the digital ones and zeros that computers read. And when books, movies, music, TV, phones, libraries, and news media all speak the same lingua franca of digital ones and zeros, they can be mixed and matched, accessed and utilized in ways never before thought possible. Consider this not-unlikely future scenario: you pause a TV news report on new treatments for heart disease to call up an animated illustration of the function of a heart valve from your network service's online encyclopedia, then video-call your doctor for a consultation. Is the device in front of you a TV, a telephone, or a computer?

As various media converge, so, too, are the industries behind them colliding on a vast new digital battlefield. The headlines tell the story: "AT&T Targets Silicon Valley," "Sega Takes Aim at Disney's World," "The King of Cable Reaches for More." In at least five great industries—computers, communications, entertainment, publishing, and consumer electronics—growth in their traditional core markets has slowed. Multimedia products and services, however, offer the promise of new markets and a virtual tsunami of profit for companies that can successfully surf the digital wave. Old corporate empires will crumble and new ones arise. And a whole new Information Age industry will emerge that will very likely become the largest in the world by the end of this decade.

"We're talking about a $3.5 *trillion* technology business by the year 2000,"—half the U.S. Gross Domestic Product!—said John Sculley, the former head of Apple Computer. "It's the mother of all industries."

And it has often seemed in the last few years as if half the corporations on the planet were scrambling for a slot at those digital teats. In the war rooms of the world's major business empires, a who's who of corporate generals are plotting their strategies, forging Machiavellian alliances and conspiring to outflank each other in an epic struggle for supremacy in these emerging Information Age markets. Like the warring feudal princes of pre-nation-state Italy, today's multimedia warriors probably give little thought to how their rivalries may prefigure the rise of an entirely new social and economic order. But they are most certainly aware that if technology is war, its principal battlefield is the American home—or more precisely, the telephone, the computer, and the television within it. And while America clearly represents the greatest prize, this battle is rapidly globalizing, with new fronts opening daily in Europe, Asia, Latin America, Canada, and Australia.

Because of the sheer size of its potential revenues, television will ultimately be the flickering focus of their contention, the medium of change and exchange, the window on a new world order in creation. From our TVs, a tidal wave of digital services will come crashing down upon us, carving a whole new landscape—often breathtaking, sometimes frightening—out of the old familiar geography of American life. Much of the new terrain will seem fertile and pleasant enough: movies-on-demand, instant access to online information libraries, video get-togethers with distant friends and family. But other regions of this new terra will feel a good deal less firma, for as always, new technology represents both opportunity and threat.

Advertisers, for instance, don't know whether to weep over the approaching death of the mass market or rejoice at the imminent birth of ten thousand new, specialized, and highly targetable niche audiences. Likewise, retailers can't decide whether to juice up their malls with amusement park attractions or just level their faux-marble behemoths and set up virtual stalls in the coming electronic bazaar. Hedging their bets, the biggest department stores have already begun to do both.

But there is much more at stake than simply markets and profits. Will hundreds of special-interest channels for every grouplet in society further deconstruct our sense of a common culture? And who can say how family and social life will be affected by the mesmerizing, 24-hour-a-day lure of interactive games and 3-D excursions into virtual-reality worlds? In some cases, age-old moral dilemmas are involved. What happens when sin dons the rather compelling party dress of interactivity and beams Tele-dildonics (remote sex play) and Virtual Vegas ("press 1 to hold, press 2 to fold") right into your living room, just a press of the clicker away?

Stay tuned. But don't expect much help in answering these questions from our emerging multimedia moguls. Says Microsoft's Gates: "It is not up to us to be the censors or referees of this [sic] media."[5] A useful reminder, perhaps, that the business of business, after all, is business. And long before we saw the fuzzy black-and-white image of the American flag, before we had the Peacock or the Eye, the very first television test pattern was the dollar sign.

Not for one moment is this fact lost on the corporate generals already engaged in the fight of their lives.

Generals like John Malone, for instance, the cowboy king of the cable industry and a man who is hardly shy about his bare-knuckle view of the dollars and sense of this new technology revolution. "All these visionaries, these pioneers, they go around hyping all these way-out high-tech ideas," he snorts. "Well, pioneers often end up with arrows in their back because, you see, a technology isn't necessarily a business. My approach is, I don't want to invent a technology first and then decide whether there's a market. I want to go the other way. I want to see where the existing revenue streams are that I can really reach and touch, and then I want to design and implement a technology to ride on those streams as cost-effectively as possible."

Malone's meat-and-potatoes brand of futurism may not have the same sex appeal as the posturings of some of the cyberhip media celebrities on today's scene. But the TCI chief makes a profound point when he scoffs at wild-eyed visionaries who spend more time on media road shows than on company cash flows. "Let 'em run around," shrugs Malone. "I'll just buy 'em out for 30 cents on the dollar."

Malone was first interviewed for this book on October 12, 1993, at his apartment on 58th Street in Manhattan. Even at eight in the morning, his place buzzed with the distracted, hurried tension of a Pentagon war room. Half-eaten doughnuts lay crumbled atop the dinette table, and a bleary-eyed, freshly showered executive grabbed one as he rushed out the door on some secret mission. As for Malone, he lounged on a chair in the living room throughout the two-hour interview, one hand stuffed in his pants pocket and the other wrapped around a styrofoam cup of cold coffee. He had the cat-that-ate-the-canary look of a high-stakes gambler with a very potent—and very secret—card up his sleeve.

As the world discovered 24 hours later, Malone's plans encompassed far more than simply being chief of the largest cable company in the world, Tele-Communications, Inc. (TCI), a kingdom that already included 1,200 cable delivery systems in 49 states, serving 11 million of America's 62 million cable TV households. Through TCI and his ancillary firm, Liberty Media, Malone also owned extensive interests in Turner Broadcasting and Cable News Network, Barry Diller's QVC Network, Home Shopping Network, the Discovery Channel, the Family Channel, American Movie Classics, Encore TV, Black Entertainment Television, Courtoom Television, the Country Music Channel, Teleport Communications, and a combined TV-and-telephone firm in England called TeleWest.

Various media accounts have portrayed Malone as "a bully boy," "an unscrupulous monopolist," and "a guy who knows how to run over people." In 1989, then Senator Al Gore even referred to Malone as the "ringleader" of a "cable Cosa Nostra" and a "shakedown" artist. His reputation was not enhanced by the publication of one of his interviews with the authors of this book, in which Malone jested that the head of the Federal Communications Commission, Reed Hundt, ought to be shot for ordering further cable rate reductions in February of 1994.[6] None of the media's disparaging portrayals of him seem to have hurt his feelings, however. Asked by one reporter to reply to charges of monopolistic practices, Malone shrugged. "When you're driving plate tectonics, you're going to squeeze people's tails."[7]

And make no mistake: "squeezing people's tails" in order to turn new technologies into profitable businesses is precisely what John Charles Custer Malone has been doing for over 20 years. In 1973, the Yale- and Johns Hopkins–educated engineer (he also holds a doctorate in operations research) left AT&T's Bell Labs for a stake in the then struggling Englewood, Colorado, cable company. There he quickly earned a reputation as a tough negotiator, bullying bankers into extending him credit and battling with city regulators over raising rates. In one classic Malone showdown his first year at TCI, he shut off all programming to the nearby town of Vail after the city council balked at higher rates, airing nothing but the names and home phone numbers of the mayor and city manager until the council caved in. By the early 1980s, Malone had also become a major customer of Michael Milken's, using junk bond financing and high cash flows to buy out some 90 percent of the smaller cable systems on the market. He would then often spin off and reacquire them in a series of highly complex financial machinations involving TCI's corporate structure. All told, Malone's TCI has invested in, partnered with, or acquired over 650 companies. By the end of 1992, according to one report, Malone managed to carry off "an incredible 482 deals, on average one every two weeks."[8]

By the late 1980s, however, Malone's strategy shifted. "It became clear," he says, "that the value of our cable systems was being driven more and more by the kind of programming we can assemble," which is another way of saying that plumbing is useless without access to a water supply. "So we started investing in programming content."

But critics claim that Malone's monopoly power flows precisely from the opposite direction—without pipes to deliver it, a water supply is about as valuable as spit. "Imagine that you have all these publishing houses but only one book chain in the United States," one report quoted a cable executive who does business with TCI as saying. "You can write the best book, but what happens if you can't get into the bookstore? John Malone is the bookstore."[9]

Malone thinks such charges make good copy but little sense. He joins many experts and pundits in pointing out that we are moving from an era of "bandwidth scarcity" to one of "bandwidth abundance" in which various multimedia delivery systems—including telephone, satellite, and wireless cable networks—will proliferate. Thus, says Malone, it will increasingly be content, not the conduit that carries it, that will provide the key competitive market differentiator and the biggest profit component of future television services. And with less than 20 percent market share of cable-viewing households—and new rivals rushing into his markets on practically a monthly basis—Malone insists that TCI's size and reach hardly give it a significant anticompetitive advantage. Monopolistic or not, however, there's little doubt that John Malone is the most powerful man in television.

Despite his image as the aggrandizing Darth Vader of the cable

TV universe, the personality and role of John Malone is far more complex. For one thing, the 54-year-old cable king is by all accounts a devoted family man, living modestly with his wife (his two children are grown) just outside of Denver, Colorado. When working out of TCI's nearby Englewood headquarters, he often drives home to have lunch with his wife, Leslie. And twice each year, in January and May, he and Leslie drive their RV (she hates to fly) to their hilltop second home above Maine's Boothbay Harbor for a month of sailing and relaxation. Some, like QVC's Barry Diller, attribute Malone's Machiavellian reputation to the fact that beneath his square-jawed and plain-spoken manner, he is so smart it can be "scary." Says *Time* magazine editor in chief Norman Pearlstine: "It's like he's playing three-dimensional chess—he's playing a completely different game." Adds Peter Barton, chief of TCI's Liberty Media unit: "Just think about a Rubik's Cube in your head. You have to remember colors and spatial relations. John's mind is even more flexible. He can spin each block on its own axis."[10]

Evil genius or not, it is precisely his ability to spin multiple future scenarios out of highly complex relationships that has made John Malone a visionary in the most real and practical of senses. It was Malone who in 1992 first coined the term "500-channel television," based on his analysis that digital compression would enable even today's 50-channel coaxial cable lines to increase their capacity by a factor of 10. When most cable industry executives insisted that interactive television could not possibly be available until at least the year 2000, Malone predicted that such service could begin to be rolled out around 1995, at least experimentally. And while most industry analysts were still arguing over who would win the war to dominate the interactive TV market—the cable giants or the telephone companies—Malone made it seem as if he had settled the whole debate with one shocking announcement.

On October 13, 1993, he took the podium at the Hotel Macklowe in Manhattan and revealed the secret he couldn't speak on the record about a day earlier. He announced that he was merging TCI with Bell Atlantic, a regional telephone company providing land-line and cellular service to 18 million customers in six eastern states. Valued at $33 billion, the deal represented the largest merger in U.S. history—and it created in one stunning stroke America's first fully integrated multimedia oligopoly. To be sure, the marriage of bad boy

Johnny Malone to Bell Atlantic's very corporate chairman, Ray Smith, did not seem at first to be a match made in heaven. But power, as Henry Kissinger used to say, is a wonderful aphrodisiac. And by combining the programming and carrying capacity of TCI's cable pipes with Bell Atlantic's expertise in billing and switching two-way interactive communications, Ray Smith and John Malone—a multimedia odd couple if ever there was one—seemed poised to command the delivery of future interactive TV and multimedia services to over 25 million homes in all the nation's one hundred principal communications markets.

Four months later, the deal collapsed—and with it, much of the wildly inflated hype surrounding the near-term prospects of not only interactive television but of the Digital Revolution itself. While the deeper implications of the TCI–Bell Atlantic breakup will be explored in Chapter 6 (and in the dramatic triptych of interviews with the chairmen of these two companies, as well as with Federal Communications Commission chairman Reed Hundt in the appendix), for now it is sufficient to note that this almost-deal of the century produced exactly the opposite of what most of the experts had predicted. Rather than usher in a new era of peaceful and cooperative convergence between the cable TV and telephone industries, it led ironically to the launching of an all-out fight for supremacy in the biggest digital markets of tomorrow. And for John Malone, the promise of dominion over the interactive television landscape of tomorrow has turned into the greatest threat to his company's future he has ever had to confront.

Much of that threat comes from none other than Malone's erstwhile merger partner: Ray Smith, CEO of phone giant Bell Atlantic. Clearly the most enterprising and farsighted of the telco leaders (just try coming up with the name of *any* other phone company executive), Smith was the first to start building a broadband network, the first to win federal approval to operate a commercial video dialtone service, the first to get court permission to sell his company's own content on that service, and the first to begin shifting his once stodgy utility toward a more entrepreneurial footing.

But underneath his new Digital Revolutionary clothing, is Ray Smith just another "Bellhead" emperor monopolist? The 58-year-old lifetime phone executive knows that this is a question on the minds of friends and foes alike, and he enjoys poking fun at his old monopolist image as much as anyone. When the authors arrived for the first interview with him, in fact, Smith pretended to be outlining secret strategy options on a giant whiteboard in his office: (1) Buy AT&T, (2) Sell Pennsylvania, (3) Retire, (4) Work for IBM (depose Gerstner), (5) Cancel subscriptions to all magazines and newspapers.

The first question, naturally, was whether Ray Smith planned to buy AT&T or sell Pennsylvania.

"No, don't use that," he pleaded. "I put that up just to amuse you. All we need is to have a rumor going around that we're going to sell Pennsylvania."

Then he definitely had no plans to sell Pennsylvania?

"Absolutely not!" Smith insisted. He smiled: "We're going to sell West Virginia."

With the preliminaries thus settled, Smith began talking about what really happened the day that the biggest deal in American history crashed and burned.

"You know what amazes me?" he said, leaning back in his chair and thinking back to his merger talks with Malone a year earlier. "There were only four people in the room that day, but there are at least 20 different versions of what happened. It's like *Rashomon*."

Was it true, as Malone has claimed, that the merger had been aborted by Bell Atlantic after Smith failed to get his full board of directors to go along with the deal?

"No, that's absolutely not true," Smith insisted. "The whole board was in favor of it. There wasn't a single voice against it. But let me tell you what *is* true. What really was going on was a struggle in the shareholder base. We have a million shareholders, and they are basically high-yield oriented. We froze the dividend, and it frightened the life out of our shareholders. And our stock, which leaped up for a while on the promise of the merger, dropped as the yield-oriented shareholders sort of pealed away.

"And so the struggle was really in the investment community," he continued. "It was not a debate on our board about whether to change into a high-growth company versus a low-growth [utility]. My cash-flow growth is faster than John's! Of course, that's not to say we didn't have cultural differences, in terms of TCI being more entrepreneurial and all. But the issue was, how do we get the cash out of our company to complete the deal without scaring off our shareholders? Because if you cut the dividend too much, then the shareholders leave and the stock drops so low that you can no longer do the deal."

This, of course, was a problem that Ray Smith knew he would face going into the deal with TCI. But he had hoped that the shareholders could be nudged along carefully. Unfortunately, Malone "lit a match in a gas-filled room," in Smith's view, when he publicly stated that Bell Atlantic would have to cut its dividend to complete the transaction.

"You see, John's approach to this issue was like his regulatory approach," Smith observed. "He didn't say, 'Shoot the shareholders'—don't quote me on that—but he was saying let's just go cut the dividend. John, being the road warrior he is, just wanted to get it over with. But that's not how you deal with regulation, and that is not how you deal with a large shareholder base."

He shrugged. "I'm more of a builder. An architect. I like to do things one brick at a time. My view is align and conquer."

So what, then, finally killed the deal?

"John's cash flow went down. Remember, when we set the deal, John's cash flow was at $200 a subscriber and we agreed to pay him about 11.75 times cash flow. But there was a cash-flow test. If his cash flow went down, as it did [after the FCC cable-rate rollbacks of February 1994], then I would give him fewer shares of my stock, which has a fixed price of $64 in the deal."

By February of 1994, because of TCI's declining cash flow, the value of its stock had dropped to barely $20 a share from its merger-fueled high of nearly $35.

"In the final meeting," recalled Smith, "we kept trying to figure out some way to make it work. John said, 'If I take this [reduced] number of shares, I'll never get my major shareholders to accept it. And there's no way you can give me the number of shares I need. You'd be paying 14 times cash flow.' And I said, 'You're right.' Finally, he said, 'Well, we can't just sit around here forever.' And I said, 'Okay, let's get [the merger breakup] over with.' "

What was his strongest memory of that day? Smith paused a moment. "I guess it's the last words he said as we separated. He said, 'Nice try, my friend.' "

While Ray Smith and John Malone appear to genuinely like each other, such sentiment has no place in war. And that's exactly what is now taking place between their two giant industries as they prepare to compete in each other's markets. Some analysts have suggested that the telcos could steal 30 percent of the $20 billion cable TV business once their video networks are up and running. Others counter that the telcos may lose 30 percent of *their* $100 billion phone business to cable-provided services. And what is Ray Smith's view of Malone's boast to the authors that he could "knock the shit out of the cost structure of the whole telephone business?"

"Oh, c'mon!" Smith snorted. "Bell Atlantic is not one business but 13 different businesses, most of them not subject to any real competition from the cable industry."

He then offered a brief breakdown of Bell Atlantic's various business operations. "We get a billion dollars of our revenues from the federal government. You're saying cable's going to take the federal government—the 25-year contract with the Pentagon that we have— that they're going to take that away? It doesn't make any sense. Cable companies aren't going to touch that. Or look at Yellow Pages. If the cable companies offer local phone services, is that going to affect our Yellow Pages business?"

Smith argues that when one really examines the portion of Bell Atlantic's $13 billion in revenues that are subject to cable competition, only about $4 billion—representing the consumer business—is actually up for grabs. The cable companies in his territory also have about $4 billion in revenues. But while Bell Atlantic reaches 100 percent of cable's customers, the cable companies only have access to approximately 60 percent of its customers—the percentage of telephone-using homes that subscribe to cable TV service.

"So actually," Smith claimed, "there is only about $3 billion they can try to get their hands on. But how successful are they likely to be? Consider the fact that Philadelphia, for example, is served by maybe 10 or 11 cable companies. Even inside the city proper there are four different cable companies. Four different ones! Now you're telling me a consumer is going to subscribe with a cable-phone service that serves only one section of the city? That's going to be a pretty hard sale. And what about power? Remember, when the power's out, so's your cable phone!"

This notion, therefore, of cable TV firms stealing the phone business out from under the telcos . . .

"It's wrong," he declared. "I would say that by the year 2000, we'll have 50 percent of the cable TV business—no doubt about it—which is why cable companies are in such a panic. Meanwhile, they won't get even three percent of telephony revenues in their best market. Not in their very, very best market. It's just not going to happen."

Ray Smith is extremely confident, as is John Malone. And like top-ranked players going *mano a mano* at a poker competition, neither seems to have noticed the arrival of wild-card players intent on reshuffling the deck.

Take Jim Clark, for example. At first glance, he seems a rather unlikely general in the Info Highway wars. Tall, blond, and rather boyish-looking for his 51 years, he has the brainy, bespectacled look of a college professor. Which is what he used to be before he became the toast of Hollywood moguls, the idol of Clinton's high-tech policy makers, the envy of every wannabe entrepreneur in the technology field, and the founder of not one but two of America's hottest technology companies.

Clark also has the distinction of being the only "general" to switch armies not once, but twice, in as many years. Six months after he was first interviewed for this book, Clark quit his post as chairman of Silicon Graphics to pursure a venture in interactive TV. Six months after that, he abandoned the TV business and launched yet another venture, Netscape Communications, to develop software for navigating the Internet, the popular network of computer networks used by millions worldwide. Clark does, however, share one quality with most other executives in this story: he feels everyone else's digital strategy is, simply put, stupid. This was made abundantly clear during this first interview for this book in August of 1993, when he was still chairman of Silicon Graphics.

"I can't tell you the number of times I've been ready to just blow out of here," he grumbled then, referring to Silicon Graphics. "You know, just take my boat down to the tropics and forget it all." He paused, saw the interviewer's surprise, and laughed. Then he leaned back, put his feet up on the desk (next to a software package titled "Civilization . . . Build an Empire that Stands the Test of Time!"), and gazed out his office window at the 17 ultrahip brick-and-glass buildings that make up Silicon Graphics' huge Mountain View, California, campus. "I'm the founder of this company," he sighed. "Big deal. It's the board that runs things, and they just don't get it. I give it six months, max; then I'm out of here."

Ironically, during the previous six months, Clark had achieved perhaps the greatest successes of his career. Silicon Graphics' 3-D visual technology had achieved worldwide acclaim thanks to the blockbuster special-effects wizardry seen in the film *Terminator 2*. And Steven Spielberg's *Jurassic Park* promised only to spotlight SGI's incredible technology even further. The company's stellar fiscal-year-end revenue results of more than $1 billion had rocketed it to the front pages of the nation's business media. And then there was President Clinton's high-profile visit to SGI (with hundreds of reporters in tow), during which he announced the administration's rather vague new technology policy and told SGI management that "government ought to work like you do." Of more practical significance for SGI's future, however, had been two recently negotiated deals—one to provide Time Warner with video servers and cable-box operating system software for an interactive TV pilot project planned for Orlando, Florida; and the other to supply Nintendo, the largest video game maker in the world, with advanced graphics technology to be used in millions of next-generation game players. Both deals had been personally nurtured by Clark himself.

So what could possibly be bothering this high school dropout from Plainview, Texas—a man who, after a stint in the navy, had managed to sweat his way to a Ph.D. in computer science, become a Stanford professor, and then design and patent the fabled "geometry engine" circuitry that turns an ordinary computer screen into a window on a 3-D virtual reality world? Here's a man who has won awards ranging from the Annual Gold Medal in Physics to Arthur Young & Company's Entrepreneur of the Year Award, a man who against all odds has succeeded in transforming himself from a dirt-poor country boy into a still-poor college professor and finally into a yacht-skippering, Mercedes-driving multimillionaire. So what, exactly, was Jim Clark's problem?

"Look," he said, "this whole digital convergence thing is really about finally baking computer technology into consumer products used by millions of ordinary people. I'm talking about interactive television, of course. And the thing is, we could have become *the* standard in operating systems for the whole interactive TV world, but we blew it."

Clark paused a moment, clearly agitated. "Imagine, a joint venture between us and TCI, which is the biggest cable company, and also with Time Warner, which is the second-biggest cable company! We could have provided the underlying software for the whole industry. But Ed [chief executive officer Edward McCracken] didn't see the importance of it. He let it slip right through our fingers."

Clark swiveled around and leaned forward on his desk, the frustration obvious behind his sharp blue eyes. "Jesus Christ, that guy . . . I mean, I had TCI and Time Warner senior executives sitting here for three straight weeks in a row. And all the while I'm trying to sell this deal—not to them, I mean to our own board! But Ed's bitching about having to put in a lousy $10 million for the venture. I mean, TCI and Time Warner, you could tell that they were just puzzled. Like, what's going on here? They'd each agreed to put up money, why shouldn't we? Basically the board was just trying to screw those guys."

He shook his head. "Anyway, what happened was by the fourth week of this shit, with Time Warner and TCI asking me, 'Jim, what's going on?' Microsoft got word of it and put a full-court press on John Malone. Microsoft kind of raised its skirt. And after that, TCI yanked the whole deal. They said, 'We're not gonna go down this road with you.' "

He paused a moment, then shrugged. "Well, I don't think TCI and Time Warner would be stupid enough to let Microsoft dominate [the operating system for] the whole interactive television business. Bill Gates, you know, he worries the hell out of these guys." As it turned out, the Time Warner–TCI–Microsoft talks went nowhere.

Jim Clark's account of the fiasco was confirmed by John Malone, who attributed the failure of negotiations to the fact that SGI was "a house divided." Malone was less forthcoming about the predatory power of Microsoft that is so widely feared in the industry. "As I see it," said Malone, with typical and not-altogether-unwarranted bluster, "the big concern is whether Bill Gates is a bigger monopolist than I am." People throughout the industry, he noted, had called to say "that if I get together with Gates it's going to be the worst thing that ever happened in history. But, you know, my goal is to make sure we have the best troops we possibly can building this system, and in my book that's Gates—if, that is, I can figure out how to do a deal with him without alienating everyone else." And since this interview, in fact, Malone has cut several deals with Microsoft, including a joint test of interactive TV technology and a $125 million

TCI investment in Microsoft Network, the online service Gates has slated for launch in the fall of 1995 and that is widely expected to eventually dominate the entire online services industry.

As for Jim Clark, he did in fact resign on January 27, 1994—exactly six months and five days after that first interview. His plans? "Oh, something in the interactive TV business," he said at the time.

But within weeks of his resignation, the mercurial Clark had reversed direction 180 degrees. Suddenly, the whole field of interactive TV appeared to him to have zero future—did the collapse of the TCI–Bell Atlantic merger that February affect his thinking at all?—and now he had become convinced that the Internet, and the Internet alone, represented the genuine promise of the Information Highway.

The pot of gold at the end of that Info Highway rainbow, of course, lies in "content," especially movies and video games and other entertainment-oriented content. Hence all the dizzy dancing around Hollywood these days, with studio executives pirouetting off to jobs at phone and video game firms, computer makers hip-hopping their way into movie production ventures, cable and phone companies leaping and twirling after studio film libraries, and investment bankers and lawyers absolutely swooning over it all as they cha-cha their way to the bank. Even ex-convicts haven't missed a beat—witness former junk bond king Michael Milken, sans toupee, tap dancing with such stars as Quincy Jones, Nastassja Kinski, and Shelley Duvall at a kickoff party for Seventh Level, his new multimedia firm aimed, he says, at developing "fun and entertaining" CD-ROM titles.

The dizziest dance of all, however, was the sensational six-month-long takeover battle for Paramount, otherwise known among digital cognoscenti as "the last studio in play." And what a spectacle it was, with more cheek-kissing, deal-hustling, rumor-slinging, and brazen party-crashing than an Oscar night victory bash at Mortons. Ostensibly the fight was between Viacom, a cable TV and entertainment company headed by 72-year-old billionaire curmudgeon Sumner Redstone, and the QVC shopping network headed by the brash, 53-year-old former Fox chairman, Barry Diller. But behind each duelist stood a long line of eager seconds—including phone companies such as NYNEX, cable giants like TCI and Comcast, and even the video store giant, Blockbuster. And "like a piece of raw meat that somebody threw in the middle of the floor," to quote one report, the Paramount fight attracted no less than a dozen of Wall Street's most powerful investment banks, which collectively received more than $20 million from the deal.[11] The prize? The studio's 1,800-film library, its Simon & Schuster book division, and its filmmaking expertise. The cost? Ten billion dollars.

One of the few entertainment figures not caught by this whole affair with either drool or spittle all over his face was Jeff Berg, head of the giant Hollywood talent and literary agency International Creative Management (ICM), which represents some 2,500 writers, directors, and actors. Sitting in his brand-new Beverly Hills office, the tall and surprisingly unpretentious (for Hollywood) 48-year-old superagent, who also co-chairs California's Governor's Council on Information Technology, displayed the quiet confidence of someone who clearly feels he's sitting in the catbird seat when it comes to the battle for content.

"People miss the point," he suggested, "if they think that Paramount was some sort of last decisive battle for control of content. Because content, finally, is the talent. It's individual writers, actors, producers, directors. They're the ones at the top of the value chain because they're the creators. So anyone who wants to fill their 500 channels ultimately has to come to the source. Our clients."

But given the enormous price paid for Paramount, couldn't someone just . . .

"Build a new studio?" he finished the question. "Even with $10 billion you couldn't develop that kind of library of films—it would take decades to build that kind of value. But for a lot less, a new player like a telephone company could start making its own movies."

Telephone companies making movies?

"Why not? They have a pretty good network, don't they? They have tremendous capital. They're already participating in the financing of films through investments. And there's no law that says studios are the only institutions that can finance or produce motion pictures. It's just that until now they've been the only ones with the institutional capability to do it efficiently. But anything's possible—Turner and HBO certainly learned how to make their own movies."

Indeed, the notion of a company like Bell Atlantic (whose only prior credits consist of some crushingly boring New Jersey safety films) making movies would seem at first to be rather an outlandish onc. But as Berg predicted in this interview, within a year three phone companies entered into a $500 million pact with Walt Disney studios to develop filmed content. And three others had teamed up with Berg's archrival, Creative Artists Agency chief Michael Ovitz, to do pretty much the same.

Jeff Berg believes the value of digital-age content goes far beyond the ability simply to attract new and additional buyers for his Hollywood clients' creative talents. He's also trolling for partners in the fertile fields of Silicon Valley. "When it comes to selling content," he observed, "the video game business is hardly a nascent market. I mean, Sega and Nintendo last year outgrossed the whole motion picture industry. It's a full-blown business, generating billions of dollars in sales."

A partnership between Hollywood and Silicon Valley, Berg noted, could offer enormous creative synergies. "The missing link in games right now," he suggested, "is the whole area of character development and narrative plot. These software developers may be able to provide the most fantastic graphics, but finally you need a story. You need characters, you need a conceptual framework, and you need a theme. So far these aspects of software grammar haven't entered into the process much. But I think certain companies are realizing that they could draw upon the talent pool of those folks who do create movies and television shows and bring their skills into the interactive software network."

Synergy between Hollywood and Silicon Valley sounds good in theory, but it may prove elusive when it comes to the actual process of creating video games and other entertainment products. Michael Backes, the Hollywood screenwriter of such hits as *Rising Sun* and a cofounder of high-flying video game start-up Rocket Science, illustrated the problem in an interview with *Wired* magazine.

"Good [movies] are really about a *single* directed point of view. A good example is the T. Rex sequence in *Jurassic Park*. It's the high point of the film: it's supremely visualized, but from a specific . . . point of view. They are grabbing you by the head and saying, 'Look here, look there,' . . . and the emotional response you have is one of unmitigated terror and utter fascination. The problem with a user-defined experience [like a video game] is that you can stare at your shoelaces rather than the T-rex, and the emotional content is diluted because the narrative drive is lost [in interactive forms of story-telling]."[12]

Still, Jeff Berg is convinced of the possibilities, at least, in a closer creative relationship between traditional filmmakers and designers of interactive games.

"It makes sense," he insisted. "I mean, what's the most success-ful noncharacter game? Tetris, probably, right? Well, what if you had a game with the addictive nature of Tetris together with strong char-acter development and a compelling plot? What would happen if you backed up all these terrifically visual games with great themes and great characters? You'd be in a whole other stratosphere."

Maybe, maybe not. But we can be certain that until interactive entertainment becomes truly compelling and wins a place for itself in the broad consumer marketplace, the most "stratospheric" aspect of the Digital Revolution will likely continue to be the hyperbole that surrounds it. This fact is in no way a criticism of Jeff Berg or any of the other heavy hitters in the new media game. A certain amount of bluster, after all, has always been the way of the entrepreneurial gladiator, whether he wields shield and sword in some ancient Roman circus or business suit and cellphone in today's Hollywood arena. But the specific alchemies of entertainment and interactivity, of technology and design, and of price versus value derived have yet to be determined. Much awaited are the Merlins of multimedia.

What precisely makes for a truly successful multimedia product, after all, is a question upon which many billions of dollars are ner-vously riding. How much will people really pay for interactive TV services? Which video games, which CD-ROM titles, which online offerings do people truly want? Indeed, the question that today haunts every media mogul, every computer magnate, every cable or telco tycoon, and every single Information Highway visionary is this: if you build it, will they come? Precious few market surveys offer much in the way of clues on this subject—certainly none that pro-vide definitive reassurance to the companies that have pledged well over $100 billion over the next decade to construct the many varied networks of switched, broadband media and communications traffic that together are loosely called the Information Highway.

As a matter of fact, most companies in this field—intoxicated with the technological possibilities, fearful of competitors leaving them behind, and desperate to get a lead in the race to command the

heights of promising future markets—are continuing to invest feverishly *against* the evidence of most market research and historical
experience.

After all, experiments with interactivity have been going on for a
long time. Even back in the 1960s, there were movies shown in
which the theater audience could press buttons and vote to affect the
storyline or the outcome. It never amounted to anything more than
a minor and short-lived avant-garde art form. Qube, another early
experiment in interactivity via cable TV, was a visionary failure
when it was tested in Ohio in the 1970s.

In the early 1990s, Time Warner offered a group of test customers
in Queens, New York, three times as many channels as were normally available. While the company learned a lot about the difficulty
of delivering such service using analog last-generation technology,
the overall consumer response to the wonderful world of 150 channels could be described as lying somewhere between a blank stare
and a yawn. Similarly, current in-room hotel TV services, with their
typical choice of anywhere from eight to more than one hundred
movies, is a rough (if only partial) model of what may be coming to
our living room TV sets in coming years. But while in-room TV is a
nice little niche business, it's no world-beater. In fact, it doesn't
even compare to frequent-flier affiliations as an incentive to attract
travelers.

Pay-Per-View television, offered through most cable systems
today—another proximate model for the near-term future of interactive television—has also consistently disappointed its enthusiasts.
Who can forget the colossal failure of NBC's 1992 Olympics "triple
cast," which invited people to pay premium prices to see much more
comprehensive coverage of Olympic events than the tightly edited
offerings on free, over-the-air TV? Here consumers made it abundantly clear that they far preferred free coverage edited for maximum
dramatic impact to having to pay for the privilege of serving as their
own sports news director and editor. Yet the occasional success of
big-name boxing match or concert events on Pay-Per-View, which
can generate tens of millions of dollars in one-night revenues, is
enough to keep hope alive in this field.

AT&T has been trying to sell people on picture phones for a quarter century without much luck—at least not yet. Home banking by
computer has for the most part been a money loser for the banks that

have offered it. Commercial online ventures such as Compuserve, Prodigy, and America Online have offered interactive services via computer for years now—many of these quite innovative and intriguing. But while they have grown rapidly of late, none has attracted the sort of revenues that can be mentioned in the same breath with those of traditional noninteractive media.

In sum, if one were to rely solely on the demonstrated consumer reaction toward interactive multimedia services to date to determine whether or not to invest in this field, one might not be altogether too bullish on the Info Highway.

But those pouring billions into Information Highway investments measure their prospects according to different yardsticks, and most *do* believe that "if you build it, they will come." For one thing, they have seen new technologies create vast consumer-driven markets where none had existed before—cable television in the 1970s, home video and video games in the 1980s, cellular telephony in the 1990s. And they certainly don't want to miss the next giant wave of opportunities for want of a little guts and vision.

But another factor driving corporate investment in the emerging digital world order is the convergence of once separate markets and industries—and all of the risks as well as the opportunities that this blurring of boundaries necessarily entails. The fact that a telephone call and a movie are now simply variations on a stream of digital ones and zeros, for instance, means that if Telephone Company A doesn't move quickly into the cable television business, then Cable Company B will use its own digital wires into the home to provide a package of voice *and* video services and thereby raid Telephone Company A's core business.

The uncertainty helping to fuel corporate investment in new media ventures also reflects the profound changes that have taken place of late in the world of business. No longer is it axiomatic that corporate wars will be won by those with the richest treasury or the largest marketing army. Nowadays, victory *can* belong to agile corporate commandos like General Magic's Marc Porat, who adroitly marshal their best technology and human resources to anticipate and adapt to a fast-changing market. In this new Age of Consortia, strategic alliances between small firms with innovative new technologies and large companies able to effectively commercialize them have come to define the corporate landscape of the 1990s. But while the new ecology of business is certainly friendlier to small firms, this does not mean that the concentrated wealth and marketing muscle of large-scale enterprises are any less critical as factors in business. Just the opposite. They provide the massive capital flows necessary to fund infrastructure development and build markets on a global scale. They offer the market-share dominance that can be leveraged through volume production and economies of scale. And they confer the power to shape the competitive environment in a way most favorable to one's own interests. Indeed, for all the talk of the decentralizing effects of digital technology—and the opportunities thereby made available to innovative young companies—it is worth noting how severely a once great company like Apple has been marginalized as a result of its declining market share.

Facilitating the multimedia investment frenzy, of course, is the underlying financial climate of the mid-1990s. Many large American corporations have been awash in cash, debt has been easy to issue at relatively low interest rates, the regulatory environment has allowed for greater industry crossover, and shareholders have generally put a premium on Information Highway investments. Against this backdrop, American business has been able to demonstrate a more visionary and long-term approach to its investments—or at least toward its Info Highway investments—than was the case in the 1980s. That is one reason why U.S. companies remain technologically in the lead in the global race to build the industries and businesses of the future.

Still, history teaches us that even the most farsighted vision and investment strategy is no guarantee that new technology will develop as planned. Alexander Graham Bell demonstrated his telephone in 1876, but it took decades before the device first appeared in business settings—and even then most experts laughed at the notion that the phone might ever become more than simply an expensive toy for a few of the idle rich. (Incidentally, Bell also wrote about the possibility of sending pictures over telephone wires, and while it's taken a good hundred years, absolutely no one is laughing at *that* prospect anymore). Similarly, in 1844 Samuel Morse wanted the government to purchase his new telegraph system and develop it as an improved mail service, but Washington was uninterested. The private-sector battle that followed to commercialize Morse's telegraph led 22 years later to the creation of the first giant monopoly in American business,

Western Union, and to the continent-wide centralization of financial markets in Wall Street.

"What Hath God Wrought?" Morse had telegraphed in his famous Baltimore-to-Washington test of the device. All in all, it was an eloquent and rather prescient statement on the unpredictability of technological change.

▪ **2** ▪

Accidental Genesis

If the U.S. does not [develop] HDTV, the country as a whole is likely to experience a continued declining world market share in automated manufacturing equipment, personal computers, and semiconductors. In addition, telecommunications and other strategically critical industries could follow. Loss of these markets will contribute to the loss of American jobs, significantly increase the U.S. trade deficit, increase the national debt, and lead to the erosion and eventual loss of a U.S. manufacturing base . . . Implicit in this decline is the United States' loss of position as a major world power.

AMERICAN ELECTRONICS ASSOCIATION
NOVEMBER 1988

It is hard to believe now, but less than a decade ago high-definition television (HDTV), a technique for offering movielike picture quality on TV, was *the* hot technology in the world, *the* economic hot button for advocates of greater U.S. competitiveness in world markets, and *the* political hot potato in Washington policy-making circles. Its development was the principal focus of research at dozens of major corporations worldwide, its promotion the single overriding concern of the Federal Communications Commission and other government bodies charged with boosting U.S. technological leadership in the world. It was a time when careers rose and fell like leaves in the wind in response to the changing political weather surrounding HDTV.

Today, HDTV is barely an afterthought on the technology agenda. The FCC is consumed with other matters—unleashing competition in the telephone and cable TV industries, and fostering the construction of new wireless communications networks to span the nation—while in policy circles the hot issue of the day is not high-definition imagery but rather the high-bandwidth social and economic implications of the coming Information Highway.

How quickly the "technology of the future" becomes the outmoded contraption of yesteryear! Yet at the time, well-informed and thoughtful people were convinced—and with good reason—that HDTV held the key to America's future.

What happened is a story well worth telling. It is first of all the soap-operatic saga of America's 20-year-long David vs. Goliath race against a supposedly invincible Japan, Inc. to find the key to the technological future—only to discover in the end that the Holy Grail was merely a mirage. It is also a parable of American stupidity and complacency somehow redeemed, at the last moment and thanks to a good measure of blind luck and Yankee ingenuity, in the accidental creation of the preconditions for the emerging Information Highway. And it is a tale that offers valuable lessons to all those (the authors included) who may be tempted to believe that the final fruits and consequences of human endeavors can be predicted with any certainty.

The serendipitous saga of HDTV should perhaps begin with the very first day of television's public existence, more than half a century ago. Witnessing a demonstration of a prototype TV at the 1939 World's Fair, a *New York Times* reporter offered this rather luminescent analysis: "The problem with television," he wrote, "is that the people must sit and keep their eyes glued on a screen; the average American family hasn't time for it." This would not be the last time that television's capacity to radically alter economic and cultural realities would foolishly be underestimated—not least by the TV industry itself.

For the first 20 years of its existence, the world of television was ruled by America. The quality of our programming was—and still is—the envy of the world. In those years also, U.S. companies like RCA, GE, Philco, Sylvania, and Magnavox led the world in the TV set manufacturing business, the competitive demands of which sparked continuing innovations in the technology, such as color broadcasting and reception. Throughout the 1950s and 1960s, the global dominance of America's TV-driven consumer electronics industry was an important factor in the nation's favorable trade balance, helping to fuel the postwar U.S. economic boom. Indeed, the robust U.S. economy made it possible for many consumers to afford the first color TVs when they were introduced in the late 1950s, despite the fact that at $1,000 they cost as much as a new Ford Fairlane car. Consumer demand, in turn, led quickly to huge economies of scale in manufacturing that drove down the price of the new color sets. But even more important, the new industry's rapid growth also funded "economies of scope"—new advances in the underlying technologies of television—that fostered the rapid emergence of new industries like computers and satellites.

In the 1970s, thanks largely to television and related technologies, the electronics industry had begun to overtake automobiles and aerospace as the nation's largest manufacturing industry. Television-inspired advances in the production of semiconductors, memory chips and circuit boards, computer systems, software, and all manner of high-tech manufacturing equipment had become the key ingredient in the unsurpassed productivity and competitiveness of U.S. industry as a whole.

But just at the peak of its success, America's TV industry began to show unmistakable signs of trouble. Under growing pressure from aggressively priced imports, many companies began to abandon the low-margin, high-risk business of TV set manufacturing. Others like RCA, the inventor of color broadcasting, sharply curtailed the sort of costly long-term investments in new technology research that are necessary to stay ahead. The fruits of any research projects that survived, meanwhile, were often licensed to the highest manufacturing bidders from abroad.

Ampex, for example, licensed its video tape recorder invention to an innovative Japanese company named Sony, which had previously shown what it could do with the American technology when it took Bell Labs' transistor (which AT&T believed had no commercial value) and turned it into a portable radio. With Ampex's hard-to-use video recorder, Sony stuck the tape into a cheap and handy cassette, thereby transforming what the Americans had scorned as a minor niche business into a worldwide mass-market gold mine.

While U.S. companies either rested on the laurels of past inventions or quit the business altogether, Japanese firms were showing the world that they were not just high-tech copycats but top-notch innovators as well. By the 1980s, the Japanese were not only making the world's best TVs and VCRs, but they had also used the profits and knowledge gained from these businesses to capture many other markets, from memory chips to computer display screens.

It is hard to believe now, but at the beginning of the 1970s, the Japanese were still not taken terribly seriously as competitors in the field of high-end technology products. To be sure, there was already a U.S. trade deficit with Japan. But it had just begun to appear and was still quite small and seemingly contained. The cumulative total U.S. trade deficit with Japan for the first three years of the decade was less than a month's trade deficit these days. Moreover, the developing acrimony between Washington and Tokyo at the time had little to do with the technology industry. The big trade fracas in 1971 was textiles.

To fully understand what long-term planning means in the context of Japanese industrial policy, it is important to note that by 1973 it was not yet even clear to Americans that Japanese companies would eventually dominate the global consumer electronics business. Most American companies in the field could sense the Japanese nipping at their heels, but believed it was a threat that could be handled through currency revaluation. (The dollar was then worth three times as much as it is today against the yen, and Americans widely believed that this factor alone accounted for much of Japan's success in exporting competitively).

So while GE, RCA, and other U.S. companies took their domination of the television-set market for granted—the Japanese were merely nettlesome upstarts in the American view—back in Tokyo, Japanese planners had no doubt that they would soon have the big, blind, and clumsy American consumer electronics companies by the throat. It was only a matter of time. The only question on their minds was what to do *after* they won the television war.

What they decided upon was a plan to reinvent television once again. The color TV revolution that overthrew the old black-and-white regime was still a fresh experience in the minds of those charged with strategic planning at Japan's Ministry of International Trade and Industry (MITI), NHK (the major national broadcasting network), and at the leading TV-set manufacturing companies. Many of these individuals had themselves risen through the ranks during a time when newly introduced color TVs were managing to attract the dollars and yen of people who already owned a perfectly good black-and-white set. And they had seen how, amid the market turmoil that inevitably results from the introduction of new technology, Japanese companies had been able to exploit a manufacturing lead in color TV sets to gain significant market share.

But in the world of television, what comes after color? To the

Japanese who asked that question in 1973, the answer seemed to be better picture quality—movie theater quality beamed into the home, to be exact. What's more, Japanese researchers believed they had found a relatively straight path to accomplishing this technological goal.

Thus was born the Japanese Hi-Vision project, aimed at developing the technology for transmitting and receiving high-definition TV—HDTV, as it later came to be known. At the core of this project was a set of standards developed by NHK known as the MUSE system. This technology promised to more than double the 525 lines of resolution typical of most television sets, change the "aspect ratio" of TV images to make them less square and more rectangular (like those in a movie theater), and utilize a variety of other mechanisms to make television fare look even more brilliantly realistic, captivating, and engrossing than before.

No one even stopped to ask themselves whether or not consumers in Japan, the United States, or anywhere else for that matter were particularly desirous of better picture quality, or how much they might be willing to pay for it. After all, the spread of color television had taken place remarkably unimpeded by price barriers. Therefore HDTV planners assumed that consumer pocketbooks would surely prove just as elastic when HDTV sets began to appear.

The Japanese were so convinced that improved picture quality would be the next big revolution in television technology that they firmly intended, regardless of what the consumer might or might not want, to stand at the forefront of it. And though they could not anticipate all the possible applications of HDTV technology that might develop down the road, they were pretty certain that if they got out in front of the next generation of TV technology, they would not only be able to drive the television market of the 1980s and 1990s, they would also be able to drive the market for new semiconductors, new displays, new satellite transmission technology, new medical imaging products, and many other emerging technologies and markets along the way.

So even as the American giants of consumer electronics began in the 1970s to be mowed down by the first generation of Japanese technological and manufacturing firepower, the Japanese had already begun developing the ammunition for their *next* generation assult on the global marketplace. Some $1.5 billion in R&D money would be poured into HDTV by the Japanese government and the private sector. And though for historical reasons they weren't involved in the space race, HDTV was for Japan the equivalent of America's moon shot.

At first, no one in America seemed to notice. The 1970s were the time when Americans first awakened to the rather startling prospect that U.S. supremacy in all fields might not forever be written in stone. The Vietnam War had sapped our confidence and skewed our economy, contributing to the first budget deficits of the postwar era. Then the oil shock of 1974 and its aftermath helped push fuel-efficient Japanese cars and energy-efficient Japanese steel to the forefront of the world market. Meanwhile, U.S. companies continued their exodus from U.S. manufacturing, rushing to Mexico, Korea, and Taiwan in search of what they thought was needed to compete with the foreigners: cheap labor.

By the mid-1970s, a flood of superior-quality foreign imports were sending business leaders and their political representatives into a panic. Looking at the TV business, where imports accounted for 25 percent of all sets sold and all but two U.S. manufacturers were gone from the scene, the business community began issuing strident calls for federal action. These found a ready response from the public. The antiforeign sentiment was not simply a matter of wounded pride. The import avalanche was soon seen as draining U.S. trade surpluses, driving up the cost of investment capital, and threatening the nation's economic future and the living standards of its citizens. But rather than roll up our sleeves and get back to work producing our own superior products, Washington took the easier road and demanded that the foreigners stop selling so many of theirs.

Thus was born the 1977 "orderly marketing agreement" on trade between the U.S., Europe, and Japan. By setting quotas on foreign imports, America was relying on blatant protectionism to help its domestic industries compete on home territory. The problem with protectionism, however—especially when it becomes a substitute for boosting the productivity and quality of domestic businesses—is that it quite often produces exactly the opposite effects of those intended. As early as 1972, for example, Sony had foreseen the political change of weather approaching and had set up its first U.S. TV set manufacturing facility near San Diego, California. Sony would be followed in later years by a host of other Japanese, European, and eventually even Korean companies.

Foreign manufacturers like Thomson of France simply bought out American TV firms or set up manufacturing facilities in the U.S. A Thomson executive (and former RCA employee before it was bought by Thomson) said, "You're better off having a foreign owner who's dedicated than a U.S. owner who doesn't give a damn." There was more than a little truth in this statement. By the late 1980s, nine out of ten TVs sold in America were built by foreign-owned plants. The sole remaining American producer, Zenith, had shifted its production—and most of its jobs—overseas.

Partly as a result of these trends, the electronics trade balance swung an astonishing $20 billion from a net surplus to a net deficit—even with various kinds of protectionism in place. Combined with similar trends in other manufacturing industries, a growing federal deficit, a drop in private savings, and steadily declining productivity growth, the effect was to sharply reduce the amount of capital available for investment. At one point in the late 1980s, U.S. capital costs were roughly four times those faced by Japanese industry. Japan's enormous advantage on capital costs—not to mention the cozy marriage of business and government interests in that country, the highly vertically integrated character of Japanese electronics companies, and a dash of predatory trade policies thrown in for good measure—all combined to make Tokyo's HDTV project seem a sure winner.

In the mid-1980s, the HDTV story began to get bloody. Having worked diligently on it for almost 15 years, the Japanese took their Hi-Vision system on the road. At a 1986 meeting of the International Radio Consultative Council in Dubrovnik, Yugoslavia (now Serbia), the Japanese proposed that their satellite-based 1,125-line HDTV system be adopted as a world standard.

Actually, two different but interlinked sets of arcane technological standards were involved, and both would soon become centerpieces of highly politicized debate. The first was the "production standard" for HDTV—that is, the technical manner in which the "high definition" look would be achieved in the original recording of HDTV content. The second was the "transmission standard"—that is, how the signals for high definition television would be generated and carried into the homes of tomorrow.

The subject of technological standards was already one capable of arousing strong political passions. The world of television itself had grown up with a 50 year history of incompatibility. The U.S. and Japan used the NTSC standard, most of Europe and the developing world used the PAL standard, and France, the Soviet Union, and many former French colonies used the SECAM standard. On top of the headaches caused by those incompatibilities, many technology policy experts of the mid-1980s were deeply concerned about the lack of standards for the emerging world of computers, operating systems, and data communications. Thus, the idea of "one global standard" for the brave new world of HDTV held a certain appeal.

Hoping to capitalize on that sentiment, the Japanese hoped to sell the rest of the world on adopting both the production and the transmission standards they had already developed. This would have made it easy for Japanese manufacturers to penetrate world markets with uniform designs, rather than having to rethink and retool for the engineering standards of each market.

Incredibly, the U.S. delegation at Dubrovnik endorsed the Japanese production standard and appeared amenable to adopting the transmission standard as well. This would not only have given over the enormously lucrative U.S. market to Japanese companies, but would have required American consumers to replace their 212 million existing TV sets with new equipment capable of receiving HDTV transmissions.

Not only was the American position at Dubrovnik a commercial blunder, it was political folly as well. U.S.–Japan issues had already become highly politicized by that time, and the notion of a sinister mercantilist Japan, Inc. trying to rob America of its birthright to technological and industrial leadership was deeply felt throughout the U.S. heartland. While American fears may have been exaggerated as a result of the anti-Japanese media and political frenzy of the late 1980s, there is little doubt that MITI and other specialists of Japanese industrial policy did, in fact, see leadership in the emerging HDTV industry as a steamroller paving the way for more Japanese jobs, exports, and profits.

Being far more phobic about Japan then Americans have ever been, the Europeans could not believe that the U.S. delegation at Dubrovnik could be so naive as to miss Japan, Inc.'s true intentions, and hand over global HDTV leadership to the Japanese just because

NHK had come up with an innovative technology for it. The Reagan-omic infatuation with laissez-faire economics was seen by the Europeans as ridiculously shortsighted and stupid—part and parcel, they felt, of the same policies that had allowed Japan to eat the market share of the American automobile industry.

This, they vowed, would never happen to European industries and jobs. Having spent years building walls of protection for their own TV manufacturers, the European Community was not about to let HDTV become Japan's Trojan horse. So to guard against the loss of their technological and industrial competitiveness, they blocked the NHK plan. Just because America had decided that its own electronics industry couldn't stand up to the Japanese juggernaut, said the Europeans, was no reason for them to lie down as well. They would be the masters of their own HDTV destiny.

"HDTV was [Japan's] ultimate weapon," insisted one Thomson executive after the meeting, "an instrument with which to squeeze their European competitors and blitzkrieg the wide-open American market—in short, move in for the kill. [Dubrovnik] was to be the new Verdun."[1]

Rather than hoist the white flag, a nine-nation European Community consortium known as Eureka Project 95—led by Dutch electronics giant Philips and Thomson of France, and backed by over a billion dollars in government and industry funding—decided to develop its own HDTV system, known as HD-MAC, using 1,250 lines of resolution.

As P. Bogels, the director of Europe's Eureka Project, would confide several years later, "The Americans strike me as sometimes quite suicidal, whereas we in Europe wish to live. Of course, we think our standard is technologically preferable to the Japanese standard. But the essence of the issue is strategy, not technology." By this, he meant that to continue to have an independent existence, European electronics companies believed they would have to do as they had done previously with earlier TV and video standards: create their own unique standard that offered indigenous manufacturers an advantage and reduced the attractiveness and accessibility of their market to outsiders.

Developing an independent HDTV strategy was not purely a defensive move on the part of the Europeans against Japan's onslaught. Seeing that the Americans had no apparent interest in establishing their own HDTV program for the U.S., the Europeans envisioned a juicy opportunity to go on the offense. By putting Eureka in motion, they could not only defend their home turf, they could compete directly with the Japanese for control of the biggest prize of all: the giant *American* HDTV market.

But before America could decide to whom it should surrender, a sudden change of heart occurred in the land that had invented television. As has so often happened in the history of technology, the change came *not* in response to the issue at hand—HDTV and American competitiveness—but to a side issue.

Motorola, along with various cellular telephone and paging companies, petitioned the FCC to assign unused television spectrum to telecommunications purposes. Since TV broadcasters weren't using their allotted spectrum fully anyway, the telecom interests had a good case. The TV broadcasters, however, regarded this move with none of the apathy they had previously shown to Japanese competition—spectrum, after all, is the bandwidth equivalent of Class A real estate—and they suddenly determined that HDTV was a matter of vital importance (at least as an argument against the reallocation request of the cellular industry).

Thus the National Association of Broadcasters petitioned the Federal Communications Commission in early 1987 to reserve available spectrum for the supposedly imminent arrival of HDTV broadcasting. If the FCC gave the spectrum to others, warned NAB President Edward Fritts, it would "preclude American broadcasters from developing HDTV as a free over-the-air service to the nation." But while the NAB petition was flowery in its invocation of the public interest, Joseph Flaherty of CBS was more candid about just whose interests were really involved:

> A terrestrial HDTV broadcast system must be devised to maintain the American system of broadcasting . . . The capability of competing [i.e., cable and satellite] home delivery systems to deliver a full quality HDTV signal emphasizes the need [for us] to . . . maintain competitive parity. A failure to provide sufficient radio frequency spectrum for the terrestrial broadcasters could put [us] in a position of irreversible inferiority.[2]

In other words, the politically potent network broadcasting industry was once again seeking safeguards against further intrusions into its markets by the cable TV industry. The FCC granted the broadcasters' petition, leading FCC chief engineer Thomas Stanley to observe, "The broadcasters played their high-definition card" and won.[3] But over the next year, the lack of any serious development work on HDTV confirmed that broadcasters were not so much interested in pursuing HDTV as they were scared to death of seeing their cushy monopoly of channel spectrum taken away if they did not.

At that time, in fact, most broadcasters actually *opposed* HDTV technology. Typical was the view of ABC's chief of broadcast operations, Julius Barnathan: "Around here, we call [HDTV] the emperor's new clothes."[4] One problem for broadcasters was expense: it was then estimated that the hardware cost alone of upgrading to HDTV would be $38 million per station—with no guarantee of increased viewership.

In early 1988, the FCC established an Advisory Committee on Advanced Television Service, headed by FCC chief Richard Wiley, and invited proposals for an HDTV system in the U.S. In essence, the government was telling broadcasters to put up or shut up—a turn of events that some broadcasters had hoped to delay. The FCC move strongly suggested that, one way or another, HDTV was going to happen. Already hammered by the rapid growth of cable and satellite TV service, broadcasters realized that if the FCC adopted Japan's Hi-Vision HDTV—thus far the only working system in the world—they were bound to lose even more market share because it was a system best supported by satellite or coaxial cable delivery.

America's broadcasters, however, had faced similar threats to their hegemony before. They knew that if HDTV had to come, they could surely devise sufficient ways to be further enriched and empowered by it—and to lobby with the FCC and Congress for solutions that helped them do so. Indeed, perhaps there was even a way broadcasters could profit from this whole nuisance of HDTV. If they developed the technological standard for it, after all, wouldn't others have to license it from them?

And so it came to be that with all the sincerity of condemned men suddenly turning to God, the major TV networks jumped on the bandwagon of electronics and communications companies working feverishly on HDTV plans. Eventually, some 23 separate HDTV proposals would be submitted to the FCC.

Little noticed amid the rising HDTV fever was one firm that did *not* submit a proposal. General Instrument (GI), a maker of satellite gear and cable TV converters, quietly began experimenting with an all-new digital form of HDTV.

The company, which specialized in non-standard technology and the conversion of signals from one format to another, had a crack team of engineers trained principally at MIT's Center for Advanced Television Studies. They knew that all the analog HDTV systems then under discussion would be incompatible with General Instrument's existing gear. The company thus planned initially only to develop a digitally based conversion process that would enable their existing equipment to interface with HDTV signals.

Having no vested interests in the HDTV debate and unafraid to fail, General Instrument dug into its digital research. "We really weren't particularly interested in HDTV per se," recalls Mat Miller, then GI's chief technology officer. "For us, HDTV was an in-house stalking horse for speeding up the work we wanted to do anyway on digital video and compression."

It was, in retrospect, a long shot—most experts at the time considered digital television to be at least a decade away from feasibility, if not longer. As one FCC consultant noted, "A lot of people were even saying it could never be done."

In the summer of 1988, the HDTV race gathered new momentum when Japan's NHK broadcast HDTV satellite coverage of the Summer Olympic Games in Seoul, South Korea. Three months later, the FCC issued its most critical ruling: any American HDTV system would have to be available to viewers in some form via traditional terrestrial broadcast on normal TV sets, as well as on future HDTV sets. And no current broadcast license-holders would be denied an HDTV license.

To be sure, this ruling made sense. With its broad geographic territory and multitude of TV stations, America was clearly not as suitable for satellite-based HDTV as was Japan, with its dense population, compact land area, and tiny handful of TV stations. But it also guaranteed that if HDTV had to come (and all signs indicated it would), at least it would come in a manner that did not directly harm the basic business of broadcasters or bolster those of the satellite and cable TV industries. By forcing the Japanese and Europeans back to their labs to squeeze their 30 megahertz satellite signals into the narrower 6 megahertz bandwidth of a broadcast channel, the FCC action bought precious time for the Americans. Given the record of complacency evidenced by the U.S. television industry over the previous 20 years, however, few expected it to make much use of it.

One man who did was Alfred Sikes, the little-known head of a backwater unit in the Commerce Department known as the National Telecommunications and Information Administration. Believing that HDTV was vitally important to America's future, the 47-year-old Sikes brought his considerable patience and organizing skills to bear on the issue. He won over his boss, Commerce Secretary Robert Mosbacher, and recruited allies in Congress. He also commissioned studies showing a huge potential market for HDTV, and pushed industry to come up with a plan to pursue that market.

Another early advocate for HDTV was Craig Fields, then the 41-year-old deputy director of the Defense Advanced Research Projects Agency (DARPA), the reclusive $1 billion Pentagon agency that has helped pioneer a number of new technologies, including the forerunner of today's Internet. Fields had a knack for getting economically important technology research projects funded by arguing that these would also help promote U.S. military and security interests. And he knew that, as a likely catalyst for advances in computer, communications, and semiconductor technologies, HDTV research could be sold to his bosses as a military necessity. Determined that America not be left behind in these areas, he initiated a small $10 million HDTV research and development program within DARPA.

By 1989, HDTV had become a red-hot political issue. The U.S. electronics industry, under pressure from Japanese competition, enlisted a small but busy legion of lobbyists to promote HDTV as the linchpin of future U.S. economic competitiveness. In May that year, the American Electronics Association (AEA) urged the formation of an industry-government consortium to spearhead HDTV development.

In some circles, HDTV was now becoming the ultimate litmus test on competitiveness. It was no longer just a television transmission system or even a technology. It had become a metaphor for jobs, for economic growth and productivity, for the trade balance, and for maintaining America's control of the top echelons of the economic food chain in an increasingly technology-driven global economy. Although today's Digital Revolution had yet to unfold and the Information Highway was not yet a meaningful phrase, a diverse array of business and government leaders shared an inchoate belief that all kinds of powerful, economically stimulating technology breakthroughs, products, services, and businesses would follow in the wake of HDTV. One study at the time suggested that if America did *not* get into the HDTV game, by the year 2010 the portion of the U.S. trade deficit attributable to HDTV and related technologies would be a staggering, unimaginable $200 billion a year.

It is useful to recall that in 1989–90, Japan seemed to Americans to be nearly invincible, and Europe, too, was a rising force in the economic world. Noticing the emphasis that Japan and Europe seemed to be placing on HDTV—and comparing those highly coordinated efforts with America's laissez-faire approach—serious advocates of American competitiveness could be forgiven for ringing a few alarm bells. Even some politicians who had never shown much interest in competitiveness issues felt compelled to speak out in favor of launching a national, federally funded HDTV project.

The political heat around HDTV turned into flames of controversy, however, when the AEA requested over $1 billion in government research grants, loans, and loan guarantees, as well as $100 million in expanded DARPA aid to help private companies kick-start their HDTV programs. In Senate hearings on HDTV, Commerce Secretary Robert Mosbacher—until then a staunch advocate for HDTV—came under sharp criticism for the AEA plan's price tag. Mosbacher, never one to miss a shift in political winds, turned around and publicly rebuked the trade group for seeking handouts from "Uncle Sugar." Mosbacher's friends contend that the AEA neglected to inform the secretary of the specifics of the plan's cost. But it is likely Mosbacher knew the rough price tag all along and simply distanced himself from the AEA when its plan was confronted with strong political opposition.

Noted Al Sikes: "That was the watershed event that caused [government support for] HDTV to decline."

The Senate hearing, however, was only the excuse, not the root cause, of HDTV's political demise. The truth is, George Bush's White House opposed any major government role in HDTV development, or indeed, any effort at rebuilding American competitiveness that smacked of "industrial policy" in the marketplace. According to one report at the time, Mosbacher was called to the White House after his Senate appearance and chewed out by the Bush troika of

Chief of Staff John Sununu, economic advisor Michael Boskin, and Budget Director Richard Darman. The message: HDTV was out, and so was anyone who pushed it too hard.[5]

"It was like a vaudeville show," Oregon Democratic Congressman Les AuCoin said. "Someone yanked [Mosbacher] with a hook."

Boskin, who would later become famous for his claim that it was all the same to the American economy if we produced potato chips or computer chips, recognized that HDTV was indeed a watershed issue. And he and the other free-market ideologues in the Bush administration wouldn't rest until they quashed any hope of government support for HDTV.

While Bush's anti-HDTV team pressed their attack on anyone who dared suggest that U.S. business competitiveness was, indeed, the proper concern of government, the senior executives of the biggest Japanese companies never took their eyes off the long-term prize.

Japanese strategists wanted to get HDTV accepted in the United States and thereby obtain all the advantages that would accrue to Japan, Inc. from exploiting the growth of a Japanese-led industry. But how to do that without worsening the already acrimonious relations between the two countries? This was a matter of sharp debate within the highest levels of Japanese business and government.

Should NHK drop its overt effort to get U.S. support for its standard and instead partner with an American company to create a seemingly American (but in actuality pro-Japanese) new standard? Should Japanese companies offer to make HDTV sets at manufacturing sites in the United States—and was this even feasible, given the problems with American manufacturing quality? Should Japanese companies partner with U.S. companies to cover themselves with an American mantle, and if so, which company would be the ideal partner: IBM, AT&T, Motorola, Intel, Texas Instruments? What about an outright acquisition of a down-on-its-luck American company like Zenith, a plan that might provide the necessary American veneer while avoiding the dangers of allowing the seemingly hapless Americans control of the manufacturing process?

A memo circulated during that time within the top ranks of one of Japan's largest electronics companies provides an unprecedented inside look at Japanese thinking not only about HDTV but about the larger field of U.S.–Japan competition as well. In a section titled "Influencing Manufacturers," the memo advises:

> U.S. manufacturers of HDTV components might be induced to support the NHK standard in return for [our] agreement to low-royalty or even free licensing of key technologies, commitments to some degree of shared North American manufacturing, and/or other attractive joint actions. Of course, those manufacturers who have quality operations and financial staying power would be most desirable for [us], but that should not be the dominant consideration. Rather, the critical question should be the likely extent of their influence on the [HDTV standard-setting] process and on what it would take to sway them . . . Though the logical extension of this line of reasoning might be for [us] to acquire [an American manufacturer] outright, the politics of such a move are all wrong. [We] must avoid the impression of "swallowing up [such a company] in a quest for HDTV domination."

As the Japanese debated strategy, their biggest worry seemed to be that the HDTV debate could spark the ultimate backlash against Japan. After all, it was precisely during this period that Japanophobia reached its peak in the United States. Sony had just announced its multibillion-dollar purchase of Columbia Pictures—an icon representing the heart of American culture—and this precipitated a whole string of acquisitions of American entertainment companies by Japanese interests that would include Matsushita's $6 billion acquisition of MCA and several others. Many Americans felt that Japan was literally taking over America.

Oddly, amid all the strategy debates in the highest echelons of Japanese power circles, one scenario never even occurred to Tokyo planners: that their basic technology for HDTV might shortly become obsolete.

As it turned out, Washington's refusal to support a major domestic thrust into HDTV was a blessing in disguise for American technology development. This, of course, was far from evident at the time. Indeed, proponents of American competitiveness sank into despair over the way HDTV was being handled and began to look for some way to spark an American entry into the field.

Enter Al Sikes again. Publicly, he stopped boosting the HDTV program. But quietly, he began campaigning for the chairmanship of the FCC, through which he felt he could more effectively drive the

HDTV program toward fruition. He succeeded in that effort, and in his first major ruling, he reaffirmed in April of 1990 the FCC's earlier decision on compatibility and made it more precise: HDTV transmissions would have to be receivable not only in their high-definition format on special HDTV sets, but also as plain old television on plain old sets. This could be done by broadcasting TV programs simultaneously as both HDTV and NTSC signals.

Nominally, this ruling was made in the interests of the American consumer—interests that the Japanese, in their very different society, had never much worried about. But at the same time, it insured that there would be no overnight rush into HDTV and that broadcasters could upgrade their own transmission equipment over time. The networks also got the FCC to double the amount of broadcast spectrum they were allocated, ostensibly so they could eventually transmit regular television simultaneously with HDTV signals. And what's more, they were assured of all this added spectrum for free! Referring to this unprecedented $1 billion license giveaway, one wag noted that "Uncle Sugar" had become "Uncle Sucker."

Craig Fields, however, was not able to avoid the wrath of Bush administration ideologues. After first trying to kill DARPA's HDTV program, Deputy Defense Secretary Donald Atwood demanded that Fields either resign, accept demotion, or be fired for "insubordination." In June of 1990, Fields left DARPA to become head of the Microelectronics & Computer Technology Corporation (MCC), a private consortium pooling technology research, where he remained for the next four years, trying through private-sector means to kick-start the high-tech renaissance he had tried to nurture at DARPA.

While Fields was bidding adieu to colleagues at DARPA, the deadline for submitting HDTV proposals to the FCC had come down to the wire. Of 23 original contenders, the FCC had winnowed the list to just 4: NHK's Hi-Vision system; a joint venture between NBC, the David Sarnoff Research Center, Philips of the Netherlands, and Thomson of France (sometimes called the "European Consortium," much to NBC's dismay); the Massachusetts Institute of Technology; and Zenith. But Sikes then extended the deadline and encouraged others with simulcast technology to come forward.

And that's when all the scores suddenly changed. Late in the evening before the final filing deadline, engineers and executives at General Instrument sat around trying to decide if they should submit their digital proposal. Among other concerns was whether it was worth the $250,000 that they would have to pay for FCC testing of the system. At literally the eleventh hour, GI's band of Davids decided to go with their instincts and challenge the media Goliaths. They rushed the next morning to file their proposal.

And so it was that on June 6, 1990—the very last day for filing HDTV system proposals—darkhorse General Instrument came seemingly out of nowhere to propose an all-digital approach to HDTV. The shock of a workable technology for digital television was heard literally around the world. Within months, three of the other four contenders had come back from their engineering labs with all-digital systems as well, Zenith forming an alliance with AT&T to do so. Only NHK stuck to its analog guns.

Looking back on General Instrument's achievement nearly four years later, TCI's John Malone expressed the sentiment of many in the cable TV and communications industries when he called it "an enormous breakthrough." Its significance, he said, was that "it made the Information Highway financially practical. The ability to capture digital video efficiently is really the reason why the Information Highway is even possible."

It is ironic that although General Instrument had not sought initially to set an HDTV standard, the scope of what it achieved went far beyond the narrow confines of HDTV. By unlocking the secret to digitizing and compressing television and by showing that even bandwidth-intensive television signals could be compressed into just another digital data stream, GI opened the door to the vast process of convergence that we now see unfolding. Today's embryonic multimedia networks and systems would probably have emerged eventually, of course, but these might not have developed under American leadership.

Observes Matt Miller: "We had some extraordinary technology at GI, but we didn't really have a monopoly on it. The fact that everybody else came back with digital proposals just a few months after ours shows that it was not extreme rocket science. Our role was to open up people's thinking in a field that had been looking inward for too long."

In retrospect, NHK's Hi-Vision system was dead as of the day of GI's filing—even if it took nearly four more years for its analog corpse to fall over. Proceeding dogmatically dead-ahead in the Japanese market, and still hoping its Hi-Vision system might yet win the U.S. competition, NHK in 1991 flipped a switch and opened what it hoped would be a new era in television history. Soon eight hours of high-definition TV would beam from satellites in the skies to the Japanese islands below. "This is a curtain-raiser for the Hi-Vision era," claimed Akio Tanii, the president of Matsushita electronics. The only problem with "Hi-Vision Day," as it was called, was that hardly anyone was watching. One reason was surely the price: the first HDTV sets cost $30,000—and a VCR to go with it initially cost a staggering $115,000!

Were Japanese businessmen crazy? Not necessarily, for during the so-called Bubble Economy of the late 1980s, conspicuous consumption had reached truly ridiculous levels—flecks of real gold served on ice cream; stodgy insurance companies laying out eight-figure sums for French paintings. The HDTV industrialists therefore assumed that a healthy number of techno-enthusiasts would ignore HDTV's initial price tag and rush to buy a set. But by 1991 the Bubble Economy had already begun to burst, and by the time the first HDTV sets hit the market, Japan's once reckless affluent consumer class had already begun to mind its yen.

Japanese HDTV suffered from a deeper problem: there was nothing to watch that could begin to warrant the investment. Sports events did look even bigger, bolder, and more lifelike on HDTV—but they looked pretty good on regular TV, too. With hardly any programming available that was specially designed to make use of HDTV's powers, NHK's most exciting offering was sumo wrestling matches. Much of the remaining HDTV-enabled broadcasting consisted of interminable hours of waterfalls, rivers, and forests. So even when prices for the equipment plummeted to "only" about five times the price of a regular TV set, consumers remained remarkably apathetic to HDTV. In the first three years of sales, only 25,000 sets were sold in all of Japan.

In mid-1993, the FCC finally drove a stake through the undead heart of NHK's Hi-Vision system by cutting it from the American competition. Six months later, even Japanese government sources began to acknowledge that the Hi-Vision system would eventually have to be abandoned. "The world trend is digital," conceded Akimasa Egawa, the director general of broadcasting in the Ministry of Posts and Telecommunications. Though an irate Japanese electronics industry association immediately demanded that Egawa retract his statement—he did so the next day—one can be sure that none of the association's members are going to be investing a lot of yen in new analog equipment or programming. Likewise, few new consumers are likely to go out and pay the current $6,000 cost of an analog high-definition television set—not when the world has so clearly gone digital.

Meanwhile in Europe, the HD-MAC system also drowned of its own dead weight in a sea of red ink and bureaucratic squabbling. "A dead duck," was how one European official described it. As for the four remaining digital HDTV players back in America, they combined forces in what is known as the Grand Alliance. In principle, they and the FCC have agreed to employ the best attributes of each system and share royalties once HDTV service is rolled out in the U.S.

When might that be? Some suggest that digital HDTV will arrive in prototype around 1998 and in significant numbers of American living rooms perhaps five years later—about the same time that commercially viable interactive TV begins to hit mass scale.

But don't hold your breath. Given the new competitive issues in television arising from interactive technology, HDTV has become an orphan issue. "The only people talking about HDTV are those who are developing it," observes John Rose, a McKinsey consultant.[6]

Well, perhaps not the *only* people. TV broadcasters discuss it, too—but (no surprise here) mainly as cover in their campaign to win FCC approval for their use of HDTV-allocated spectrum to other than HDTV uses. These include the broadcast of multiple pay-per-view channels, as well as information, home shopping and banking, and E-mail services.

In the end, it may turn out that HDTV is a niche technology best suited not to the living room but to medical imaging, military reconnaissance, and other fields where fine resolution matters most. But whether or not a broad audience of consumers at home ever gravitates toward it, HDTV has already played its historic role as the midwife to the Digital Revolution.

It is now clear that June 6, 1990, marked the critical turning point in the long drama of high-definition television—and, as with the D day invasion of Europe exactly 46 years earlier, everything that followed was mere epilogue. On that day, General Instrument—the "little engine that could"—not only came from out of nowhere to reach the top of the HDTV mountain, but with digital technology as its fuel, it also inadvertently triggered an avalanche of invention and investment and industrial convergence that is still crashing down upon the American landscape, carving out that road to the future we now call the Information Highway.

Looking back at HDTV's 20-year march, one cannot help but marvel at the many ironies that lay strewn across its path. High-definition television was meant to be the Holy Grail of picture quality, yet that is absolutely the least of what HDTV development has given the world. Indeed, with digital television technology now energizing the growth of a host of new interactive programs and services, it hardly matters at all if HDTV is ever beamed to our TV screens. In a digital world, you can scratch the "HD" from HDTV and few would ever know the difference.

Then, too, there's the irony of a Japan that made all the right moves, that strategically assessed the importance of this new television technology, and spent vast resources on its development, only to discover in a cruel twist of fate that it would have been better off sticking its head in the sand for 20 years as America had done. One way to gauge the scope of Japan's tragedy would be to imagine those nineteenth-century pioneers who had sweat the best years of their lives laying track on the Transcontinental Railroad suddenly looking up, just as they hammered the last spike in the last stretch of track, to see a passenger jet flying overhead.

And finally, there's the irony of the U.S. government, firm in its opposition to any intervention in technology development and industrial policy, nonetheless managing by a largely unconscious mix of policy action and inaction to open the way for U.S. technology to regain world leadership.

The moral of the HDTV story would *seem* to be that government cannot successfully plan the development of industries. If so, then they ought to stay out of the way and let the creativity of entrepreneurs and the dynamism of the marketplace drive technology's development.

But HDTV may be a more complex tale than it appears. Let us give the techno-libertarian opponents of government involvement their due: the Digital Revolution was born and has been able to flourish in the United States precisely because there was no government-directed program seeking a single outcome. In contrast, digital technology was observably stifled in Japan and Europe by the dogmatic monoliths of industrial policy and its predefined goals.

But is this a fair summary not just of the HDTV story but of the general process of technology development as a whole? Prior to HDTV, the Japanese certainly had their share of winners in picking technologies to support, and the Europeans have had a few notable successes as well. Does HDTV show that those approaches are now dead? What if Japanese planners learn the lesson of HDTV and, choosing not to throw the baby out with the bathwater, merely recalibrate their approach to technology policy to make it more fluid and innovative but still government directed? Will they still be on the wrong road, or will they become more competitive with American norms as a result?

And while we're at it, let's not overstate what the HDTV case tells us about the inability of government to set intelligent policy for technology. After all, it was an American government agency—the FCC—that determined that an HDTV standard was needed. It then set up the process and the rules for choosing one. That government-established process then provided the goal and the opportunity for General Instrument's pathbreaking work. Ultimately, it was that same process that recognized the validity of the digital approach and set the stage for the rapid unfolding of the other fronts of the Digital Revolution.

By a certain syllogism, therefore, government *has* played a more important and more positive role in shaping the foundations of American success in new technologies than the dominant chorus of techno-liberterians would like us to think. (Government, incidentally, via the forerunner organization to Craig Fields's DARPA, was the initiator of what is now known as the Internet, the success of which is now so often—and so mistakenly—attributed to the spontaneous generational powers of loosely knit individuals working independently of government). Even so caustic a critic of government policy as John Malone says that the FCC's "decision to go for digital rather than screw around with analog" was a powerful and important one.

Time and experience will tell us more about the right and wrong things government can do in this new era of technology development. It is too early to draw a permanent conclusion. But HDTV is surely a worthwhile cautionary tale about government trying to do too much (as in the case of Japan and the EC) and about grand business plans being launched toward goals consumers do not necessarily desire (HDTV's improved picture quality).

More than that, the story of HDTV tells us much about the protean quality of the Digital Revolution. With new digital technologies emerging faster than the marketplace can absorb them, no intelligent forecaster can be fixated on any single end point. Everything will change, everything will be subject to surprises, corporate alliances will rise and fall. To be sure, from today's standpoint it seems absurd that only five years ago government and the media were singularly focused on HDTV's supposed importance to U.S. economic competitiveness. But let us at least consider the possibility that *today's* infatuation with *interactive* TV might look just as absurd five years from now.

The Digital Revolution is a process, not a product. It is evolutionary and proceeds, often fitfully, along an unpredictable path. We should all learn some humility in trying to forecast its development. Let us leave room in our imagination for unforeseen events, low-probability scenarios, surprising responses from consumers, innovations by little-known companies, and unexpected competition from other countries.

Anything can happen, and probably will, in a world where dark-horse contenders such as General Instrument can come seemingly out of nowhere to humble a once invincible Japan, Inc.

▪ 3 ▪

The Rabbit in the Hat

Imagine, if you will, that Ford has just introduced a new car with a revolutionary steering mechanism that significantly reduces accidents and driver error. According to the company, its engineers set out to design an automobile with the most efficient precision-response steering system possible. The fruit of their efforts is the new Ford Handler, a car with approximately five times the handling capability of an ordinary vehicle.

Your curiosity piqued, you visit the local Ford dealership to examine the new vehicle. The salesman tries his best to project the casual diffidence that is typical showroom style these days, but it's obvious he can barely contain his excitement as he ushers you into the showroom. There, a new black Ford Handler shines like mirrored steel under the pinpoint lighting from above.

"Wait'll you feel this baby under your fingers," gushes the salesman, opening the door with a flourish and guiding you into the rich leather seating. You slide inside and instinctively reach for the wheel . . . but there's a computer keyboard mounted on the dashboard instead!

"Hey, I know it's a little different," he explains. "But our engineers say it's much more efficient this way . . . I can give you the data. You get five times more maneuverability and a quicker response to road hazards when you've got ten fingers working these keys instead of just two hands trying to jerk around some old-fashioned steering wheel."

The salesman pauses, waiting for you to say something.

"She's a beauty, isn't she?" he offers hopefully.

You suppose the man forgot to take his medication, and begin to climb out of the car.

"Uh—wait—" the salesman stammers, glancing around conspiratorially. "Listen, between you and me, I'm prepared to work with you on the price here."

A beat. You look up at him, intrigued. "Really . . . how much?"

And so it goes—a day in the life of NerdWorld, a planet totally ruled by engineers.[1] Now, most people would say that NerdWorld is entirely different from our own world. Here, no industry would ever dream of designing anything as absurdly counterintuitive as a car without a steering wheel, right?

No industry, that is, except the computer industry. Only in the computer industry is it considered customary to sell products that produce mind-boggling confusion and distress in a significant percentage of people who attempt to use them. Only in the computer industry can one witness the unabashed retailing of supposedly user-friendly products that require instruction manuals hundreds of pages long. Only in the computer industry does one hear the phrase "real-world solutions" applied to devices that can only be operated by navigating through a bizarre simulated maze that has no likeness to anything in the known physical universe.

As a refugee from NerdWorld, David Leffler is well acquainted with the computer industry's penchant for designing gadgets that seem perfectly logical to engineers and patently insane to ordinary people. As the head of the user testing lab at General Magic, Leffler's job is making sure that the company's trailblazing software works—or more to the point, that ordinary people can use it to communicate, send messages, find information, or conduct transactions without suffering a brain seizure. Toward this end, he tested over 900 people during a two-year period, computer users and novices alike, accumulating in the process a library full of detailed responses from his test subjects on the strengths and shortcomings of the software. One could say that Leffler is a glutton for feedback.

Which is why, at approximately 12:29 P.M. on January 6, 1994, the six-foot-six, 45-year-old Leffler was squirming anxiously in his chair in the front row of the Yerba Buena Ballroom at the San Francisco Marriott. The mother of all feedback sessions was about to begin. In exactly one minute, General Magic would publicly demonstrate for the first time its new Magic Cap and Telescript software before a standing-room-only crowd of more than three thousand people.

Leffler turned around and looked back at the crowd. People were crammed into every chair; they were standing in the aisles and sitting cross-legged on the floor. Most were either dedicated Mac-Heads—devotees of Apple's Macintosh computer—or else Mac software developers, Mac equipment suppliers, and Mac groupies of all stripes. To Leffler, it seemed like old home week on NerdWorld. Though he couldn't be sure, he thought he detected a certain skeptical air drifting like a mild breeze up and down the aisles. Perhaps this was only to be expected in an industry where hype so often outstrips performance. He himself had witnessed many product introductions in the past where a few well-timed snickers had served as a useful laxative to the bloated pretensions of executives daring to fancy their company the "next Apple" or the "next Microsoft." Leffler hoped that General Magic would not make *that* mistake.

General Magic had chosen this venue, the MacWorld Expo, to unveil its new technology because this is where it felt most at home. General Magic's principal executives had once worked at Apple, and its star programmers, Bill Atkinson and Andy Hertzfeld—who had designed the original Macintosh that was introduced at a MacWorld Expo exactly 10 years earlier—were revered by these people as heroes. And though MacHeads generally find it difficult to conceive of any technology more profound or liberating than their own, they were also immensely curious about the details of Bill and Andy's latest excellent adventure in software design. Much more than public relations was at stake here. In the audience were some of the best software designers in the business, and their support in developing third-party application programs for General Magic's new technology platform would be critical to the company's success.

The lights dimmed and a hush fell over the room. Bill and Andy took the stage, accompanied by marketing vice president Joanna Hoffman, another former member of the original Macintosh design team. After a brief introduction by Hoffman, Andy stepped forward—and for those who have never witnessed this short and round forty-something leprechaun in action, suffice it to say he is a sight to behold.

"When we started four years ago, our goal was to reinvent telephony," Hertzfeld began. "We wanted to cut through the awful complexities of electronic communications and make it as easy as using a phone. We wanted the average person to be able to really use digital technology with no prior instruction, with no need for an instruction manual.

"But how do you do that?" he asked, his voice beginning to rise as he hopped around on the stage. "How do you build something that people already know how to use before they've ever even used it?" His arms were now gyrating about so excitedly it seemed he might rotate up and off the stage. "Our solution was to create an entirely new interface between people and computers. One in which the world you see on the screen is as congruent as possible with the real world in which you live. One where all you need to know is the intuition and experience you've already gained in life."

He paused for breath and tugged on his T-shirt. "Well, for four years we've worked behind a curtain of secrecy. Now it's time to lift the curtain!" With that, a curtain rose behind him to reveal a giant projection screen. And as the audience watched spellbound, Andy Hertzfeld began spinning his tale of the new electronic world in creation.

Though Leffler had no way of knowing it, industry analysts would later hail General Magic's technology as a breakthrough in high-tech, low-maintenance computing for ordinary consumers. "The era of intelligent computer networks for the masses is officially underway," declared the *Wall Street Journal*.

To be sure, General Magic is only one of the leaders of the "usability" movement in high-tech, though it is probably the most interesting and well known of these. And company officials have consistently cautioned that widespread public use of digital technology was still years away. But there is no denying that in some important measure, General Magic's achievement suggests that the computer industry, having finally set its sights on the broad consumer market, has come to an historic juncture in the development of the Information Highway.

Every historic juncture, of course, represents the coming together of diverse and once separate roads. Some of these roads are paved with the vision and sweat of upstart innovators such as General Magic. Others are chiseled out of the social landscape by the inexorable march of economic and scientific development. And then there are those surprising and serendipitous pathways carved out of the odd accidents and blind luck of fickle fate.

Had IBM in the 1970s and 1980s, for instance, not blinded itself to the revolutionary potential of the microprocessor and the personal computer, Silicon Valley might never have become midwife to hundreds of visionary technology companies like Apple and General Magic, and once proud Big Blue might not now be reduced to sucking out the last of its phlegmatic mainframe revenues. Then, too, had IBM not fumbled so badly, college-dropout-turned-Microsoft-boss Bill Gates might today be flipping burgers instead of clipping coupons with his fellow billionaire and friend, investor Warren Buffet.

And had Apple Computer listened to former employees Andy Hertzfeld, Bill Atkinson, and Marc Porat about building a *communications*-oriented handheld device instead of a gadget for note taking, its brain-damaged Newton would have been mercifully aborted in its first trimester of development, and General Magic might never have been born.

Such grand and aerial views of history's multiple converging pathways, however, were not on David Leffler's mind as he watched Hertzfeld work his magic on stage. He was thinking back instead to the long-ago origins of this day and to all the struggle and sacrifice it took to get here. For if the truth be told, only weeks before this event Leffler had serious doubts that they could even pull it off.

"I was having horrible tests," he recalls. "I mean, horrible to the point where I was embarrassed right into the floor. The engineers would be saying the software was fine. But under the scrutiny of real users, it just didn't work. Frankly, it scared the shit out of me. The software wasn't ready, and I was skeptical that it'd ever be ready in time."

Skepticism, to be sure, is essential to a test manager's job. As Leffler points out, it's one thing for an engineer to come up with a great idea for a computer program, quite another to actually construct one that people want to use. A test manager has to know the difference and see to it that the gap between concept and use, promise and performance is as narrow as possible. But this is not always an easy task.

During the seven years he had worked at Apple Computer, Leffler had helped force the reluctant cancellation of eight promising development projects after test results revealed serious usability problems. He recalls that on one project, a database program for the Macintosh code-named Silver Surfer, he spoke up at a meeting chaired by marketing manager Jean-Louis Gassee to announce that the program crashed in 25 percent of tests, causing the loss of data. Gassee's reaction was not particularly unusual for a marketing executive: he warned that anyone leaking word of Silver Surfer's "little snags" could expect to be fired. Gassee, however, must later have pondered the liability that might accrue to Apple from selling a product that caused customers' business records to vanish forever into some sort of cyberspace Bermuda Triangle because three days later he dropped Silver Surfer from the product line.

Even more than the usual quotient of skepticism, however, was required when Leffler quit Apple to join General Magic. For one thing—and this may come as a surprise to many people—virtually no computer company before General Magic had ever integrated systematic user testing into the actual design process of its products. At Apple, Leffler's role was confined to determining whether the product worked, not whether typical customers could easily use it or obtain any real benefit by doing so. What's more, even such limited user testing was done only after the product was basically finished and ready to be shipped, not during the early design stage when user feedback might have enabled the engineers to alter its features or simplify its use. At General Magic, however, Leffler was hired specifically to ensure that what the company eventually shipped was what customers wanted to use, not what the engineers wanted to build. His job title rather outspokenly reflected this mandate: User Champion.

"There were a lot of fights," Leffler concedes. "A lot of what I call 'religious' issues, you know, where the engineers want to do things a certain way because that's how they've always been done. I'd argue that we can't do it like we did it in the computer business. This has got to be accessible to *normal* people. But sometimes engineers tend to get this really entrenched attitude. Like, what's the problem? You just touch your nose with your left hand and hit your knee with your right elbow and it'll work fine! But if I sit down with them, show them tapes of 10 people all having the same problem, then usually we get the problem fixed. Irrefutable proof is kind of hard to argue with."

Ironically, by temperament Leffler is anything but the gladiator type. His colleagues universally describe him as "good-natured," "unassuming," even "gentle." And one would never guess, given his lanky laid-back surfer looks, that Leffler would have such an abiding passion for minutiae.

"Most people would be bored to tears by my job," he smiles. "But I love it. I love the redundancy." Sitting in his office, surrounded by videotapes of user sessions, he describes the testing process in a way that gives it a kind of Sherlock Holmesian quality. "We had this problem that kept coming up in the testing," he explains, "where, in order to send a message to someone, after you'd typed in their name you were supposed to touch the DONE button, and then go on to write the message. But a lot of people, after they entered the name, they just would not touch the DONE button to move on to the next step. It got to the point where I'd be testing someone, and I'd say to myself, 'Okay, she's not going to touch that button—she'll touch any button but the DONE button.' And sure enough, she wouldn't do it. I couldn't figure it out at first. Was the button too big, too small, was it incorrectly placed on the screen? I love a mystery like that because often it'll turn out that the word is actually Lithuanian for 'Don't do it' or something. Then I'll go back to my records and sure enough, the people having the problem are all Lithuanians."

As it turned out, DONE might as well have been a Lithuanian word, given that it's a term familiar in context only to computer users. Closer examination revealed that people with computer experience understood the meaning of the DONE button. Nontechnical people, however, took it to mean they wanted to quit the task entirely when, in fact, they had only just entered the recipient's name and hadn't even started to write the message yet. So they refused to hit that button. Finally, the engineers changed the button to read ACCEPT—as in, "Yes, the name I've just entered is correct, so let's move on to the next part of the task."

Leffler takes great pride in the rigorous methodology of his usability testing program, as well as in the fact that the user feedback data he compiled was pivotal in the 13 major revisions of the software prior to its official release. During each two-hour test, the subject sat in a small office in front of a desk, upon which sat a working mock-up of the communicator loaded with Magic's software. As the user navigated through the program, attempting to send an electronic message or schedule a meeting, a video camera mounted in the ceiling above recorded the process. Leffler, meanwhile, sat on the other side of a two-way mirror in the adjoining office, communicating with the test subject through a microphone, and recording his observations with a word processor. The word processor was programmed to give him a time-stamp from the VCR, thereby allowing him to later correlate his notes to the appropriate segment of the video test record. He also charted the ease or difficulty in using each software feature on a scale from zero (no problems) to three (needed assistance), comparing the averages for each update of the software with those of the previous version.

Early on in the testing process, Leffler discovered that those people who had used computers before tended to underreport the level of distress they were having using the software. "I'd watch people suffering through it and I'd ask how it was going. 'Uh, I really liked it a lot,' they'd say. 'It was great.' But I could tell it was horrible."

He thought at first that such underreporting was the result of many of the early test subjects being family members or friends of General Magic employees. "I thought maybe they just didn't want to be negative," he recalls. He later concluded it was because they had been conditioned by experience to expect a certain level of distress when using technology. "People who've used computers think it's normal to have the machine *not* do what you want. They think it's normal to feel frustrated and stupid when using a computer."

He shakes his head and laughs. "It's totally different with non-technical people. They let you know when they feel like picking up the device and throwing it against the wall. Of course, with these people you have to do a lot more preparation before the test. I mean, with your average person who's never touched a computer and hopes never to touch one, that person is worried that if they touch the wrong button the ICBMs are going to go off and nuke Russia or something. So I'd let them know what to expect, reassure them that if the machine crashes it's not their problem, it's ours because it means we still haven't built it right."

The fear and loathing many people have for computers stems in no small measure from the fact that, until now, the only way to use one has been to master a user interface that is fundamentally at odds with their experience of the real world. Take the basic notion of Windows, the Microsoft operating system that runs on 80 percent of the world's computers. People who have never seen a Microsoft "window" have no idea what it is. For them, the computer screen has been cut out and replaced by strange panels of mysterious pictographic symbols representing application programs. Similarly, the Macintosh's much-vaunted Desktop graphical user interface depicts tiny folders arranged across the screen, and inside these folders are other folders containing application programs and files.

To get any work done with either computer system, one first has to understand the concept of an "application"—the action you wish to perform, such as communicating with another computer—and then grasp the notion of a "file"—the particular message you wish to communicate. Leave aside for the moment the difficulty many people have even finding the applications they want inside the Macintosh desktop folders or Windows program groups, and then matching these to appropriate files archived in various directories. More important is the fact that such a cleavage between action and goal—grammatically speaking, the separation of subject and verb from the object of that verb—violates our instinctive manner of interacting with the world. If real life operated in such fashion, a pedestrian would attempt to get out of the way of an oncoming bus thus: first, decide to perform some sort of action, as opposed to remaining inert like a deer caught in headlights; second, choose from a whole menu of possible actions, such as SCREAM or CRY or PRAY, an action called MOVE!; third, decide what to perform that MOVE! action upon—in this case your feet, dummy, so you can jump out of the way!

The practical effect of such a byzantine approach is that one must devote considerable effort not to the task for which the computer was purchased—that is, writing or sending messages—but instead to manipulating the user interface in an often frustrating attempt to get the machine to work. Artist and technology researcher Brenda Laurel has compared the experience of using a computer to going to a theater and having to watch the projector instead of the movie.

It's no wonder, then, that after 15 high-profile years on the market, computers are still found in barely one-third of American homes or that more than a third of all adults are afraid even to touch one.[2] In contrast, two electronics devices that have been on the market roughly the same length of time, microwaves and VCRs, are owned by 81 percent and 80 percent of households respectively. While in one sense the comparison is unfair—microwaves and VCRs are utility and entertainment products whereas computers only claim to be—this difference in market penetration certainly owes much to the maddening difficulty people endure when using computers.

"You want to find out how user-friendly the Macintosh or Windows computer really is?" suggests David Leffler. "Just stick one in front of your mom and say, 'Okay, Mom, write a message and send it to another computer.' Now, that computer may be connected to a phone line and have a modem built into it. It may have writing software built into it. And it may have a communications program. But I guarantee you—my mom, at least, is sure as hell not going to be able to do it."

In contrast, Magic Cap's interface mimics the real world that people have known all their lives. It offers the user 3-D images of three physical locations: the DESK in an office, the HALLWAY containing various utility rooms, and the DOWNTOWN main street full of shops and services. Each location displays various real-life objects—a phone on the DESK, for example. Simply touch the phone with a finger or plastic stylus and Magic Cap automatically activates that function, without the user needing to know anything about computers or application programs or files. The genius of Magic Cap's approach is that one doesn't have to be a genius to use it. The same technique has been used by auto companies since the Model T: rather than having to know how to increase fuel intake, adjust carburetion, and accelerate piston action, drivers simply press the gas pedal harder to go faster.

When first turned on, a handheld device or computer running Magic Cap displays the DESK in the office. The DESK contains a telephone, a Rolodex, a datebook, a postcard for sending messages, and a notebook for writing to-do lists and memos. As in real life, drawers in the front of the DESK hold stationery and a calculator. An in-box and out-box hanging on the wall show whether any messages have arrived for you or need sending to someone else. In the corner stands a file cabinet for storing messages and other documents for later retrieval. At the bottom of the screen is a pictograph bar showing various utilities. Touch the picture of a keyboard, for example, and an imaginary keyboard pops up on the screen, enabling you to type rather than handwrite a document with the stylus.

The function of the datebook illustrates how Magic Cap is designed to handle much of the complexity of computerized communications itself rather than force it upon the user. To schedule a meeting, first touch the datebook. The image of a real-life daytimer pops up on the screen, and after choosing a time and date, you name the individual with whom you want to meet. Magic Cap then automatically searches your Rolodex for that person's E-mail address, writes a standardized memo requesting the meeting with YES and NO RSVP buttons on it, and then zips it electronically to the recipient. If that person finds the meeting time acceptable, he or she merely touches the YES button and an RSVP is sent back to you confirming the meeting and automatically scheduling it into both of your datebooks.

The second location, the HALLWAY, is accessed by touching the word "hallway" at the top of the screen. It depicts doors to various rooms. Tap on the library door to enter a room containing reference material. Tap on the game room door to go inside and play video games. The HALLWAY is infinitely extensible in both directions, enabling the user to create as many rooms as desired. An accounting room, for example, might hold your business or personal financial records, as well as programs for automatically trading stocks or getting quotes.

The HALLWAY is also decorated with paintings and furniture, which you can alter at your leisure. While these design elements appear nonfunctional, they do serve a purpose: in the same way you might locate your room in a real-life hotel hallway—just past the stairwell, for instance, or next to the ice machine—the HALLWAY furnishings in Magic Cap act as subliminal landmarks for users who may have customized their HALLWAY with a large assortment of rooms. Similarly, sound effects convey information that also aid the user— hearing a slurping sound as your memo flies into the out-box confirms that it is, indeed, being faxed or E-mailed to the recipient. These little touches help personalize the software and make it more enjoyable. But more significantly, they attempt to recreate not only the physical world in which we live but also the specific and often subtle cues we use to help us navigate that world and manipulate the objects in it.

DOWNTOWN is where third-party services and products can be accessed electronically. Some of these were available in early commercial releases of communicators using Magic Cap, and more will be added in later versions. As you scroll down main street (by touching the arrow in the street), you pass a travel agency, a department store, and perhaps a bank just as you would if strolling along a real downtown street. Tap on the travel agency building, and you'll be taken inside to check flight schedules or make reservations. Tap on a store, and you'll find yourself moving down the aisles on a virtual shopping tour. Your purchases will be automatically billed to your credit card if you choose. Again, DOWNTOWN is wholly customizable, and its main street buildings reflect the particular services you have chosen to sign up for.

"The effort put into this, does it come through to people?" wonders General Magic cofounder and Software Wizard Andy Hertzfeld. "I don't know, maybe it's like what they say about movies—you don't see the money and work that went into it up on the screen."

For Hertzfeld and most of the 40 or so key programmers on General Magic's development teams, that effort consisted of several years of 90- to 100-hour work weeks. The motivational factors were complex, of course, and included stock options (as well as, in Hertzfeld's case, a 9.5 percent ownership stake valued at nearly $25 million at the time of Magic's public stock offering in early 1995). But having stood at the intersection of science and business more than once in his career—at Apple, at Frox TV, and at Radius, Inc.—Hertzfeld feels that financial rewards alone could not have produced the results achieved by the company's development efforts.

"Sure, money's a factor," he agrees. "But very few of us are doing this primarily for money. It's about getting the chance to be artists, about creating something new and incredibly great and knowing that you're way past just being competitive because you're three steps ahead of the rest of the industry. I mean, how did Picasso know what the next brush stroke should be? I'm sure he didn't say, 'Oh, if I paint it this way I get more money.' It was a need inside him. That feeling of walking on untrammeled snow."

He pauses a moment, mindful perhaps that he has just compared programming to art. "A lot of people can't see how it can be like art. Can an engineer be Picasso? It's just that I think that what goes into creating good software is that same vision and passion an artist has.

To do any significant thing in this world, the coin of the realm has got to be your vision, your passion, and your time."

As Thomas Edison once noted, however, invention is 10 percent inspiration and 90 percent perspiration. "There were really three secrets to making it work," Hertzfeld confides. "Iterate, iterate, iterate. This is why the user testing is so important. Because when I'm creating, I'm not saying, 'This is the way it has to be.' I'm saying, 'This is my best guess of what it should be.' And then I try it on myself. I would say that 80 percent of the things I try on myself, I can tell they're not good enough. But finally I get to the point where I think, 'Boy, this is pretty good.' Then I go to the next level, which is showing it to Bill."

He smiles. "Now about half the time when I think it's good enough, Bill doesn't. And so it's back to the drawing board. Then we get to the point where Bill and I both think it's pretty good. And not just Bill—I've learned to trust his judgment—but anyone who's around, who's within earshot. Other programmers, my girlfriend, her kid. Anyway, once we think it's really pretty good, then it gets into the user-testing process."

He shakes his head and laughs. "Yeah, and user testing is where we find out it's still not good enough."

The user-testing process was especially critical for General Magic because of the nature of their audience. "We're aiming this stuff at a huge breadth of people with no experience whatsoever in using technology," notes Leffler. "So if you come from the computer world, like I do, you have to question all your assumptions. And you have to pay close attention to cultural and gender differences, too."

He offers an example. "There's not much room on the screen [of a handheld communicator], so some of the buttons people have to touch are very small. The way we had it at first, when you touched a button, it would highlight in a darker color and that's how you could tell it'd been activated. Well, the men had no trouble. But the women did. They couldn't tell if they'd hit the button properly.

"Now, it turns out that men use the tip of their finger to initiate a button," he continues. "That's just what men do. So even if the button is small, their fingertip is smaller and they can see they've highlighted it. But women touch a button with the large, flat ball of their finger. They almost never use their fingertip to touch things because even if they don't have long fingernails now, they had them in the past. So women learn never to touch anything with their fingertips because they might chip a nail, or crack it, or whatever. The engineers, being mostly men, designed a button that didn't really take into account that women might use their fingers differently than the men do."

How was the button problem resolved?

"Well, first we had to do some research. I asked Leanne Clement—she's our info goddess—for help. So she goes out [electronically]—she knows where every little bit of information in the world is practically—and she finds this study by Ford, which at one point had these women come in and help them design their car. And based on the women's input, Ford recessed their door handles so women wouldn't break their fingernails opening the door. And they brought out the knobs a bit, so women with nails could grasp them more easily. Anyway, based on that and other studies about button design, we came up with the idea of creating a corona effect. A starburst sort of thing. So in addition to highlighting the button, now we have this starburst-corona extending out when you touch the button. You can see it even if you're using the flat of your finger."

User testing also revealed the need to pay attention to age differences. "On a regular computer screen, black text on a gray background looks great, and that's how we did our text at first. But people over 40 had trouble reading it because our screen's a lot smaller. Also its a non-backlit LCD [liquid crystal display], so the resolution and contrast isn't as good. So Leanne found some studies—in the United States there's been a study done on almost everything—and we learned that combining uppercase with lowercase letters with descenders is more readable in small type, especially in poor lighting conditions."

In the end, building software that did not require an instruction manual meant spending thousands of hours of labor time to perfect such seemingly minor software elements as the highlighting of a button activator or the choice of text used—"accept" versus "done," for example. Similar attention was also paid to such nonfunctional aesthetic issues as the look of the phone, datebook, and other objects displayed in Magic Cap. This was the province of 40-year-old software artist Susan Kare, who ten years earlier designed much of the look and feel of the Macintosh user interface.

"We gave a lot of thought to how the telephone and the desk and all that should look," Kare recalls. "If you go into an office today, you'll probably see these very modern desks that look like Herman Miller work surfaces. And the file cabinets will have those molded plastic drawers. But when you call up an image in your mind of a phone or a file cabinet or a desk, it's probably not the latest or the most modern design. I think when people picture a desk, they picture one that has drawers. When they think of a phone, it's probably a push-button phone but not one of these super high-tech ones. That's what I wanted to recreate—the images that people have in their minds."

Kare, who comes from a traditional art background, designed the company logo—a smiling rabbit peeking out of a top hat. Though she was insistent that her work at Magic is a "team effort," she is also clearly guided by her own finely tuned sensibility to the pulse of popular imagery.

"Go into people's homes and usually you won't find the most modern furniture designs," she observes. "It may not be Ethan Allen, but it's also probably not too trendy, either. People tend to surround themselves with things that make them feel comfortable. So our designs should help make this technology understandable and comfortable for people."

To help make the software comfortable, a key ingredient in the alchemy of Magic's interface design is its customizability. "It should be able to reflect the way you as an individual live and work," insists Leffler. "If you're left-handed, you should be able to move the phone over to the other side of the desk. You should be able to shift everything around."

The point being that when the interface becomes intimate enough, familiar enough, it stops being a barrier. You don't have to negotiate it or struggle with it any more than you have to struggle with your real desk in real life. The interface disappears, and you can just do your work.

Or as Brenda Laurel might say, you can just sit back and enjoy the movie instead of hassling with the projector.

If the Magic Cap interface allows one to focus more clearly on the tasks at hand (rather than the process of trying to carry out those tasks), then Telescript's "intelligent agents" offer the tools for accomplishing those tasks, venturing into cyberspace on various missions on the user's behalf. By issuing English-language commands—for example, search out and retrieve news articles on a particular subject; locate the best cross-country air fares; or redeliver an E-mail message to the recipient's fax machine if it remains unread for a specified period of time—a Telescript agent can be dispatched to accomplish relatively complex tasks without the user needing to master the skills of a programmer or experienced network surfer.

The implications of Telescript's agent technology for the future are enormous. Because it requires only that users connect with a remote network long enough to dispatch an agent into it, the technology greatly reduces network costs and eliminates the need for information transfers to take place in real time while "the meter is running." It also cares not a whit what type of PC, communication program, or network one is using—it can even transfer agents over non-Telescript-enabled networks—and thus functions as a kind of universal translator between the world's disparate computing environments. It is especially valuable in the fast-growing field of wireless communications, where limited bandwidth and low transmission speeds make Telescript a cost-effective solution to the problem of network overhead. And in a broader economic sense, Telescript and similar agent software being developed by other firms also have the potential to alter the nature of commerce and the workings of the marketplace quite profoundly.

One thing is certain: Telescript is the key to General Magic's fortunes. Noted a 1994 white paper by one consulting firm: "The Yankee Group believes the long-term importance and viability of General Magic's technologies depend upon Telescript. Magic Cap may be an exciting, user-friendly, and downright enjoyable interface for [personal communicators], but it is the paradigm-shifting nature of Telescript that means the most."[3] Ironically, Telescript only came to General Magic through an odd bit of serendipity.

"Out of complete left field, [Magic CEO] Marc Porat called me one day," recalls Rich Miller, coinventor along with Jim White of the Telescript programming language. "I had known him I guess going on 25 years, since our days in graduate school at Stanford. Anyway, this was in October of 1990, and he said he needed someone to help him with the communications part of Magic's story. He wanted me to come in as a consultant, help them create a group, set up the commercial strategy and all that."

At the time, Miller and White ran a small consultancy, Rapport Communications. They had each led distinguished careers in the communications field—White is generally credited with being the father of E-mail, and Miller had just served as president of the Electronic Mail Association—but now, with the explosion of processor power and bandwidth capability, they saw the opportunity to create something that was, in Miller's words, "totally new."

"We had already had discussions with British Telecom at the time," he explains. "Our ideas were pretty radical—I mean *really* radical. British Telecom just didn't get it."

After a series of meetings in Palo Alto, California, in December of 1990, Miller came to the realization that General Magic, with its vision of a truly consumer-oriented interface and communications service, would be "the most wonderful place" to take something as revolutionary as the Telescript communications language.

"Jim and I had just left a meeting with Marc, and as I recall, we were having a beer at Scott's Seafood. We were talking about Magic, how great it was, and that's when we decided to let them know about Telescript. So, we went back and said, 'Uh, we've got something that's probably worth trying . . . just some ideas, you know, that we've been working on for a while.' "

The rest, as they say, is history. It's a history, however, whose true promise will only be fulfilled if the marriage of interface and communications technologies such as Magic Cap and Telescript actually make the Information Highway easy enough for the average American to drive on. And bear in mind, the company's interface design is only partly successful—the authors' mothers were unable to send an electronic message using a Magic Cap–based device without some coaching (though in fairness it should be noted they would have refused to even try using a Windows-based device). Nonetheless, as a first effort, the team at General Magic has certainly helped bring us closer to the day when ordinary citizens can use complex technologies as easily as they use a phone, a TV, or a pen and paper.

Observes Leffler: "It would have been pretty trivial to design just another program for the computer market. But trying to design a consumer product that lets ordinary people use this technology— now *that's* hard."

Harder still will be the struggle to build a viable business from these technologies. While General Magic had initially predicted fairly strong consumer purchases of personal communicators, by the time Sony launched its Magic Link device in September of 1994—to rave reviews but, unfortunately, slow sales—expectations had already been trimmed back considerably. Sony, in fact, decided to target its Magic Link only at that small segment of business users known as "mobile professionals."

In part, this change in strategy and expectation reflected the more level-headed approach that had already emerged throughout corporate America regarding the near-term prospects for Info Highway products and services. Yes, the Information Highway *was* being built, but by the middle of 1994 it had become evident that the construction process was going to be a lot more painful and take a good deal longer—a decade at least, rather than a few years—than had been imagined during the techno-glory days of 1993.

The retreat in expectations, however, also reflected the reality of Sony's actual product in hand. The Magic Link suffered from a difficult-to-read screen, little or no wireless capability, slow communications speed, and a text input method that, while making innovative use of Magic Cap's "virtual" keyboard, was still too slow and cumbersome for anything but brief memo-writing and messaging purposes. Even more limiting was the dearth of truly useful things that could be done with the device. While improvements in device functionality and a greater availability of services are sure to come with future product releases, these will necessarily require a good deal of time and effort before General Magic's vision comes nearer to being fulfilled.

Then, too, there is the matter of price. Sony's Magic Link retailed for slightly less than $1,000 when released, more than double the price most analysts believe is necessary in order to achieve wide consumer acceptance. Motorola's General Magic–based Envoy communicator, released in early 1995 with enhanced wireless capability, was priced near $1,500 and has also been meeting with only marginal results. Matsushita and others are readying their own versions of Magic-based devices for eventual release.

A large consumer market for personal communicators, it seems, will likely have to wait until the end of the decade or even beyond, when functionality improves, prices drop to a few hundred dollars, and new and more-relevant services become available. But in the meantime, General Magic–based communicators have already begun to gain a small foothold in the Fortune 1,000, says a study by Forrester Research.[4] That this market will be slow to develop is hardly surprising. It took three years, after all, for sales of camcorders and audio CDs to exceed one million units annually, and VCRs and color TVs needed seven and nine years respectively to reach similar sales levels. Nonetheless, a study by Montgomery Securities envisions a $10 billion market in personal communicator hardware, software, and services by the year 2000.[5]

Probably the most critical factor in General Magic's success will be the dynamics of competition that eventually take shape in the communicator business. Four other companies—GO, EO, Momenta, and Slate—have all vaporized as a result of weak product technology, high prices, and an immature market. Apple's Newton, after a series of facelifts, still struggles to survive, but its prospects are not good, and its difficulties are only compounded by Apple's increasing marginalization in the PC business. Tandy's Zoomer, based on the GeoWorks operating system, is a cute little device for doing pretty much nothing of value, but then it's priced accordingly at the low end of the market and therefore doesn't present much of a threat to General Magic.

That leaves giant Microsoft, whose Winpad operating system for personal communicators had to go back to the engineering lab in late 1994 owing to various unspecified problems with the technology. Will Microsoft come roaring back with a revised Winpad and, by virtue of its size and clout, simply swallow the personal communicator market as it has so many others? Or will Bill Gates decide that General Magic's technology and early market position would require too heavy an investment on his part to overcome, and simply license Telescript instead?

It is known that in late 1994 Bill Gates had asked to meet with Marc Porat, who told the authors he preferred to hold off on talks "until we establish ourselves a bit more." In any event, it is unlikely that the long-term competitive dynamics of this new industry will coalesce into coherent shape until the late 1990s.

Whatever the future holds for General Magic and others in this new arena, the company's efforts reflect and inspire a new direction for the computer industry. Is it mere chance that other companies, including Microsoft, have also focused strenuous efforts toward making their products more usable? Microsoft's Bob, in fact, is a simplified user interface similar to Magic Cap in the sense that it, too, depicts real-world objects that signify various tasks the user can perform—for example, click on the image of the telephone on a desk and the communications application is launched. Two important differences separate Bob and Magic Cap, however.

First, in the usual Microsoft fashion, Bob is an incredibly awkward and memory-hogging system, requiring 8 megabytes of main memory and 30 megabytes of storage just to run. That's twice the memory capacity of most computers purchased in 1994. And second, the use of patronizingly cute cartoon characters such as Ruby the Parrot and Scuzz the Rat as guides is annoyingly distracting and indicates that for all its good intentions, Microsoft still doesn't have much of a clue about the consumer market.

"Microsoft misunderstands the whole problem novice users are having with their new computers," observed Gina Smith, the *San Francisco Examiner*'s "Inside Silicon Valley" columnist. "It isn't that they're too childish or unsophisticated to figure things out. It's that current interfaces like Microsoft Windows are hopelessly confusing and complicated for them. There's got to be a better way, but I don't think Bob is it."[6]

Smith also quoted Microsoft insiders who indicated that opposition to Bob was squelched when it was first being developed. "Most of [us] were floored," said one Microsoft employee. "We couldn't believe the idea of having these characters would ever make it through the approval process." So why did it get approved? "There was this widespread feeling at Microsoft that the consumer market was different, but they didn't know how," said Smith's source. In the end, it was a matter of needing to come up with *something*—combined with "excellent timing."

And not a moment too soon, either. For as computer companies have pushed their wares into mass-market channels, they have increasingly met with anger and resistance from mass-market buyers unable to use those products. In an article titled "Ho, Ho, Ho, Crash!", *Time* magazine warned that record Christmas 1994 sales would, owing to usability problems, be followed by the "Year of the Returns."[7]

Thanks in part to the work of firms like General Magic, "usability" has now become an industry buzzword. Or as David Leffler might say, "We're not in NerdWorld anymore."

PART TWO

A Kingdom of Riches

∎ **4** ∎

The Internet Reconsidered

Stop thinking about it as the Information Highway and start thinking about
it as the marketing superhighway. Doesn't it sound better already?

DON LOGAN, PRESIDENT AND
CEO OF TIME, INC., TO THE
ASSOCIATION OF NATIONAL ADVERTISERS

There truly is something exhilarating, even liberating, about navigating around the Internet. The sensation is akin to what a child might feel entering a hugely overstocked candy store without adult supervision, and suddenly realizing the *everything* in sight is free!

To give an example, imagine that you're writing a book on the Information Highway, and you're curious about what sort of helpful information might be available online. So you log on to *HotWired*, an all-electronic "magazine" affiliated with the print version of *Wired* (and only one of hundreds of thousands of publishing sites on the Internet).

The first thing you see on your computer screen is *HotWired*'s "What's New" page.[1] One item reads: "Vanderbilt University business school professors Donna Hoffman and Tom Novak explore the future of commerce in a virtual world."[2] You think this could be interesting, so you position your mouse over the blue-highlighted item and . . .

Click.

Hoffman and Novak's article, "The Challenges of Electronic Commerce," appears on the screen. Before reading it, though, you'd like to know a bit more about the source. You position your mouse atop the authors' names and . . .

Click.

You're suddenly in a computer at Tennessee's Vanderbilt University. You see a summary of the authors' credentials, some examples of research they've published, and various announcements concerning the Vanderbilt program. The screen also displays their photos, next to which are two small pictures of microphones . . .

Click.

"Hi, this is Donna Hoffman," a voice announces. "Glad you could visit."

Who says the Internet isn't user-friendly?

Click.

You're back to the Hoffman and Novak article again. You begin reading, scrolling down the page as you go, finding that their analysis does, indeed, offer some good food for thought. You notice that various words in the text are also highlighted in blue—*efficient channel, electronic commerce, pricing*—any of which could, if you click on them with your mouse, take you off on all sorts of fascinating tangents to other computers and publishing sites all over the world. But you're on deadline, so you put your mouse on the word *successful* in hopes of getting a quick summation of the likely factors for success in electronic commerce.

Click.

Ooops. You've landed in a computer maintained by the Tenagra Corporation of Virginia, which just announced its Internet Marketing Success awards for 1994. The top award goes to Pizza Hut, which distinguished itself by . . .

Click.

Okay, Hoffman and Novak's article is back on screen again. You spot a highlighted word that you hadn't noticed before—*demographics*—and give that one a try . . .

Click.

Up comes a page produced by the Graphics, Visualization and Usability Center at the Georgia Institute of Technology. Beautiful full-color pie charts appear on the screen. And these paint a surprising profile of users of the Internet's most popular region, the World Wide Web:[3]

- Only 15.5 percent of users are women.
- The median age of users is 29 years, average age 35.
- Approximately two-thirds are students, faculty, researchers, or technical professionals.

Now *that's* interesting—why are there so few women online?

The profile is not much different at the commercial online services such as America Online, where one might have expected their ease of access would have attracted a broader audience. Here, too, (with the lone exception of Prodigy, which we will address later) only 15–20 percent of users are female.

What's more, cyberspace also appears to be nearly devoid of consumers. Barely 10 percent of all online users, in fact, employ the medium for home banking, shopping, or other consumer-oriented purposes.[4] Rather, users spend most of their time online exchanging electronic mail, participating in discussion groups, called "newsgroups," or "chatting" with others in various forums, including those devoted to romance and sex like the "Flirts Nook" on America Online (although given the demographics, one wonders precisely *who* these guys are flirting with).

All of which suggests an interesting dilemma for the thousands of businesses now stampeding to set up shop on the Internet: how do they intend to create an online shopper's paradise when the people who actually do most of the shopping in America—women and mainstream consumers—seem to have so little interest in going online?

To be sure, millions of people *have* flocked to this boisterous amalgam of 5 million host computers linked by 40,000 networks that we call the Internet. Worldwide usage is now estimated somewhere between 15 and 30 million people. And the hundreds of Internet books and thousands of newspaper, magazine, and TV stories about cyberspace certainly attest to its allure.

For those who have ventured online, the Internet represents an entirely new form of human communication—perhaps the only mass communications medium in history that has not descended *to* the people from on high, but rather has emerged largely *from* the people, spontaneously, from below.

And while interactive TV networks are still only in the earliest stages of construction, the Internet already offers a fully functioning (albeit bandwidth-limited) Information Highway. As such, it has provided an extraordinary opportunity to test out new and emergent forms of media and entertainment, community and politics, trade and commerce. In effect, the Internet has become the principal R&D lab of the Digital Revolution itself, a sort of planet-wide petri dish in which key genetic strands of twenty-first-century society are already germinating.

But where is the experiment leading? Is the Internet about to become a vast new commercial market for consumer goods and services, as many pundits predict? Will it also serve eventually as the principal vehicle for large-scale corporate financial transactions and business-to-business data traffic?

No one really knows for sure, of course. But just as we can extrapolate the character of the future adult from the already distinct, if not yet fully formed, personality of the adolescent, perhaps we can also envision something of the Internet's future by identifying the core characteristics of its "personality" today:

> *Free. Egalitarian. Decentralized. Ad hoc. Open and peer-to-peer. Experimental. Autonomous. Anarchic.*

These words make up the lexicon of the cyberspace frontier, and it is remarkable how closely they parallel those which once described America's last great frontier, the Old West of the nineteenth century. The words evoke a certain sense of openness, of untrammeled spaces and unfenced ground, and of opportunity mixed with risk.

Notice, however, how sharply these words contrast with the hard-headed vocabulary of business and commerce:

> *For profit. Hierarchical. Systematized. Planned. Proprietary. Pragmatic. Accountable. Organized and reliable.*

This is more than simply word play here. There appears, in fact, to be a core conflict of values between the basic nature of the Internet and the demands of organized, large-scale commerce. One side or the other must give, and this fact naturally frames questions concerning the Internet's future in a new light, to wit:

Can the Internet's wild frontier be tamed and made "safe" for Big Business?

If so, what happens to the venturesome spirit, the raw and imaginative experimentalism that makes the Internet such a unique communications and cultural medium?

And if not—if the Internet cannot be molded into the chief communications backbone, the principal transmission belt for the major industrial engines of America's nearly $7 trillion economy—what, then, *is* its future?

It might be helpful to approach these questions by exploring what it is about the Internet that has generated in the popular imagination such an aura of excitement and luminescent promise.

Perhaps the most important quality of the Internet is that it is the most dynamic and wide-ranging interactive mass medium in history. *You* decide what you want to do on it, when you want to do it, whether you want to do it alone or with others, and so forth. Interactivity, of course, is a basic premise of all Info Highway projects you wouldn't want a highway where you couldn't choose your own route and destination, after all. But to a far greater degree than currently envisioned in most interactive TV schemes, the Internet offers a panoramic range of interactive choices that can be tailored to any individual's preferences. You can get information on almost any subject and in any degree of complexity; "chat" in real time with pen pals anywhere on earth; "listen" to or participate in discussions about almost any topic, interest or hobby under the sun; publish manifestos; sell your services; trade software; find, copy, and print out interesting books, articles, or documents; organize clubs and interest groups; meet your dream date; compete against others in games and contests; and collect your mail. And all this doesn't even scratch the surface.

Even so, the Internet is still only a crude Info Highway. Its narrow bandwidth pipes don't allow it to fully utilize the rich multimedia potential of full-motion video and sound. Hence the vast majority of Internet traffic still consists of alphanumeric, keyboard-entered text. But while upgrading these pipes to carry the high-bandwidth multimedia transmissions promised by future interactive TV networks will be costly and difficult—some say impossible—at least *this* network is up and running *today*.

The premise of personal interactive choice is widely thought of as revolutionary—almost a rebellion against centralized, hierarchical, industrial society and a by-product of digital technology's natural tendency to promote decentralized, nonhierarchical social relations and organizational forms. Since Gutenberg, printed media (and later radio and television) descended to us from on high. We sat and read (or listened and watched). Now, however, we can interact from the ground up: we can search and access planet-wide libraries of media according to our individual level of interest and sophistication. We can manipulate, store, clip, skip, fast-forward, reverse, send, order, buy, connect, annotate, question, or criticize media as *we* choose and in the way we choose. As the world itself adapts to the growing preeminence of information in social and economic life, the Internet and other interactive networks allow us to shape the media to a far greater degree than ever before and to use them in accordance with our own individual vision.

In some ways, however, interactivity is rather less revolutionary than it looks. We have *always* interacted with the media—that's what our minds, our intelligence, and our imaginations do for a living. Interactive media have also existed for far longer than many imagine, albeit in simpler form. Letters to the editor have existed for centuries, call-in talk radio for 40 years, 800-number telephone services and information database searching for 20 years, and television home shopping for a decade. Using an encyclopedia or a library to get information the old-fashioned way is pretty interactive; so, too, is looking through a newspaper—clipping sale coupons, underlining items of interest, calling phone numbers mentioned for further information, skipping the story about Bosnia in order to read the one about China, ignoring the Giants box score but poring over the Dodgers.

Indeed, the Internet is compelling *not* primarily because interactivity itself is so revolutionary—the human desire to interact with the world around us is actually quite traditional. Rather it is because the nature of interactive exchange on the Internet is so much more far-reaching in scope and dimensionalized in form and substance than anything that has existed in media before.

Accessing the Internet via a desktop computer, a modem, and a telephone line, many people spend their time using the network for the purposes imagined by the computer scientists who developed it in the 1970s and 1980s: scientific exchanges, university communications, and intergovernmental relations. Others engage in high-speed bursts of profound political discourse or perhaps lengthy metadebates about the future of mankind (or more likely the future of the Internet—for all the millions of people online, it still feels strangely like a small and somewhat secret club).

Still others, meanwhile, travel down the back alleys of sex chat. In the more than one hundred interviews conducted for this book, in fact, perhaps half the experts consulted alluded at some point in the discussion to the historic relationship between pornography and new media. "Dirty" pictures were one of the engines of photography and film development in the late nineteenth and early twentieth centuries. X-rated movies drove the diffusion of VCRs into the home in the 1980s. And now, on the Internet, sex has its place as well. Still, of the 20 most popular newsgroups on the Internet in June of 1995, only three were devoted to sex: in 3rd place, ALT.SEX (330,000 readers); in 16th place, ALT.SEX.VOYEURISM (with 150,000 readers); and in 17th place, ALT.SEX.EXHIBITIONISM (with 150,000 readers). More prevalent among the top 20 newsgroups were those focused on computers or on popular TV shows such as *The Simpsons*.[5]

The growth of sex chat reflects some of the social problems of the new technology for which no good answers yet exist. Children, for example, who are old enough to use online services may not be old enough or mature enough to understand what's happening when they are lured into sexual conversation. Commercial services like America Online have rules against open sexual discussion in their children's forums—and they advise strict parental control of the child's online activities—but these rules have proven difficult to enforce because the very anonymity of cyberspace enables pedophiles and child pornographers to lurk online, often posing as children themselves. (In his first foray online, the 12-year-old child of one of the authors "chatted" with a supposed kid who eventually asked him, "Are you wearing an athletic supporter?")

Out in the wild vastness of the Internet itself, beyond the all-too-permeable fences erected by commercial services to protect their young users, there are no controls at all. Unlike America Online or Prodigy, the Internet has no governing authority, no board of directors, no rule-making bodies of any sort except for those that assign domain (or site) names to companies and institutions that establish computer nodes on the Net. This is basic to the Internet's appeal, of course—net surfers jealously guard both their freedom of speech and their right to roam the wide-open digital spaces as they see fit. But it means that the Net is strictly an off-road environment. There are no stoplights or traffic dividers and absolutely no crossing guards.

All of which raises unique and troubling questions regarding traditional ethical standards as well as basic constitutional guarantees of freedom of expression. As Robert Rossney, the "Online" columnist for the *San Francisco Chronicle*, has written: "This is America, darn it, and I have the right to say whatever I want. Except that maybe it's not America. You may have *said* it in America, but in 15 minutes, when your message gets to England, you may be breaking anti-blasphemy laws. You don't even want to think about what happens when your message gets to Saudia Arabia."[6] Rossney went on to address the core dilemma:

> [The Internet] is not the public airwaves. It's thousands of computers, each belonging to someone else. Thomas Jefferson was a pretty forward-thinking guy, and it's possible that he intended the First Amendment to guarantee you the right to circulate copies of your dirty stories on computers belonging to Carnegie Mellon University. But on the other hand, maybe he didn't. And [what if] you post messages on my computer but I don't like what you say and [delete them]. Am I violating your rights yet?

Controversies such as these have already produced some celebrated legal cases, including one in 1994 in which a lawyer sued Prodigy for *not preventing* the posting of what he claimed was a libelous message. Similar demands that online services act as policemen and be held liable for the content carried on their services are contained in Nebraska Senator James Exon's proposed Communications Decency Act of 1995. In his unthinking rush to address public concern over pornography on the Internet, however, the senator seems not to have considered the fact that a law imposing fines of up to $100,000 and jail terms of up to two years on anyone who "makes, transmits, or otherwise makes available" words or images deemed offensive is not only constitutionally objectionable but, as a practical matter, absolutely unenforceable. Can you imagine the police attempting to monitor our private phone conversations in a (certainly vain) effort to stamp out cuss words? This is, quite literally, what the good senator would have the FBI attempt to do on the Internet.

As Brock Meeks, the ace reporter for *Interactive Week* who covered the Senate proceedings on Exon's bill, noted in his self-published Internet newsletter, *CyberWire Dispatch,* "The bill is flawed from the outset. While a 12-year-old can sneak a peek at *Playboy* at his local 7-11 or drool while reading the graphic descriptions of blow jobs in a Danielle Steele novel at Crown Books, the same type of material will land you in jail under this bill." Meeks added a humorous but telling anecdote to his report. Excusing himself from the Communications Decency Act debate for a moment, Meeks went to the Senate men's room which is, he noted, "just down the hall from where this august body of lawmakers was holding forth on how to shape the future of telecommunications." There he found the walls covered with all sorts of pornography depicting "anatomically correct, if slightly exaggerated, sketches of homoerotic acts [as well as] photos from sexually explicit gay men's magazines." As he left the wash-room, he passed a youngster about 10 years old—doubtless present that day to witness his lawmakers in action—entering a graffiti-covered stall with what Mecks termed a "pained" look on his face.

Flawed, perhaps, but it didn't stop the Senate from passing the Communications Decency Act by an 84–16 margin. But prospects for the bill's subsequent passage by the House looked bleak when, toward the end of June 1995, even family values advocate Newt Gingrich publicly opposed it.

In early July, however, Senator Exon's bill got a shot in the arm when *Time* magazine hit the newsstands with a special "Cyberporn" issue. "There's an awful lot of porn online," *Time* shrieked—and make no mistake, given the dark and frightening image *Time* used on its cover, of a wide-eyed child terrorized by a computer, this *was* a shriek. The story went on to report as fact that on the portion of the Internet known as Usenet, "83.5 percent of the pictures were pornographic." The magazine based its exclusive story on what it called "an exhaustive study of online porn" conducted by an under-graduate student, Martin Rimm, at Carnegie Mellon University.

Time's "Cyberporn" cover story was picked up by ABC's *Night-line* and other media. It was also seized upon by the Christian Coali-tion and by Senator Grassley of Iowa, who cited *Time*'s "83.5 percent" porno rate in support of the Exon bill's limits on freedom of speech over the Internet.

The only problem was, *Time*'s "83.5 percent" figure was utterly and completely false. The study upon which *Time* based its story focused not on pornography on the Internet per se, but principally upon images available on adult bulletin board systems, known as BBSs, which specifically cater to those seeking pornography. And as *Time* (and the study's author) conceded, pornographic images in fact represent only about 3 percent of all traffic on the Usenet—and the Usenet itself represents only 11.5 percent of all traffic on the In-ternet.

Once we do the math, we get a rather different picture of the extent of the cyberporn threat—only about one-half of 1 percent of all Internet communications, in fact, are devoted to pornography. One might well find a higher rate of pornography at the local magazine store—or even in the workaday world of business. Indeed, if you like surveys, consider the one in the July 1995 issue of *Sales & Marketing Management* magazine showing that 49 percent of salesmen routinely take their customers to topless bars to cement their deals.

The *Time* story was a classic case in point of media sensationalizing with regard to the Internet. The magazine's editors were informed at least a week before publication that the Rimm study appeared to be seriously flawed. For one thing, Rimm's study had never been submitted for peer review—a red flag if ever there was one, especially for a study of such purported significance. And once the experts—including Professors Hoffman and Novak of Vanderbilt, probably the nation's top authorities on online usage patterns—examined Rimm's study in detail, they found it riddled with misrepresentation, manipulation, lack of objectivity, and methodological flaws. Even Rimm's own faculty advisor and at least one of the researchers who worked with Rimm distanced themselves from the study.

But *Time* ignored the warnings and failed to conduct journalistic due diligence on its "Cyberporn" "exclusive." This was especially troubling given that *Time* surely knew its story could directly affect the prospects for pending legislation that might alter national policy regarding electronic free speech for decades to come. But the chance to sell magazines by sensationalizing an issue—especially regarding a subject such as cyberspace that few Americans yet know much about firsthand—was simply too hard to pass up.

The ironic thing about *Time*'s portrayal of cyberspace as a den of iniquity is that the Internet actually served as a center of grass-roots research and debate that eventually led to the debunking of *Time*'s story.

In the week before and after publication, some 1,000 messages and items of information were exchanged between lawyers, academicians, journalists, and ordinary citizens on the Well, a small online service frequented by some of America's leading journalists and media experts. They worked together to uncover the truth behind the *Time* story and Rimm's study, and in so doing, illustrated the changing dynamics of media and public opinion in this new era. Just a few years ago, the chief recourse in dealing with media misinformation was perhaps a letter to the editor. Now, through the miracle of digital ones and zeros, it has become possible in some situations for citizens outside the media to take matters into their own hands, ferret out the truth, spark media coverage, and influence public opinion. No longer does the mainstream media have a sole monopoly on public discourse.

The fundamental point underlying all this is that the Internet and new technology are not the source of our nation's problems—they merely add new and sometimes troubling dimensions to the problems we already face throughout society.

This is not to suggest, of course, that the concern many citizens have over the proliferation of pornography and other apparent assaults upon traditional family values is entirely misplaced. People are right to be worried—who wouldn't be, looking at our high divorce rate or the rising numbers of unwed teenage mothers and single parent families? And we do not mean to imply that the Internet plays *no* role in helping to promulgate the tastes of those who, for example, believe that barnyard bestiality is a healthy expression of human sexuality. What's more, for all the talk of pornography getting into the hands of children, it is equally unnerving to imagine several million adults so socially alienated and lost in sexual obsession that they spend their time masturbating in front of their computers while our society—Rome, as it were—burns around us.

But two critical points bear reiterating. First, the Internet only reflects the anomie in our society—it does not cause it. And second, the threat to children from cyberporn in particular pales beside the dangers they face every day in the real world just going to school: gangs, drunk drivers, guns, drugs, deranged street people, sexual assault—and don't forget the rack of X-rated magazines at the neighborhood liquor store.

Indeed, whether we're speaking of cyberspace or of the real life conditions in nearly every city and town in America, raising kids these days—not to mention trying to nurture in them a moral and ethical code conducive to good citizenship in a free society—is fraught with dangers that previous generations of parents never had to face.

In any event, precisely because the Internet is such a new and controversial mirror for society, it does tend to attract more than its fair share of attention when politicians go looking for scapegoats for today's problems. In the wake of the Oklahoma City bombing in April 1995, for example, a number of political initiatives were proposed that would grant the FBI expanded powers to conduct surveillance on the Internet, and in doing so, create significant threats to the first amendment freedoms of citizens. Again, it was Brock Meeks who provided the best report of a May 11, 1995, hearing of the Senate Subcommittee on Terrorism, Technology, and Government Information called to investigate "The Availability of Bomb Making Information on the Internet." He cited the testimony that day— ignored in most other national media coverage—of a law professor who pointed out that similar information on how to make explosives can be found on pages 275–282 of Volume 21 of the 1986 edition of the Encyclopedia Britannica. On page 279 of the volume is a description of the Ammonium Nitrate–fuel oil bomb used by the right-wing terrorists in Oklahoma City. What's more, Meeks reported, even the Department of Agriculture Forestry Service publishes a *Blaster's Handbook* that also includes a recipe for the Ammonium Nitrate–fuel oil bomb.

The point, of course, is that child pornography and bomb making can be carried out with the aid of all kinds of technology, not just the Internet. Compared to the phone or the postal system, the Internet may offer a bit more anonymity and reach to people who engage in such activities. But we could shut down cyberspace tomorrow and rip out every single computer in the country and we'd still have Americans sexually exploiting, libeling, harassing, and blowing each other up in ever-increasing numbers. That's because the real culprit is not technology but the deep-rooted alienation people feel from each other and from their institutions, and this is reflected in the erosion of the common values and public responsibilities that have always kept this nation glued together. When the foundation and the walls of your house are collapsing before your very eyes, it's really rather silly to worry about installing new locks on your doors.

While obscenity and right-wing organizing on the Net get all the attention (especially in election years), issues regarding copyright and intellectual property protection may prove to be more important economically and more difficult to resolve. Forget for a moment the problem of extraterritoriality—the Internet respects no national borders—and whether users in other countries can or even should be bound somehow by U.S. patent and copyright laws. Forget also the ability of anyone in cyberspace to download, if he or she so wishes, a copyrighted image or text and then appropriate it without paying the owner. One can do the same in the real world, of course, but theft is a lot more difficult (and risky) in a bookstore made of bricks than it is in one made of electrons—especially when the thief himself is merely a burst of invisible electrons. One of the thorniest problems is Net culture itself, which not only upholds the paramount right of the individual to publish and distribute anything he or she desires, but further asserts that "all information wants to be free." Though many Net users go absolutely ballistic when their postings are quoted in the press without their explicit permission, oftentimes they don't extend these ownership rights to others. So how does the creator of original work, especially one whose livelihood depends on being paid for that work, enforce his or her copyright out in the limitless Net badlands?

New questions seem to arise every day. What about the bad, even sometimes dangerous, medical advice dispensed in health newsgroups? What about stock manipulation in financial newsgroups? The Internet is not only a source of information but of *misinformation* as well.

This homegrown, antiauthoritarian Net culture is in many ways a natural byproduct of the origins of the Internet as a Pentagon-inspired backup communications system in the event of a nuclear attack. Its power was intentionally decentralized so that it could withstand the kind of direct hit that would decapitate a more centrally controlled network. The dispersed and unruly nature of the Internet is only reinforced, of course, by the software system that controls the network's underlying operations. Indeed, the same openness and flexibility of the Unix operating system and the TCP/IP communications protocol that has allowed a planet full of incompatible computers and networks to bypass any sort of central manager or translator and talk to each other across almost any physical channel—from phone lines to cable TV setups to satellite and fiber-optic links—also makes it extremely difficult to enforce standards or rules of any kind. Simply put, the Internet is ungovernable.

Anyone sufficiently adept in the Unix operating system can send objectionable messages or intrusive advertisements to millions of people at once. Likewise, that same person could send cancel or delete commands (called "cancelbots") that erase messages posted by anyone else anywhere—even one posted by the president of the United States. Hackers can track messages, snoop on them, intercept unencrypted transactions, or even break into other computers and steal or scramble confidential information. Out on the digital frontier, you can pretty much do whatever you want—and, for the most part, there's no sheriff or posse to stop you.

All anyone can do is build a kind of "fort" around their computer system to stop unauthorized access. But as a number of major companies have discovered to their chagrin, even such "firewalls," as they're called, are only partially effective against a truly dedicated hacker. In February of 1995, for example, after stealing 20,000 credit card numbers from the subscriber list at the nation's largest Internet access provider, the long-sought outlaw hacker, Kevin Mitnick, was finally arrested by the FBI. The FBI was only able to get their man because the even more highly skilled computer expert Tsutomo Shimomura, a researcher at the San Diego Supercomputer Center, decided to trace and catch the thief after Mitnick had broken into Shimomura's home computer. The high-noon-in-cyberspace drama of the Mitnick case—two lone gunfighters shooting it out with bits and bytes—made it front-page news in the *New York Times*, and a book and movie are also reportedly in the works. But the extent of the Internet's security problems run far deeper.

The Computer Emergency Response Team (CERT), which monitors Internet security problems from its headquarters at Carnegie Mellon University, reported 2,241 Internet security breaches in 1994, twice as many as in 1993.[7] And even more disturbing, the government concedes that in 1994 alone, hackers successfully compromised 350 separate Defense Department computer systems. According to some experts, the total number of incidents of hacker intrusions into defense systems over the last few years may be as high as 300,000.[8] One does not need to be a gung-ho, flag-waving jingoist to be made uneasy by the thought of tattooed, postadolescent digital scofflaws running around cyberspace selling U.S. defense plans and nuclear secrets to the highest bidder.

"The Internet is like a bad neighborhood where a lot of people are looking for trouble," says Ray Ozzie of Iris Associates, a software company. "It's wild out there."[9] While a bit one-sided, this statement highlights the ineffectiveness of anticrime efforts on the Internet.

Adds Jim McMahon, a veteran of the San Jose Police Department, who heads a four-person high-tech crime unit responsible for investigating computer crimes in the heart of Silicon Valley: "I would no more drop my kid off on the Internet than I would at midnight in Golden Gate Park in San Francisco. In my home, if children are logging on to an outside network, either my wife or I am next to them. We guide them as to what they watch on TV, what books they read; this is no different. I see a lot of parents abdicating this responsibility. They think their kid is safe. It couldn't be farther from the truth."

Nonetheless, despite troubling issues concerning security, obscenity, libel, and copyright protection, the social value of the Internet is more than redeemed by the many thousands upon thousands of thoughtful discussion groups, wide-ranging knowledge libraries, creative and useful services, and close-knit "virtual communities" that have grown up spontaneously over the years. Indeed, even the most rudimentary exploration of the Net cannot help but evoke a powerful sense of the vast diversity and richness of human experience in its newest medium of expression.

It may be true, as the now famous *New Yorker* cartoon put it, that "on the Internet no one knows you're a dog." But in this dog-eat-dog world, in which life has become so fragmented, isolated, and rootless for so many of us, the electronic frontier has offered a new home of sorts for tens of thousands, perhaps millions, of people. Deep and lasting friendships, even marriages, have been crafted out of the raw digital material of a Net connection. Victims of corporate downsizing have been able to launch sustainable businesses in cyberspace when pounding the pavement for a job proved fruitless. And in an anonymous world in which one in five citizens moves every year—and where church, community, and even family are all too often replaced by the lonely midnight flickering of the TV set—the Net can offer companionship and belonging in "virtual communities" (whose spirit is often made flesh through subsequent get-togethers) that are as genuine and meaningful as any that exist in the real world.

If the Internet is, in truth, a grand bazaar of ideas and spirit, it is also now becoming a bazaar in the original sense as well—an organized oasis where products and services can be bought and sold and where new and mutually beneficial trading relationships can be formed. Even the smallest sampling of cyberspace enterprises suggests that the Internet is sprouting all sorts of new forms of commerce and new models of business.

Publishers who have gone online on the Web, for instance, have created entirely new kinds of "books" and "magazines," and new ways in which these can be accessed, experienced, and appreciated. *HotWired*, described earlier in this discussion, offers innovative samplings of digitized art, music, and video in a format that stretches traditional boundaries between print, audio, and visual media. (Cognizant of this fact, *HotWired* calls its magazine a "cyberstation" and its various sections "channels.") The Gutenberg Project is building an electronic library with a wealth of titles such as *Alice's Adventures in Wonderland* that are no longer covered by copyright protection. Stephen King has sold his own short stories directly to consumers on the Web. Who, after all, needs the publisher, printer, sales rep, and bookstore as middlemen in cyberspace? HarperCollins Publishers now offers more than 10,000 books and software titles for sale through its online bookstore, and McGraw-Hill's "Titlebank" likewise sells some 9,000 professional and educational books. Other, more radical experiments in book marketing are also under way, such as Random House's 1995 offering of free electronic versions of Michael Wolff's *Netguide* in the hopes that online distribution will expand rather than dilute sales of the print version.

Because the barriers to entry are so low in electronic commerce, the variety of experiments in marketing, sales, distribution, and transaction processing is mind-boggling. Some start-up ventures with little money for marketing, for example, have used the Internet to inexpensively distribute free samples of their product and thereby bootstrapped themselves into multimillion-dollar corporations. Millions of free copies of Doom, a 3-D shoot-'em-up computer game, were distributed online by Id Software. The company asked only that customers send in $45 for an enhanced version of the game if they liked what they saw. According to press accounts, more than 100,000 people apparently did exactly that.

Marketing has, indeed, moved in new directions along the digital frontier. Historically, advertising has followed a "one-to-many" model, filling our televisions, newspapers, and mailboxes with messages that shout in one way or another in order to be heard above the din and clutter of competing ads. Such an approach would violate Internet cultural norms ("Netiquette"), and would also very likely cripple the Net with a barrage of bandwidth-clogging advertising images. As Vanderbilt professors Hoffman and Novak suggest, a new model for Internet-based marketing is needed—one that follows a "many-to-many" approach.

"The Web presents a fundamentally different environment for marketing activities than traditional media, dooming to failure the old one-to-many advertising approaches which assume a passive, captive audience," they write. "Virtually every aspect of Internet-based marketing strategy—including advertising, pricing, word-of-mouth influence, distribution channels, and product development—differs from the manner in which firms are used to doing business."[10]

Hoffman and Novak argue that the potential of this new medium to provide an efficient channel for business is great. They cite early studies indicating that marketing through conventional channels may be four times as expensive as marketing over the Internet, and quote one source suggesting that marketing on the Web portion of the Internet results in "ten times as many units sold with one-tenth the advertising budget."

But studies of Net advertising and marketing are still largely anecdotal and rudimentary owing to the experimental stage of these efforts. In terms of real dollars and cents, Net commerce is still more a dream than a reality. Still, the opportunities in this field may be substantial, or at least so believe the thousands of businesses already actively exploring electronic ventures.

Marketing on the Net, aside from being lower in cost, offers another and potentially even more powerful advantage for businesses: they will know exactly how many times their ad or promotion has been read or seen—and, with users' permission, they'll be able to gather valuable information about the demographics and interests of potential customers and follow up with more targeted promotional efforts.

In a whole variety of ways, electronic commerce offers businesses potentially large competitive advantages in terms of cost reduction, inventory control, market outreach, targeted promotion, customization of products, time to market for new products or services, transaction completion, and the streamlining and more efficient coordination of business processes themselves. Electronic funds transfer enables businesses to greatly speed up payments and receipts while at the same time reducing errors as well as the costs of paper handling and storage. Enterprise integration allows businesses to integrate suppliers and shippers vertically into the organization while at the same time increasing collaboration between various departments within the firm. In short, electronic commerce combines the speed, efficiency, and global reach of computer and communication technologies with the creativity and adaptability of people in ways that enhance productivity and create new market opportunities.

The advantages of electronic-mediated commerce are available not only to "virtual" enterprises—those that exist only in cyberspace—but also to traditional bricks-and-mortar businesses that use electronic systems to speed up and better manage their operations. In the 1980s, for example, Wal-Mart invested heavily in computer and satellite communications networks linking each point-of-sale terminal in all its stores to distribution centers and to corporate headquarters in Bentonville, Arkansas. Individual stores were given the authority and the technology to place electronic orders directly with suppliers. This allowed Wal-Mart to reduce its inventory restocking time from an industry average of six weeks to just 36 hours. Combined with the fact that each store could now automatically track what was selling and what wasn't, the company was able to keep its stores stocked and its prices low even as it expanded rapidly to become the number-one retailer in America. In December of 1994, Wal-Mart became the first mass-market retail chain to offer interactive home shopping services over an online network, in this case to residents of Phoenix, Arizona, who subscribe to America Online.

Clearly, electronic commerce potentially offers enormous advantages for businesses and consumers. And cyberspace may eventually turn out to be the greatest new market opportunity in history. But while predictions of hundreds of billions in online revenues abound, the reality is that consumer spending for content, goods, and services on the Internet actually amounted to a grand total of only $13 million in 1994. That's barely 1.5 percent of the $843 million derived that year from the sale of Internet-related hardware, software, consulting services, and access fees.[11]

In other words, there's a lot more money being made selling access *to* the Internet than there is selling anything actually *on* the Internet itself. Similarly, consumer purchases on the commercial services amounted to some $35 million out of total industry revenues of $708 million in 1994.[12]

Still, Net commerce is young, and market researcher SIMBA Information predicts it will grow by an astounding 6,000 percent to become a $1 billion a year industry by the end of this decade. Of course, that will still be only half the size of today's market for blow dryers, but it's a start.

Not much to write home about, to be sure. Still, there is no other way to commence the long march to the commercial cyberspace cornucopia of tomorrow except by beginning with a few halting dings of the virtual cash register at Pizza Hut online, so there is no point in being discouraged. One should, however, be cognizant of the challenges that must be faced *before* a truly mass consumer market can be created online.

One of these challenges, of course, is to broaden the population mix online. As noted earlier, women and consumers make up only about 15 percent of online users, and this demographic weakness has not been altered much even by the cyberspace growth spurt of recent years. What's more, the striking similarity in online demographics between women and ordinary consumers makes perfect sense. Women's needs and buying habits, after all, largely shape the consumer marketplace. And besides being the predominant consumers of media in the U.S., women also make the key buying decisions in many if not most consumer product categories. According to the American Mass Retail Association, 73 percent of all primary shoppers in America— whether for groceries, apparel, or durable goods— are women.

So why such a dearth of women and consumers online? Certainly part of the explanation, at least where women are concerned, lies in the harassment women often receive in cyberspace. As Fran Maier, a cyberspace marketing executive puts it, "On some services, simply identifying yourself as a woman is the virtual equivalent of walking into a cowboy bar wearing a Wonderbra, boots, and not much else."[13]

Significantly, Prodigy's higher-than-average 35 percent female subscribership may be due in part to its family-oriented approach and strict antiobscenity policies, as well as to its more active development of consumer services.

Even in Internet discussion groups that focus on women's issues, however, there is still a boys' club atmosphere in much of cyberspace. One researcher at Simon Fraser University in Vancouver, British Columbia, pegged the population of the ALT.FEMINISM newsgroup at 11 percent women, 83 percent men, and 6 percent undeterminable.[14]

But the larger explanation, supported by many studies, is that women and mainstream consumers have little interest in computers per se—as high-tech toys or as the stuff of a hobbyist's fancy—but view them instead as simply tools. It's not that going online is too complex a task for women or ordinary consumers to master. It's that they have yet to find much in the way of practical and compelling benefits for doing so.

The truth is, online services today offer precious little of real, tangible value to people in the form of convenience, service, or practical solutions to daily life problems. You may be able to chat with the *Star Trek: Voyager* crew or read a movie review, but you are not able to reserve movie tickets online. You can search back issues of the nation's top parenting magazines, but you can't search a database of local baby-sitters and contact one. You can download *Consumer Reports*, but you can't find a local repairman online to fix your water heater. You can order a computer from a dealer in Montana, but you can't download discount grocery coupons for diapers or cereal redeemable at your local supermarket.

The paucity of tangible, daily-life value in most of today's cyberspace offerings may explain why only 6 percent of U.S. households subscribe to an online service—and even more telling, why more than half of even the homes that *have* modem-equipped computers don't. Among those who do subscribe, as many as 50 percent may drop the service in any given year.[15]

Fran Maier's San Francisco–based company, Electric Classifieds, Inc. (ECI), hopes to make cyberspace more appealing by offering a service that provides some practical value and that ordinary consumers also already understand: online classifieds. America Online and other commercial networks already offer some classified services, of course, but these are limited by their geographically undifferentiated and often sparse database of listings. But by partnering with print media, whose $13 billion classified ad business generates nearly 30 percent of newspaper revenues, Electric Classifieds intends to launch regionally based classified services (such as JOBS.COM, AUTO.COM, and HOUSING.COM) that combine the advantages of interactive technology—intelligent search capability, faster response time, and a rich multimedia environment—with the existing practical benefits of print classifieds.

ECI's first service is MATCH.COM, an online interactive personals ad service that, aside from providing the advantages of interactivity, also offers a more welcoming environment for women as well as the safety and security so often lacking in other relationship services. Relationships, of course, may not offer the quantifiable benefits of a job or a place to live, but they are central to people's daily lives. Indeed, printed relationship ads constitute the fastest-growing sector of the classified business today. According to SIMBA, "Personals are the 'killer application' among classifieds."[16]

Online classifieds are only one example of the kinds of consumer-oriented services that need to be built. Another (and one likely to attract more women to the online world) would be an electronic grocery coupon service. Instead of laboriously searching newspapers for coupons to clip, value-conscious shoppers would be able to log on to a network, type in "cat food" or "cereal," and have all available coupons for those products downloaded to their computers. Such a service would also benefit coupon providers, who today must suffer the expense of printing over 320 billion coupons annually only to see less than a fortieth of them redeemed. Manufacturers and stores would also no doubt love the chance to build a comprehensive database of shopper preferences in order to more effectively target their future promotions.

Despite the best efforts of companies like Electric Classifieds, however, it will take time—probably five years or more—before cyberspace can attract the critical mass of women and consumers necessary to outgrow its niche status and become a genuine mass market industry.

One factor limiting the Internet's growth as a mass commercial medium, of course, is technology. Only 10 percent of users of the World Wide Web, for example, have modems fast enough to access the Web's rich graphical capabilities at acceptable speeds.[17] And as for the core trunk lines that carry the bulk of Internet data traffic today, even using the Mbone (Multicast Backbone) protocol that allows Internet transmission of digital video and CD-quality audio signals, as of mid-1995, these could barely support 100 simultaneous real-time video sessions.

"People say the Internet is carrying multimedia today," scoffs Bob

Metcalfe, who invented the Ethernet network protocol at Xerox PARC in the early 1970s and is regarded as one of the world's top networking experts. "But dogs can walk on their hind legs, too."

In other words, the Internet is not yet ready to support the bandwidth-rich applications that will be needed to facilitate large-scale consumer commerce on the Net. But even when it is—say, by 1997–1998—the key issue is and will continue to be developing more compelling services.

"The different services are now challenging themselves to come up with creative [services]," noted Lisa Johnson, an analyst with market researcher Link Resources. With only [6] percent of U.S. homes now online, she added, "what appears to be lacking is the compelling content that is going to [grow] the subscriber base and generate usage."[18]

Added ECI's Fran Maier, "Ultimately, unless we can offer something to the average consumer, cyberspace may wind up becoming the biggest zero-billion-dollar business and the most exciting fading cultural fad in history."

The key word there, of course, is *ultimately*. In the meantime, there are plenty of opportunities to develop rich businesses that appeal to the existing, largely male, and upscale population of the Internet. Indeed, when more than 800,000 people visit Penthouse Online in just its first week—and are willing to spend, at 30 cents per minute, the dollar a pop it takes to download nude photos—that tells you something about the benefits of knowing your market well.

Another online company that truly knows its market is Underground.Net, headed by Serry Osmena-Ruegg and Charles Como. Recognizing that among the largest groups of online users are 18–24-year-olds whose access is provided free by their colleges and universities, the firm creates sites on the World Wide Web for rock groups such as Megadeth, Van Halen, and Sky Cries Mary, and for Capitol Records and other entertainment industry companies. It has also organized live events and concerts online, attracting as sponsors such youth-oriented consumer product companies as Coca-Cola and Tower Records. Its Megadeth site, called *Megadeth Arizona* because that was where the band recorded its *Youthanasia* album, was generating some 90,000 log-ins per day soon after it opened. Users could download song lyrics or photos of the band, read their diaries, play interactive games, enter sweepstakes, or view short video clips of live concerts.

"Internet users, especially in our audience, don't want to simply look at an advertisement or download a graphic," observed Underground.Net's Osmena-Ruegg. "They won't go to a site that's static—that's like looking at a billboard in traffic or turning a page in a magazine. They want a place to 'hang out' online, someplace that's cool, fun, active, and interesting. If you want to market on the Net, then you've got to remember that this audience is young."

In the real world, of course, such advice would be considered obvious—a no-brainer, as it were, that hardly needed mentioning. But many otherwise-enterprising companies seem to think that somehow the basic rules of marketing and merchandising don't apply in cyberspace. They concentrate their efforts on boosting the technological sophistication of their services, for instance, rather than on developing effective *brands* backed by strong, targeted marketing.

Indeed, as a percentage of total operating expenses, marketing budgets at many firms developing Internet commerce applications are far below what is considered appropriate at consumer product companies. Customer research and other marketing functions generally receive short shrift, while staff resources are focused on product development and engineering. Indeed, the CEO of one firm told the authors he would be more willing to share with competitors the names of talented marketing people than he would the names of top engineering talent. Often missing in the virtual mall, it seems, is the customer-centric orientation that guides the business strategies of real-world retailers and marketers.

Andrea Werboff is a highly regarded consumer marketing consultant whose clients include Silicon Valley start-up eShop, Inc., a firm developing an online shopping mall in conjunction with 800-FLOWERS, Tower Records, The Good Guys electronics stores, and other name-brand retailers. Werboff has also worked with such consumer marketing powerhouses as Quaker Oats and Levi's.

"I've found that high-tech companies tend to confuse the concept of consumer-friendly *products* with consumer-driven *marketing*. They pump money into making their product look better or easier to use, when the real task is to show people why they should even want to shop online in the first place. I mean, everyone knows what hot cereal is and how to use it—we all have spoons, right? But creating consumer awareness and demand for shopping in cyberspace requires that you educate the market about exactly what this is, why they should do it—and why they should do it at *your* online mall as opposed to the other guy's—and then really be able to deliver on your promise of added value."

She pauses a moment, then adds: "We've got to stop thinking of online commerce as a technology business, and start thinking about it like any other consumer-driven retailing or merchandising operation."

As Gene DeRose of Jupiter Communications, a consulting firm, put it: "Long sought and sorely missed, the talent, tools, and integrated marketing savvy [of] the traditional mainstream media will increase the appeal of online services and intensify what is already becoming fierce competition among major service providers."[19] Such mainstream content companies, DeRose points out, are already rushing to the online world in droves for three reasons: the low cost of entry, the promise of a ready-made market, and the assurance of near-term revenues in contrast to the longer-term (and more uncertain) prospects of future interactive TV profits.

Indeed, everyone who is anyone in media, technology, and communications seems to be "going online" these days. From Rupert Murdoch's News Corp. to Bill Gates's Microsoft, and from Bell Atlantic to Apple Computer to AT&T—perhaps a dozen major companies are scrambling to grab a piece of the lucrative online pie by launching networks of their own. The same trend is also unfolding in Europe and Asia, where telephone, computer, publishing, and entertainment companies are rushing to unveil online services.

Potentially the most important of these ventures will be Microsoft's online service, which thanks to a deal with Web software maker Spyglass and the purchase of an interest in Internet access provider Uunet will also offer access to the Internet. With its enormous marketing clout and its direct hooks into 80 percent of all computers, Microsoft could quickly become the dominant Internet access provider. Scary though the thought is of yet another Microsoft monopoly in an Information Age industry, Bill Gates's online juggernaut will certainly improve the chances of cyberspace becoming more of a mass consumer marketplace. As Allen Weiner, principal analyst for online strategies at the market research firm Dataquest, notes: "They have fired a salvo at the online information providers and at the Internet service providers as well. They are going to force everyone to look at their strategies."[20]

And, indeed, they already have. After Bill Gates's announced intention to purchase personal finance software maker Intuit for $1.5 billion (the deal was later scuttled in the wake of a Justice Dept. antitrust suit), Microsoft's agreement with Visa a month later to develop software enabling credit card users to shop online, and most important, its announcement of its own online network, the financial services industry suddenly awoke to the fact that the once "virtual" online banking and shopping fields were not only possibly about to become real businesses but Microsoft-dominated ones at that. In response, a number of banking and financial services firms have also joined the online gold rush, hoping to carve out a position before Microsoft owns all the territory. BankAmerica and Mastercard, for example, have teamed up with Internet software developer Netscape to develop a system enabling credit card users to purchase goods online without fear that their card numbers will be stolen by hackers. BankAmerica, the nation's second-largest bank, has also joined with NationsBank, the country's fourth-largest, to purchase and market a home banking software program called Managing Your Money, a competitor to Intuit's Quicken.

"This is obviously a major power play," noted William Bluestein, an analyst at Forrester Research. "It's clearly a response by these banks to the fear of having their lunch eaten by Microsoft in cyberspace."[21] It's also a signal that sooner or later the major players in retail banking and consumer products and services will establish marketing and sales locations in cyberspace.

And what then? When the Internet is finally ready for prime time—when the technology works well enough and at fast enough speeds, when enough people have the equipment and skills needed to access it, and when enough genuinely consumer-oriented services and stores have been created—what will we have gained? Ladies and gentlemen, we offer you (drum roll, please) *the shopping mall*!

You see the problem? What's really new, where's the added value? To be sure, some products and services seem to be ready made for the online environment. FTD-type flower orders and phone-in theater or concert ticket sales, for example, let customers at last *see* what they were buying. Products in which a high information content is involved in the sale—wine, say, or perhaps certain high-end consumer electronics—also appear well-suited to cyberspace, where shoppers can obtain information often more easily than in real stores and can automatically compare prices between a variety of vendors as well.

But in general, Internet marketers and retailers will discover that unless they can offer consumers significantly greater convenience, noticeably lower prices, or dramatically improved service, there is simply no reason in the world why anyone with any sense would venture into the unfamiliar territory of a virtual store when there's a perfectly good *real* one down the street.

One virtual business that seems to be capitalizing on the added-convenience factor is the online supermarket. Chicago-based Peapod, for example, offers the convenience of ordering groceries online and having them delivered without the hassle of standing in line behind (it always seems) the lady with a fistful of coupons. Peapod users can compare items by category, brand, size, price, and unit cost. And online shoppers say the time savings each week more than makes up for the cost of the service. Apparently, this claim is true, for Peapod reported triple-digit growth in 1995.

This sort of added convenience is of considerable value in a society such as ours that is becoming ever-more complex and stressful. Remember when you didn't have to make a month-long research project out of buying a coffee maker or a bottle of vitamins or even pet food, for God's sake? To the extent that online shopping makes obtaining life's necessities more convenient or exploits the new technology to offer substantial added value to people's daily lives in other ways, it will become an important though secondary force in a complex retailing and commercial environment that, even in the future, will remain dominated by in-person, face-to-face transactions.

By the end of this decade, then, it is likely that the Internet will have become a thriving multibillion-dollar bazaar for consumer goods and services. But what is far less certain is whether it can be effectively molded to serve corporate America's key financial and business-to-business requirements.

As we noted early in this discussion, this question is of paramount importance in determining the ultimate character of the Internet and its future role in society. And it is our belief that it will *not* become the principal Information Highway that corporate America depends upon for its most critical data and financial traffic.

The reasons for this are several, all more or less stemming from the fact that the Internet was expressly designed and created *not* to be an efficiently managed, tightly organized, and secure network in the first place. As noted earlier, it was built specifically to be invulnerable to any centrally targeted, decapitating nuclear strike.

And guess what? The plan worked! Trying to knock down the Internet would be like trying to shoot out the lights in the aurora borealis.

But at the same time, trying to make all the Internet's disparate parts work together smoothly and efficiently would be akin to trying to herd five million cats. Good luck!

Indeed, you wouldn't want to bet a $10 *billion* priority funds transfer on those five million cats—er, host computers—acting in concert to ensure the transaction is processed securely and speedily ahead of John Q. Citizen's $10 cheese-and-pepperoni order from Pizza Hut Online.

One barrier to corporate reliance on the Internet is that in many ways it is still more a dirt road than a paved superhighway. In the mid-1980s, the Internet was updated by the addition of a high-speed backbone link, called NFS Net and funded by the National Science Foundation, which served to enhance communication between various governmental, academic, and scientific research institutions. But even so, there are still not enough high-capacity lines carrying Internet traffic today, and as a result its speed and bandwidth are too low-end for high-end corporate traffic.

What's more, some degradation of network operation may result from the April 1995 privatization of the Internet and the withdrawal of government's $12 billion annual subsidy. When the NFS backbone is fully disconnected, three private communications carriers—Pacific Bell, Ameritech, and Sprint—are due to take up the slack. Metropolitan Fiber Systems will operate a fourth network hub. The Pacific Bell and Ameritech hubs, however, are based on a technology called ATM (Asynchronous Transfer Mode), which, although universally touted as the switching technology of choice for interactive systems, has not yet been actually proven capable of handling large volumes of high-speed data traffic. This, combined with the continuing explosion of new users, could place severe strains upon what is, in fact, already a congested and jerry-rigged system.

"I don't think anyone has large amounts of confidence that [it] will work as advertised," observed Edward M. Velmetti, vice president for research at MSEN, Inc., an Internet services provider.[22]

Then there's the problem of security. As noted earlier, the greatest threat to Internet security comes from hackers who are able to utilize weaknesses in the Unix operating system to penetrate corporate gateways and enter the heart of a firm's internal network. But an additional problem lies in the control and allocation of internal network resources for the company's most urgent and mission-critical tasks.

Proprietary software solutions to the external threat are being developed by firms such as Novell, whose NetWare software manages internal computer networks for some 30 million corporate users. Because these solutions run under Netware rather than Unix, hackers will have a harder time using the usual Unix tricks to break through. Firewalls are also needed to ensure protection against unauthorized access. Rudimentary security measures are not expected to be widely implemented on the Internet before 1996–1997.

Before connecting their tightly controlled internal networks to the wild and woolly world of the Internet, large corporations will likewise want to be able to control, regulate, and allocate their employees' access to the Net. Again, 1996–1997 seems to be the time when most experts feel such administrative control functions will be widely available to corporate users of the Internet.

A third and crucial barrier to corporate use of the Internet is the lack of comprehensive information locating services. "There is no standard way of finding anything, no easy way of turning data into knowledge," notes industry pundit Robert X. Cringely. "Right now what we have is a library without a Dewey decimal system."

Also lacking are basic directory services, which are critical to business-to-business communications. If an employee of General Motors' legal department wished to send a secure encrypted document—a contract for multimillion-dollar computer services, for example—to his counterpart at IBM, he would need to locate the electronic "address" and "public key" de-encryption number for that employee. Many believe that the Internet is highly unlikely to ever be able to support this service owing to its fragmented, unregulated, and insecure architecture. And it is equally unlikely that IBM would ever distribute this sort of information about its 250,000 employees to any and all roaming about in the Internet badlands.

Finally, no matter what steps a corporation may take to control and manage access *into* the corporation and *out to* the Internet, there is still the problem of what happens to messages, transaction orders, legal documents, and electronic funds once they're *in transit* on the Internet. Company A and Company B may well be able to send a flurry of encrypted documents about their secret upcoming merger back and forth over the Internet, but Hacker C will likely be able to spot the unusual level of traffic between the two companies and possibly sell that information to Stockbroker D. In short, as many a wagon train full of forty-niners discovered enroute to their gold rush dreams 130 years ago, in between those eastern farms and the hills of California there lies a long, long stretch of "Indian country."

Given all the costs, uncertainties, and time associated with trying to make the Internet "corporate-ready," the development of private "Internets" such as AT&T's Netware Connect service may well offer a more secure and economical avenue for high-risk or priority transactions and services within the corporate world. AT&T Netware Connect will actually consist of a tightly managed web of secure business networks that also offer high-performance business services and applications. These include robust directory services; information sharing as well as information access controls within the company; multilayered security, firewall, authentication, and encryption ability; 24-hour system monitoring and disaster-recovery provisions; and messaging gateways to other networks, including the Internet.

Major firms with the ability to pay for such full-service, top-of-the-line systems as AT&T Netware Connect are unlikely to rely on the Internet for their priority or high-risk traffic, even when basic security firewalls and encryption capabilities are widely deployed sometime in 1997 or 1998. Instead, most business transactions conducted on the Internet will probably involve low-risk information like consumer transactions, marketing and advertising, noncritical data exchange, intracompany workflow, and nonstrategic collaborative engineering and planning between companies, suppliers, and customers.

As Dale Kutnick, president of the Meta Group, puts it: "The 'premium' Internets that Big Business will build for its mission-critical operations will be to the 'mass' Internet what Federal Express is to the Post Office."

One hopes the Internet's future service will be a good deal better than that which we get from our outmoded postal system. But even if we have to put up with the occasional misrouted E-mail or sluggish video download or bothersome hacker, the good news is that the Internet, in addition to becoming a vibrant new bazaar of consumer goods and services, will continue to offer all the vast diversity of thought and richness of experience that has already made it such an exciting new frontier of millennial society.

And best of all, it'll probably still have a bit of the call of the wild in its soul.

▪ 5 ▪

Monster Experiment

Maybe it's just the power of suggestion that derives from being in proximity to Disney World, Universal Studios, and the other vast stretches of real estate devoted to fantasy and entertainment in Orlando. But there is something steamy, sultry, and vaguely surreal about the atmosphere in the headquarters of what Time Warner calls its Full Service Network in Maitland, Florida.

The lagoon outside the office park is reminiscent of the landscape in the Disney jungle cruise ride. Gazing out at it, you almost expect to hear the tour guide's patter: "Don't worry about the friendly hippos. They're only dangerous when they wiggle their ears. Uh-oh, look out: they're wiggling!"

Inside, on this particular day in the early stages of the project, the feel is less Disneyesque and more that of Jurassic Park—fascinating, futuristic, even a bit foreboding. Engineers scurry about, hooking up air conditioners to keep the computers happy. In the war room, consultants drink coffee from styrofoam cups, wolf down chicken salad sandwiches practically whole, and review flow charts for software systems that will calculate royalties, billables, and payables— all for a business that doesn't yet exist. A large, powerful computer "server" sits unopened in an empty room. It is fresh off the loading dock, still in its crate, which is stamped with the logo of its maker,

Silicon Graphics. One almost imagines that it contains a caged baby velociraptor, what with everyone assuring the visitor that they know what they're doing and most certainly have all the variables of this monster experiment under control. But do they?

Tom Feige, the charismatic 43-year-old president of the Full Service Network, exudes confidence and energy. He's a risk taker and a pioneer. He's seen the future, and though he seems cognizant of its challenges and its complexities, Feige insists he and his team can make it work. Time Warner CEO Gerald Levin says he is "betting the company" on it. That's more than a little pressure on Mr. Feige.

From the *Sports Illustrated* swimsuit issue to the movie reviews in *Entertainment Weekly*—and from Warner Brothers movies to the various magazine divisions and the book publishing arm—every asset in the Time Warner empire is being scrutinized for its suitability as an interactive multimedia product. "Obviously, that's part of the attraction of being here," said Feige. "What we're doing has immense, immense potential."

What they're doing is attempting to construct the most ambitious of all the many announced interactive television trials in the U.S. Time Warner was among the first to announce a major interactive TV trial. Later, throughout 1993 and 1994, announcements of other pioneering tests by other companies popped up all over. By the end of 1994, in fact, there were fifteen well-publicized and much-hyped interactive TV trials announced by major telephone and cable companies in selected test markets from Omaha to Alexandria, Virginia, and from Seattle to Toms River, New Jersey. Similar initiatives undertaken by smaller companies brought the announced total to over 40—although many of these are now delayed or have otherwise fallen by the wayside. From the United Kingdom to Japan, Korea, and Singapore, similar experiments are also now in motion.

Each trial envisions a different mix of programming choices, relies on different technological architectures, is backed by different corporate alliances with different investment philosophies, and seeks to answer a somewhat different set of market questions about precisely what consumers want and will pay for. But Time Warner's Orlando project is the only one to have been conceived from the start as a top-of-the-line, spare-no-expense test of interactive television's full (current) potential. It is the equivalent of a gold-plated moon shot, now widely recognized as an extremely and overly ambitious attempt to do too much too soon.

The first planned step in Time Warner's approach was to deliver the service to four thousand test homes in the northern suburbs of Orlando. Traveling from a central server in the Maitland office, over a hybrid network of coaxial cable and fiber-optic wires, into powerful "set-top boxes," and then onto the familiar living-room TV screen, the experimental Full Service Network hoped to offer the most amazing and diverse set of on-screen programming choices in entertainment, information, education, and home and business services any consumer had ever seen. A navigation system—operated via an intelligent supercharged remote—will supposedly allow the customer to move seamlessly through windows and menus full of choices, sort them out, and customize the available programming to his or her own interests and needs.

From that point on, Feige said, long before the test was operational, the answer to every question about what the service ultimately will and won't offer, including what services people will actually want and how these will be priced and paid for, is the same: "The customer will decide." But does this outlook reflect the Full Service Network team's scientific objectivity or their avoidance of sticky issues?

When the FSN, as it is known around Maitland, was unveiled by Time Warner in 1993, it was by far the best articulated vision of what the interactive system of the future might look like. FSN seemed both a technologist's and a marketing man's dream.

Reality has a way of redrawing grand visions, however. While quantum leaps have been made in the technology for handling the massive storage and switching complexity required to allow thousands of different homes to access thousands of different programs simultaneously, it's one thing to say the technology is feasible but quite another to actually make it work. Indeed, the critical tasks are considerably more complicated than Time Warner's gung-ho engineers thought back in 1993.

Back then, they assumed the key challenges would lie in making the navigational software easy to use and in managing the complex procedures for billing customers and collecting royalties from service providers. But now it turns out that the core system technology itself is far from perfected. The Silicon Graphics "media servers," for example—powerful computers stored with video libraries that are supposed to route all the simultaneous movie-on-demand requests to their proper recipients—are, like *Jurassic Park*'s baby raptor in a crate, a lot less manageable than first thought.

"The real challenge of [media servers] is in the software," explained Jim Barton of Silicon Graphics' Media Systems Division. "I need to know I can deliver a [video] stream on time, glitch free, with no jitter." Before the server can deliver the video, however, the latter has to be stored. "Time Warner hadn't thought about how much storage was needed," Barton conceded, referring to the huge amounts of space on a digital storage unit used by a movie. "They're spending a lot more money on disk drives than on computers."

Technology that is graceful in the lab and a bit club-footed in the real world is only one problem. Critics also question the relevance of FSN to the real-world economics of Info Highway construction. Silicon Graphics' set-top boxes alone cost $3,000 each—six times the upper limit of price considered financially practical for real-world deployment. The argument, of course, is that the cost curve will plunge as mass deployment gets under way. But mass deployment also puts new storage and switching requirements on the system, thereby generating new costs.

These costs and technical problems—not to mention more than a year of repeated delays in FSN's launch—have dampened much of the initial feverish enthusiasm for Time Warner's Orlando experiment. Skepticism has grown, both inside and outside the company. And Gerald Levin appears to have toned down some of his earlier comments about "betting the company" on FSN.

Today, he implies that the hype about the Info Highway was fueled by Wall Street, which has now soured on the near-term prospects for major returns from the technologies and businesses about which it had formerly been so enthusiastic. As a result, Levin acknowledges a shift in direction to the telephone side of Time Warner's growth strategy while still professing his intent to plow "full-speed ahead" with FSN.

"Now, Time Warner is a Phone Company" was how *Business Week* titled an article in a late 1994 issue. It noted that Levin had concluded that "the telephone business may have a more predictable payoff than such exotic services as interactive home shopping or video games." As a result, the company's pitches to Wall Street analysts have lately begun "trumpeting the promise of the phone business while giving its once highly hyped Orlando cable system only a perfunctory mention."[1] But while Levin may have retailored his company's strategy to suit Wall Street's changing fashions—not to mention the fact that even its interactive TV strategy was always aimed partly at getting into the phone business via cable TV wires— Levin is a dreamer still dreaming the big dream about interactive TV.

In December of 1994, after many delays and a good deal of downsizing of its original plan, Time Warner finally flipped its FSN switch and let the interactivity roll—to exactly five homes. In a symbolic moment that will probably *not* rank with the famous first words of Samuel F. B. Morse by telegraph or Alexander Graham Bell by telephone, Time Warner's Levin, ensconced in a Florida hotel room, was shown on the front page of the *New York Times* playing an on-screen card game interactively with the Willard family in the test community a few miles away. In addition to card and video games, the system offered test homes a choice of 36 movies and a chance to shop from the Spiegel catalog, Eddie Bauer, Crate and Barrel, and several other retailers, along with the U.S. Post Office (selling stamps) and Chrysler (selling cars)—all contained in a "virtual" on-screen mall.

It was all rather underwhelming, considering the hype of the previous two years. The next year would witness major improvements to the system, but as Time Warner's senior engineer Jim Chiddix put it, the Orlando FSN project is best thought of as a prototype—"a time machine pointing to the future"—and a very rough one at that.

Despite its primitive implementation, Time Warner's basic vision for FSN—and, in a curious way, its problems deploying it—are very much worth considering. While it's true that the technology being employed in Orlando is far too expensive for nationwide use, at least until equipment costs come down later this decade, the FSN experiment offers an intriguing peek at what the interactive communications world of the early twenty-first century might look like.

Jim Chiddix has been installing and designing cable systems for most of his adult life. He worked on the architectural details of several earlier Time Warner forays into expanded service, such as an experiment with 150 channels in the early 1990s in Queens, New York. Chiddix concedes that interactive TV is an evolutionary technology and that the company's plans for it are evolutionary as well. But "in Florida," says Chiddix, "we have one piece of the company's portfolio that attempts to leap all the way to where the technology will ultimately go."

That end point is to break down the walls of even the much-talked-about 500-channel universe and offer instead virtually *unlimited* channel capacity. "Five hundred channels is a horrible idea—no one wants 500 channels," says Hal Wolf, who is charged with overseeing the development of programming and content for FSN. The Full Service Network, he explains, is part of the postchannel world where there is essentially only one channel—the "me" channel.

Taking advantage of breakthroughs in digitization, compression, and bandwidth capacity, the FSN world was conceived as one in which thousands upon thousands—perhaps tens of thousands—of choices in programming and services could be called up at any time. The FSN customer would be liberated from the constraints not only of traditional channels but also from the lowest-common-denominator programming the networks have traditionally beamed over those channels in order to attract mass audiences and large advertising revenues. The customer would also be freed from the constraints of time. In the parlance of the interactive television world, the customer will be able to "time shift" and access any program without regard to when it was originally broadcast.

Theoretically, the time-shifted world of vast media servers, sophisticated switches, and broadband wires in the home is a world in which a simple digital truth—that voice, text, video, and music are all just "bits" to be mixed and matched as desired—gives citizens extraordinary power over how, when, and in what form they get their information, communicate, or are entertained. Virtually anything that has ever been on videotape could be made available. In fact, virtually anything in print, on radio or TV, in the computer, or transmitted by telephone could be digitized and televised into the home. Programming chief Wolf says such a service could theoretically offer a "communicopia."

Or in the words of Time Warner CEO Gerald Levin back when he was "betting the company" on FSN:

> Our new electronic superhighway will change the way people use television. By having the consumer access unlimited services, the Full Service

Network will render irrelevant the notion of sequential channels on a TV set . . . The losers will be those who decide that they can wait and watch, that there is no urgency involved, that they can go on working and producing in splendid isolation from a technology that will transform the way people live, work, entertain, and educate themselves.[2]

If the FSN vision is ever fully realized, the "communicopia" will include the following:

▪ Hundreds, and eventually thousands, of movies resident in the system's servers and available at the touch of a few buttons—in other words, the equivalent of a well-stocked video store. Because these movies will be downloaded electronically through the system, *this* video store will never "run out." Everything is indexed by a superfast and (hopefully) easy-to-use navigational database that lets you pick from a menu you yourself have defined: a list of all movies available starring Marilyn Monroe; a list of all available Westerns, or perhaps just those starring John Wayne; a list of all the latest releases—make that just the new releases that got two thumbs up from Siskel and Ebert. The list appears, you punch the appropriate number on your remote, and voilà, you're at the movies! You'll be able to pause, rewind, and enjoy what engineer Chiddix calls "the full functionality of a VCR"—but without the hassle of going out to rent a tape, finding it out of stock, or having to remember to return it on time.

▪ Hundreds, and eventually thousands, of TV shows—reaching beyond the spectrum of today's current programming back in time to the archives and even across borders to other cultures. You will be able to see your favorite *I Love Lucy* and *Mary Tyler Moore* reruns or that episode of *Seinfeld* you missed last week. The Time Warner crew are especially enthused about the possibility of time shifting as a means of doing away not only with the fixed-time nature of television broadcasting, but the difficulty of programming a VCR to record a show that otherwise would be missed as well. "You get stuck in traffic on your way home from work and miss the 6:00 evening news?" says Wolf. "No problem. You can come home and call it up *when you want to see it.*" Your friends tell you about a great episode of *60 Minutes* you missed the night before? Again, no problem.

▪ Hundreds of sporting events—not just the local team's games but *any* games televised anywhere. Or for that matter, any games that have *ever* been televised. (How about watching the 1969 Super Bowl again, or the 1951 World Series?) Ditto for rock concerts and music videos.

▪ Hundreds of video games, downloadable from the Full Service Network either for individual use or for play during real-time competition with others on-screen.

▪ A panoply of educational videos for children—*Sesame Street* on demand—plus how-to videos for adults, video lectures, conferences, and special events. Informational videos of all kinds, from picking the right Caribbean vacation island to previewing homes available for sale in the local real estate market.

▪ Self-broadcasting of any videotaped event. From the local school play to your cinema verité camcorder movies, anything could be put up on the system for viewing by any interested party in much the same fashion as Internet and online service users post and exchange text messages and World Wide Web "home pages" today.

▪ Home shopping of the highest order—not simply the drone of cubic zirconium telethons but classy catalogs and sophisticated "virtual stores" on screen. The system is programmed to remember your size, your Visa card number, and your shipping address. Stored video images of yourself let you "try on" clothes on-screen . . . a "virtual supermarket" lets you walk down the aisles and point at products, pick them up to read their labels, and then order them for delivery to your home the next day . . . detailed infomercials about everything from cars to computers allow you to peruse product specifications and prices at your own pace, asking your own questions and getting your own answers. Want to see what a Jeep Cherokee looks like in red with a beige interior? Just click the remote.

▪ A plethora of services, including home banking, interactive on-screen investment advice and transactions, retirement planning videos and check-balancing software, personalized restaurant reservation services, concert and theater ticket ordering, video classifieds, a video personals matchmaking service, video E-mail to friends and family, and a video yellow pages of available services.

▪ Interactive news and information, including on-screen newspapers integrating text with video ("If you'd like to read the text of the president's speech on health care reform, press 1; if you'd like to see videotaped highlights from it, press 2; if you'd like to see last night's *Nightline* discussion of it, press 3"), and customized newspaper and TV reports ("Show me yesterday's news reports about why Microsoft's stock plunged").

▪ Plus, a variety of services that have more to do with the telephone than television. The services imagined by Time Warner as part of FSN are of both the POTS and PANS varieties. POTS (Plain Old Telephone Service) means that regular local telephone service could now be brought to you by Time Warner instead of your local telephone company. PANS (Pretty Amazing New Stuff) means all sorts of video calling, video conferencing, video telecommuting, competitive video games with picture-in-picture communications, and much more.

If Time Warner (or any other cable TV or telephone company) can, in fact, offer all the above services anytime soon—and if consumers could, indeed, access all of them easily with a remote control command—one could imagine the development of an interactive services industry of immense scale and scope. The costs of building such a system nationwide, however, are inestimable. There is more than a little uncertainty concerning the efficacy of the technology in real-world applications, how quickly equipment costs will decline when mass deployment begins, how imminent deregulation of the cable and phone industries will affect capital investment and deployment plans, and how rapidly customers will embrace (and pay for) the new services.

In 1993, however, Time Warner's early guess on the cost of wiring its own 7 million cable subscribers to near FSN quality interactivity was reportedly about $6 billion—or about $850-plus per home. Amortized over three years, the company figured it would have to raise each subscriber's bill by $25 a month. This $25 a month may, at first blush, seem like a trivial amount, especially to business and media types who can easily spend $25 a day on taxi fares in New York just going to Information Highway seminars. But in a country where people have long been accustomed to free TV—and where consumers are incensed already over the $30 a month that, on average, they're paying for basic cable *now*—squeezing that extra $25 from most people would seem a dubious proposition. The few objective studies done on this subject, in fact, suggest that people are not willing to pay much more than $10 additionally per month.[3]

What's more, FSN's financial model appears to understate greatly the true expense of Info Highway construction. Many experts now peg the aggregate costs to the cable and phone companies of connecting all of America's 98 million homes to an FSN-style interactive network at over $200 billion—perhaps a good deal more. At $200 billion, just to use an oft-cited reference point, the cost is about $2,000 per home, making it necessary to boost cable revenues by $55, not $25, a month. This includes the cost of the media servers and switching technology that will store and forward movies and other content on demand, the hybrid networks of fiber-optic wire and coaxial cable used to deliver it to the home, the TV set-top boxes required to decode and display the content, and the system software needed to navigate the network.

And then there's this wrinkle: in the first torrid days of Info Highway fever back in 1993, many engineers, marketers, executives, and technology pundits alike believed that the bandwidth and switching capabilities necessary to support an FSN-style vision on a mass scale were within easy reach. It now seems that the technological infrastructure is still years away from being able to deliver *thousands* of programming choices to *hundreds of thousands* of people in a major city simultaneously. It's coming—especially via fiber, which is being laid to the "curb" in some neighborhoods and even to the home itself in a few cases. Many techno-visionaries are already thinking about a world in which bandwidth is nearly free because of its abundance. But if that day ever comes, it won't be until the latter years of the *next* decade—a blink in the eye of history, perhaps, but a life-and-death eternity for any business that projects near-term costs and revenues for their interactive network investments.

The limits of today's commercial technology, in turn, dictate that the first interactive trials must necessarily offer a far more limited choice of programming than had been previously envisioned. Quantity, at a certain point, becomes a quality. If, for example, the video-on-demand system only offers 50 movie choices, then the video store has not effectively been replaced. A video-on-demand menu probably needs to offer at least a thousand movies—with flawless transmission and ease of use—at prices not much higher than video store rentals before consumers will begin choosing in large numbers to get video-on-demand at home rather than trudge to Blockbuster.

Riding this long on-ramp to the future, interactive service providers will have to finance high infrastructure costs on the back of a less-than-robust set of programming choices offered to a consumer market that isn't even sure it wants to spend $25 (let alone $55) a month extra.

So how to avoid a possible shortfall that could match the federal government's yearly budget deficit?

Enter the magic of advertising. And not just any advertising, either. Time Warner's vision of Info Highway pricing involves a new breed of interactive, highly targeted advertising and marketing that is as different from traditional mass-market Madison Avenue peddling as digital bits are from old-fashioned analog wave forms.

"By the year 2000 we will be getting *a hundred dollars* more per month from every cable household than we were in 1993," said Feige, "but the consumer won't have to pay for it." Or, at least, for most of it. Sketching a picture of the cyber-advertising Time Warner envisions, Feige suggested that watching a newly released video on demand might ordinarily cost three or four dollars. But if you agree to watch a half-hour infomercial from the local Lexus dealer, you might get three *free* movies credited to your account—paid for, of course, by the Lexus dealer who wants to get your attention.

How will they know you're really watching? You might have to hit a few buttons on your remote at some strategic point in the infomercial to let them know you're there and the advertiser is getting his money's worth. Actually, for the advertiser, it's *more* than his money's worth. He used to wonder whether you were really watching or going to get a sandwich instead. Now he not only knows you are watching—he knows you are watching *carefully*.

Certain products will become incredibly tempting to buy in this new regime. You see a music video you like? Just press the order button. The set-top box already knows your credit card number and your shipping instructions, so the CD is automatically dispatched (as is, automatically, a small royalty to Time Warner unless it is a Warner Music CD, in which case all the better for the company). Watching a movie and feel like a pizza? Just click on the Domino's Pizza icon in the corner of your screen and select your topping. Domino's instantly knows not only that you want pepperoni, it also knows which of its outlets is nearest your home.

If home shopping becomes pervasive, Time Warner will get a small cut of each transaction. Thus, if the notion of the "virtual supermarket" catches on—and if customers really will sit in front of their TVs and order the soup, toothpaste, and laundry detergent they need from on-screen menus—Time Warner will suddenly own a piece of every family's grocery bill.

The new advertising world is one of never-ending marketing partnerships, incentives, and customer rewards; it is a world where the logic of the frequent flyer plan drives all merchandising. Watch this commercial, get a free chance to watch a World Series game. Press some buttons that tell an advertiser your grocery-buying habits, and your set-top printer spits out valuable free coupons.

The leap from bait to hook will be much easier in this new technology of advertising. Need the directions to the store nearest you? Press the buttons, click the mouse, and again your set-top printer goes to work delivering information, coupons, and even prizes.

For advertisers, the cost of providing such premiums is more than recouped by the chance to target their promotions to specific audiences and *know* that they are reaching them. If you are Saab's marketing team and you want to do a pitch aimed at attracting Volvo owners, you buy a list of Volvo owners and you run your ad just to the TV systems in *those homes*. While the cost per home may be greater, you pay far less in total costs because you aren't wasting the vast majority of advertising dollars on people who drive Chevys and have no intention of buying either a Saab or a Volvo.

Thus, the most important element in the new media equation may not be the superhighway itself but the supermarket growing up alongside it, argues John Sculley. The ability to shift the communications paradigm away from one-to-many and toward one-to-one is the basis for a full-blown reordering of the huge retailing and consumer spending sectors of the economy.

Advertising and marketing have been a bit slow to embrace this revolution and more than a bit skeptical about its prospects. After all, it requires them to invent new communications forms that creatively and appropriately use the new technology. This in turn requires that they break with their old mass scale assumptions about television. But there is a growing sense that such a change is necessary, and some highly creative work has begun.

"You can jump in early and help create this exciting new medium, or you can let the world pass you by and find yourself operating the best darned buggy-whip business on Madison Avenue," Bell Atlantic

CEO Ray Smith told a conference of advertising executives in early 1995.[4] Indeed, today's cleverest designers, graphic artists, and pitchmen are now rushing to invent exciting new Web sites, spurring the greatest creative race in the advertising and marketing disciplines we have seen at least since the sixties.

All this leads, of course, to major questions about the structure of business in the future, as well as the shape of the future society that revolves around it. Shopping malls, for example, will continue to occupy an important place in retailing because many people enjoy the social experience of the mall. But some of the retailers in those malls may well discover that they need to offer more of an *entertainment* experience if they want to attract shoppers who otherwise could simply buy their products on-screen—and at lower prices, too, since home-shopping merchants can factor out of their cost structure the huge expense of mall real estate and in-store operations.

Indeed, given the stakes, the next decade will surely witness an escalating "battle of the malls" between virtual and traditional retailing. After all, some 68 percent of U.S. economic activity involves personal consumption. If even 2 percent of that goes online, a brand-new $80 billion industry will have come into existence, transforming the consumer market in its wake.

Interactive advertising also raises much more troubling issues about the potentially insidious social effects of micromarketing. With our personal choices and preferences pouring into easily cross-indexed advertising and marketing databases, how much will businesses end up knowing about us? And how might they use that information against us in their efforts to "program" our buying habits? As one Time Warner executive admits, most people would be scared to death if they knew how much the operators of cable, telephone, credit card, and mail order companies *already* knew about them.

How will the differences between classes, races, genders, and age groups be manipulated by marketers, and with what effect on society as a whole? Where once our homes were our castles, with each of us relatively secure from intrusions upon our privacy, will we now become interactive ducks in a consumerist shooting gallery, easy targets for a new breed of digital marketing hotshots?

The Full Service Network also opens up philosophical questions about whether, as human beings, we wish only to be exposed to products and services we have already specified an interest in, or whether we want and need the stimulation of browsing. And what if future customized TV diminishes our opportunity not only to browse advertisements but to be serendipitously exposed to news, information, and *ideas* that we have not already preselected?

What effect will spending even more time looking at the world through the inherently visual, fragmentary, and impressionistic window of the television have upon reading, logical thought, and reasoned social discourse? Will social involvements diminish even further and alienation from public life increase? Will we become a nation of dilettantes who have a smattering of views and emotions about everything (at least everything that can be covered by CNN and MTV in 22 minutes), and yet a deep-seated understanding—which comes from experience, study, and reflection—of nothing?

Of course, it is possible society will avoid having to come to grips with these issues because the interactive revolution will fail, crushed under the weight of its own hype and unable to deliver enough profit to justify its costs. Certainly, there are those who think that is the message of most of the interactive TV trials. Apple CEO Michael H. Spindler carved out a platform for himself as an Info Highway debunker when he declared that the technology was simply never going to be good enough to deliver what people will expect of it. Saying there was "no need" for an Information Superhighway, Spindler saw little value in 500 channels when "60 are enough."[5]

No matter what corporate spokesmen for the companies involved may say, the interactive trials conducted by Time Warner and others to date have been uniformly disappointing. Aside from gross technical glitches experienced regularly by every system tested, some of the early high expectations have been, shall we say, "downsized" after confronting the realities of consumer response. One report of an interactive TV trial undertaken by TCI, AT&T, and US West in Littleton, Colorado, for example, summed up the results this way: "The companies collectively paid about $10 million to learn that participants, who were offered more than 1,000 movies on demand at prices competitive with video store rentals, watched on average only 2.5 movies per month. This is almost 50 percent *lower* than the national average for video rentals" from traditional video stores![6]

Most cable subscribers already have pay-per-view capabilities to watch movies, yet few utilize the service with any regularity. According to one recent study, in fact, less than 20 percent of cable viewers watch pay-per-view movies.[7]

Indeed, while there has been much talk about total entertainment spending greatly expanding when people have the equivalent of a video store, a first-run movie theater, and a shopping mall inside their TVs, the reality is that neither consumers' discretionary income nor their time is likely to grow by much, if at all, in coming years. Says Scott Sassa, president of Turner Entertainment: "You may have 500 channels instead of 50, but you won't get ten times as many people willing to pay a penny more for what they get over the air for free. If you really look at the growth in household income from 1970 to today, it was a second income that fueled it. And we've tapped that one out. So it's not as if this pie is just going to keep expanding."

But disappointing as some of the test results may be, it is important to remember that they are simply early-stage experiments. The response to a still-thin set of programming and service choices, delivered via an imperfect technology infrastructure to consumers not yet accustomed to using their TVs as interactive devices, should not be viewed as indicative of the later potential for success. In this, today's fledgling interactive TV systems are only following the trail blazed by the telegraph, the telephone, and other technologies before them. Each had to plod through years of slow growth before large numbers of people began to grasp their use and value, and businesses based on them took off.

"The best minds haven't worked on the problem yet," because interactive TV is still in its infancy, notes a report by the Austin, Texas–based consulting group WPTC. Until there are customers, standards, and ways of producing content and applications at low entry costs, "Interactive services will be a weak offering on the digital broadband infrastructure . . . Although the network will be built and there will be other applications, the truly creative interactive content delivered by the network operators will not appear until the twenty-first century."[8]

Until that time, most of what we'll see on interactive TV will be limited to movies-on-demand. Even this business is more likely to be movies on "near demand" for the next several years as kinks in the various systems are slowly worked out and consumer demand gradually ramps up. In this arena, the players will not only be the traditional cable TV firms but also their arch enemies, the regional telephone companies. Bell Atlantic, in league with Hollywood talent agent Michael Ovitz and two other phone companies, claims to have amassed an impressive mix of 700 hours of programming for its yet-to-be-deployed interactive television service. The Stargazer system, as it is called, will reportedly offer 200 new and classic movies; 120 episodes of recent and classic television sitcoms, dramas, talk shows, and news specials; 45 sports, comedy, and music performances.

Time Warner's Gerald Levin says he is not worried about the phone companies stealing his interactive thunder. Nor would he disagree that the truly powerful growth markets for interactive TV lie well down the road. But he dismisses those who think interactive TV will never amount to much.

"The same kind of minds that denounced Galileo as a heretic, ridiculed Edison's notion of an electric-powered light, and dismissed the Wright brothers' ideas as a crackpot scheme have turned their sights on the new medium of interactivity," Levin notes, insisting that over time the naysayers will be proven wrong. "Interactivity is going to change how consumers view the world."[9]

▪ 6 ▪

Reach Out and Crush Someone

Like a good slap in the face, the February 1994 collapse of the proposed merger between John Malone's TCI and telephone megacorp Bell Atlantic brought a sharp halt to all the delirious swooning in 1993 over the supposedly imminent convergence of Information Age industries. After a year of frenzied merger activity, the likes of which had not been seen since the late 1980s, the Bell Atlantic–TCI crack-up proved to be just the antidote needed to cool the hyperbolic fevers of convergence-itis.

Not that convergence is merely a mirage on the corporate landscape—far from it. Digital technology does, indeed, tend to blur the old boundaries between industries and markets by distilling the content of our communications, entertainment, media, and publishing into their common constituent elements—digital ones and zeros—and then alchemizing them into new economic possibilities. To exploit these new opportunities, companies have found that by combining their skills and resources with one another they can achieve powerful synergies and risk-sharing advantages.

Convergence, however, is only one of the manifold phenomena at work in the political economy of today's world, and not even the most powerful or fundamental one at that. Indeed, just because we are entering the digital new world order, we should not delude ourselves

147

into believing that somehow the laws of capitalism (and of modern nation-state politics) have been suspended.

In the case of Bell Atlantic and TCI, the blending of their technologies and financial resources would certainly have benefited both companies and speeded the birth of the Information Highway. But however sensible such a marriage of convenience may have seemed when it was announced in October 1993, the real-world stresses of capitalist economics—the splintering forces of competition, the constraints of federal regulation, the fickleness of the financial markets, and the strikingly incompatible commercial dynamics of the phone and cable industries—all conspired to tear the Bell Atlantic–TCI union asunder before the happy couple could even reach the altar.

Unfortunate, perhaps, but there it is. It now looks like the building of a new communications infrastructure for the next century will be marked by a protracted war between these two powerful industries, perhaps through the rest of this century. To be sure, cable and phone companies may again try to forge large-scale mergers, especially if the regulatory climate becomes more favorable for such combinations and if developing market conditions favor the cross-industry clustering of customers, technology assets, and financial resources to achieve scale and market share. Wireless cable and direct-broadcast satellite networks will also add new complexity to the competition, as will PCS and the rebirth of the broadcast networks. By the year 2000 or so, the outline of America's Information Highways could well resemble the political map of the former Yugoslavia—i.e., an oligopoly of a few imperial network powers and their allies battling for control of key market enclaves in a continuous division and re-division of the spoils.

It's not all bad news for Info Highway aficionados, however. Although Make Love, Not War is no longer the watchword for relations between cable and phone companies, each side will very likely now be screwing each other with enough abandon in coming years to keep most digital voyeurs delightfully entertained. Besides, a good fight makes for good copy, as trend-setting *Wired* magazine recognized when it illustrated the authors' interviews with TCI chief John Malone and Bell Atlantic CEO Ray Smith with enhanced cover photos of the two as Mel Gibson's Road Warrior (Malone) and Arnold Schwarzeneggar's Conan the Barbarian (Smith).

But there is much more of interest here than simply the Sturm und Drang of a big industrial slugfest. The cable-telco wars offer an extraordinary window through which we can observe at close range the process by which capitalism aims the arrow of technological change. Here, in the heat of battle between these two powerful, high-profile industries, we have a rare opportunity to examine the ways in which the dynamics of market competition—the ways each side faces its multiple challenges and deploys its differing talents and resources—shape today's technological possibilities into tomorrow's economic and social realities.

No matter which companies ultimately dominate, the American people may take comfort in the fact that amid all the corporate back-stabbing and headline-grabbing, all the buyouts and breakups and make-ups, a foundation *is* being laid for a new and exciting communications infrastructure for the next century. And in the process, the cable-telco rivalry will inevitably open up for public debate vital questions about their differing models of the nature and functioning of these networks that America needs to address.

The cable industry's "gatekeeping" system, developed under conditions of video bandwidth scarcity, dictates that conduit owners reserve their limited channel space primarily for the largest mass-market programmers—MTV, HBO, CNN, and the like—whose shows generate the biggest revenues. This naturally results in a plethora of depressingly similar and often banal offerings. Though technology will enable future TV sets to broadcast as well as receive programming—beaming your child's birthday video to grandma, for example, or televising your own neighborhood arts and entertainment channel—the top-down gatekeeping model would inevitably tend to stifle the grassroots, peer-to-peer programming and video communication that digital technology makes possible.

The "open" networks of the regional Bell operating companies (RBOCs), in contrast, arose in a regulated environment in which copper-wire voice bandwidth was cheap and ubiquitous. In this system, users connect not only to each other but also to virtually any service provider, no matter how small or marginal. The phone company just provides the connection service—it generally doesn't take a piece of the action or otherwise involve itself in the content of communications. Its decentralized architecture is also far better suited to the sort of diverse, grassroots-oriented, people-to-people communication that digital technology makes possible.

By throwing the spotlight on their different network models, the cable-telco rivalry naturally raises public policy questions over how to ensure that the interactive networks of tomorrow are open and accessible to all. The Electronic Frontier Foundation, a Washington public-interest group concerned with communications policy, insists that only federal action can "preserve the democratic character of our society as we move into the Information Age." As one of the organization's early statements noted:

> The switched nature of advanced digital network technology offers to end the spectrum and channel scarcity problem altogether. If new network services are deployed with adequate down- and upstream capacity, and allow point-to-point communication, then each user of the network can be both an information consumer and publisher. Network architecture which is truly peer-to-peer can help produce in digital media the kind of information diversity that exists today only in the print media. If network access is guaranteed, as is the case in the public switched telephone network, the need for content providers to negotiate for air time and channel allocation will be eliminated.[1]

It is important to digress here and discuss the growing debate over whether government should even be involved in settling such public policy questions or in establishing competitive ground rules for such strategic industries as telecommunications. Of those who argue most strongly against any such federal role, one of the most articulate is the author George Gilder, whose utopian perspective we discussed in the introduction to this book. Gilder argues that, owing to the capitalist law of supply and demand, the future abundance of bandwidth will *automatically* lead to a diverse and open Info Highway modeled along the lines of today's phone networks. "The most open networks will dominate," writes Gilder, "and the [gatekeeping] networks will wither." But he warns that this ideal scenario can only come to pass if Washington stops trying to regulate the cable and telephone industries and simply allows the free market to work unobstructed. "An information superhighway cannot be built under a canopy of federal [regulatory] tariffs, price controls, mandates, and allocated markets," Gilder insists.[2]

One problem with Gilder's view is that while an age of unlimited and virtually free bandwidth may lie years off in the future, broadband networks are being built in the real world of today, where bandwidth is scarce and those who control it wish to gain as much leverage from that fact as possible. To neglect the public interest today simply on the promise that all will be taken care of tomorrow is irresponsible, akin to disarming today in anticipation of future world peace.

But a more crucial flaw in Gilder's analysis is that he confuses free market *tendencies* with actual market *realities*. It is certainly true that the eventual abundance of multimedia bandwidth will tend to diminish the economic incentive for an Info Highway run along gatekeeping lines. After all, it will be much harder to monopolize supply—in this case, of bandwidth—when there's more than enough of that supply to meet demand. But it is equally true that in the real world of capitalist competition, the law of supply and demand has never *by itself* prevented businesses from monopolizing supply, rigging markets, gouging prices, or otherwise skunking the consumer whenever they can.

Ironically, the open telco-style networks that Gilder claims will be the natural fruit of free-market beneficence are, at least in the telephone business, anything but market-driven creations. They are the deliberate product of such federal regulatory action as the "common carrier" and "universal access" provisions of the 1934 Communications Act and the 1982 Consent Decree that broke up AT&T. Indeed, for most of American telephony history, Ma Bell ran one of the most ruthless vertically integrated monopolies the world has ever seen. Remember when it was actually *illegal* to use anything other than an AT&T phone? It required a Justice Department lawsuit in the 1950s and finally action by the Federal Communications Commission in 1968 to give consumers any choice about what telephones they could use.

The underlying presumption of Gilder's argument is that the marketplace, if left to its own devices, will always reach and maintain an equilibrium state of free and open competition. "Every innovation gives its owner a temporary monopoly," concedes Gilder, and he is correct to point out that temporary monopolies (usually enforced by patents) are frequently essential to the rapid funding and early growth of new industries. But is it appropriate to view the 25-year-old cable TV business—let alone the century-old telephone industry—as emerging sectors in which innovation can occur only on the basis of monopoly profits and carte blanche freedom from federal regulation?

What Gilder fails to recognize is that tendencies toward both competition *and* monopolization coexist in the market, and that the latter is an especially strong drive not so much in the emergent phase of industries but rather in their later stages of consolidation and maturation. One need only contrast the early days of the cable TV, computer operating systems, and telephone businesses, when competition was prevalent, with the situation that prevails in these industries today, in which one or at most a few giant companies have managed to secure a stranglehold on their markets. Does anyone seriously believe Gilder's claim, for instance, that Microsoft has outgrown its "temporary" monopoly and is now "at the twilight of its dominance"?[3] Most experts, whether or not they favor government action to limit Microsoft's power, at least concur that the software giant is expanding its hegemony over its most critical markets while continuously reaching into new ones.

In Gilder's idealized view, any government effort aimed at "preventing the dominance of successful technologies—sustaining an artificial diversity—is anticompetitive [and] wantonly destructive of the future of the economy." To begin with, the absolutism of Gilder's notion here—that regardless of the circumstances, government action always perverts the otherwise natural and beneficent effects of free market forces—is highly questionable. Furthermore, what about cases where it is the government itself that has created and sustained anticompetitive monopolies—e.g., cable TV and phone companies—by means of federal law, FCC policy, and government grants of exclusive licenses? Here in the real world, federal intervention has already distorted the marketplace, and the question now is what to do about it. It is difficult to imagine how government, having created an unlevel playing field in the first place, would truly be promoting free competition by totally absenting itself from the game now, thereby giving certain competitive victory to the monopolies it had previously nurtured. Any federal withdrawal from communications must be executed in such a way that key chokepoints in the system, such as local phone exchange access, are opened up to genuine competition rather than left to remain under the sole control of today's regional telephone monopolies.

When Gilder says, "There is no way [government] can demonize the cable industry and micro-manage telecom without direly damaging all its hopes for an information superhighway and thus the best prospects for the future of the U.S. economy," he makes a valid point about the dangers of overregulation. History offers plenty of examples here and abroad of how governments have squashed progress under the boot of overcentralized planning, overambitious social engineering, and overly rigid bureaucratic procedure. What's more, the dizzying complexity of modern society, with all its multiple and interlinked forces, only increases the chances that unforeseen harm may result from even the most well-intentioned regulatory policy decisions. This is especially true when such policies are not subjected to the sort of dynamic scrutiny and reevaluation that has unfortunately been lacking in federal communications policy. It is only prudent, then, to acknowledge that the bigger and more unpredictable the industrial tiger—and they don't get much bigger than the $300 billion U.S. telecommunications business—the more cautious Washington ought to be in poking it with the stick of national policy.

Nonetheless, when Gilder suggests that *all* government regulation of the marketplace is anticompetitive and harmful to innovation, he ignores not only the reality of markets as they are actually structured but the lessons of economic history as well. To be sure, as a *general* rule the free market does tend to promote innovation, reduce prices, and enhance the public interest. Following the expiration of AT&T's early patents in 1894, for example, competition between Ma Bell and some 6,000 independent phone companies led to the two greatest innovations in early telephone technology: the loading coil and the electronic repeater, which greatly reduced the cost and extended the distance over which a voice signal could travel. These inventions were developed not by AT&T but by independent inventors.[4]

But history also records that government action can sometimes be a powerful catalyst for advancing the public interest and for injecting innovation into sclerotic and monopolized markets. By 1913, for example, AT&T had managed to buy out or destroy most of its national competitors and was on the verge of becoming America's sole telecommunications monopoly. The only barrier to absolute AT&T hegemony was the continued survival of independent local phone companies that served millions of customers. These firms were being slowly crushed, however, because Ma Bell refused to let them interconnect their local lines with AT&T's long-distance network—the only one in existence. As a result, the development of a truly national telephone service was roadblocked. But faced with a huge public outcry and threats from Washington to break up the company under provisions of the Sherman Antitrust Act, AT&T finally agreed to let independent providers interconnect, and to subject itself to federal regulation as a public utility. The net result was the establishment, at long last, of a fully integrated national phone service for all citizens, and the emergence of the modern era of communications.[5]

But federal intervention, even to free an industry from an innovation-stifling bottleneck, can often create a whole new set of problems (just as free competition can sometimes lead to monopoly). So 57 years later, the FCC was finally forced to loosen the stranglehold that AT&T, with federal support, had secured over America's communications industry. Had MCI, Sprint, and other alternative service providers not been allowed to enter the telecommunications field, it is doubtful that long distance service would be as low cost or high quality as it is today. And it is even more doubtful that the diversity of services and innovation that we now see in telecommunications would ever have come about.

The cellular phone industry, for example, might well have been stillborn. Arguing precisely this point, Reed Hundt, President Clinton's chair of the Federal Communications Commission, describes how 20 years ago, AT&T went before the FCC with a plan to "develop" cellular technology. "They said cellular might be a good idea or a bad idea . . . it's hard to figure out," notes Hundt. "So ATT said, 'Give us 40 megahertz and an exclusive license, and we'll try it out. But our estimates are that there will only be 900,000 cellular users by the end of the century.'"

Instead, he adds, "The Commission said, 'We'll create 50 megahertz and divide it into two licenses of 25 megahertz each.' AT&T was broken up during the period of this debate in the 1970s and early 1980s. So the FCC ultimately gave one regional license to each of AT&T's children, the Baby Bells, and another to regional cellular pioneers like Craig McCaw.

"And that," notes Hundt, "is how a duopoly was created in cellular—one that's been very price competitive, by the way. This duopoly earned enough money for the industry to enable them to build out a whole system. And that's a big plus. Cellular is now a ubiquitous service with 17 million subscribers instead of the 900,000

AT&T forecast. And we still have a long way to go before the end of the century."

In other words, says Hundt, "What AT&T wouldn't have accomplished, government intervention, to a greater degree, has accomplished. The [FCC-mandated] duopoly has built a universal system and it has gotten prices down so that in many parts of the country, it is cheaper to install cellular service than to maintain the wired infrastructure."

Dogmatic and purist theories about the workings of economies, whether of the left or the right, certainly make for neat and tidy polemics. But they are far less useful in accurately predicting the real-world effects of either unfettered market forces or government intervention upon the ever evolving (and only partially understood) dynamics of economic life. As with almost everything else in society, cause and effect are always conditioned by time, place, and circumstance.

The futurist and free market advocate Alvin Toffler, a leading voice together with George Gilder in the "Magna Carta for Cyberspace" project sponsored by the Progress and Freedom Foundation (generally regarded as Newt Gingrich's think tank), has noted that government intervention can even occasionally save a slumbering, monopolized industry from its own stagnancy. In his little-known yet seminal study of AT&T, *The Adaptive Corporation,* Toffler wrote: "A truly 21st century communications system could not be built by an oversized, overcentralized and overconstrained organization of the kind AT&T was before the great break-up. To have kept AT&T's old structure would have guaranteed America's loss, before long, of its claim to the world's most advanced telecommunications." The author of *Future Shock, The Third Wave,* and *Power Shift* went on to place the question of government's proper role in context:

> I have publicly urged, again and again, that market forces be allowed to work in communications and other fields. But to recognize the creative forces of the marketplace is not to deny the need for some policy coordination that reaches beyond the scope of any individual company. Communications is too important to be left entirely to the short-term pressures of competition. Nor should the future of communications be determined entirely by economic considerations. Communications, above all, is a social act. It is inherently cultural, political, psychologi-

cal. To regulate (or deregulate) telecommunications for narrowly economic reasons is to lose sight of its primal importance. Telecommunications is part of the glue that must hold us together in a world that is
quaking with change and fragmentation.[6]

It's one thing, of course, to recognize that government can at times
intervene positively in the marketplace, quite another to determine
the precise shape, manner, and extent of that intervention and accurately predict its effects. The vast complexity and increasing globalization of today's markets, in fact, *require* that we reject old liberal
notions of wise, all-knowing federal officials and policy wonks safely
micromanaging the economy. But how, and under what conditions,
government intervention is needed to help steer the wheels of commerce so that the indispensable wealth-creating engine of private
profit is neither choked off nor allowed to overrun the best interests
of society is a question that no one has yet fully answered.

For now, it is enough to acknowledge that when it comes to an
enterprise as far-reaching in its social and economic implications as
the Information Highway, it is imperative that the citizenry have a
voice in determining how and in whose interests it will be financed,
built, and operated. We are dealing, after all, with a technology that
has the potential to become either a profoundly liberating and revitalizing force in society or a grave threat to personal liberty and the
human spirit. It is not recommended that we trust the outcome solely
to corporate accountants and investment bankers.

The bankers, in any event, are otherwise occupied down in the
fiber-optic trenches, helping the telephone and cable companies
marshal their armies for the coming clash of the infrastructure titans.
While the strategic battle over major metropolitan markets has yet to
be fully joined, the skirmishing has already begun, with each side
testing its forces and nibbling at its opponent's territory.

Throughout 1994, telephone and cable TV companies announced
plans to wire more than 20 million homes for interactive television
by the end of the decade. Included in these announcements were
promises to hook up four million homes by the end of 1995, but
these ambitious goals seem highly dubious, considering that only a
handful of American households had been wired for even the most
bare-bones interactive service by the summer of 1995. Underneath
all the posturing, however, cable and telephone companies *are* com-

mitting billions of dollars toward the construction of their Info Highway networks.

Significantly, though, cable and telco spending for Information Highway construction does not seem to be motivated by any near-term expectation of major revenue returns from multimedia services. In Bell Atlantic's Section 214 FCC application for a three-million-customer zone in its planned network, for example, the company projected interactive service revenues of only $1 billion by the year 2004. That's peanuts compared to the nearly $12 billion Bell Atlantic derived in 1994 from its basic phone business.[7]

So why the frenzy to build these advanced networks? The answer lies not so much in tomorrow's promise of profits from interactive services but rather in today's reality of nearly $200 billion in combined telephone and cable TV revenues. As a result of ongoing federal and state action to open cable TV and phone markets to competition—as well as recent court decisions allowing cable companies to launch telephone services and vice versa—all those billions upon billions of dollars are now ripe for plundering. The major players in each industry, therefore, feel compelled to develop an advanced network, both in order to defend their own turf as well as to be able to mount assaults on the lucrative territory of others.

Notes a report by the Austin-based consulting firm WPTC: "Interactive services [are not required] in justifying the digital broadband infrastructure buildout. The network upgrade is required by market pressures."[8]

These existing markets, especially the huge $100 billion local telephone business, also offer the only sure capital source for funding the development of interactive TV services when they are later introduced. As the head of one cable company's new telephony venture puts it, "We believe the introduction of telephone service is the only revenue stream that can justify [building an interactive] system."[9]

In other words, "It's telephony, stupid!"

Says Time Warner Communications president Tom Morrow (a man with a fortuitous name if ever there was one): "The money today is in telephone service. As far as video-on-demand and other interactive services go, we *think* there's money there. But we *know* there's money in phone service."

The local telephone business is, by virtue of its size and near-term availability, the most hotly contested focus of cable-telco competition. And the most lucrative chunk of that business is the $24 billion—25 percent of sales and one-third of profits—derived from "access charges" paid by long-distance firms to connect to local customers. NYNEX, as just one example, concedes that while the actual cost of providing such local access is only half a cent per minute, its federally mandated monopoly of the local market enables it to charge seven times that amount.[10] Furthermore, while long-distance phone rates have fallen 40 percent owing to increased competition since the breakup of AT&T a decade ago, the telcos' 99 percent monopoly control of local phone service has allowed them to *boost* their rates by an average of more than 250 percent for regulated basic services, and by 650 percent for deregulated services such as wiring and installation, according to a study by the research firm New Networks Institute.[11] The study claimed the RBOCs have overcharged consumers by $75 billion in the last decade.[12]

Given the opportunities for discounting telco pricing, cable systems clearly offer an "invasion path," as TCI's John Malone puts it, into these fertile fields of local telephony. One of the first raiding parties has already been dispatched by Time Warner, which plans to offer cut-rate phone service over its cable lines in Rochester, New York, by the end of 1995. It has also hired AT&T, at a cost of $200 million, to install cable telephony equipment for use in Rochester and eventually in 25 other cities. Industry-wide, cable firms announced plans to purchase $2 billion in such equipment during 1994.

The cable "invasion path" has also attracted telephone company raiding parties seeking to pilfer the home markets of rival telcos. SBC Communications (formerly Southwestern Bell) and US West, for example, intend to deploy their cable subsidiaries to raid the telephony markets of rivals Bell Atlantic and Bell South respectively. But by and large, the battle lines are between cable and telephone firms.

Taunted Tom Morrow: "If, as I expect, our phone service works better and is cheaper than the telcos', we'll cannibalize their business so fast they won't know what hit 'em. This isn't a good business, this is a *great* business!"

The former chairman of NYNEX in New England, Paul C. O'Brien, said he was unafraid of the cable challenge: "We welcome our friends in the cable TV business. We think they are going to find [telephony] more difficult than some anticipate. It is capital intensive and requires the ability to switch, time, and bill calls. We think they will find it challenging. So let the games begin."[13]

Likewise, Bell Atlantic chairman Ray Smith scoffs at the notion of cable companies successfully capturing major segments of his phone business. "Cable is not where our competition will come from," he declares. "The competition's going to come from AT&T and wireless, not from cable companies reequipping their ancient and crappy systems."

Despite Smith's and O'Brien's confident statements, the Baby Bells are clearly worried about not only cable but other threats as well to their federally protected revenue reserve, and they are responding in several ways. First, the telcos are fighting hard to enter the $65 billion long-distance market, which they appear likely to be allowed to do within a few years given a new Republican-controlled Congress that seems quite favorable to their interests. Second, they are cutting costs—the seven RBOCs laid off over 120,000 workers in 1993 and 1994, and more cuts are likely. Third, the RBOCs have rapidly begun combining their cellular businesses in order to meet the challenge from long-distance company links with wireless and cable firms, such as AT&T's buyout of McCaw Cellular and Sprint's alliance with TCI and Comcast, that menace their "local access" profits and threaten their expansion into the new wireless PCS (Personal Communication Services) spectrum. The linkup of the cellular operations of NYNEX, US West, Bell Atlantic, and Airtouch Communications (Pacific Telesis's cellular spin-off) in 1994 created a formidable third power in nationwide wireless and long-distance telephony, fully capable of competing with Sprint-TCI and AT&T-McCaw.

But at the end of the day—or rather, by the end of this century—the only way for the RBOCs to maintain their market hegemony, let alone expand into new markets, is to enter the interactive TV and new digital services business and try to poach customers from other regions, as well as from the cable TV and other industries. As Fred Salerno, vice chairman of NYNEX, observes: "If we do nothing, we can expect an erosion in our residential telephone market share of 40 percent over the next decade," as cable and long-distance companies start offering local phone service. That would translate into a loss of $1.6 billion in annual revenues in NYNEX's New York and

New England markets. But on the other hand, if NYNEX invests now in interactive networks, "then we'd lose only 15 to 20 percent of the telephone market share in our region."[14]

To be sure, the telcos aren't the only ones facing new competitive pressures. Some 99 percent of all cable TV systems also enjoy monopoly control in their markets. But on July 6, 1994, the bell began to toll as well for the cable oligarchs. The FCC gave Bell Atlantic the go-ahead to offer cable TV service to 38,000 homes and businesses in Toms River, New Jersey. Nearly two dozen other RBOC requests to offer similar cable service were waiting in the wings for FCC approval in early 1995.

"That cowboy's all hat and no cattle," scoffed Comcast President Brian Roberts in reference to telephone company plans to launch competitive television services. But no amount of tough talk can hide the real concern over new competition felt within cable industry ranks. Indeed, even Cablevision Systems, a cable firm, has announced its intention to raid the New Jersey territory of rival cabler Comcast Corp. This last move, said one media analyst, was "like throwing a grenade into the tent of the cable sheiks."

It's a mad, mad digital world today, and who precisely is attacking (or, conversely, partnering with) whom is a question that requires a new answer on practically a daily basis. Yet despite the thick fog of war shrouding the cable-telco battlefield in confusion, most Wall Street pundits and industry analysts in 1994 and 1995 were placing their bets on the telephone companies to come up winners in the war for network supremacy. As one industry dealmaker put it: "The cable industry is [going to be] steamrollered by the phone companies."[15]

Usually cited were two telco advantages over the cable companies: more advanced technology and more money. Closer examination, however, suggests that there may be far less to the telcos' supposed advantages than meets the eye.

True, the phone companies have far more experience operating the complex hardware and software necessary for digitally switched networks. And true, they have deployed fiber-optic lines nine times as extensive as those of the cable industry.[16] What's more, they enjoy a major advantage in "glueware," the enormously complex systems used to track and bill millions of customers for their service. But the telcos also have a profound technology weakness in their bread-and-butter technology: the copper-wire lines running into their customers' homes. Copper's bandwidth is simply too narrow, at least with today's technology, to carry the range of broadcast-quality video services customer expect.

The cable industry, in contrast, already possesses an infrastructure that transmits video over high-bandwidth coaxial cable lines into 63 million homes and can be easily extended to connect 95 percent of U.S. households. Those clunky black cables can potentially carry a gigahertz of communications power, or 250,000 times the capacity of a typical four-kilohertz copper phone line.[17] Digital modulation techniques enable coaxial cable to pour six gigabits of voice, data, and video per second—equal to five hundred channels of movies, shopping, and other services—into or out of the home at once. These coaxial cables could even be configured to do away with preset channels altogether and instead offer a personal and customizable "Me Channel" to access all sources of information and entertainment.

The problem for the cable companies is that while coaxial cables are clearly robust enough in theory to carry interactive services, fiber-optic hubs and "back office" digital switching systems must first be installed if these are to be transformed from dumb, one-way firehoses of mass media into intelligent two-way access conduits to the coming digital cornucopia. Cable companies are actively developing this technology, which they plan to deploy first in the online services business through cable modems capable of delivering Internet-based multimedia to PC users at better than 200 times the speed of existing telephone modems. Why target PC customers rather than their traditional TV customers? The reason is simple: this is where the money is today, whereas the fledgling interactive TV business won't even begin to generate revenues for several years.

As for the phone companies, they have considered using interim technologies such as ADSL (Asymmetric Digital Subscriber Line) to solve their problem of narrow bandwidth. But ADSL offers only one one-hundredth the capacity of a coaxial cable line and can't yet carry live television broadcasts. So while the RBOCs keep trying to massage their copper-line technology, they have concentrated their efforts on two alternative approaches: one is to lay fiber-optic lines to curbside nodes linking 20 or so homes, at a cost of nearly $1,000 per home; the other is to deploy high-capacity fiber to neighborhood hubs linking up to 500 homes and then redistribute the signals from there to each home using coaxial cable lines, at a cost of perhaps $800 per home. As of late 1994, most RBOCs were taking the hybrid fiber-coax approach. But with costs coming down for fiber-to-the-curb systems—and the interactive potential of wireless cable systems uncertain but looking more attractive, this began to change in early 1995.

Indeed, in April of 1995, Bell Atlantic withdrew its FCC application for hybrid fiber-coax systems—not because it was losing interest in interactive TV, as some pundits suggested, but because the company felt the cost for a more robust fiber-to-the-curb system had become competitive with that of the hybrid fiber-coax approach. The same month, Bell Atlantic also bought a wireless cable TV firm, signaling its intention to have available several alternative systems for the delivery of interactive TV service even before its fiber network is deployed.

"It's going to be built differently in every town," explains Bell Atlantic's Smith. "That's the part that hasn't been grasped yet. The way it's been reported to date is that we are all going to put out hybrid fiber-coax and connect it to a so-and-so with a micronet. Like there's a grand plan. Of course, that's ridiculous. It's that old manufacturing model—create one automobile design and then make a hundred million cars that all look the same. But that's never how things of this sort get deployed."

As for the cable companies, upgrading their networks will surely prove a complex and slow process, especially with the industry's capital investment pool—highly leveraged against cash flows—somewhat constrained by the 1994 cable rate rollbacks ordered by the FCC. Still, early estimates that the industry would lose $3 billion in 1994 revenues because of the rollbacks proved exaggerated. Though TCI and Time Warner did scale back their capital spending plans, the industry began bouncing back within months of the FCC action, and industry losses ultimately totaled less than half of the $3 billion that had been expected.[18] In fact, the FCC pressure also had the ironic and unintended effect of boosting industry competitiveness by spurring a new wave of mergers between cable firms seeking to "cluster" their markets in order to cope with reduced cash flows and prepare for the new threat of the RBOCs' planned TV ventures.

The error made by overly bullish pro-telco analysts is that they focus too narrowly on which industry has access to the most advanced technology—clearly, the phone companies do—when they ought to be considering which industry can most easily overcome its technological shortcomings and deploy a working interactive network most quickly. In this regard, the cable companies would seem to be not quite so disadvantaged as many believe. They merely have to add some electronics, albeit advanced electronics, to make their networks fully interactive, whereas the telcos actually have to lay new cable, with all the time delays and physical construction costs involved in digging up streets, climbing utility poles, and punching holes through the walls of tens of millions of homes in order to string those lines.

To appreciate exactly what such a massive undertaking can entail for a phone company, consider the little town of Milpitas, California, a bedroom community of 56,000 south of San Francisco. There, Pacific Telesis had planned to offer its first-ever showcase test of interactive TV to one thousand of the city's residents. But as one newspaper reported, "When city officials looked at Pacific Telesis's plans, they saw open trenches along 60 miles of city streets, a four-month traffic nightmare, broken water mains and a huge overtime bill."[19] The plan also required digging trenches through homeowners' yards in order to lay new cable into each home.

Calling PacTel's rewiring project "mind-boggling," city officials demanded $1.2 million from the phone company for extra building inspectors and traffic monitors as well as for lost revenues caused by the disruption of business. They also asked PacTel to provide the same sort of franchise fees and public service guarantees that cable firms are required by law to provide but from which the telcos are currently exempt. (Franchise fees are vital to cash-starved cities in California, which currently receive $150 million a year in such payments from cable operators.) And if all this wasn't enough, consumer groups also jumped into the fray, opposing the plan on the grounds that PacTel would force current phone customers to pay the high capital costs of the new video network.

After repeated delays and much arguing between the city and phone company officials, PacTel finally called off the entire Milpitas test. "We didn't expect any city just to roll over and say do whatever you want," noted Craig Watts, a PacTel spokesman. "But what we didn't expect from Milpitas was the quantity of issues they kept bringing up and the amount of time that it's taken to move [the plan] forward." Despite having shot itself in the foot in Milpitas, however, PacTel appeared ready to shoot itself in the other foot when it announced that the company would move immediately to a commercial rollout of interactive TV services statewide.

How PacTel intends to accomplish that is very much a mystery, however, given that the imbroglio in Milpitas is hardly a fluke. "A lot of communities are in the same situation that Milpitas is in," observed David Jones, legislative director for the League of California Cities. Representatives of 14 other cities, in fact, attended a special Milpitas City Council meeting to question PacTel's statewide rewiring plans, and leaders of 10 other cities have already met with phone company representatives directly to discuss their coming construction headaches. How PacTel responds to their concerns will determine whether it gets its building permits or is instead buried under the sort of lengthy delays for which city bureaucrats are famous.[20]

Now, replicate Pacific Telesis's Milpitas experience to tens of thousands of municipalities nationwide—or just imagine NYNEX trying to get permission from New York City officials to dig up and rewire all of Manhattan—and the telcos' vaunted technology advantage begins to lose a bit of its charm. Bell Atlantic's Ray Smith, however, insists that such construction roadblocks are exaggerated.

"I think Milpitas was an anomaly," Smith says. "Maybe what happened was an overreaction by the city council or something. In any case, we know how to build so you hardly even know we're there. We have a construction permit for Dover [Township, New Jersey, the site of Bell Atlantic's first interactive trial], and if you polled the people in Dover and asked, 'What cataclysmic thing is going on here?' they wouldn't know what it was. In Morris County [New Jersey], in fact, people are virtually cheering . . . it's like the Persian Gulf War or something and everyone's waving Bell Atlantic flags saying, 'Please come! Please come!'"

Cheering, no less?

"Sure," Smith insists, "because they see us as finally bringing decent cable TV service. We've had people calling us, asking how soon they can sign up for our cable service. I mean, look. I live in Montgomery County [Maryland]. Just this week, my cable TV service has been out for three days. Fortunately it wasn't out on Monday when the Steelers were on *Monday Night Football,* but it went out Tuesday, and today's Friday! We get terrible cable service, really lousy service. And everybody says so."

Even if Ray Smith is right, and the RBOC construction plans breeze through most of the nation's clotted city bureaucracies without a hitch, there is still the cost to consider. Even under the best of circumstances, an estimated 79 percent of network costs lie in the fabled "last mile"—the wire connection to the home. The cable companies have largely laid those connections over the last two decades.[21] That means the telcos will have to spend roughly four times more than cable firms to upgrade their systems.

Which brings us to the telcos' supposed financial advantage. Together the RBOCs have announced bold plans to spend nearly $80 billion dollars—four times the total revenues for the whole cable industry—to build advanced networks during the next decade. The numbers seem staggering at first glance. But when one takes a close look at these plans, the telcos' high-stakes investment scheme begins to look rather like a shell game.

When Bell Atlantic, for example, announced in 1994 that it would spend $11 billion by 1999 to build an interactive video network, the company neglected to mention that this included the $2 billion a year— $10 billion total—it *already* planned to spend on basic capital upgrades to its existing infrastructure. In other words, the plan involved only $1 billion in net new spending over the next five years. As a report in the *Wall Street Journal* noted, "[The telcos] are so infected with multimedia fever that they are issuing news releases portraying even basic capital upgrades as a boon to the national mission of building an information highway."[22] To be sure, such routine upgrades would certainly support the future video network Bell Atlantic hopes to build. But how the company hopes to achieve its stated goal of wiring 10 million homes by 1999 with fiber or fiber-coax links is still unclear, given that $1 billion in new spending is barely enough to hook up one in ten of these homes.

This same sort of financial huffing and puffing can be seen at the other regional phone carriers as well. In 1994, Pacific Telesis loudly trumpeted its plan to spend $16 billion by the year 2001 to build a California network that would "help customers in their daily lives, learning, shopping, playing," according to a company press release. But an analysis of the company's previous capital spending profile suggests the company would have spent $14 billion of that amount anyway, without wiring for multimedia service.

Similarly, Southern New England Telephone touted its 1994 announcement of a $4.4 billion interactive spending program with near space-shot hyperbole. "Our vision for Connecticut just took a giant leap forward," boasted a company press release. But whoops . . . SNET forgot to mention that these outlays will occur over a 15-year period, which means the company will be spending only $30 million a year more than its current expenditures. That basically buys them fiber-coax deployment to 30,000 customers a year—and perhaps a full-page ad in the *Hartford Courant* to tout their "giant leap" forward toward interactivity. At this rate, SNET will need 110 years to wire the whole state at current costs.

It would seem, then, that at least some of the "interactivity" in the telcos' Info Highway plans is concentrated in their public relations departments, which churn out what they think Wall Street and the public want to hear—or at least what they wanted to hear in 1993– 94, when investors attached a hefty premium to the stock of companies involved in Info Highway businesses. An analyst with the consulting firm Yankee Group framed it starkly in 1994: "The bull that's being thrown around is unreal. It's all hype."[23]

Well, perhaps not *all* hype, but the point is well taken. A superficial glance at the telcos' balance sheets might suggest an *overwhelming* financial superiority over the cable industry. But a host of factors—from the telcos' far greater costs in deploying their new networks to their inability to finance those costs by taking on the sort of debt loads typical of the cable industry—suggests that the RBOC financial advantage may be less than it seems.

In any event, with deregulation of the local telephony cash cow now on the horizon, the RBOCs' no-risk glory days are numbered. Besides having to spend four times more than cable firms to upgrade their networks, the telcos will also have to take billions of dollars in charges against their balance sheets in order to write off their $100 billion in outdated copper-wire networks, only 40 percent of which have been depreciated. In 1994, US West was the first to take such a write-off. Bell Atlantic followed suit and posted $2 billion in equipment write-off charges and another $100 million to cover the cost of laying off 5,600 workers.

"The cost cutting in the telephone industry is a daily event because of the expectation of rising competition and plans for network upgrades," explained Frank Governali, a CS First Boston Corp. analyst.[24] While hiking competitiveness in terms of operating costs, however, such cutbacks may end up eroding the telcos' clear advantage in customer service. Colorado's Public Utilities Commission, for example, charged US West in 1994 with violating state guidelines following sharp declines in service practices in the wake of the company's "reengineering" cutbacks.

"They may have gone over some line," concedes Bell Atlantic's Smith, who doesn't believe that RBOC streamlining efforts jeopardize their competitive advantage over cable in customer service. "But just because US West has a couple of problems, that doesn't compare to [the fact that] cable companies [are] considered the worst service providers in the community. I don't remember my telephone ever going out. We've got such a competitive advantage over cable because of our service reputation that we'll get 15 percent of video market share just by putting out our shingle."

Actually, they could get more than that. According to the highly regarded market research firm Odyssey, which specializes in examining the relationship between consumers, technology, and in-home information and entertainment, "fifty-five percent of U.S. households with cable television say they would be *very likely* to switch to a different cable provider if they simply were offered a competitive price." What's more, among those considered most likely to try new technologies such as interactive television, over 70 percent said they would be "very likely to switch."[25]

The study's results, if broadly accurate, could pave the way for major telco inroads into the cable TV business. But it is not altogether clear that they can beat the cable companies when it comes to the ultimate litmus test: price. And almost every market study has shown that no matter how interested consumers are in interactive TV, they are not willing (or able) to pay much for it.

Clearly, the RBOCs would love to be able to pass on some of the costs of deploying these new networks in order to be price competitive with the cable industry. But current regulations prohibit the phone companies from financing new services out of existing subscriber revenues, even though they are notorious for sidestepping such constraints, as a General Accounting Office report noted when it found the FCC had failed to audit telco accounting practices ade-

quately and prevent illegal cross-subsidization.[26] And now the telcos
are coming under an even closer scrutiny as they prepare to launch
their new video dialtone networks. Stung by the GAO report, for
instance, the FCC conducted its own audit with the help of the accounting firm of Ernst & Young. It resulted in a March 3, 1995,
"show cause" order from the FCC charging the RBOCs with having
"misstated" their long distance access costs, and four weeks later,
an FCC order to roll back access charges by nearly 3 percent, or
about $500 million for all the bell companies.

In the final analysis, it's not just the amount of money the RBOCs
have that matters—it's how effectively they're able to use it. And
in this regard, their record has been less than thrilling. Apart from
successful cellular and overseas ventures, the telcos have wasted
huge amounts of money on enterprises outside their core telephone
business, from computer retail stores (NYNEX) to financial services
(US West) and even, incredibly, to an interior design service (SBC
Communications). As Michael Noll, dean of the Annenberg School
of Communications at the University of Southern California, put it:
"Most of their new ventures have not turned out very well."[27]

Hardly a surprise, given that Baby Bells have never had to face
competition before, thanks to their court-protected monopoly of local
phone service. Can telco executives, who even jokingly refer to
themselves as "Bellheads," now become entrepreneurs? The experience of AT&T—once the mecca for Bellhead-istas everywhere, but
today known by the moniker 1-800-GUTS—suggests that entrepreneurialism can, indeed, take root in a once regulated monopoly. But
it requires a good deal more than simply replacing a few people at
the top, as Pacific Telesis did in 1994 when it appointed 41-year-old
David Dorman, a veteran of the grueling long-distance wars while a
Sprint executive, to be its new CEO in 1994.

Indeed, it's one thing to graft a shark's head onto the slow-moving
body of an RBOC whale, quite another to actually turn a bloated sea
grazer into a hunter-killer. And here the RBOCs will have to swim a
lot of ocean before they can hope to match the aggressive speed and
savvy of cable firms. For starters, the telcos must reorganize their
geographic operating divisions into strategic business units that
focus on markets and customers in order to bring their enormous
financial and technology assets to bear as effective competitive
weapons against the cable companies. The latter use their far more

limited resources twice as efficiently as the RBOCs, generating a fifth of the telcos' revenues with only one-tenth the capital.[28]

Are the telcos truly prepared to shed their monopoly ways and compete in the uncharted world of interactive TV?

"I don't think their culture makes them competitive, and that's their big vulnerability," argues cable magnate John Malone. "Sure, any one RBOC has got as much revenue as the whole cable industry put together. And sure, they're very powerful politically. But they've lived as protected monopolies in a regulated environment all these years and never had to face competition of any kind. So, yeah, the RBOCs have a lot of money, but in order to use it they have to change their whole way of doing business."

Naturally, Bell Atlantic's Smith takes a different view: "I know what they say about the old Bellhead mentality—and it's true!" he laughs. "I remember the old days in the sixties when we had a rule for everything, including the correct way to hold a pencil. We even had a written rule that said, 'Before you go to a meeting, always go to the bathroom, even if you don't have to.'"

He pauses a moment for emphasis. "Well, those days are gone, at least here at Bell Atlantic. It's become clear that all the old givens— like 'monopolies are forever'—no longer apply. Which is why we've been working very, very hard for over five years now to transform ourselves. The world's changing, and we intend to manage that change."

One wild card in the cable-telco contest is how the communications reform process will play itself out over the next few years. The first rewrite of telecom law since 1934 was derailed in the 1994 Congress after the RBOCs balked at a provision requiring that competition exist in local phone markets before they be allowed to enter the long-distance business. Senate Commerce Committee Chairman Ernest Hollings (Democrat, South Carolina), for years a telco supporter, accused the RBOCs of holding telecom reform "hostage" and blasted their lobbying tactics. "The Bell companies engage in a political onslaught of misrepresentation and outright fraud," the senator wrote in a letter to Senate Majority Leader George Mitchell (Democrat, Maine). "They state that all they want is to compete when all they want is to control. They are determined to keep and extend their monopoly or kill the bill."[29]

As we write this, Republican-led efforts in the Congress to cobble together a telecom bill may yet result in passage of some sort of piecemeal package of reforms that would generally favor the interests of the RBOCs. After all, having spent $3.1 million versus the long distance industry's $1.7 million in the congressional campaigns of 1993 and 1994, the telcos' political action committees will certainly expect to get their money's worth from the new Republican majority on Capitol Hill.[30]

But the bill being debated in the summer of 1995 has already been watered down, compromised, and obfuscated on every major issue. Whatever eventually passes will hardly address the real need for deregulation and reform in communications. At best, any bill that is passed will give deregulation a modest push, while throwing all the truly difficult and controversial issues into the court system and the state legislatures.

Buried deep within the arcane complexities of the current version of the telecom reform legislation are literally hundreds of "land mines"—special interest favors, confusing new regulations, and small passages with unimagined implications. One perfect example is a provision that would usurp the traditional rights municipalities have had to supervise RBOC construction projects and be compensated for damages, lost business, and use of local resources. The federal government would, in effect, take control of the traditional rights of eminent domain that states and cities have had. This is one of the greatest attempted extensions of federal power in recent memory—yet the enabling passages of the bill are so well hidden that they have escaped public debate, even in a political climate when practically everything else the federal government tries to do is being seen as an abridgement of states' rights.

In any event, thousands of cities and towns are not about to roll over and play dead in the face of what could be hundreds of millions of dollars in costs to support the RBOCs' interactive network construction projects. On this issue, and so many others, the passage of new legislation will mark the beginning of the political and legal fight, not the end.

Nonetheless, the deregulation process itself is inexorable, whether it is carried out in Congress or in the courts and state legislatures. Sooner or later, most if not all of the major U.S. communications markets will be opened to competition.

Then we will discover that the most decisive factor in the cable-telco rivalry is neither technology, money, nor regulation. Rather, the key crucibles of success in the competition to come will be the quality of the new interactive products and services that each industry offers as well as their expertise in marketing these to consumers.

Within a few years, according to NYNEX's Fred Salerno, both cable and telco networks "will probably be very robust and almost equal. The differentiating factor [will be] content. How do you package content and how do you market these packages to the consumer? These will be the major drivers of success in the business."[31]

And therein lies the cable industry's chief advantage. They have already acquired more than a quarter century of experience in developing content and marketing that content in various ways to customers. To be sure, cable firms have enjoyed anticompetitive monopolies. But even so, they can rightly claim more than a little marketing expertise—after all, they convinced 62 million households to *pay* for television service that, at least in limited form, could have been had free over the air. As even NYNEX's Salerno acknowledges, "Right now, if you had to rate cable companies versus telephone companies, I think you would find that cable companies do a better job marketing to consumers."

Only very recently, in fact, have local phone companies even considered the frightening possibility that they might have to actually compete one day for customers. Can the RBOCs now develop the necessary skills to compete with cable firms in the packaging and marketing of communications and entertainment services? It remains to be seen. Clearly, the telcos are willing to spend heavily to buy or develop their own filmed content—NYNEX invested $1.2 billion to help Viacom acquire Paramount; Bell Atlantic, NYNEX, and Pacific Telesis put up $300 million to create a new company to produce films and TV shows under the guidance of Hollywood superagent Michael Ovitz; and Ameritech, BellSouth, and SBC Communications have put $500 million into another film venture with Walt Disney Studios.

"We feel it is absolutely necessary to be involved with a content provider," said NYNEX's Salerno. Noted Ray Smith of Bell Atlantic: "We will be ideally positioned to compete in this new market." And added Ameritech executive vice president W. Patrick Campbell: "We want to be out front and make sure that our [entertainment] package is superior."[32]

But as any movie executive can attest, developing and then marketing entertainment that truly captures the popular imagination requires an extremely subtle and instinctive feeling for the popular mood—a sensibility often acquired only after many years spent trying to blend the artistic talents of writers, producers, and actors with the commercial dynamics of the entertainment business and then testing the results with the public. Like voodoo, it's a craft that is both intuitive and inexplicable. It is not the sort of thing one can simply purchase by investing in Paramount's or any other studio's existing film library.

Disney Chairman Michael Eisner addressed this point following his licensing deal with the three Baby Bells. While acknowledging the role that new technology had played in bringing together the three communications firms with his Hollywood studio, Eisner notes that, "At the same time, the essence of entertainment will not change. What has always counted is the story and the skill with which it is told."[33]

In the short term—the next five to ten years or so—the shape of the competitive battlefield between the cable TV and telephone industries will most likely resemble that envisioned by Bob Kavner, the former multimedia chief at AT&T. "I suspect that the RBOCs will tend to predominate in communications services, which is their strength," he said in an interview shortly before leaving to join Michael Ovitz's Creative Artists talent agency in Hollywood. "The cable companies will dominate in entertainment. Each industry will probably retain most of its market share in their core businesses, and this will naturally exert a kind of gravitational pull on their expansion into new markets. The big question will be at the margins between their two traditional markets—who will get more of whose business?"

If that is true, then Tom Feige, head of Time Warner's Full Service Network in Orlando, Florida, believes the smart money should be placed on the cable companies to come out ahead. "Some of these telephone guys are a little slow," he observed. "One of them told me recently that his expectation was that the cable companies will get 30 percent of the phone business and the phone companies will get 30 percent of the cable business—and this guy seemed to think that was a pretty good deal for them. "But, hey, I'll take that any day," Feige added. "I mean, 30 percent of their business is $33 billion, whereas 30 percent of our business is only $6 billion. That's a hell of a good deal for us."

Not surprisingly, Ray Smith disagrees strongly. "Oh, for Christ's sake!" he retorts. "This notion that cable companies will get 30 percent of the $100 billion telephone business, whereas we'll only get 30 percent of cable's $20 billion business—that's ridiculous. It won't be dollar-for-dollar. It'll be ten-to-one in our favor."

Ultimately, what will determine the winners and losers of this high-stakes battle for network supremacy is not so much the innate differences between the two industries—their respective resources and capabilities, for instance—but the skill and strategic vision with which individual companies within each industry *deploy* those resources and capabilities in the marketplace. In the end, it will be the most creative, aggressive, and far-sighted companies in *both* industries—the TCIs and Bell Atlantics—who are likely to prevail, while those who adapt too slowly or gamble unwisely may not only lose market share but even disappear altogether into mergers or bankruptcies.

What's more, there will be new and perhaps surprising candidates entering the fray, nipping at the heels of the TCIs and Bell Atlantics. These dark-horse contenders—satellite delivery systems, PCS-based providers, Internet-based services, and even foreign telephone and television companies—could well spark new realignments in the telephony and interactive TV competition. At the very least, they'll certainly keep the existing players on their toes.

"The real bottom line," observes NYNEX's O'Brien, "is that none of us—not the telcos, not the cable companies, not the broadcasters, not the advertising agencies—none of us can stand still."

▪ 7 ▪

The Games People Play

Think back to last Christmas. After little Jason and Jennifer had opened their presents, blown away a few cyborgs with their new $400 video game machine, and fiddled with the $150 worth of CD-ROM educational programs you had bought them (assuming you figured out how to install these on your new $1,500 computer), do you remember what happened next?

If your home is like most, the kids probably tired of their high-tech gadgets after a few hours. By early afternoon, Jason was lying on the living-room rug, holding his $5 Mighty Morphin Power Rangers action figure six inches in front of his face and watching, in his mind's eye, the little morph man karate-chop the evil Goldar into mincemeat (all the while accompanying himself with those incredible "KA-POW!" and "YE-AAH!" sound effects of his). As for Jennifer, she was probably absorbed with her $15 Barbie, chatting to imaginary friends in her little singsong voice as she dressed the enduring icon of girlhood first for work and then for a night on the town with Ken.

But then again, maybe that's not how it was at your house. Perhaps your kids simply spent the afternoon sitting inside the imaginary clubhouse they had built out of cardboard boxes—the ones the video game machine and computer had come packed in—and deciding which of their friends they would and would not let into their club.

In any event, it's a safe bet that if you're a parent, you have more than once rolled your eyes at the money you have spent on high-tech toys only to discover that even the most advanced technology in the world ultimately is no match for the imaginative power of a little child's mind.

To be sure, video games and CD-ROMs have achieved showcase status in the Digital Revolution largely because of their sometimes-breathtaking fusion of photo-realistic imagery, high-quality sound, and full-motion video into new entertainment and educational experiences. Some of these products are stunningly creative, especially educational titles such as *A Passion for Art*, a CD-ROM that combines the high-quality visuals of a PBS TV documentary on impressionism with interactive tools that allow users to customize their own tour of the Barnes Collection. Some, like *A Passage to Vietnam*, are so creative and inviting that you want to spend time exploring their many customizable paths, even if you don't have that kind of time in your life.

What's more, unlike interactive TV or online services, video game and CD-ROM publishing have already developed into mass market industries with well-defined sales channels and customer bases in the millions. Which explains, of course, why almost every major publisher, movie studio, television outfit, and computer company has set up a "new media" unit to pursue either interactive games or CD-ROMs or both.

But all that said, it's important to remember that no interactive technology in the world offers anywhere near the price-performance benefits of the human imagination. Our minds require neither electricity nor batteries (though three squares a day appears to improve performance), they are fully portable, and with regular use they'll last a lifetime without ever breaking down or becoming obsolete.

And talk about simulated 3-D visuals—our minds beat anything else on the market by a light-year!

All this is worth bearing in mind as we listen to some of the more breathless claims about interactive technology radically reshaping education and entertainment and, indeed, human experience itself in the years ahead. The truth is, even digital technology has its limits and no digital 3-D adventure or simulated learning environment will ever match the emotional and illuminative power of the dreamscapes conjured by our minds. Long into the future, children will still toss aside their overpriced toys and crawl under cardboard boxes to imagine worlds of wonder.

In the world of business, too, digital technology also has its limits. It cannot sell an otherwise weak product, make a bad business plan work, or salvage inept marketing programs, inadequate channel distribution, and inappropriate pricing strategies. Neither can it magically vanquish competitors who have stronger brands nor surmount the demographic and income barriers that tend to define and limit one's core market.

One would think that all this would be self-evident, but it apparently is not—at least not in the interactive video game and CD-ROM industries. Here we find that all too often sound business strategy and a healthy respect for the real-world demands of the consumer marketplace have been cast aside and replaced by the glassy-eyed worship of new technology. This disease—let's call it "competitive technophilia"—has already crippled the hopes of at least one exciting new video game company that succumbed to it, and in the multimedia CD-ROM business, now threatens to reverse the early successes of the industry itself.

Consider the video game business, the only interactive medium to date to have achieved genuine mass-market success. In 1993, a peak year for video game sales, U.S. revenues soared to $6 billion ($15 billion worldwide), making the game industry bigger than Hollywood's box office and almost as rich as the music business. Video game rentals comprised an additional $1 billion business, with Blockbuster alone renting 100,000 video games a day. That year, over one-third of all American households—including two-thirds of those with kids—possessed video game machines.[1]

As Lee Isgur, director of the securities firm Jeffries & Company, put it in 1993: "You can talk all you want about the electronic highway and video-on-demand, but the only place anyone has sold anything interactive is in games."[2]

Isgur was referring, of course, to *mass-market* sales and billion-dollar-plus revenues, and at the time he made the remark, he was right. Cable and phone giants may have been hyperventilating over the prospect of dialing for interactive TV dollars. Internet and online services firms may have been dreaming of cybersurfing a tsunami of digital profits. But video game giants Sega and Nintendo were already raking in billions of dollars annually, and had been doing so since before most people had ever heard of the Information Highway.

Video games became the first interactive media product to hit pay dirt in the mass consumer market because, for one thing, they are incredibly simple to operate. Just plug it in and push the power button—as easy as a toaster. What's more, the use-value of video games was exceptionally high: they offered hours of fun at a relatively affordable price.

But now, just when so much of the world is waxing euphoric about interactive media of all types, the video game industry that first blazed the trail to digital riches finds itself at a crossroads in its development. The glory days of triple-digit growth have come to an end, at least temporarily. A period of consolidation, shakeouts, and even retrenchment has begun as game companies struggle to find new ways to expand their customer base, market and distribute their products more broadly and effectively, and compete for customers on a global scale.

"The whole industry is slowing," noted Jeffrey Camp, an analyst at Jardine Fleming Japan, Ltd. In 1994, video game receipts dropped sharply to about $5 billion—the first downturn in the game industry's history.[3]

Why the retrenchment? Part of the game industry's problem is that there are only so many pre-adolescent and teenage boys in America. "They already have 75 percent saturation among teenage boys," noted analyst Camp, and game companies have so far been largely unsuccessful in reaching beyond this testosterone-soaked core market to attract girls or adults in large numbers. At the same time, the industry is introducing a new generation of far more powerful game machines, often employing graphically richer CD-ROM discs instead of traditional cartridges, and as a result consumers have slowed their purchases of older game machine systems in anticipation of the new machines' arrival.

One game mogul attempting to navigate this uncertain territory is Trip Hawkins, 40, a man with the good looks and persuasive style of a natural-born salesman. A legend in the game business, Hawkins became a millionaire at 30, thanks to the success of Electronic Arts, the game software company he cofounded in the 1980s. He could easily have rested on his laurels, living off the interest alone from the sale of his stock options, but in late 1992 he decided to embark on a new and risky adventure. And because of his reputation, Hawkins was able to convince a great many sophisticated investors to go along on that adventure with him.

Developing a new technology that supposedly outstripped the performance and photo-realism of existing game machines by a factor of 50, Trip Hawkins launched the 3DO Company. He did not plan to actually make anything. Rather, he licensed 3DO's hardware technology to outside manufacturers, such as Matsushita and Sanyo, and recruited independent software developers to design games for the new system.

Before getting under way, however, Hawkins put together a top-notch "strategic alliance" of investors, including Matsushita, AT&T, and Time Warner. Strategic alliances, of course, are all the rage in the multimedia business, but they don't necessarily guarantee a company's success. As industry wag John Dvorak put it, "Nowadays anyone with a decent Rolodex can line up so-called strategic partners."[4] Still, 3DO's alliance did generate a great deal of buzz.

Hawkins decided to translate this (much-cultivated) buzz around 3DO's "revolutionary" technology and its "world-class" strategic partners into something more bankable. In May 1993, he took 3DO public at $15 a share, raising over $47 million for operations and expansion. The stock quickly soared to a price in the high $40s— despite the fact that 3DO had not booked any sales. Since then, the stock has declined to around $13, where it has hovered since.

At the time, there were those who blasted 3DO's public stock offering as a "concept" sale, unsupported by revenues, earnings, or any of the other usual indicators of a growing business. This criticism, however, missed the point. 3DO's problem was not that it was selling a concept. Its problem was that the concept itself was fatally flawed.

Here's the 3DO concept, or strategy, as outlined by Hawkins himself: "The way we're going to fight against competition is we're going to make sure that we maintain a technology lead."

It is strange that Hawkins would bet his company on the hope of always maintaining a technology lead, given all his years of experience in an industry where the lifespan of such leads is usually measured in months. Be that as it may, Hawkins's technophiliac strategy was soon reflected in every aspect of 3DO's business plan, from pricing and product development to marketing and distribution.

Take pricing. When 3DO's game players, manufactured under Matsushita's Panasonic label, finally hit the store shelves in late 1993, their price was $700—or about *seven times* the cost of competing (albeit less powerful) machines. Sales were so disastrous that Panasonic reduced the price three times over the next year, finally settling in at $400. Carrying a price that was still three to four times above the competition, 3DO machines failed to attract the sales levels Hawkins had expected. By early 1994, having lost more than $50 million since the company's launch, 3DO was forced to seek new financing from its partners. Amid much grumbling—AT&T refused to pony up additional cash—the company managed to secure $37 million more from its investors, including $12.4 million chipped in by Hawkins himself.

In two interviews for this book, Trip Hawkins dismissed with unflappable cheerfulness even the possibility that there might be a screw or two loose in 3DO's business plan.

"We think that even at $699, it was a remarkably low price, considering how powerful the technology is and how much better it is than the alternatives," Hawkins argued.

Such exquisite insensitivity to irony was a consistent subtext of each of Hawkins's interviews for this book. This was particularly true of the first interview, for which he had requested that the general line of questioning first be submitted in writing.

"Hello . . . this is Trip Hawkins," said a voice at the other end of the phone late one evening several weeks later. "I'd like to respond to your questions."

When asked to hold just a moment so a pen and notebook could be retrieved, he asserted it wouldn't be necessary. "Actually," he said, "I'd rather dictate my responses directly to your answering machine."

Answering machine?

"Yeah, I'd actually prefer it that way."

[Long pause.] O-o-o-kay.

He then hung up and redialed. The author's answering machine clicked on—BEEP!—and Trip Hawkins commenced the, er, "interview."

"Okay," he began, "You asked whether there's a danger that new interactive game technology will get in the way of people interacting with each other. Actually, I think it's just the opposite. I think what I'm trying to do with my work is really encourage *more* social interaction."

Hawkins paused briefly to consider the next question, apparently unaware of the contradiction between what he had just said and his insistence on delivering a speech to an answering machine rather than "socially interact" with his interviewer.

Then Hawkins resumed his monologue. After a half hour more of virtual Q and A, he thanked the author and hung up.

BEEP!

In a subsequent (this time, face-to-face) interview, the 3DO chairman again responded to questions about the company's pricing strategy with characteristic aplomb.

"If you look at other successful consumer media, their interactive price points, adjusted for inflation, were even higher," he said. "Typically between $1,500 and $2,000."

Interactive price-point?

"Yeah, the real issue is not the absolute price," he asserted. "The real issue is, What is the intrinsic experience you get out of the product?"

Actually, the real issue *is* the price. Or to put it another way, How much are consumers generally willing to pay for a video game machine? In a 1994 survey of game industry analysts, most expressed the view that price was the most critical factor in the success of a hardware platform.[5] And according to analysts, that price had to be around $200 or less—preferably around $100.

Hawkins is certainly correct to point out that VCRs, audio CD players, and even calculators all commanded steep prices when first introduced. But that was when each of these devices represented a totally new category of consumer product and hadn't yet developed sufficient manufacturing volume to push down prices. 3DO, on the other hand, is not introducing its product into an immature or embryonic market. It faces the challenge of carving out a survivable niche in an already mature game market dominated by the largest consumer electronics powerhouses on the planet. Sony, for example, generates more revenue in half a day than 3DO did in all of 1994.

As Dvorak observed at the time, "[3DO] promoters have no grasp of what consumers can afford. Ask anyone closely involved in 3DO when last they stepped into Kmart. They're as out of touch as poor George Bush was when he played the Gomer and yelped upon seeing a laser scanner at a grocery store checkout counter."[6]

The same myopia displayed in 3DO's pricing practices was also shown in Hawkins's careless dismissal of potential competition. "Sure, we have to be concerned about technologies that could leapfrog over 3DO," he conceded. "But we've got a big jump over what's out there by a factor of about 50. So somebody's not only going to have to catch up with us, they'd have to surpass us, because after a while we'll have a pretty significant momentum."

And whose technologies, exactly, might leapfrog 3DO?

"You [might] think of a Silicon Graphics," he shrugged. "They have the right technology, but they've never been able to make it cheap, and they don't know how to relate to the software industry the way we do. And they're also behind us in terms of their schedule."

Actually, even at the time of these interviews, Silicon Graphics was cementing an alliance aimed at blending its world-leading graphics technology with the video game know-how of industry giant Nintendo in a game machine that would offer movielike images superior to those of the 3DO unit. The Nintendo–Silicon Graphics machine, the Ultra64, is slated for an early 1996 launch—and at a price of only $250! Also in the works were 3DO-killing game machines from U.S. market leader Sega (called Saturn and released in May 1995) and from Sony (called the Playstation and slated for a late 1995 launch).

As for Hawkins's claim that his far more successful rivals "don't know how to relate to the software industry like we do," they would (given 3DO's software record) no doubt happily agree with him on that score. In the fall of 1994, it seems, Hawkins sparked a mutiny among the software developers most crucial to the company's survival by unilaterally (and some say illegally) doubling from $3 to $6 the royalty 3DO charges developers for each of their game titles sold. Hawkins conceded the action may have antagonized developers, but he claimed it was necessary to offset losses by the machine's hardware manufacturers that by then had ballooned upward of $200 million.

In typical fashion, however, Hawkins put a positive spin on the developer revolt. "Everyone [would have been] much worse off" without the royalty increase, he said, adding, "Some developers felt

I misled them [and] they're going to call me a lot of names. But I still love them."[7]

Replied Tom Zito, CEO of Digital Pictures, a California CD-ROM firm that was among the first to develop software for 3DO: "We have consulted with our attorneys."[8]

Facing weak sales, steep losses, and even a rebellion within his own ranks, Hawkins never really confronted the fact that, sooner or later, his technology edge and lead time in the market would evaporate. Was he at all concerned that such global video game and electronics powerhouses as Sega, Nintendo, and Sony would shortly try to snuff out his candle?

"The video game guys," Hawkins snorted, "they're pretty much in the toy business." The way he used the word "toy," it sounded like a slur.

It is precisely Sega's and Nintendo's appreciation of the clear affinity between the toy and video game markets, however, that has enabled them to sell 65 *million* game machines worldwide—many of these in toy stores. Both companies know that what they are really selling is entertainment, not technology, and both target an audience that is young and has little discretionary income of its own. Both industries also rely on low pricing and broad retail distribution (for example, Kmart, Wal-Mart, and Toys "R" Us) to reach a mass audience. So alike are the toy and video game businesses that executives freely move back and forth between the two industries.

Hawkins, meanwhile, has consistently sacrificed market penetration in favor of a high-priced appeal to that small segment of "early adopter" technophiles attracted to the latest in "revolutionary" hardware. Fine if you're Sharper Image; not so fine if you're looking for a mass market among kids. 3DO's sticker-shocking pricing has also shut it out of perhaps three-quarters of the retail outlets that carry Sega and Nintendo gear. And as for 3DO's corporate leadership, you guessed it: there is no one on board with any serious toy industry experience.

3DO investors were somewhat cheered in the middle of 1994, however, by the news that Hawkins had finally cut a deal with Wal-Mart to carry his $400 machines. Analysts wondered if the deal signaled, at long last, a change in 3DO's techno-elitist strategy.

"We are well positioned," Hawkins told reporters, "because this business is moving away from being a toy business and becoming a high-technology business."

Ooops, there he goes again. . . .

By the end of 1994, Trip Hawkins was again using the occasion of bad news—the layoff of a sixth of his workforce in a cost-cutting move—to announce an "upswing" in the company's fortunes. Said the 3DO chairman: "We now want to focus the majority of our efforts on expanding the success we are having."

The man truly is unflappable. Having been right earlier in his career with Electronic Arts, Hawkins (like so many other techno-visionaries) is unable to grasp the fact that the real world moves to its own rhythms rather than to his personal rhapsodies. Blinded by the brilliance of what he felt was an unshakable technology advantage, Hawkins believed he was not bound by the long-established commercial dynamics of the video game business.

As Keith Benjamin, an analyst at Robertson Stephens & Company, observed: "Trip thinks he can maintain a technical lead. But the challenge isn't tech, it's marketing."

By mid-1995, here's where Trip Hawkins stood: eighteen months after the first 3DO machine had hit the market with a dull thud, 3DO could count barely 500,000 machines sold. Most of these—350,000 to be exact—were sold in Japan, where 3DO might at first appear to have been moderately successful until you compare its sales to the one million Playstations sold by Sony in the first six months of 1995 alone. Most experts believe 3DO must sell a million units total by year-end 1995 to stay in the race with industry giants Sega and Nintendo.

Can 3DO do it? Opinions vary. Says Lee Isgur, the Jefferies & Company analyst (and a personal friend of Trip's): "They've got enough capital to carry them through the fiscal year. If they push their installed base to one million units by the end of 1995—and it's certainly not out of the question at all—then I think 3DO will be on strong ground."

But Kathy Klotz, an analyst at Dataquest, sees it differently: "Let's look at reality, shall we? Their installed base is too small. They don't seem to understand the business model of this industry. I'd say everything hinges on how they do this next Christmas. And with the new Sega and Sony platforms entering the market, I'd be surprised if they make it."

Some see AT&T's decision in mid-1995 to sell its stake in 3DO as a sign that even Trip's backers are bailing out. But Trip counters that "AT&T's decision to sell its modest 2.5 percent interest in 3DO was part of AT&T's overall strategy to pull back on multimedia across the board, focusing instead on wireless communications."

Not true. To be sure, AT&T did also cancel its Edge modem deal with Sega, but meanwhile it has boosted its stake in the game-playing enterprise Imagination Network to 100 percent ownership. And through its venture capital unit, AT&T Ventures, the telecommunications giant also maintains sizable investments in Spectrum Holobyte, Knowledge Adventure, and other multimedia companies.

Then there's the continuing price competition that 3DO faces in the market. "I will agree that [you] make some legitimate points about the degree of competition and price pressure in the market," Trip concedes in arguing about his company's future. But he noted that since the company adjusted its strategy, "several retailers are selling 3DO machines at an effective price of $299 with bundled software."

That certainly may help 3DO sales, although it all depends upon what Trip means by "several retailers." Will the $299 price be widely available in mass-market channels? Or is Trip merely talking about a few electronics boutiques carrying his machines at that price?

Then there's 3DO's new M2 technology, which has gotten some good reviews. But despite Trip's insistence that M2 will enable 3DO to outshine the new competing machines from Nintendo, Sega, and Sony, it must again be pointed out that the challenge in this business is still marketing, not technology.

So, the bottom line on 3DO's future? To put it bluntly, everything hinges on Christmas 1995. If the company truly abandons its techno-centered strategy and markets the hell out of its machines—and if somehow the competition stumbles—then who knows, Trip may once again defy the naysayers. But that prospect appears unlikely.

Says Dataquest analyst Bruce Ryon: "I think 3DO will be a footnote in the history of the business."[9]

Contrast 3DO's approach with that of Sega, which relies not only on technological improvements but especially on continual innovations in marketing and distribution to keep pace with a fast-changing marketplace. As recently as 1990, Sega's larger rival, Nintendo, held a near-monopoly lock on the U.S. game business. But it grew complacent, was late in upgrading its product line, and its marketing was lame compared to Sega's far hipper approach to American youth. Sega was also more aggressive in reaching out to mass-market retailers, signing up Kmart, Wal-Mart, and Blockbuster video and thereby adding 6,500 new outlets for its products. By Christmas 1993, Sega had managed to surpass Nintendo as the dominant player in the hotly contested U.S. market. Much of the credit for Sega's success, incidentally, goes to Sega of America CEO Tom Kalinske, the former head of Mattel and a man with extensive experience in the very same toy business that 3DO's Trip Hawkins scorns.

Today, Sega is pushing forward on two fronts. First, the company is aggressively marketing its new Saturn machine, though at nearly $400, the price is felt by many (even within Sega) to be too high to achieve significant penetration of the U.S. market. Sega's boldest venture, however, may be Sega TV, a new marketing and distribution venture being developed in conjunction with cable industry leaders TCI and Time Warner.

Before his August 1994 departure for Mattel, Sega's Doug Glen discussed the new Sega channel.[10] As with all Sega products, one of Sega TV's key features will be ease of use.

"[Simplicity] goes a long way toward explaining why video game machines have been so enormously successful," Glen explained. "Consumers like an apparatus that is simple to use, foolproof, that you can bang on, pour Coca-Cola on—and it still keeps working. [They] have no tolerance for bugs. This is a very important consideration to keep in mind while developing the broadband networks of the future. These services have to be bug-free. They have to be non-frustrating from the beginning."

Outlining the reasons for Sega's move into interactive television, Glen first of all cited the huge size of the video game business. "This is an enormous market for some sort of [online] consumption," he explained. "Sega's strategy is pretty simple. We want to build an electronic distribution system immediately. Consumers are going to be looking for familiar brand names. And by getting lots of Sega [owners] onto electronic distribution services early, we're going to have a running start in the market."

How will the channel work? "Consumers will pay a few dollars a month," said Glen, "and they get a couple thousand dollars worth of games to choose from. This is a mass market because it's deliverable to every Sega owner whose home is cabled. That's 10 million or more such owners."

More than a way of distributing games electronically, the Sega channel is also a marketing tool. "We've done a lot of research," he said, "and the hottest features of the Sega Channel—in addition to value—are the previews of unreleased games and insider tips. An awful lot of people who are cable subscribers also said that this channel is sufficient reason to go out and buy a Genesis. That wasn't too surprising. What was surprising? In interviewing a lot of house-holds that had a Sega but no cable service, we discovered that these households thought our product was a good enough reason to have cable installed."

This, Glen observed, was an important incentive for TCI and Time Warner. "From the cable operator's point of view," he noted, "our channel is more than just a profitable and attractive service. It also offers the kind of leverage that operators just might need to [help them] get into the 30 percent of households not presently served by cable."

Time will tell if Glen is right. But clearly Sega TV represents the sort of creative, consumer-oriented emphasis on branding, market-ing, and distribution that is becoming ever more essential in today's marketplace.

Or to paraphrase the old Starkist commercial: "Sorry, Trip! It's not the guy selling the most innovative technology, but the guy who sells his technology most innovatively, who wins."

Ultimately, the key challenge facing all video game companies is how to develop new sources of revenue in a market that appears to be near saturation. Sega TV is one effort in this direction, of course, but Sega and other firms are also seeking ways to expand the demo-graphics of the game-playing population beyond its current young male core (Nintendo doesn't call its handheld device Game Boy for nothing). Sega committed $1.5 million in 1994 and organized a five-person task force toward the development of gender-neutral or girl-oriented games such as Crystal's Pony Tale and Baby Boom. Critics, however, point out that of the few "girl games" produced by develop-ers so far, such as one based on Barbie doll characters, most neither relate to girls' real interests nor offer positive role models.

"Barbie goes to the mall to get ready for a dream date and she

gets pelted with tennis balls—a very popular antic with males,"
cracked Renee Courington, director of product marketing for Sanctu-
ary Woods, a game developer with a more highbrow and high-minded
strategy than most.[11]

It is unlikely, of course, that girls will ever flock in large numbers
to shoot-'em-up or crash-and-burn games. After all, evolution seems
not to have placed a high priority on females developing combat-
and dominance-seeking skills as the chief means of propagating
their genes. But it is possible to imagine the growth of a game market
built around girls' social interests, sports, and competitions that depend less upon violent conquests as a motivator.

As for adult gaming habits, these seem not to be easily transferable to the video game realm (although undoubtedly there is *some*
money to be made here). Indeed, the most popular noncasino adult
games—cards, chess, Trivial Pursuit, Pictionary, etc.—depend upon
social interactions during game play, not motor reflex skills, for en-
joyment.

It is precisely this universal human desire to *share* the fun of game
play, however, that may offer the most exciting opportunity for large-
scale revenue growth in the video game market. This, at least, is the
belief of Catapult Entertainment, a California start-up company that
has created technology that allows Sega or Nintendo game owners in
separate locations to play competitively *against each other* rather
than simply against their machines.

"We believe the missing 'killer application' for the entertainment
software world is not better graphics [or] processing power . . . but
real-time, low-cost connectivity," says Catapult's president and
CEO, Adam Grosser. Catapult's modem—cheap and widely available in such outlets as Kay Bee Toy Stores and Kmart, incidentally,
and advertised on TV shows like *The Simpsons*—connects game
players via ordinary phone lines to its XBAND network, and then
matches players of similar skill levels against each other, handling
all the processing and real-time transmission of back-and-forth game
play in the background.

As Grosser notes, "Until now, the vast majority of video games . . .
have been played against the game machine, not other people. As a
result, interest in a particular game title tends to wane quickly."
In fact, consumer research conducted by Blockbuster Entertainment
found that frequent game players cited "the lack of a comparably

skilled person to play" as the number-one reason for dissatisfaction with the existing video game world.[12]

Other companies are also rushing into the "networked gaming" field. AT&T's Imagination Network, Microsoft's PlayerNet, and GTE's game-networking alliance with Nintendo all will attempt to exploit this burgeoning opportunity.

That there may very well be a significant business opportunity in shared interactive game play conducted over communication networks is strongly, albeit indirectly, supported by the explosive growth of the Internet and various online services (see Chapter 4). Simply put, people want to connect. Indeed, if there is a single driving urge underlying all the excitement over the coming Information Highway, it is this desire for greater connectedness—for the ability to reach out, anytime and anywhere, and communicate with others or find whatever product, service, or information you need.

Ironically, the magnet of connectivity propelling the growth of interactive media may ultimately limit the growth of the newly born CD-ROM industry. CD-ROMs, after all, are simply a distribution medium for content. By the end of the decade, the question may be, Why purchase a fixed and rigid piece of plastic—a CD-ROM encyclopedia, for instance—when you can access a frequently updated online encyclopedia over your network much more cheaply?

This is not to suggest that all those shiny CD-ROM discs in video, book, and computer stores will one day be used as coasters, or that the hundreds of CD-ROM businesses just now coming into their own are about to go the way of the blacksmith. It's simply that in a world where networks will soon be able to transmit libraries of text, sound, and image quickly and inexpensively upon request, publishers of CD-ROMs, as well as books and periodicals, will increasingly move their most appropriate titles into the online world.

To survive long enough to be around for the transition, however, the CD-ROM industry must first confront some major potholes lying in its path toward Info Highway riches.

On the one hand, sales figures show that CD-ROMs are, indeed, becoming a mass-market business. Although surveys vary widely, the best estimates show CD-ROM hardware and software sales skyrocketing. At the end of 1994, the number of CD-ROM players sold more than doubled from 1993 to between 12 and 16 million, depending on whose data one wishes to believe.[13] While statistics are even more slippery concerning CD-ROM software—two dueling research firms estimated 1994 consumer CD-ROM software sales in the U.S. variously at either $202 million or $648 million—there is no doubt that growth in the CD-ROM market has been astonishing.[14] Indeed, according to the market research firm Dataquest, total shipments of CD-ROM titles surged to nearly 54 million worldwide in 1994, up from less than 17 million the year before.[15]

But when one looks beneath the rosy statistics—the phenomenal sales numbers, the frenetic Wall Street new media investment binge, and the launch of some four thousand CD-ROM businesses over the last two years—one sees deep signs of trouble in the industry. Indeed, a consumer backlash appears to be building that, in the words of one CD-ROM executive, could "close off our window of market opportunity."[16]

Consider the industry's so-called skyrocketing sales. The fact is, only 34 percent of all CD-ROMs "sold" are actually purchased by consumers at retail prices. Most are more or less given away—"bundled" in with CD-ROM–equipped PCs as a sales incentive.[17] And not only are most CD-ROM sales bundled, an unusually high percentage of those that are purchased retail end up being returned by dissatisfied customers. One highly regarded industry newsletter reported that in 1994 over 25 percent of CD-ROMs purchased were being returned, nearly double the 13 percent return rate in the recorded music business.[18] Some estimates have the 1995 return rate running at 50 percent. The problem has become serious enough for some distributors to boost the percentage of developer money they set aside to help offset returns.

Are CD-ROM publishers gearing up for a demand that, in terms of consumers' willingness to pay, is simply not there?

A Dataquest survey found that 54 percent of consumers sampled had no intention of buying CD-ROMs beyond those that came bundled free with their multimedia PCs. Yet another survey found that 40 percent of CD-ROM owners said they had quit using their devices.[19]

What's going on here? Part of the problem is that it is nearly impossible for most people to get their computers to play all their CD-ROM titles, many of which require users to reconfigure the computer's IRQs, DMA channels, sound, and video card settings to work.

If you aren't sure what an IRQ or DMA channel is, much less how to reconfigure them, then you probably understand the problem here.

1994 Christmas sales of Walt Disney's eagerly awaited *Lion King* CD-ROM were followed by a near revolt of disc owners unable to get it to work on their computers. "The software is full of bugs and will not install on people's machines without some sort of sound fix from Disney," wrote one angry user on the Prodigy online service. Similar messages were posted by nearly one thousand people on America Online and on the Internet newsgroup REC.ARTS.DISNEY. Pleading for patience, harried Disney spokeswoman Amy Malsin said, "We've been able to pretty much guarantee satisfaction for any customer who makes it through to our phone line."[20]

Not exactly reassuring, is she—especially given the fact that 85 percent of calls to customer support lines these days get a busy signal. As one industry newsletter asked: "How are consumers who are used to true plug-and-play consumer electronics—a CD audio disc plays in any audio CD player and a videocassette in any VCR—supposed to make an informed purchase amidst this chaos?"[21]

Microsoft's new Windows 95 operating system is supposed to improve the plug-and-play capabilities of CD-ROMs. But there's another, more worrisome, source of consumer dissatisfaction: most CD-ROMs, to be frank, are painfully boring. Their plots are weak, their characters not compelling, and their visual production values are generally poor compared to television and filmed entertainment.

"The problem with most [CD-ROMs] is that they still work better as traditional books," insists Robert Gelman, a multimedia developer and consultant. "I may be in sparsely populated territory here, but I want [CD-ROMs] that inspire me to create, that give me new insights, that open doors which traditional media never could."[22]

Notes Lee Isgur of Jeffries & Company: "I would say people are not satisfied with over 50 percent of the CD software that they get. At the moment, the overall quality is fairly low. A lot of it is boring."[23] Adds Mark Stahlman of New Media Associates, a consulting firm: "Many [CD-ROMs] are hard-pressed to deliver even a minute's worth of interesting information or entertainment."[24]

And this, even more than the difficulty people have using CD-ROMs, is the Achilles' heel of the industry. Indeed, we believe that the fundamental limiting factor in the CD-ROM industry's efforts to build a mass-market business is the lack of genuinely satisfying content. Consumers do not want technology, nor do they want interactivity per se. They want an immersive, emotionally compelling (or truly informative) *experience*.

This point was echoed by Microsoft executive Linda Stone during her talk at the 1995 Technology, Entertainment and Design (TED) Conference in California. "The difference between CD-ROMs today and good storytelling is the difference between Similac and mother's milk," said Stone. "Right now, people are relying on focus groups to develop CD-ROMs. But you can't do art and experience that way."

The need for better-quality content helps explain the shift in the industry's center of gravity from Silicon Valley—where microprocessors and 3-D graphics algorithms are the subjects of lunch conversation—to Hollywood, where the three secrets of a successful movie have always come down to "story, story, and story." There, despite all the shallowness of a get-rich-quick industry, filmmakers still somehow manage to take our deepest human urges—expressed in archetypal myths and noble legends and everyday dreams of boy-meets-girl—and magically embody them in stories and characters that capture our imaginations.

Say what you will about Hollywood—and there's plenty of negative things to say—but it is still true, as the Academy Award–winning co-writer of *Witness*, Bill Kelly, once said, that "this town still knows how to make a movie with real heart."

Heart, of course, is not the only thing Hollywood can offer the CD-ROM business. There's also the matter of money. Current financial models in the industry make it extremely difficult for developers and publishers to make any money in the business. The cost to produce a CD-ROM title now runs between $500,000 and $1 million or more—a big reach for an industry in which only a few developers make over $1 million in annual revenues. Indeed, Gistics, Inc., a consulting firm, found that 96 percent of the 912 CD-ROM software developers it surveyed in 1994 were unprofitable.[25]

Let's break the financial model down, using an actual budget from a well-known CD-ROM developer. As is typical, this developer has an "affiliate-label" deal under which a major distributor uses its sales force to push the product into stores. The CD-ROM's retail price was $49.95, less a 55 percent discount to the retailer, netting a wholesale price of $22.47. From this, the developer deducts 22 percent for the distributor and then a cost of goods (manufacturing, packaging, and documentation) of $4 per disk. Thus for every title sold the developer receives only $13.53.

Hence, *just to break even* on a rather modest development budget of $500,000, this developer has to sell 36,955 copies of the disk. The break-even number, of course, still doesn't cover the cost of marketing (about $250,000), let alone salaries, overhead, shipping, returns, etc. And don't forget, the life cycle of the product is only one year at best. And we're not even talking about profit yet!

Only a very, very few CD-ROM titles will sell anywhere near that number of copies. Of the 2,057 CD-ROM titles tracked by market research firm PC Data, Inc., in fact, 20 percent sold less than 10 copies. Given that stores usually stock less than 500 CD-ROMs, one can only guess at the fate of the thousands of other titles that can't get shelf space.

So what effect will this squeeze have on an industry so dispersed among small start-ups that even the king of the hill, Microsoft, commands only 15 percent market share? "The year of the shakeout" is coming, says the president of one CD-ROM publishing company.[26]

And it's not only the independent developers who are being hurt. Even an established company like Comptons New Media had to lay off 30 percent of its workforce and cut the number of titles it sells by more than 80 percent in early 1995. Apple Computer quit the business entirely.

Financial pressures, no less than the need for higher-caliber creative talent, is inexorably pushing the CD-ROM business into Hollywood's orbit. This convergence was highlighted most dramatically in March 1995 by the formation of Dreamworks Interactive, a $30 million joint venture between CD-ROM market leader Microsoft and Dreamworks SKG, the new Hollywood studio formed by Steven Spielberg, Jeffrey Katzenberg, and David Geffen. The deal created "a marketing powerhouse," noted one reporter. "Consider the strength and size of Microsoft, the world's largest software company, and the prowess of Katzenberg, who [while at the Walt Disney company] turned the 1992 movie *Aladdin* into a launch pad for everything from pencils to pajamas to dolls to books."[27]

Other film studios such as Paramount, Sony, Fox, and Turner are also venturing into the CD-ROM field. By tapping into Hollywood's financial and talent resources—not to mention its sophisticated marketing and distribution muscle—CD-ROM developers hope to survive the looming shakeout and sell into mass-market channels. This is especially true of the game and "edutainment" developers, whereas publishers of how-to or reference CD-ROMs and of titles serving the information needs of businesses are obviously less in need of Hollywood's creative coattails.

An interesting crosscurrent to the Hollywood-ization of the CD-ROM industry, however, is suggested by Rick Smolan, a photojournalist and CD-ROM publisher whose *From Alice to Ocean* and *Passage to Vietnam* are popular and highly innovative CD-ROM titles. "The CD-ROM world is very interesting right now because nobody knows how to do it," he says. "The playing field is leveled by creativity, not money. Time Warner, with all their millions, has not been able to come up with anything that's terribly compelling, but Robin and Rand Miller, working out of a basement in Spokane, invented *Myst*, which is a big hit."[28]

Indeed, Time Warner's interactive media group lost $30 million in 1994 and failed to produce a single hit title. Viacom's New Media division lost $7 million in 1994. And Sony's multimedia operation is reorganizing and reevaluating its strategy after suffering major losses as well.

Not even Hollywood, it seems, can fully vaccinate the multimedia industry from the squeeze it now faces. A year from now there will be a lot fewer—and a lot bigger—companies dividing up the CD-ROM market. And the market itself will increasingly cleave into a few profitable consumer segments—children's education, games, and reference. Business-to-business CD-ROM applications will continue to grow as well, mainly in such areas as directories and parts catalogues.

Big questions, however, hang over the long-term direction of the CD-ROM medium. Right now, "CD-ROMs are training wheels," notes photojournalist Smolan. "They're an interim stage."

But even so, says developer Robert Gelman, "CD-ROMs fulfill a valid need for the industry today." Besides helping to sell the current generation of computer hardware and software, he suggests that of far greater importance is the fact that they also help "presell the consuming public on the concept of TV you can interact with."[29]

▪ 8 ▪

Smart TV, or a PC
in Drag?

Not long ago, a San Francisco newspaper used a half-page composite photo to illustrate an article about the rapid growth of personal computer sales to the home.[1] It showed a 1950s-era family gathered happily in the living room around what was then the new family entertainment appliance, the television.

Closer inspection, however, revealed that something was wrong with this picture. The editors had replaced the boxy TV of the period with a giant computer screen, in front of which sat an enormous five-foot-long keyboard. The point, of course, was to humorously suggest that personal computers might soon become the primary home entertainment appliance.

But will they? Do the surge of home PC sales and the burgeoning use of online networks and multimedia CD-ROMs suggest that computers are about to supplant the ubiquitous (and much maligned) television as the centerpiece of family fun and conversation in America's living rooms?

If true, this would obviously signal an unprecedented transformation in American social life. Couch potatoes would become an endangered species, reduced to gathering in small hobbyist circles and bemoaning the loss of their once proud status as the butt of late-night talk show jokes. We would all become more informed, more

194

productive, less prone to overeating—and, of course, much better typists (thanks to the keyboard). Soon we would be renowned the world over not as a nation of beer-guzzling, football-watching Biffs, but as a morally superior, knowledge-loving culture of interesting and very slender people. Even the French would have to stop turning their noses up at us. And best of all, we would no longer have to suffer the sight of those smug Kill Your Television bumper stickers on the cars of self-righteous snits who try to imply that they read a lot more books (and a lot more uplifting ones at that) than we do.

There are many virtues to this notion that computers are about to replace the TV as America's principal living-room window on the world. Unfortunately, as we shall see, a realistic chance of this happening anytime in the foreseeable future is not one of them.

The debate over PC versus TV does, however, offer an intriguing vantage point from which to view the many challenges confronting the computer industry today. As metaphor, it gets to the heart of the technological change process: do new media replace old or merely infuse them with new possibilities, expanded capabilities? And as a practical matter, it helps to illuminate the divergent strategies being pursued by PC companies today—including Microsoft, the industry's most powerful company—in their pursuit of new, high-growth markets.

More than any other business, the personal computer industry has come to symbolize the great ideals of Yankee ingenuity, entrepreneurial capitalism, and economic progress. In less than 20 years, it has grown from a small collection of garage hobbyists into one of the greatest wealth-creating forces in modern history. Its economic impact goes far beyond the nearly $116 billion in revenues expected from PC hardware and software sales in 1995. It has also been the proximate cause of profound changes in the structure and internal life of American business and in the basic building blocks of commercial activity itself, from sales and marketing to manufacturing and distribution.

How ironic, then, that even as the computer's digital vocabulary of ones and zeros becomes the lingua franca of the whole economy, the PC business finds itself facing a very difficult challenge. On the one hand, growth in the PC industry's core desktop office computing market is slowing and its profit margins shrinking. Yet on the other, few if any PC companies have any experience navigating the consumer markets where the highest growth is expected in the future.

This is not to say that there are no growth areas left in traditional PC markets. The enterprise computing sector—communications networks for businesses, media servers and databases to circulate information through these networks, and "groupware" to help employees collaboratively use that information—is experiencing rapid growth as rigid corporate hierarchies flatten into decentralized work teams. But the maturation and commoditization of the core computer business of stand-alone PCs and word processing/spreadsheet software has closed the once wide-open window of high-growth opportunity enjoyed by the computer firms during the 1980s.

Whither, then, the computer industry?

"The next ten years in computing are going to be driven by automating the consumer experience," explains Bruce Lupatkin, a financial analyst at Hambrecht & Quist, a San Francisco–based investment firm. Charles Ferguson, a consultant based in Cambridge, Massachusetts, adds: "The conventional computer industry is going to be the funky, behind-the-times part of the [technology] business."[2]

Jim Clark is the founder and former chairman of Silicon Graphics (SGI), one of the fastest-growing computer companies in America. In early 1994, believing that the only real future for computing lay in the consumer market, Clark resigned from SGI in a dispute with the company's CEO, Ed McCracken. Since then, McCracken has changed his views and is also now pushing SGI toward consumer markets. But today, while both men view the consumer market as the Zion of the industry's future, what this actually means—in terms of what products to build and which corporate strategy to pursue—is radically different for each man.

During an interview shortly before his resignation, Jim Clark outlined what his differences with McCracken were at that time. "The interactive TV market is where Silicon Valley should be headed," Clark argued. "But Ed and the management felt the interactive TV business was frivolous. His attitude was, 'We don't make televisions. We make technical computers. We're the fastest-growing company in that market, so why do we need the consumer market?'

"What he didn't see," Clark added, "is that there are tremendous synergies from being part of a volume market. If your computers are used in consumer products, it becomes a standard—which then helps sell more of your computers. It takes volume to set standards. But there's this tendency to say, 'Hey, we've got a perfectly good little market in front of us and we make a fat profit from it. Why rock the boat?'

"Now to me, that's shortsighted," he went on. "Apple could have had 30 or 40 percent of the PC market instead of 10 percent. But they chose to take those high, fat profit margins just like SGI does now. And in the end they drove the company into the ground by letting Microsoft beat them on volume. As Apple found out, profits have a way of disappearing when the other guy sets the standard."

In Clark's view, the problem with most computer companies is that "their managements only see existing markets. They ask you, 'What is the size of this new market you propose?' And if it doesn't exist yet, they say, 'I'm not going to go for a zero-size market!' The irony is, the consumer technology market, which is only beginning to emerge, is the only hope for our industry. Anyone in this business who doesn't see that is dead in the multimedia water, so to speak. It's that simple."

For Clark, the mathematics of the emerging market for interactive TV seemed compelling. "Why battle it out over a market that's relatively small?" he insisted. "I mean, SGI probably sold tens of thousands of units last year. For PC companies, maybe it was tens of millions of units. But if you get your technology into consumer products . . . well, Nintendo and Sega and other video game companies have sold something like a quarter of a *billion* game cartridges. And with interactive TV, we're talking about maybe 100 million set-top boxes just in the U.S. So that's why I pushed those deals with Time Warner and with Nintendo, to get us into interactive TV and video games."

Ultimately, he contended, "All the trends show that computers and consumer electronics are going to be shared technologies. This whole digital convergence thing is really about finally being able to bake computer technology into consumer products used by millions of people."

It is perhaps characteristic of the times that less than six months later, Clark was labeling interactive TV dead on arrival—a totally impractical conduit for the Information Highway. He had found a new Zion for his mass-market dreams: the Internet, that vast anarchic network of computer networks used by millions worldwide. So he launched a new venture to develop navigational software, much needed owing to the Internet's byzantine complexity. And he made a bold prediction: "By mid-1995," he declared, "there will be more Internet users than cable TV subscribers."

We now know, of course, that Jim Clark was wrong. Today the Internet is used by perhaps 30 million people—though experts sharply disagree on the exact number—of which no more than 3.5 to 5 million are mainstream consumers as opposed to academics or technical professionals. Cable TV viewers, meanwhile, number about 150 million in 63 million subscribing homes. But whatever the numbers, there is no disputing the fact that usage of the Internet and commercial online services has exploded in recent years. This, of course, strongly supports Clark's belief that the Internet is truly becoming a mass medium. But it is quite a leap from there, as we shall see, to the notion that the PC is about to supplant the TV as America's principal media device.

Those same six months, meanwhile, had also witnessed the near-religious conversion of Ed McCracken from naysayer to evangelist for interactive TV and the consumer market. Under McCracken, SGI has leveraged its unrivaled leadership in 3-D graphics into a $1.5 billion company. Its "visual computing" technology is highly valued not only in technical and scientific work—everything from designing cars at Ford to crunching them between the realistic-looking jaws of a T. Rex in Steven Spielberg's *Jurassic Park*—but also in the interactive TV and video game markets as well.

Clark claims credit for SGI's 1993 agreements with Time Warner to provide video servers and TV set-tops for its Orlando video trials, as well as with Nintendo to provide SGI graphics chips for the game giant's new Ultra64 machine (which could earn SGI $300 million in royalties by 1998). But it was McCracken, after Clark's departure, who orchestrated the company's high-profile pacts with AT&T to help sell SGI video servers, with Nippon Telegraph and Telephone to employ SGI servers in interactive TV trials in Japan, and with Sony, which is using SGI graphics chips in its first-ever video game machine. And today it is McCracken who is pushing SGI toward a future in which he sees the majority of Americans using their living-room TVs—the most ubiquitous, simplest-to-operate appliance (next to the phone) in the home—as their principal vehicles for cruising the Information Highway.

As McCracken points out, until recently the computer industry was driven by the demands of the business market. "If I were to pick out the top four or five projects that stimulate the technology directions for our company, now they're almost all entertainment. The real battleground is consumer electronics. It's the video game. It's the set-top boxes. It's the digital televisions."[3]

So here we have two men who, by all accounts, hate each other's guts and who have marched off, like duelists, in completely opposite directions to find their mass-market utopia. Their conflict reflects two sharply divergent visions of how the PC industry must reinvent itself to compete in the digital new world order.

While visionaries duel, hurling hype and hyperbole at each other to bolster their own vested interests, the voices of reason lie more in the intelligent middle. To many in the industry, in fact, the whole PC versus TV debate is silly. Larry Ellison, CEO of $2 billion database software giant Oracle, put it this way: "That's like trying to figure out what's going to be more successful, the stove or the refrigerator. PCs, personal communicators, smart televisions—[all] will be attached to the Information Highway."[4]

True enough. Just as they do today, people in the future will continue to use a multiplicity of devices to communicate, entertain themselves, and get their work done. In one sense, therefore, Ellison is absolutely right to call the PC versus TV debate "bizarre and ridiculous."

But if it's such a nonissue, why won't the PC versus TV debate go away? Why does it keep resurfacing in the boardrooms and product labs of America's biggest computer firms? The reason is, when it comes time to bet your company on the pursuit of one particular business strategy—and on the decision to build a specific set of products for a specific market—hard choices must be made.

Jim Clark and Ed McCracken have already made theirs. And so, apparently, has Larry Ellison, whose "agnosticism" regarding the PC versus TV debate has led his company to wage competitive war on two fronts: to become the preeminent supplier of media servers and set-top software for interactive TV networks on the one hand, and a major vendor of PC-based software for managing data and video news over the Internet on the other. Hence, Ellison is attempting to mine the riches of PC-based applications today, while also preparing for the day when TV-based interactive services begin to be rolled out tomorrow. Despite his two-pronged approach, Ellison leaves little doubt as to where he thinks the greatest mass-market revenues from interactivity will ultimately be found. "The Internet is very low-speed," he points out. "So the idea that the Internet will ever be the primary multimedia hookup into the home is sheer nonsense."[5]

If Larry Ellison is betting, at least over the long term, that television does have a mass-market future, then Andy Grove, CEO of $10 billion Intel Corporation, the world's largest computer-chip maker, has lined up squarely on the side of those who think television is dead. "The PC is it," declares Grove. "That sums up Intel's business plan and rallying cry."[6]

"Some think the information superhighway will come through their TV," Grove proclaimed in an ad plugging his keynote speech at the PC Expo convention in 1994. "[But] the information tool of the future is on your desk. Not in your living room."[7] Grove apparently missed the irony of his free offer of a videotape of his speech—online services carried only a summary of it—which could only be viewed, of course, on a TV set. Despite that oversight, Andy Grove continues to boast that the personal computer is going to "eat" the TV, which he calls a mere "toy."

It's worth recalling that similar hubris was displayed by IBM in the late 1970s when Andy Grove and his then tiny Intel Corp. dared to suggest that the newfangled personal computer—also scorned as a mere "toy"—would soon become the principal productivity tool for business.

Be that as it may, under the hard-charging leadership of 59-year-old émigré chip monk Grove, otherwise known as "the Mad Hungarian," Intel is investing an astonishing one-third of its total revenues on developing new products to make the PC dominant in the consumer market. That's a rather weighty vote in the PC's favor because Intel is the most profitable company of its size in the world. And its size is doubling every two years.

According to one glowing business magazine profile on Intel, the company intends to "take over your home even more completely than it has already conquered your office."[8] How exactly does it intend to do this? The magazine featured four new "Smart TV" products from

Intel that will supposedly let consumers "shop for shoes, watch the news, rent a movie, or buy a CD" from their homes.

But wait a minute . . . once again, there seems to be something wrong with the picture—or more precisely, with all four photos the magazine used to illustrate "Desktop TV." Each depicted a computer and keyboard, and in a little corner of the PC's monitor, a two-inch-square video image. One showed a Cable News Network shot of Secretary of State Warren Christopher above the caption "Watch the News!"

One wonders, Why go to all that trouble just to cram the TV news into a tiny box on our PC screens? We've already got TVs! Sure, there's a growing market in offices for PCs that can archive and display television news. But if Andy Grove really wants to offer the mass of consumers digital interactive TV at home, where most people would watch it, why not just toss the keyboard, crack open the computer, pry out the chips, and hook these up to the TVs people already have, as Oracle and Silicon Graphics are doing?

What's being offered to consumers here is not "Smart TV" but a PC in drag. As computer industry leader Michael Dell notes, "Yes, you could make a PC that also [receives] TV, but at those prices why would you want to?"[9] Good point. If this is really how Andy Grove intends to "eat" the TV, he's probably going to develop a major case of indigestion.

It's not hard to imagine one of Grove's motivations for endorsing the PC as Info Highway vehicle of choice. Intel's enormous capital investment and line-of-business expertise is a compelling enough reason to try to push his PCs into the consumer marketplace. But as Intel's 1994 Pentium chip fiasco showed, doing business in the consumer market requires technology companies to fundamentally restructure their old ways of doing business. Can anyone imagine Nabisco even attempting to sell vitamin-fortified cereal lacking some of its promised vitamins—and then, once the truth was revealed, requiring customers to prove that they would personally suffer demonstrable harm from the lack of said vitamins before any refund is granted? This is what Intel did after the Pentium problem first surfaced.

Computer industry analyst Richard A. Shaffer points out the very different character of the computer and consumer media industries, the latter of which includes television:[10]

The computer industry sells productivity.	The media business sells information/entertainment.
In the computer industry, revenues come from sales. Somebody buys a Mac or a PC and that's it.	In the media business, revenue has more the character of an annuity stream.
The computer industry depends on business-to-business sales.	Most media revenue comes directly from consumers.
Computers follow a manufacturing business model.	The media tend to look more like a distribution business.

As Shaffer sums it up: "Interactive media is not a tool like a word processor. Those who buy it want an experience. It's more Broadway show than spreadsheet."

The differences between the two industries are not simply cultural. They reflect fundamentally different commercial dynamics. This fact is often ignored, however, by TV's naysayers, including the author George Gilder, who once again jumps into the debate on the future of technology with both feet planted firmly in the sky. Combining utopian economics with statistical sleight-of-hand to promote his views, Gilder argues that the PC is the only viable interactive device in the home and that any thought of TV playing a role in the Info Highway is bunk.

"The computer industry is converging with the television industry in the same sense that the automobile converged with the horse," wrote Gilder in one influential business magazine. "Making the boob tube into an interactive hive of theater, museum, classroom, banking system, shopping center, post office, and communicator is contrary to the nature of the box." Indeed, said Gilder, multimedia PCs are going to "usurp phones, televisions, and video game players entirely."[11] To back up his view, Gilder attempted to prove, first of all, that PCs are fast becoming the gadget of choice among consumers, and second, that the most powerful leaders of the computer business agree with him that the TV is dead as a platform for building the interactive future.

As to his first claim, Gilder asserted that the PC business is already outstripping the film and TV business in revenues—as if this has much to do with the relative popularity of PCs and TVs among the public. Even so, his claim is unsupported by the facts. Gilder asserted that 1992 computer sales totaled $161 billion against $104

billion for film and TV entertainment. He neglected to mention, however, that only $66 billion of that figure represented sales of PC
hardware and software. (1995 sales are expected to reach $93 bil-
lion.) The rest reflected sales of mainframe computers and related
corporate computer services that have nothing to do with PCs or
consumers.[12] Even with soaring PC sales, it is important to note that
well over half of all PC hardware sales and over two-thirds of software sales are derived from the office and home-office business markets, not the home consumer market.

On the other side of the equation, meanwhile, when the $6 billion
in *TV-based* video game sales that Gilder so neatly squirreled into
his "computer" figures is put back in its proper category, the film
and TV market actually totals $110 billion. Furthermore, film and
television entertainment are only the core of a much larger $232
billion media business—and a $341 billion entertainment in-
dustry.[13]

To be sure, dollar sales of home computers have now equaled
those for color televisions. While this sales growth excites PC enthusiasts who see the TV being toppled as the primary home entertainment device, it's important to note that far more TVs are still being
sold than computers—*they just cost a lot less.* In fact, 25.4 million
color TVs were sold in the U.S. in 1994, at an average price of $293,
compared to 6.7 million home PCs priced at $1,200 each.[14]

Perhaps recognizing that comparative measures of PC and TV industry revenues are hardly the best gauge of consumer usage of each
device, Gilder tackles actual home penetration rates—but with a
twist. First he cites industry studies showing PCs present in over 30
percent of American homes. Of course, this figure does not tell us
that only 9 percent of households had *multimedia* computers—the
kind obviously needed for the interactivity Gilder talks about.[15] But
in any event, instead of comparing the PC home penetration rate to
that of the TV, Gilder employs sleight-of-hand and poses the question: "How long will it take before [interactive TVs] are in 30 percent
of American homes?"[16]

Actually, as Gilder is well aware, 63 percent of U.S. homes already receive cable TV service. True, those TVs must be outfitted
with new digital set-top decoders—and the networks that link them
must be upgraded with fiber-optic and digital switches—before they
can receive interactive programming. But the same is true for today's

computers, the vast majority of which do not have the capacity to process data at video speeds (let alone meet FCC requirements for closed captioning and the like). Likewise, today's slow-speed, low-bandwidth PC networks such as the Internet need upgrading before they can offer high-quality interactive multimedia and video service. Indeed, a San Diego user inadvertently shut down most international access to the Internet not long ago when he broadcast an audiovisual test pattern over the network. According to one estimate, it would in theory take only 50 to 100 full-motion video signals to swamp the entire information-carrying capacity of the Internet.[17]

The truth of the matter is, *neither TVs nor PCs* are presently equipped to receive interactive multimedia transmitted over networks. As for the comparative cost of upgrading each device—a critical factor in consumer acceptance—even with all the uncertainty over the future prices of TV set-tops and video-capable computers, for many years to come it is going to be *significantly cheaper* to install an interactive set-top box atop a TV than it will be to buy a multimedia computer with a 27-inch television-ready screen, which is the average size preferred by consumers.

There's yet another issue that Gilder sidesteps, and it's one that historians and businesspeople alike recognize as critical in shaping the manner and speed with which new technologies are adopted by consumers: ease of use. A key reason for the prevalence of TVs and VCRs in American homes is that their form and function are so easily understandable. (Granted, many people do have problems *programming* a VCR, but even a complete idiot can figure out how to stick a rented movie in the VCR and punch the play button.) PCs, in contrast, can be a nightmare for the average consumer. "This is the only business in the world in which people take home a product and [can't use it] one-third of the time," concedes Richard Thoman of IBM.[18]

With about a third of PCs sold now going into the home, PC vendors are coming to realize just how difficult they truly are for most people to use. How do they know? Simple. Microsoft reportedly receives about 750,000 calls for help from frustrated consumers every month. Dell gets close to 500,000 calls monthly. IBM answers 200,000 calls and third-party support lines field another 100,000 calls every month. To this one must also add perhaps another

500,000 calls each month to all the many thousands of smaller-sized PC hardware and software vendors in America.[19]

Even these staggering numbers, however, don't begin to reflect the true extent of consumer difficulty with PCs. As studies conducted by market researcher Robert Johnson at Dataquest reveal, only one in seven customer support calls at midday even get through to a technical support operator. About 85 percent reach a busy signal. We may be talking here about half a million cries for computer help each day!

In assessing which device—the PC or TV—is most likely to be used by the majority of Americans to drive the Info Highway, perhaps it would be useful to look at the question from the notoriously practical point of view of the average consumer: Which would you rather have go on the blink—your PC's CD-ROM or your TV's VCR?

Here's what the instructions for Microsoft's PC-based Encarta encyclopedia say about dealing with a CD-ROM that won't play (grammar and spelling are Microsoft's):

> Make sure that the Encarta program is looking for the compact disc on the correct drive. Check that ENCARTA.INI file in the WINDOWS directory. The section called [94Options] should have an entry called "BookPath". The path should be set to the \encyc95\ directory on the drive that your CD-ROM appears as. For example, if your CD-ROM drive is drive D:, the entry would appear like the following:

> > [94Options]
> > BookPath = D:\encyc94\

Now, compare the above with a Sharp VCR manual's instructions for handling a videotape that won't play:

> Make sure the power cord is plugged in.

People who are enthralled with the wonders of computers often forget that most other folks don't necessarily feel the same way. As SGI's Ed McCracken notes, "Obviously, everyone's PC and workstation is going to be connected to the [Information Highway]. So that takes care of the 10 to 20 percent of the population who have PCs and workstations. Now, how are we going to deal with the other 80 percent?"

Precisely. Any clear-headed analysis of the factors shaping the adoption of new technologies, from cost and ease of use to installed base among consumers, suggests that while PC use is certainly growing rapidly in the home, it is not about to kill off the television anytime soon. In fact, the TV—or a device that more closely resembles a living-room TV than a desktop computer—will probably be the chief interactive window on the world for most Americans.

TV itself, of course, will be transformed and will incorporate many of the attributes of computers and other interactive communications devices. At the same time, PCs will become easier to use and will increasingly take on entertainment as well as information capabilities.

But for many years to come, there will still be significant differences in the form, function, and principal uses to which TVs and PCs are put. The far greater usability and approchability of television suggests that the Information Highway will, at least in its earliest decades and along its most heavily populated byways, be built around the extended metaphor of the living room TV set.

Interactive TV networks, however, are still several years away from practical mass deployment, which means that *for the present* the only truly viable commercial business in interactive services still lies with the PC. This is why cable giant Tele-Communications, Inc. has invested $125 million in Microsoft's new online service, the Microsoft Network, and why TCI and others are developing cable modems that enable PC users to receive high-speed, high-bandwidth video and other multimedia services over the Internet.

But when interactive TV finally becomes practical—and it probably will by the end of this decade—the "80 percent" of us that McCracken speaks about will constitute a market and a constituency for digital-age products and services that will dwarf those for the PC. To be sure, the most information-rich and ennobling of interactive services will doubtless gravitate toward the world of the PC, as will the bulk of today's affluent and technology-conversant social classes. But for some years to come the vast middle of America will only gain access to the wonders of the Information Highway through tools that have the familiarity and ease of use of television.

In other words, for good or ill, in the real world television is still the medium of the masses. This is what interactive TV naysayers like George Gilder obfuscate with all their utopian forecasts and statistical tricks.

As the futurist Paul Saffo observed: "The problem with advocates like Gilder is that they use facts the way a drunk uses a lamppost—for support rather than illumination."

Which pretty much says it all—except, perhaps, for a final comment on yet another Gilderian sleight-of-hand. He claims that Microsoft chairman Bill Gates rejects the TV as an Info Highway access device. "Gates has fiercely focused Microsoft on the PC culture," says Gilder, adding that Gates has committed the company to "the CD-ROM market as an alternative to TV." Gilder then quotes from *New Yorker* writer John Seabrook's interview with Gates in which the software mogul notes that the Info Highway will offer services that more closely resemble the interactivity of the phone network than the one-way, passive reception of old-style television—"more like the Library of Congress," Gates said, "but with an easy way to find things." True enough, of course, but Gilder twists his meaning to imply that Gates is actually *opposed* to interactive TV itself when all he is really saying is that today's old-style TV will become tomorrow's two-way interactive TV.

"Gates doesn't even own a TV set," Gilder informs us (slyly neglecting to mention that a centerpiece of Gates's new $30 million mansion near Seattle is a battery of high-definition TV screens). The point, claims Gilder, is that the most powerful man in the computer business and the richest man in America is absolutely, positively "not interested" in interactive TV.[20]

Unfortunately, someone must have forgotten to inform Bill Gates of this fact, because the poor misguided fellow is constantly running around giving speeches, talking to reporters, and signing interactive TV mega-deals with the likes of cable TV giant TCI and set-top box maker General Instrument that strongly suggest just the opposite is true.

Indeed, in the three-month period following the publication of Gilder's comments in 1994, Bill Gates announced the following interactive TV deals: a contract with Compaq Computer to build video servers for interactive TV networks; a deal with the Japanese telecommunications giant NTT to cooperate on the testing and deployment of video servers and software for interactive TV networks; a pact with Rogers Cablesystems of Canada to license and deploy Microsoft software in Rogers's cable TV networks; and an agreement with TCI, the largest cable television company in the world, to deploy Microsoft's video servers and software in upcoming TCI tests of interactive TV service in Seattle and Denver.

By mid-1995, Gates had signed deals with 13 additional companies to either test or supply software and services for Microsoft's planned interactive television network, called Microsoft Interactive Television, or MITV. These included CUC International, ESPN, Time Warner, AT&T, Samsung, Bell Atlantic, Pacific Telesis, and even the U.S. Postal Service. Gates revealed also that Microsoft intended to recruit 100 companies by the end of 1995 for its interactive TV venture. On top of all that, he announced a strategic partnership with television broadcaster NBC.

Does this sound like a man who's "not interested" in interactive TV?

Gates has also been quite public about his interest in interactive TV. At the 1994 TED (Technology, Entertainment & Design) Conference in San Jose, he noted, "What I wanted to do in terms of showing some of the interactive TV work we're doing is to suggest some of its breadth. It's a system that won't be hard to use. I mean, people say it's hard to program a VCR. Okay, I suppose it is. So let's make [interactive TV] easier than that."

He went on to explain some of the features Microsoft will offer in interactive TV. "You'll be able to surf around and see all the shows that are interesting," he said. "We've got [TV navigators] where you can see all the different things that are on, where you can pick something related to a particular topic. Now sometimes you'll get to a show that'll have a special little logo on it . . . that interactive logo says that if you just push a button you can get more information. Another thing we've got is the [ability] to get [video] messages from people. So we really are starting to look at applications that are more driven by communication than just by passive viewing."

Gates also took an appropriately two-sided view of the PC versus TV debate at the conference. "People ask, 'Is it a PC or is it a TV?'" he observed. But, "today's TV [and] today's PC are completely inadequate." Instead, Gates envisioned a variety of Info Highway devices. "If you think of somebody's den," he explained, "that's a device more akin to the PC today. If you move to the living room . . . that's a device more akin to what the TV set is today."

More recently, in his keynote speech at the Comdex trade show in November of 1994, Gates screened a Microsoft video that outlined his vision of life in the year 2005. The high-quality video presented several vignettes—a teenager doing his homework online via computer, a cops-and-robbers caper involving smart wallets and video carphones—but time and again the video returned to a living-room scene involving an upper-middle-class mom using a remote control device to channel surf a huge, interactive, easy-to-navigate *TV set!*

(It is interesting to note that Gates did *not* distribute his presentation over the Internet. He did, however, produce a *videotaped* version of his keynote, which reportedly sold several hundred thousand copies.)

Although Microsoft obviously foresees a big business down the road in interactive television, it is wisely focusing the bulk of its consumer efforts today on PC products and services. 1995 will witness the debut of the company's new online service, the launch of an easy-to-use home computer interface called "Bob" that incorporates some of the same approaches developed by General Magic in their Magic Cap interface for personal communicators, and the rollout of some 100 consumer CD-ROM titles. But as company spokesman Mike Maples concedes, even a wildly successful business in PC-based consumer products and services would still not account for more than 10 percent of the company's overall revenues by 1997.[21]

For the truly significant revenue growth Microsoft needs to maintain its current phenomenal growth trajectory, it must look elsewhere. Until now, the bulk of company revenues has come from application software sales to the business market. Revenue growth in this core sector, however, has slowed from an historic 50 percent rate to 25 percent annually.[22] As industry analyst Denise Caruso notes: "Corporate computing isn't exactly a growth industry anymore, and Microsoft itself is responsible for driving down the prices of its cash cow—applications software—to maintain its market dominance. If the company doesn't move forward, it is only a matter of time before it begins to slide."[23]

This view was echoed by Microsoft's Steve Ballmer, vice president for sales and marketing. "We are really worried about saturation," Ballmer told analysts in 1994. "How many times do people have to buy a spreadsheet? Just once."

To be sure, Gates has high hopes that his Windows NT–based

networking software will strike it rich in the fast-growing enterprise computing market. And the Windows95 update of Microsoft's operating system will certainly generate billions in revenue over the next several years.

But ultimately, Bill Gates aims at a far, far bigger target. He wants Microsoft code to control the transactional guts of the entire Information Highway, managing the flow of traffic not only from PCs and TVs but also from new wireless communicators and any other kind of intelligent device. In short, Microsoft wants a cut of most everything sold or transmitted on the Info Highway: every minute spent online, every check paid via home banking, every item purchased from a home shopping network, every video-on-demand rented over interactive TV, and every business-to-business transaction carried out electronically. In Gates's vision, no bits should traverse the Info Highway without Microsoft taking a nice royalty byte out of it. Gates intends to transform his company from a $5 billion packaged-goods vendor into a $20 billion Info Highway "utility" that derives a guaranteed continuing revenue stream simply from the highway's daily use by millions of people.

"The Information Highway will generate a higher volume of transactions than anything has to date," says Gates, "and we're proposing that Windows be at the center, servicing all those transactions."[24]

Can he do it? Can his company, which already controls the software guts of 80 percent of the world's computers, now leverage that power into a far more lucrative dominion over the transactional heart of tomorrow's mass-market interactive products and services?

As analyst Caruso cautions, the PC-industry model that Microsoft is familiar with may not work so well in promising high-volume transaction-based technologies such as interactive TV or online services. "Unlike the PC business, where it has great influence over all the links of a relatively short chain, Microsoft has no inherent influence in the large and existing infrastructures it wants to penetrate (cable networks, telcos, and content providers)," Caruso notes. "But it *is* Microsoft. That's good news to those who feel the urge to connect with a sophisticated software provider, and bad news to those fearful of indentured servitude."[25]

Microsoft's commanding position in PC software unquestionably gives it a huge competitive advantage. Apart from the "monopoly rents" Gates derives from his chokehold on operating systems, obeisance to his Windows standard also gives him the power to shape the direction of development at most of America's 30,000 software companies. These companies that have tried to escape Microsoft's orbit by creating new software applications for new markets have usually crashed and burned after Gates later saw the profit potential others had created and bullied his way to supremacy in them. Among the majors, only a few companies—Novell in networking, Oracle and Sybase in databases, and Lotus in workflow software—have managed to resist the Gates juggernaut. And they are under increasing assault from the Microsoft empire. To borrow an old axiom once said of IBM, no one has ever been fired for buying Microsoft.

Notice, however, that this *used* to be said about IBM. For it is a law of business (and of life, for that matter) that all success contains within it the seeds of future failure. Just as the huge size and weight that once gave the dinosaurs mastery of the earth eventually slowed their ability to adapt to changes in the environment, IBM itself is proof that even the most fearsome giants of the business jungle can end up in the tar pits of corporate history if they're not careful. Or as another famous axiom has it, the bigger they are, the harder they fall.

Indeed, there are some signs that the dark power of Redmond may have limits. Bill Gates's tentacles have so far been unable to get much of a chokehold on the fast-growing enterprise computing market, despite the aggressive pricing and marketing of his Johnny-come-lately (and apparently inferior) products in this sector. A new version of Windows due in 1996 could well be a serious contender for the enterprise market, however.

Likewise, the company faces challenges in pursuit of its stated goal of becoming the dominant power in CD-ROM publishing. "I don't think Microsoft will ever dominate the content business as thoroughly as [it does] the operating systems or word processing or spreadsheet businesses," noted Charles H. Finne, a multimedia analyst with the investment bankers Volpe, Welty & Company. As in the book or record business, a key to success in the content field lies in building partnerships with writers, artists, filmmakers, and other owners of content. But as Nick Arnett, president of the consulting firm Multimedia Computing Corp., pointed out: "Name a significant Microsoft partnership that has worked out for the partner."[26]

As for the media server and set-top software business for interactive TV, the successes of Oracle, SGI, Hewlett-Packard, and other competitors must be cause for concern to Gates. Oracle in particular has taken an early lead in the race to supply interactive TV command-and-control software. The battle between Gates and Oracle chief Larry Ellison, in fact, has always been about more than money. Ellison, a billionaire like Gates and just as maniacal a competitor, never loses an opportunity to taunt his opponent. Says Ellison acidly: "I don't object to Microsoft's monopoly, I object to Microsoft's mediocrity."

In his struggle for dominance in the interactive TV field, Gates may find himself in a bind because Microsoft's huge capital commitment (and nearly 100-million-unit installed base) for Windows creates a powerful disincentive against the company abandoning that architecture as it moves into the interactive TV business. His Tiger media server software, a networked Windows-like system that delivers streams of video and other content to TV set-top boxes, has received some favorable reviews, including from cable TV chief John Malone of TCI. But Gates's set-top box software and user interface were still in development as of early 1995. Especially in the user interface area, Microsoft's reputation for producing, in the words of *Fortune* magazine, "inelegant products that are frequently inferior to the competition and for bringing them to market way behind schedule" could spell trouble for the company.

It's one thing to sell buggy products to experienced computer users—sadly, they're used to it. But if Microsoft tries foisting anything resembling today's bewildering computer software upon tomorrow's interactive TV viewers—most of whom have never had the pleasure of coping with a Windows "General Protection Fault" error message—Mr. Bill could fall flat on his interface.

Recognizing this, perhaps, the company is reportedly hard at work on efforts to develop a new and truly easy-to-use interface for controlling the interactive TVs and other consumer supergadgets of the future. The only problem here is that Bill Gates, while a brilliant strategist and an awesome competitor, is a lousy innovator. From the original DOS operating system (bought for $50,000 from another company) to Windows itself (some say "inspired by," others say "copied from," Apple's Macintosh interface), Gates has built an empire upon other people's inventions. Microsoft, it turns out, has invented precious little on its own.

What's more, when Microsoft *has* invented software for consumer products, it has had more than a few failures. Remember MSX (short for Microsoft Extended Basic)? It was supposed to become *the* operating system standard for video game machines—or so Gates claimed when he announced it with much pomp and circumstance back in the mid-1980s. Suffice it to say that MSX has taken its place alongside turn-of-the-century airplanes with flapping wings—and will soon be joined by Gates's next-century brainstorm, a $9 billion network of 840 satellites providing wireless communications to penniless masses in Africa and Asia who presumably need to call their stockbrokers—as one of the truly great dumb ideas of our time. ("God save us, it's the stupidest damn thing I've ever heard of," said John Pike, the director of the Federation of American Scientists' Space Policy Project when he first heard of the Gates satellite plan, known as Teledesic.[27])

Microsoft, of course, could always try to team up with or even acquire a company that *can* build the right technology. It tried to do just that, in fact, with Ken Kaplan, president of Microware Systems Corporation, a small privately held software firm in Des Moines, Iowa. According to reports, Kaplan was the recipient of a rather unwelcome Gates buyout offer some time back. But Kaplan was unwilling to sell his interface software, called DAVID (Digital Audio Video Interactive Decoder), to the Goliath from Redmond. The result of their dealings was that "Bill Gates's picture earned a place of honor on Ken Kaplan's dartboard."[28]

Instead, by late 1994 Microware had taken a strong lead over Microsoft, licensing its DAVID operating software to 20 manufacturers of set-top boxes, including IBM, Philips, Zenith, Fujitsu, and Mitsubishi. Microware software is also slated for use in various Bell Atlantic, Cox Cable, Telecom Australia, and Hong Kong Telecom trials of interactive TV. Also significant was the partnership Microware forged last year with Macromedia, the PC industry's leading maker of multimedia authoring tools, to modify multimedia PC programs so they can be run on interactive TV networks.

Assessing Microsoft's performance to date in developing interactive TV software, Microware's Kaplan had this to say: "I just think Gates is too late."

What Kaplan forgets, however, is that Microsoft *loves* harvesting markets that others have seeded. And time and again, the company has shown it is fully capable of muscling its way into *any* business it chooses. With his immense capital and technology resources—and with his fingers locked in a death grip around the throat of the computer software industry—Bill Gates ventures out into the risky new territory of consumerland with a mighty arsenal.

But while Gates may point with pride to Microsoft's leadership in interactive media publishing, there's a world of difference between developing a specialty product for a few million CD-ROM users and creating entertainment and information products and services that can engage a hefty share of America's 250 million television viewers. Still, the company has consistently demonstrated an enviable capacity to adapt to, and eventually dominate, new markets.

To reassure critics, Gates insists he has no interest (for now) in acquiring part of a television network or film studio. But he has, as we all know, already launched a joint venture *with* such a studio— and probably the most powerful one at that (DreamWorks SKG). "We *do* want to provide software tools to help people make movies," Gates explained, "but you won't see us making movies ourselves. Anything we do . . . would *all* be on the interactive side."[29] In other words, while Gates may forge deals with entertainment companies, these will be solely for the purpose of licensing or developing media interactive CD-ROMs or online services.

Or so he claims. But don't bet on Bill Gates limiting his appetite for entertainment content for long, given his and his company's vast wealth and the growing primacy of content in technology development.

It would be wrong, of course, to begrudge Bill Gates his success or deny the pivotal role Microsoft has played in building an industry that has become the world leader in innovation and wealth-creating capacity. Indeed, America's best hopes for economic revitalization rest in large measure on the technology industry and the dazzling entrepreneurship that Gates has come to represent.

But there is another side to the Bill Gates success story that demands our thoughtful attention: monopoly.

Until recently, most in the business community were reluctant to challenge Gates's power publicly. Even the U.S. Justice Department, which carried out a lengthy antitrust investigation, did not in the end dare to stand up to Gates, and in 1994 signed a consent decree that was so utterly and obsequiously servile to Microsoft's interests that

federal judge Stanley Sporkin took the unprecedented step of over-
turning it. Stung by Sporkin's decision (and apparently not content
with simply brownnosing Gates), America's top "trust buster," Anne
Bingaman, then decided to get tough—on Microsoft's *behalf!* She
and Microsoft joined together—talk about unprecedented!—to appeal the judge's decision and restore the feeble consent decree.

That Bill Gates's hegemony does, indeed, have a chilling effect
on the industry was only highlighted by the manner in which a group
of rival companies challenged Microsoft's 1994 takeover of software
firm Intuit on antitrust grounds. When they submitted evidence to
the Justice Department showing that the Intuit buyout gave Microsoft
control of 90 percent of the personal-finance market, they at first
only dared do so *anonymously.* And when they challenged the Microsoft consent decree itself in U.S. District Court, they again did so
anonymously.[30] It seems their challenge had an effect, for in what
appeared to be an effort to resuscitate its slavish image, the Justice
Department later filed suit to block the Intuit merger. Bill Gates
himself ultimately backed down from his stated commitment to go
all-out to fight the government's anti-monopoly case, and withdrew
his offer to buy Intuit.

But while Gates resigned from the Intuit battle (reappropriating
the $2 billion earmarked for the Intuit acquisition to internal devel-
opment of Microsoft's own household financial software), it was
a strategic retreat designed to try to outflank the government's
traditional-thinking trust-busters in the much bigger battle over Microsoft Network. This is Microsoft's own proprietary online service
that will not only compete directly with major commercial online
services, but will have a major leg up on the competition because it
will come "bundled" into the next version of the Windows operating
system.

One could argue that Gates merely threw the government and his
critics a bone by dropping his intended acquisition of Intuit. In doing
so, he deflected scrutiny away from his foray into the wider world of
online commerce.

All of this only highlights the central problem with Microsoft and
the future of digital technology. Whether or not the company has
willfully violated antitrust laws or conspired to engage in illegal
business practices, its monopoly control of computer operating systems and certain key application software programs give it a natural
platform from which to gain domination of a whole variety of new

technologies, services, and markets as they come on stream. We can't know in advance all the ways Microsoft might exploit or abuse its monopoly position, as most of these businesses are still in their infancy or not yet born. But we can observe an increasingly strong correlation between the growth of Microsoft's power and the disappearance of competitors in several niches.

In his defense, Gates rightly points out that the so-called "anti-competitive" practices Microsoft is accused of—pre-announcing future products far in advance of shipment to hurt the sales of competitors' current products—are standard operating procedure in the software industry. Indeed, they have been employed to great effect over the years by two of Microsoft's chief competitors (and anonymous accusers), Apple and Sun Microsystems. And as for the charge that his company derives competitive advantages from the success of its flagship Windows product, Gates is also correct to point out that just like any company that takes risks and invests resources in a venture, Microsoft is certainly entitled to the fruits of its success.

The truth is, it's not necessarily bad behavior on Microsoft's part that makes it such a cause of concern to many in technology and new media circles these days. It's simply the company's objective size, expansionist goals, and unrivaled hegemony over the direction of technological development in America that worries people.

Says Matt Kursh, the CEO of Internet commerce company eShop: "Basically, Microsoft has become an unelected, de facto government, and that spells trouble. Because Gates absolutely controls the operating system business, he can issue an upgrade to Windows every few years and 60 million people have to fork over the money or be left behind. In other words, *he's got the right to tax*. What's more, he's got the right of eminent domain because he's got effective control over the real estate on your hard disk."

Another critic is Scott McNealy, CEO of computer workstation manufacturer Sun Microsystems: "I'm the world's biggest advocate of free markets and open competition," says McNealy. "But when someone achieves a monopoly in a particular market, it is no longer a free market but a controlled economy. And you know what happens when you have a controlled economy. Everybody winds up driving Trabants"—a reference to the former East Germany's national car.[31]

A third voice of concern, ironically, is Andy Grove of Intel, whose company has benefited probably more than any other from Microsoft's control of the software industry: "Whenever there is something new that is developing, like the telephone system or the PC or now this [Information] Highway, someone, or some company, has to take the lead. Yet at a certain point, when the utility becomes so all-encompassing, society has a legitimate right to limit the dominating company's influence. But it's very hard to argue that it needs to be or can be regulated today."[32]

Grove is certainly correct to point out the difficulty of assessing the extent to which Microsoft has now become an obstacle to, rather than an enabler of, technological innovation and wealth creation. Clearly, many within and without the industry are deeply concerned about Gates's growing ability to dictate the shape and direction of much of our nation's technological future. But what, if anything, can or should be done about Microsoft's expanding power is the subject of much debate but little clarity.

Simplistic calls for industrial-era government trust-busting do not take into account the complexity of today's multifaceted and technology-driven markets. For all the wealth and power of Microsoft, hundreds of new and exciting technology companies *are* still born each year. Equally simplistic, however, are demands that the government ignore Microsoft's dominance and expansionism and leave the market utterly to its own devices. For entrepreneurialism that thrives only so long as it serves (or defers to) one master will inevitably become marginalized and wither on the vine.

In any event, it is unclear whether market forces by themselves are any longer enough to check Microsoft's power. Some form of societal intervention may be needed, be it the severing of the company's operating system business from its applications and transactional services endeavors, or perhaps the imposition of a modified version of the cable TV industry's 30 percent rule that would limit the market share that Microsoft may control in any of its lines of business. In the current Republican-dominated political climate, however, federal intervention would appear to be a very remote possibility.

Yet society does have a vital interest in whether Bill Gates is able to impose his vision of an Information Highway dominated by Microsoft tollbooths at every junction. For Gates's vision is that of a modern-day robber baron who has invented almost nothing yet owns practically everything—or at least many of the decisive chokepoints of America's technological future. And his is the vision of a man with reportedly few social skills and even fewer social concerns about the deeper meaning and implications of the enormous revolutionary forces being unleashed by digital technology.

As a 1995 *Fortune* magazine cover story asked, Is there anything Bill Gates doesn't want? A better question might have been, Is there any good to come from so much power being concentrated in the hands of such a man?

Here is a man best symbolized, say some, by his lifelong infatuation for (and predilection to dress up as) the Great Gatsby, the fictional antihero who possessed wealth and power but was incapable of infusing his life with meaning or soul because he did not know where to find these things within himself. Here is a man who is described by those who know him as "the most surprisingly conscience-free individual I've ever met," "dangerous," and "not the kind of person you want building the social network of the future."[33]

As one writer who has profiled Gates asks, "Would we vote for a man who sometimes behaves like a ten-year-old boy to be the principal architect of the way we communicate with each other in the future?"[34]

There are those who insist that the Great Gatesby is simply a businessman, and that he makes no claim to intellectual or moral leadership. All the more reason why it is very much in the national interest that Bill Gates and Microsoft not be allowed to single-handedly monopolize so life-changing a social and economic force as tomorrow's Information Highway.

Even absent government intervention, however, there is still some reason to be optimistic about a technology future without Bill Gates at its helm. The consumer market, after all, presents Gates with a challenge he has not faced in more than a decade: *a fair, competitive fight.*

Indeed, like the grammar school bully who finally graduates to the big-city high school, Bill Gates is about to find himself in a whole new playground, facing for the first time others just as big and tough as he—bigger and tougher, in fact, and far more experienced in the rough-and-tumble rules of the consumer game. Don't forget, Microsoft still garners only half the revenues in a year that Sony commands in a single quarter. In this new environment, then, it may be that Bill

Gates is unable to maintain the gross predominance of power he has been accustomed to in the past.

This would not necessarily mean that Microsoft is about to wither or grow smaller. It's just that, for Bill Gates—and, indeed, for the entire computer industry he has so long dominated—the world is about to get a lot bigger.

· 9 ·

An Interesting Place to Go

Remember that burst of liberation we all felt the first time we got into a car and had the personal power to go anywhere? I submit it required three preconditions then, just as the Info Highway requires three now.

Number one, you need a great vehicle. One you can jump into and drive easily. These will be easy-to-use computers, intelligent TVs, personal communicators, and so on.

Second, the roads have to be reasonably good. The digital networks we're building have to be pretty easy to navigate around on.

And third and most important, you need an interesting place to go. At the end of the day, the vehicle and the road are merely the means to satisfy the impulse, the liberating impulse to go somewhere.

But *where* you want to go is the most important thing.

MARC PORAT
GENERAL MAGIC, INC.

"Where do you want to go today?"

That's the tag line for Microsoft's $100 million 1995 ad campaign, and since it would be churlish to suggest that once again Bill Gates has lifted a good idea from someone else, let's focus instead on how superbly Porat's and Gates's metaphor captures the core enigma around which the fate of today's new digital businesses will be decided.

To wit: what do people really want from all this wonderful new multimedia technology?

Do we want movies on demand, last week's episode of *Seinfeld,* or perhaps a video game we can play with a friend across town? Would we like to have 24-hour-a-day access to libraries of information and education, or the convenience of home shopping and online banking? What about video phone service (or would we rather not have to worry about how we look when we pick up the phone)? And for the sporting among us, how about some remote Las Vegas casino action—or perhaps something more lascivious, like a bit of interactive X-rated action—all from the privacy of our living-room televisions?

The truth is, nobody knows what people want or what they'll be willing to pay for it. Indeed, we can't even be sure precisely where the technology will take us, let alone what we'll want to do with it once we get there. Yet the uncertainty over what kinds of interactive entertainment and information services people truly desire—or, indeed, if they really want these at all—has hardly slowed the stampede of mergers, acquisitions, investments, and strategic alliances now charging across corporate America. Consider a few of the highlights of this merger mania in recent years.

During 1993's "cable is hot" phase, three regional telephone firms decide to buy all or part of three cable TV companies—including John Malone's TCI for $33 billion. Their aim is to get into the video business, and not so incidentally, to raid the phone markets of fellow telcos. Two of these deals crash and burn, however, so those telcos later team up with four other telcos in two separate tripartite alliances, each of which launches its own film development venture—one with a Hollywood studio (Disney), the other with a Hollywood talent agency (CAA)—to compete against the same cable companies they had previously tried to buy.

Got that so far? Good, because around this time the "studios are hot" phase begins. Viacom, a major owner of cable TV systems, starts a bitter brawl between a dozen telco, cable, and entertainment firms—during which, in a classic case of the pot calling the kettle black, Viacom chairman Sumner Redstone files a lawsuit charging fellow cable magnate John Malone with monopolistic practices—and finally buys Paramount's vast library of film and book properties for $10 billion, ostensibly in order to offer these over its cable TV systems. Whereupon Mr. Redstone turns around and offers to sell those very same cable TV systems to none other than . . . you guessed it, a consortium ruled by John Malone (whose Liberty Media division, incidentally, had backed QVC home shopping magnate Barry Diller's attempt to steal Paramount from under Sumner Redstone's nose)! But the deal fizzles.

Still with us? Great, because now comes the aborted "networks are hot" phase in 1994. Zirconium trinket salesman Diller, fresh from his bruising defeat in the Paramount bloodbath, tries to buy the majestic (and much larger) CBS television network for $5 billion, but before he can complete the deal, he is himself bought out by his two major shareholders. One of these (surprise!) is our old friend John Malone, Diller's fickle ally in the Paramount war and a man who always seems to turn up wherever money is changing hands. The brouhaha over CBS, meanwhile, stokes the network feeding frenzy even more, and soon Time Warner is sniffing around NBC. But Time Warner's creditors balk at adding to the company's already staggering debt load, so the company drops its grab at NBC and, somewhat petulantly, turns around and blocks cable czar Ted Turner (whose company is 19 percent owned by Time Warner) from spending its own debt-leveraged $5 billion to buy NBC. Then Time Warner starts casting about for someone to buy out its own stake in the irrepressible Mr. Turner.

Are we having fun yet? Good, because by the end of 1994, software companies have suddenly started popping up all over Wall Street radar screens. Cap Cities/ABC, feeling its Wheaties after the "networks are hot" phase, launches a new media division and a joint venture with video game developer Electronic Arts, while TCI's Malone never one to sit out a hand, strikes a similar deal with Acclaim Entertainment to market video games over cable TV.

Bill Gates's giant Microsoft, meanwhile, having lost the personal finance software wars against tiny Intuit's Quicken program, opts to swallow the victor for $1.5 billion worth of stock, which soon becomes $2 billion as Microsoft's own shares rise through the roof. This prompts suicidal depressions, of course, among ex-Intuit employees who had quit years before when Intuit was on the ropes rather than accept CEO Scott Cook's offer of stock in lieu of salary. It also causes severe heartburn in the banking industry, which suddenly realizes that the coming launch of Microsoft's 100-megaton online network, combined with Intuit's finance program, amounts to a preemptive strike against their dreams of dominating the future home banking business. While the Justice Department sues to block the Microsoft-Intuit deal, and Gates eventually backs down rather than try to prove in court the rather hard to prove case that he's *not* trying to monopolize another application software market, the big banks scramble in search of their own alternative to Microsoft's growing power. BankAmerica and NationsBank go in together to snap up a third-rate financial software firm, MECA, which they bill as their vehicle for adapting antiquated banking practices to the increasingly electronic home environment. "Not all dinosaurs roll over and die," barks one banker, "Some of 'em can run real fast and bite the hell out of you."[1]

And speaking of fast-running, sharp-toothed dinosaurs, old IBM—looking for a new lease on life in a world of increasingly networked computers and flush with cash after CEO Lou Gerstner's remarkable turnaround of the company—suddenly bares its teeth in a hostile takeover bid for workgroup software leader Lotus. After playing hard to get for a few days, the hitherto coy Lotus finally decides her scaly suitor is not such a bad dinosaur after all when IBM sweetens its marriage proposal to a phenomenal $3 billion.

Meanwhile, having already trolled their lines through just about every digital watering hole in America, the dealmakers decide in the spring of 1995 to rebait their hooks and go fishing once again in Hollywood. Japanese electronics giant Matsushita, barely on speaking terms with the management of the MCA studios it had bought for $6 billion just a few years earlier, decides to cure its Tinseltown headache the American way—by dumping the company. And who of all people should step up to the newly vacated MCA plate but the scion of the Seagram liquor empire, young Edgar Bronfman, who always wanted to be in the movies. Thanks to his daddy's farsighted diversification into oil and chemicals, Edgar can now trade most of the company's $10 billion interest in DuPont for MCA instead.

While Bronfman Jr. is making this switch (to mostly negative reviews from staid shareholders), he has his eye on a plot twist that will make MCA far more valuable—a potential distribution agreement with DreamWorks SKG, which has just been launched by the three most bankable moguls in Hollywood, Steven Spielberg, ex-Disney exec Jeffrey Katzenberg, and music maven David Geffen. The first new Hollywood studio in 50 years, DreamWorks is so hot and so hyped that investors and bankers are lined up out the door to provide the founders nearly $2 billion in equity and debt financing based on little collateral other than the three amigos' huge reputations.

Speaking of reputations, Rupert Murdoch's legendary prowess at turning depressed media properties into delirious successes—he owns Fox studios and a host of money-gushing media firms around the globe—attracts the attention of telephone giant MCI, which has been feeling rather depressed itself of late since the collapse of its never-consummated marriage to fading wireless star Nextel. So MCI offers Mr. Murdoch $2 billion for . . . well, as best as the analysts can figure, just for the right to be friends.

But wait! This storm of deal-making seems like minor weather when a hurricane of mergers strikes in August 1995. During one week, Disney buys Capital Cities' ABC network for $19 billion, the second largest merger in U.S. history; Westinghouse ponies up $5 billion for CBS (and rumors heat up about Turner and NBC); newspaper giant Gannett (*USA Today*) ventures into TV by acquiring Multimedia, Inc.; the $2-billion TCI-Viacom deal is revived with John Malone's acquisition of old enemy Sumner Redstone's West Coast cable systems; computer networking leader 3Com's bid for Chipcom is threatened by Cabletron's counter-offer; Broderbund teases educational software leader Learning Company into its fold with a $500-million offer; and even the unsexy business of business forms gets a makeover with Moore Corp.'s $1.3-billion purchase of Wallace Computer Services. Convergence isn't a phenomenon; it's an eye-popping, stark raving adventure in global economic transformation.

Don't worry if you're confused, for even Wall Street finds this Machiavellian merger mania—the biggest in U.S. history, approximately one deal every single hour of every day of the year except Sundays—often impossibly byzantine. But there *is* a logical thread running through these deals: the quest for content.

This quest—for the movies, books, video games, TV shows, and other interactive information, communications, and financial services of tomorrow—has now become a driving force behind the post-industrial realignment in the U.S. economy. It is not only propelling once-stodgy corporations in radical new directions but midwifing as well the birth of literally thousands of small technology start-ups and multimedia development companies. And though the price and size of most of these content-driven deals may have declined somewhat from the glory days of 1993—Disney's $19-billion purchase of ABC excepted—this probably has more to do with anxious investors and accountants slapping a bit more economic sense into their deal-hungry CEOs than with any lessening of corporate America's belief that content is the key to success and power in the coming digital era.

Indeed, most chief executives today recognize that just as control of natural resources and manufacturing capacity once drove wealth creation during the industrial era, today it is knowledge resources—

content and all the skills and talent that go into creating and marketing it—that have become the fulcrum of wealth in the emerging information economy. Though there is certainly a good deal of hype (and fear of being left out) involved in the current deal frenzy, the quest for content is based fundamentally upon very sound economic reasoning.

Content, after all, has come increasingly to represent the highest-value-added component of products and services these days. It is also highly leverageable, offering multiple opportunities for syndication, resale, and the creation of continuing revenue streams not found, for example, in the hardware business. And because the bits and bytes of content are translatable into so many forms—from books to movies to video games and CD-ROMS—it can serve as a magic key that enables its owners to unlock the doors to a variety of new markets and new businesses to which they otherwise would never have had access.

On the other hand, the content business also carries risks not found in other sorts of ventures. To a commodity widget manufacturer, a profit can be expected so long as one's widgets are of decent quality and one provides fair service at a competitive price. Not so in the creative (unpredictable and ambiguous) world of content.

After all, what makes for a successful movie? This is a question that Hollywood executives have spent literally billions of dollars trying to answer to no avail. They hire proven box-office stars, directors, and writers. They run countless focus groups to pretest audience reaction. And they spend more on advertising and marketing today than it once cost to produce an entire film a decade ago.

And what happens? They release a *Last Action Hero* and it bombs at the box office. Go figure.

"It's not for the faint of heart," concedes cable TV and Hollywood magnate Ted Turner. "You can make 10 movies at $40 million a pop, and only one of them can make money. You have to have the heart and mind of a gambler," he added, and still, "the odds are you'll lose."[2] Indeed, of the 332 films released in 1994, fewer than a third will make a profit.

Well, that's showbiz! And one man who understands the vagaries of turning movie magic into box-office gold as much if not more than any other is Sony Corporation of America chief Mickey Schulhof. "The thing to remember," says the physicist turned entertainment mogul who oversees all of Sony's U.S. operations, including its Columbia and Tri-Star film studios, "is that creative talent is not a fungible resource. The factors that allow a book writer or screenwriter to tap into the public psyche, to understand human emotions, is limited to a handful of people. A businessman can't force it. All he can do is, one, hire people who can sniff out and locate talent, and two, distribute the product created by the talent."

In other words, you can buy a vineyard, but that won't necessarily make you a vintner, let alone a wine master.

Schulhof has directed the Japanese electronics giant's push into the content in recent years, taking charge of the company's film studios and recorded music enterprise and directing its entry into the multimedia CD-ROM business as well. Underlying all his actions was a strategy that Sony used to call synergy—until the word was written out of the corporate vocabulary owing to overuse and less-than-impressive results. But the basic concept of trying to alchemize the company's electronics "hardware" and content "software" assets into a seamless engine of success was a pioneering one, a recognition of the convergence of once disparate industries in the digital age.

The origins of Sony's approach actually predate the digital technology revolution itself, going back over 15 years to the company's traumatic experience with the then fledgling VCR business. In the 1970s, when VCRs first hit the market, two competing formats emerged: first, Sony's pioneering Beta, and then VHS. Experts at the time all agreed that Beta, which offered better image and sound quality than Matsushita's VHS format, was the superior technology. Yet in a few years' time, the technologically inferior VHS blew Beta completely out of the market.

Why? Ultimately, it came down to the fact that all the good movies had ended up on VHS! Matsushita had pushed its VHS standard aggressively into the marketplace, winning the backing of other VCR makers as well as the film studios, which had rushed to license their films for the increasingly popular VHS format. Sony had bet on the superior technology to win the day, forgetting that consumers don't really care about technology per se; they just want to curl up on the couch and watch a good movie.

In the years that followed, Sony executives thought long and hard about the meaning of the Beta disaster. They had an awakening of sorts, and heard the voice of God—or was it simply the sound of 80 million cash registers going *ding!* each and every time a VHS video tape deck was sold in the U.S.? In any event, they realized that Sony must stop thinking of itself as an electronics company and start seeing itself as an *entertainment* company. For without entertaining content, consumers have little reason to buy the Sony hardware to play it on. With it, however, Sony hardware could be pushed into the market more forcefully.

Having learned a bitter lesson, Sony's leaders vowed never again to be stuck on a hardware canoe without a software paddle. Akio Morita, Sony's visionary founder, and his protege, Norio Ohga (a former opera singer turned businessman), were determined to buy software assets.

Sony's first major acquisition was CBS Records, one of the preeminent American record labels, for $2 billion in 1988. This was a business Sony knew well, having long been CBS Records' partner in Japan. Music, and even more broadly sound, were bred in Sony's bones—even the corporate name, Sony, was invented by Akio Morita to resonate with the English word "sound." So although the famous photograph of the time showing Akio Morita embracing pop singer Cindi Lauper was a shocking image to some, the Sony–CBS Records marriage, given Sony's experience with both music software and hardware (radios, Walkmans, and CD players), was actually not very astonishing at all. Indeed, it has proven to be not only an outstanding source of strategic leverage for Sony in the electronics and entertainment industries, but a barn-burning financial success as well.

The same, however, cannot be said for Sony's 1989 acquisition of Columbia Pictures, and various other related Hollywood acquisitions and investments that cost the company around $4 billion. The movie strategy was similar to that which guided Sony's music venture, and it represented the same antidote to the Betamax trauma of the past: if you own the content, you can drive the format. At least that's the theory. But the distance between theory and practice is greater in Hollywood than anywhere else, it seems. And thereby hangs some important object lessons about the central but terribly quixotic role played by entertainment in this era of digital convergence.

When Sony acquired Columbia it was in fact a troubled movie studio sorely in need of turnaround. Even so, the U.S. media chose to play up the purchase as some kind of Japanese theft of an American cultural icon. This only added to rising fears in the late 1980s about Japan's seemingly unstoppable economic juggernaut. Having bought large U.S. stakes in everything from real estate to manufacturing and even government securities, was Japan, Inc. now about to "Japan-icize" American culture as well? In fact, Sony took a hands-off approach to its Hollywood assets, preferring to allow Mickey Schulhof and his all-American team of Hollywood moguls to work their magic. After all, Sony reasoned, to understand entertainment one must come from the culture of America, the center of the creative universe of content.

How, then, to explain Sony's stunning announcement in November of 1994 that it was taking a $3.2 billion write-off on the value of its Hollywood studios? How could a company that had committed such heavy resources to the content business have failed so dramatically to profit from it?

To hear it from the *Wall Street Journal* and *New York Times*, which (gleefully) offered strikingly similar analyses on their front pages, the answer can be summed up in one word: Japan. "Sony's humbling and expensive foray into Hollywood highlights the dangers facing the Japanese who enter the entertainment industry," chortled the *Journal*. "A stark symbol of the reversal of fortunes of corporate Japan!" snickered the *Times*.

Japan-bashing makes good copy, of course, but in focusing on the Japanese element of the equation the media may have failed to appreciate how Sony's problems in Hollywood merely reflect larger challenges faced by *all* who attempt to develop content amid the new digital realities.

In retrospect, of course, it is now clear that Sony allowed its American management team—headed by Jon Peters and Peter Guber, two of the most erratic and profligate producers in Tinseltown—to go far beyond even Hollywood's traditional lack of cost controls. Taking nearly $1 billion in personal salaries, contract buyouts and so-called production deals from Sony, Guber and Peters also overbid for every script and big-name star within reach. Yet despite their previous successes with films like *Batman* and *Rainman,* once Peters and Guber arrived at Columbia all their excesses failed to buy them a single blockbuster hit in five years.

How ironic that the same media that once warned of the dangers of Japanese corporate intervention in Hollywood creative decisions now criticized Sony's top brass for not intervening enough in the affairs of its two kamikaze moguls. But it would be a mistake to think Peters and Guber were the only hotdogs running film studios in La-La land. The entertainment industry is rife with "creative executives" just as likely to end up in Heidi Fleiss's little black book as in daily *Variety*'s box-office winners chart.

Indeed, Sony's difficulties in harvesting big bucks from its synergy strategy is hardly unique. No company, Japanese or American, has yet managed to find the pot of gold at the end of the "convergence" rainbow—not Time Warner, not Viacom, not anyone. But the pot of gold still exerts its attraction. Even Sony—the company that should, according to the media, be quite averse to chasing rainbows anymore—is still at the forefront of efforts to synergize hardware and software successfully. This says something both about Sony as well as the pot of gold.

Indeed, after the stunning 1994 write-down, the pundits expected Sony to dump its entertainment assets in a fire sale, or at least to sweep out its key American management personnel. But this hasn't happened. While Guber and Peters have departed, Mickey Schulhof remains at the helm. To be sure, the "bubble economy" in Hollywood has burst and Sony is proceeding much more cautiously these days. But its basic commitment to both traditional filmed entertainment as well as new interactive media remains strong.

What many American "experts" on the situation don't realize is that Sony's financial losses, while unpalatable, are still ultimately digestible for a company of Sony's size and scale. And this is where Sony's cultural heritage does come into play. For all the corporate pain caused by its Hollywood misadventures, Sony exemplifies the Japanese traits of persistence and patience in achieving long-term goals. Coupled with the fact that Sony's acquisition of CBS Records has been such a stunning success, Sony's commitment to keep itself at the forefront of innovation suggests that the company is unlikely to cut and run from the Hollywood scene any time soon. Indeed, early in 1995 Sony began showing signs of a modest turnaround in its film business. While a joint venture or even a partial asset sale remains an option for Sony in riding out these losses, ultimately the company's recent problems are not going to deter it from owning a major seat at the table when the Digital Revolution's kingdom of riches materializes.

One lesson of Sony's Hollywood experience is that there are no get-rich-quick ways to generate large-scale sustainable success from the potential synergies between hardware and software, between technology and content. It will prove to be a protracted and difficult challenge for all who attempt it. This fact loomed large over the proceedings of the Western Cable Show held in Anaheim, California, in December 1994. Indeed, the 2,500 executives who attended seemed quite bewildered not only over how their industry could meet the synergy challenge but also over exactly what the nature of their industry really was anymore.

"Calling us the cable industry has become an anachronism," noted Ted Turner. "We need a new name for what we are doing."[3] TCI's Malone agreed: "This is not the same business anymore."[4]

Indeed, it is not. One symbol of the changes being wrought by digital technology was the fact that telephone and computer companies attended the show for the first time.

"It's a mistake to call cable 'cable' and telephone 'telephone,'" suggested Glen Jones, president and CEO of Denver-based Jones Intercable. "Both industries are like shadows merging into night at sunset."[5]

A rather poetic remark, to be sure, from someone who would have been called a conduit salesman a year or two ago. But such are the mental effects induced when trade show debates shift their focus from the finer points of coaxial cable noise reduction technology to the less quantifiable and far more elusive subject of content. With the boundaries between their once disparate industries blurring, the chief executives in Anaheim were inclined to wax profound about the new competitive landscape before them. (The authors here wish to point out that one of the Digital Revolution's central laws is that the more uncertain one is about exactly how to profit from digital technology, the more lyrical one becomes in describing it.)

"We're entering a renaissance of creativity," proclaimed Bob Kavner, the former AT&T executive who is now a principal at Hollywood's Creative Artists Agency.

"Imagination will rule the marketplace," swooned the ever-inspiring Glen Jones.

"[The] huge growth industry will be the creation of intellectual property that can be exploited," gushed Stuart Johnson, group president of large business and information services at the Bell Atlantic telephone company.

On this last point, conference attendees all agreed that interactive services offer enormous opportunities for capturing a goodly portion of the hundreds of billions of dollars now spent on entertainment, media, and advertising. As poet-in-residence Glen Jones put it, "The home market is like a garden where we can go and pick vegetables."

Among those most ripe for picking are the $12 billion videotape rental market; the $5 billion video game business; the $47 billion traffic in books, magazines, and newspapers; the $57 billion catalog shopping sector; and the $130 billion advertising business.[6] But that's only an introduction to the digital economy's new business opportunities.

Legal gambling, for example, is already a $30 billion business that draws 90 million casino visits a year from a third of all households in America. Illegal sports and horse betting, as well as the cards and numbers rackets, generate an additional $43 billion a year.[7] If online gambling were legalized—and considering that 37 states already operate legal lotteries and the rest are under intense and growing pressure to do so, this seems an eventual certainty—it could become bigger than the existing movie, books, recorded music, and park and arcade businesses combined.

But as James Burke of the Learning Channel's *Connections* cautions, "How do we even know people really want all this stuff?"

A good question, to which there is unfortunately no good answer. Though numerous market surveys have been conducted to try to determine the demand for promised Info Highway services, the results have been contradictory to say the least. A survey of one thousand adults conducted by Louis Harris and Associates, for example, found interactive entertainment such as movies on demand and home shopping to be far less appealing to consumers than had been expected.[8] But another survey conducted for computer maker Hewlett-Packard found movies on demand to be among the most popular of promised Info Highway services.[9] The disparity stems not so much from any bias in their respective survey questions as from the fact that queries about services that do not yet exist are, by their nature, unlikely to yield very reliable data.

As a general barometer of consumer attitudes toward interactive services, however, most surveys seem to endorse the notion that consumers would like movies on demand, time-shifted news and sports on demand, and certain episodes of favorite "evergreen" shows like

I Love Lucy—so long as these are priced reasonably. As to what "reasonable pricing" means, one of the better surveys suggested that most people would subscribe to an interactive service if it cost no more than $5 to $10 extra per month.[10] The number of willing subscribers drops sharply above that price.

In any event, while "the jury is out on whether the economics make sense," as TCI's Malone puts it, the many advertiser-supported schemes now under consideration (see Chapter 5) suggest that at least some basic services will be priced quite affordably. Such heavy advertiser involvement, however, could uncover barriers even greater than cost to widespread consumer adoption.

"We've found that people don't like intrusions into their homes," observed Dennis Boyce, a senior partner with KMR Group, a Chicago-based research group. "They tend to resent telephone solicitations and to feel their names and addresses have been sold to too many advertisers. They don't want salespeople coming to their homes."[11]

Will people want interactive marketers "coming into their home" via their TV or PC, gathering all sorts of data on what shows they watch, what products they buy—and even, perhaps, on whom they correspond with electronically?

Today's consumers may be many things—impulsive, status conscious, susceptible to gimmicks—but they are not fools. The notion that one's home is one's castle runs deep in American consciousness, and virtually all opinion surveys that address this topic reveal extremely high levels of public concern about privacy. Thus, content providers who ignore the need to provide strict privacy guarantees along with their interactive service offerings may well find the doors to consumers' homes slammed in their faces.

Assuming their privacy concerns are at least partially addressed—a reasonable assumption, for marketers are no fools, either—and that the pricing models for interactive service are attractive to a fairly broad demographic swath of the consuming public, what *can* we say about the likely factors that will determine success in the content business?

With all due respect to Marshall McLuhan's brilliant analysis that the medium of public discourse affects the character of that discourse, it's still the *message*, not the medium that counts most of all.

Entertainment, whether of the digital interactive sort or merely the plain old-fashioned kind, has always and will always be defined principally by its capacity to engage human beings in an *emotionally compelling experience*. This will be no less true in the farthest reaches of tomorrow's virtual universe than it was 35,000 years ago in the narrow confines of the caves of Altamira, upon whose walls early humans painted their awe-inspiring images of the hunt.

But somehow, the notion that interactivity itself is the goal rather than simply a tool has gained far too much currency these days. "I think sometimes people look at false indicators," notes the president of Ted Turner's worldwide entertainment empire, Scott Sassa: "Take CD-ROMS. Everybody's harping about getting movielike images in CD-ROM games. But [the computer game] Tetris has no movielike images, and yet you see all these people hooked. So movielike images don't matter. What matters is playability in games. It's the same with movies. If they're going to be successful, they've got to engage me. They've got to give me an immersive experience."

All popular entertainment shares this characteristic. While movies and novels may teach a moral lesson or offer a message, fundamentally they engage our emotions, enabling us to escape the confines of our own subjectivity and enter the consciousness, as it were, of the characters. We don't just observe the protagonists; we "feel" what it is like to be them. To accomplish its emotion-engaging task, drama usually has a beginning, a middle, and an end—first setting the stage, then pulling the audience into the conflict, and finally resolving it. This structure, of course, is not simply a Hollywood convention. It goes back to Aristotle and beyond to the dawn of history, where it is found in the storytelling traditions of diverse cultures. That all popular drama exhibits this common characteristic suggests that our response to it is hardwired in the human brain.

As for trendy interactive movies, whose plots and character development can be altered by viewers at their whim, these are unlikely ever to become more than a minor art form and novelty business. To randomize either the structure or narrative thread of a story is to unstitch the tapestry of emotional experience it creates.

"What if crowds during Shakespeare's time had decided whether Lady Macbeth should wash her hands or not?" asks Penn Jillette, half of the comedy team Penn & Teller and a commentator on new media. "This [eviscerates] art. More endings don't make for a better narrative."[12]

Adds Scott Sassa: "Good movies are made by good storytellers, by people who know how to engage us and take us along on an experience. Even the guys who are great sports producers are all great storytellers. *Monday Night Football* was a hit because Roone Arledge was a great storyteller, and he had a great on-camera storyteller, Howard Cosell, who was able to set the drama."

This explains in part why there was so much excitement over the formation of the new DreamWorks studio by Steven Spielberg, David Geffen, and Jeffrey Katzenberg in 1994. No one can top these three amigos, especially Spielberg, when it comes to creating cultural works that capture and engage our imaginations. For all Spielberg's special effects, his stories always rely on a traditional Aristotelean narrative structure and strong characters to transport audiences into exciting and emotionally engaging adventures.

In reaching for new technological heights, too many digital pioneers lose sight of the *human factors* that are the core of the entertainment experience. Nowhere is this more evident than in the so-called experience industry itself, otherwise known as the virtual reality attraction or high-tech thrill business. The "thrills" here offer a preview of some of the more banal entertainment we may be receiving over our interactive TVs later this decade.

Virtual reality, for those readers not glued to the cutting edge of their seats, used to mean something fairly specific back in the 1980s when it first emerged. Back then, it referred to the use of highly sophisticated computerized simulation tools to fool human sensory perception and make people feel that they were immersed in an experience—and able to interact with it—when they were not actually experiencing anything in a physical sense at all. Flight simulators were an early example of VR technology which, by providing a reasonably real enough approximation of what it was like to fly a plane, proved useful in the training of pilots. Since then, VR technology has advanced to the point where, through the use of software-controlled goggles and motion-sensing gloves and headgear, one can simulate the sights, sounds, and feel of experience that seem at least minimally to resemble the real thing—the smoke and confusion of a tank battle in the Iraqi desert, say, or the sight and even the *feel* of blood vessels and tissues as you cut through them in simulated surgery.

Clearly, virtual reality technology has many potential applications, from skills training to interior design. But while technologists point to its social uses, entrepreneurs have focused on virtual reality's potential to generate some very real and bankable economic realities. Indeed, VR has nowadays become more a marketing buzzword than a science. It is liberally applied to almost any game, ride, or attraction that induces some sort of faux sensory perception. And to hear enthusiastic entrepreneurs and investors talk, virtual reality attractions are the Disneylands of the twenty-first century, the urban entertainments of the future, the travel industry of tomorrow.

Among the most notable of these attractions is the $50 million virtual thrill ride that is the centerpiece of the Egyptian-themed Luxor Hotel in Las Vegas, which opened amid much fanfare in 1994. With its high-tech visual illusions and synchronized motion computers, the Secrets of the Luxor Pyramid ride is supposed to drive a stake through the heart of any earthbound experience. Indeed, the hotel's promotional material makes it sound like a genuine cyberspace adventure—more mysterious than a Moroccan bazaar, more sensual than a night in Paris, more thrilling than a rafting trip down *The River Wild*, and more real than . . . well, than *reality* itself.

"Your adventure begins on a hair-raising, falling elevator which descends to a dazzling ancient temple discovered two miles beneath Luxor." You will "search for a mysterious crystal obelisk containing the secrets of the universe. You will board a levitating vehicle for a thrilling high-impact adventure ride through the temple's maze. Experience an explosive battle with evil forces . . . and narrowly escape death in your return to the surface."[13]

Nice copy, eh? A bit overdone, but that's Vegas for you. In any event, the attraction—designed by movie special-effects wizard Douglas Trumbull of *2001: A Space Odyssey* and *Close Encounters* fame—promised nothing less than the very latest in high-tech adventure, a new standard in virtual thrill rides, the absolute cutting edge in interactive entertainment.

Actually, Secrets of the Luxor Pyramid is not one but three (three! three!) rides in one. The first phase of the experience consists of standing in line—apparently, among all the special effects Mr. Trumbull was able to design, the elimination of long waiting lines was not one. So that your time will not be wasted, however, video monitors attempt to bring participants up to speed on the story in which they are about to become immersed. Unfortunately, most people are unable to determine the gist of this story or the relationships between its characters because they are only in line long enough to view the video loops half a dozen times, and sadly, this is not enough time to make sense of it.

But no matter, the "experience" is what counts. And this is what it consists of: In episode one, the "hair-raising" elevator ride to a "dazzling ancient temple" two miles underground is rather more conducive to graying one's hair rather than raising it. It amounts to nothing more than a great deal of disembodied and annoying shouting, followed by a sudden stop. The remainder of episode one is spent trying vainly to figure out what is going on.

Episode two involves a badly done fake TV talk show taking place in the present, in which two characters named Colonel Claggert, Mac, and Carina talk melodramatically about some sort of "mystery." To judge from the bored chatter in the audience, the only mystery here is what these characters were really talking about. Of the "fabulous 3-D vision" of the magical crystal obelisk that one is supposed to behold, there truly is not much to report. Most of the audience is too busy trying to get the dimestore-quality 3-D glasses they have been given to work properly.

As for episode three—the "dazzling special-effects journey to the end of the world and back"—for most in the strapped-in and swaying audience, it feels more like a journey to the edge of nausea and back. That all of the contrasting heaven-and-hell images of mankind's future are displayed on the world's tallest movie screen certainly does not help matters.

To be fair, some of the imagery is interesting. But the execution of this virtual fantasy is so poor as to thoroughly distract the audience from appreciating it. One sees walls, one sees seat backs, and almost incidentally, one sees seven-story close-ups of extremely bad acting on a screen that is inexplicably taller than it is wide.

After it's over, more than a few participants report that the ride was without a doubt the dumbest experience to which they have ever (willingly) subjected themselves. They say it ranks right up there with watching water evaporate.

The error of Luxor's high-tech entertainment experiment is that its technology is employed as a *substitute* for experience rather than as a tool for enhancing it. As a result, it serves only to bludgeon rather than excite the senses, to exhaust rather than stimulate the imagination, to vulgarize rather than celebrate mankind and his creations.

In contrast, arguably the single best attraction in all of virtual reality–crazed Las Vegas is the pirate battle enacted several times a day in a lagoon in front of the Treasure Island Hotel. With much shooting and sword fighting and acrobatic jumping from sinking ships, real actors stage a brief but engaging drama about a band of pirates who attack a British navy frigate. In the heroic finale of the show, both ships are set on fire and sunk.

Now, presumably a fair amount of technology is at work here—creating the ersatz fire, operating the massive hydraulic lifts that sink and then raise the two life-size ships. But here the technology is used appropriately—as *enhancement* rather than substitute for an intrinsically rich experience—and it is invisible to the spectators, who in any case are far too engrossed on the drama unfolding before them to care how it's done. It's a nice spectacle, a pretty good piece of street theater, and most of all, it reflects the sort of clever and creative evocation of old-fashioned human emotions that is common to all good entertainment.

Respect for the emotional magnets that engage the human psyche will prove invaluable not just in the entertainment business per se, but also in the creation of such consumer-oriented services as online shopping. There is much at stake here, for if even two percent of the $2 trillion in consumer retail spending can be captured online, that's a $40 billion business—about the size of today's entire U.S. cable television business. But as any retailer can attest, the art of the sale involves a good deal more than simply offering goods to the market.

Consider the nature of shopping. Ever since the earliest markets, when Abdul rode his camel across the desert to haggle with Farouz in the oasis bazaar, shopping has always embodied more than the acquisition of life's necessities. Its attraction for people has depended upon the way it evokes and satisfies two basic human impulses.

Shopping first of all offers a feast of the senses. For Abdul, this meant brightly colored cloth wafting in the dust-choked air, the cries of street vendors and the braying of donkeys, the smell of smoky lamb grilling over coal.

Today, we call this a *compelling shopping experience.*

Then, too, shopping offers the opportunity for serendipitous discovery. Abdul may think he needs only one jug of olive oil, but Farouz has a proposition. "Tell you what, my friend," Farouz whispers confidentially. "If you buy two jugs—and for you, of course, my first price, last price, and only price is always the friend's price— then you may also have this beautiful red cloth at no cost for your wife, Insh'allah. When she sees it she will forever praise your generosity and shrewdness as a businessman."

Today, we call this *merchandising*.

Such were the visceral gravitational forces that pulled people into the bazaar in olden days, and their attractive power remains undimmed today. Yet how to embody these human dynamics in tomorrow's cyberspace bazaars is a question that today's digital merchants have only begun to ponder.

eShop, Inc. of San Mateo, California, is one company that has given this issue a good deal of thought. It sells software to electronic retailers and online services that enables them to not only offer their electronic shoppers an enhanced online experience but to actively merchandise their wares as well.

"So much of what is envisioned as electronic commerce is really just a scrolling list of products," says eShop's 30-year-old CEO, Matt Kursh. "That may be fine for certain things, like discount software. But that's not selling; it's taking orders. And it won't work in the mass market."

eShop's software system allows merchants to custom design the look and approach of their virtual stores, offering their own branded shopping environment to consumers through online and (eventually) cable TV services. It has licensed its technology to merchants—800-FLOWERS, Tower Records, and Lands End are three early customers—who have set up shop on AT&T's new PersonaLink service.

Using eShop's graphical software, retailers can create a simulated real-world shop, with 3-D views of navigable aisles and of merchandise that can be manipulated by the shopper through the click of a mouse button.

Observes 800-FLOWERS's Elaine Rubin: "With eShop, we were able to create a real-world visual metaphor—but with a twist. We didn't think duplicating the look of a flower shop was as important as trying to recreate the moods and emotions that usually motivate the purchase of flowers. So we designed an interface oriented around various emotional occasions: click on the 'birthday party,' for instance, and you're greeted with the sights and sounds of a party, where you can see various flower arrangements that are appropriate to that occasion and make a purchase if you want."

eShop's software also allows merchants to create Personal Shopping Assistants—digital sales clerks with distinct "personalities" and scriptable behavior—that provide information and service to individual shoppers. Finally, the technology allows for detailed customer tracking and profiling data that enables retailers to target certain customers for specialized promotions.

"It'll tell us if a customer lingered over an item but didn't buy it," explained 800-FLOWERS's Rubin. "The next time that person enters our online store, the Personal Shopping Assistant can offer the same item to that customer for 10 percent off and maybe close the sale."

It's one thing, of course, to sign up for a Macy's credit card and later receive promotions in the mail. But it's an altogether different story when Macy's can record the dollar amounts and nature of our entire transactional history online and then cross-reference this with our income, credit card, medical, and marital history, our interactive television program choices, and possibly even a log of all our electronic mail. Do we want anyone, let alone someone we owe money to, knowing us *that* well?

"The privacy concerns are huge," concedes Kursh. "Normally we don't meddle in how merchants use our software— how they price or promote their products, for instance. But I don't think we can abdicate our responsibilities in this area. So we've built in the ability for the consumer to shut off profiling and tracking by the merchant."

By taking the high road on this issue, eShop has shown that it recognizes the deep attachment most Americans feel to their personal privacy and to fair play in the marketplace. Will others involved in building the new digital bazaar show the same foresight? And for that matter, how will the vast body of consumer protection and product safety laws built up over the last half century be applied to what is still the no-man's-land of cyberspace? These are cyberspace issues that will likely require the intervention of government to resolve, just as they did in the world of bricks and mortar.

The emotional links between entertainment and shopping extend to many other forms of digital content as well. In some cases, especially online information services, business will find that success depends upon also offering consumers some tangible and practical value in the form of choice, convenience, or solutions to daily-life problems.

"[Online services] are not about some intergalactic out-of-body experience," says US West chief executive Dick McCormick, speaking of the burgeoning online information business. "It's as simple as the microwave oven—it should help us do things more conveniently."[14]

What many content developers have yet to recognize, however, is that such convenience, service, or solutions to daily-life problems must quite often be *local* in character.

Home, family, job, neighborhood, city—these are the arenas in which people spend the majority of their daily lives. So far, though, the major commercial online services—America Online, Prodigy, and Compuserve—have been unable to offer much value in these *local* arenas.

Their classifieds are usually undifferentiated by locality or region, and therefore have only limited value. Their job listings are rarely the best place to look if you need to find work anywhere within a thousand miles of your home. Their entertainment and lifestyle forums cannot tell you what movies are playing in town, how to reserve a local campground space, or when a table might be available at your favorite restaurant. Their consumer services don't provide references for local contractors and repairmen, nor can they help you lodge a complaint with the local Better Business Bureau. Their reference services will show you how to obtain vast volumes from the Library of Congress but often not so much as a periodical from your local library. You can't get your driver's license renewed, protest your parking tickets, register to vote, or file an action in small claims court. And while their political forums can tell you how to E-mail the president of the United States, they usually can't put you in touch with your city councilman.

One industry that is surprisingly well positioned to exploit this opportunity in locally oriented services is the newspaper business. To be sure, most analysts believe that newspapers are primarily victims rather than beneficiaries of the technological changes taking place in the media. In their view, newspaper companies such as Gannett or Newhouse cannot leverage their profitable local news and classified and retail advertising operations into a digital media business. As a result, say the experts, newspaper companies have only three options: (1) attempt to erect as many barriers as possible to the cannibalization of their businesses by new electronic media products and services; (2) expand into cable TV, book, data collection, or other content-related activities with more national scope; or (3) become suppliers of information to national online networks.

The pundits just don't get it. The long-term limiting factor in online service industry growth is the lack of services that appeal to mass-market consumers and women. And newspaper companies, perhaps in partnership with national online services, are more capable than anyone of developing services that offer practical value to mainstream consumers where they need it the most—in their daily, *local* lives.

Local services already exist, of course, mostly in the form of special-interest bulletin boards and the like. Newspaper companies, too, have launched local services, but these have met with little success. The *San Jose Mercury News,* for example—the paper of record in California's Silicon Valley—operates an online service whose subscribership is only "in the thousands," according to spokesman Barry Parr, in the most computer-literate region of the nation. Why? One explanation is that the service mainly just recreates its *content* online—a dubious "solution" at best to an even more dubious mass-market "need" for more detailed or customized news.

What's needed instead is a consumer-oriented service that recreates not the newspaper's content but it's *historic role* online—as town square, citizen resource, community forum, and civic glue.

Local newspapers could use their profitable databases of local news and classified and retail advertising to develop advertiser-supported "town square" online services. And national newspaper chains like Gannett, Newhouse, or Knight-Ridder could use their strong national brands to create whole networks of local "town square" services that offer real value where people need it the most, to wit:

▪ Consumer Action—file suit for small claims court, check contractors' board and Better Business Bureau reports, file consumer complaints, get referrals to legal services providers and consumer-aid organizations.

▪ The Classifieds—search for products and services by type,

price, and location; see photo classifieds of autos for sale and apartments for rent; send out "Requests for Proposals" for needed services or repairs.

▪ City Hall—obtain government forms, pay taxes and parking fines, renew drivers' licenses, register to vote, reach city officials, comment on pending legislation, request action by various city departments (e.g., health or building inspections, animal control services).

▪ Exploring the City—make reservations for theaters, restaurants, and concerts; view cultural events listings, customized maps, and searchable directions; access tour, hotel, and tourist information.

▪ Shopping—download grocery discount coupons of choice, register for bridal gifts, shop at virtual malls and stores, search for products/services by item, price, or location.

▪ Sports and Recreation—reserve picnic areas and campgrounds, sign up for youth or amateur sports leagues and summer camps, buy tickets to sporting events, get stats on high school, college, and professional teams or players.

▪ Schools and Education—search out adult or continuing education programs, register for schools and classes, read minutes of school board meetings, check test-score ratings of local elementary and secondary schools.

▪ Resources and Services—get referrals to health, family, and other services; find out where to volunteer.

▪ Neighborhood Watch—request nonemergency police services (e.g., parking control), review area-by-area crime reports and missing persons and police "wanted" profiles, see listings of local neighborhood watch activities.

▪ The Social Scene—get information on church, club, and library activities; browse through the personals (including photo/video personals); access chat lines and an E-mail "post office."

The above examples of online service offerings, of course, help address only one of the challenges faced by media developers—the need to *localize* content. And we have already discussed the necessity of putting *human factors* at the forefront of any ventures in entertainment and shopping. But no matter what type of digital content is at issue, developers will need three keys to unlock the gates to the kingdom of riches: copyright, branding, and leverage.

One man who has a profound appreciation of the ways in which these three elements work together to drive success in the content business is Scott Sassa, the 35-year-old president of Turner Entertainment. Sitting in his offices, which used to house the Creative Artists Agency before it relocated to its new I. M. Pei–designed building, Sassa seems more the multimedia artist type in his jeans and T-shirt than a typical Hollywood mogul. His Hollywood career took off in 1986 when, at the tender age of 26, he developed the original business plan for the phenomenally successful Fox TV network. Today he sits in charge of a dozen film and TV enterprises, and when he speaks, it's with the voice of someone well versed in the art of the deal.

"Our business basically has two areas. The first is the creation of good copyrights. Entertainment companies—whether they do video games, movies, or TV—are always looking for that Holy Grail, that killer copyright. Whether it's Mortal Kombat or The Mask, Forest Gump, or Seinfeld. The second side of it is developing a system that leverages your content further, higher, faster than anybody else so as to maximize the value chain."

He offers as case in point the classic movie *Snow White*, which had just been released on video. "It's probably the best animated movie ever done. Walt Disney was great at the first part—creating the product. Then Katzenberg and Eisner created a second level of activity that extended the value chain. They took movies like *Little Mermaid*—which are good but aren't *Snow White*—and put them out on video, ran them on cable, released them in foreign markets, and licensed and merchandised toys based on the characters."

This is a new Hollywood, Sassa explains, one very different from the more self-contained entertainment business of 20 or 30 years ago. "Back then, it was just the copyright. You lived or died on the one-time success or failure of your copyright. Today these businesses are very complicated. They're vertically integrated, horizontally integrated. And every copyright that starts out anywhere in the system gets leveraged every which way imaginable."

As example, he mentions the projects being piggybacked onto Turner's *Jonny Quest* adventure cartoon series, which he describes as *"Home Alone* meets *Indiana Jones."*

"We're coordinating new episodes of the *Jonny Quest* cartoons with the development of a live-action feature film with [*Lethal*

Weapon director] Dick Donner and also as TV specials," he explains. "And we've got a fully integrated consumer products program to sell video games and T-shirts, Jonny Quest bikes and sneakers, and things like that. So basically that's what we're all about—creating a good copyright and then leveraging the hell out of it."

Why Hollywood's new emphasis on leverage? "Partly, it has to do with the huge cost of building these major, killer copyrights," Sassa notes. "But also, the entertainment business is becoming as segmented as a third-world country. On the one hand you have a few huge, very prosperous copyrights. You have your *Mask* [produced by Turner-owned New Line Cinema], your *Jurassic Park, True Lies, Clear and Present Danger,* and other hundred-million-dollar hits. And then you have successful little movies like *Four Weddings and a Funeral* and *Barcelona.* There's not a lot in between. Nowadays it seems that a few movies do over $100 million at the box office. And then a lot tank well under $40 million. But you don't have a lot of midrange movies. It's almost like they either take off or they don't."

This fragmentation of media markets, he believes, will only intensify. "So any company has first of all got to have the capital to build those big *Jurassic Park* copyrights. And second, it's got to have the wherewithal to get the value out of them because the entry cost is so high."

One of the oft-repeated promises of the Information Highway, however, is that new technology will lead to a vast explosion of new content production and distribution. Not only will consumers be able to receive what they want on demand, they'll also be able to publish or broadcast whatever they want via their interactive TVs and PCs. Doesn't this shift the center of gravity in entertainment content away from Hollywood and mitigate against the need for such capital-intensive enterprises as he describes?

"Just the opposite," says Sassa. "Sure, there'll be more room at the grassroots level, and a lot of new, small content developers will jump in. But there'll be so much information and entertainment and choice out there, there'll be a new problem. How does any show break through, really grab public attention? How does the consumer choose?"

Branding?

He nods. "Branding. Why do Disney animated movies do better than anybody else's? First, because they're great. And second, because we've come to know and trust the Disney animated movie brand. That's the value added. Think about it: what's the scarce commodity of the nineties? Time. With all the new choices, who has the time to watch everything, go to every movie? So by making sure that we're able to leverage our assets to create brands, we're able to make people's time more valuable. That's the new paradigm for success."

This "new paradigm for success" also helps to explain Turner's interest in acquiring one of the three broadcast networks, despite the fact that these were given up for dead by many experts until recently, having suffered a one-third loss of their audience over the past 20 years to cable TV and other new media. Once again, the issue is leverage.

"Obviously, the networks have been damaged over the years by some erosion of their audience," he concedes. "But we still think they're a good business. They still have the only beachfront, class-A real estate there is. And they have scale economics that nobody else comes close to."

Beachfront property?

"Sure, look at it this way: we own Castle Rock now, which produces *Seinfeld*. Now, I could argue with you that if we had owned it a few years back, we could have just created *Seinfeld*, and at far less cost, and run it on our cable systems. But we all know that *Seinfeld* would never have made it onto the cover of *Time* magazine. Only the networks can create that kind of cultural phenomenon."

Indeed, with all the choices in cable and syndication, the networks still command extraordinary audiences. Their prime-time shows—*Seinfeld, Home Improvement, Monday Night Football,* the Superbowl—all have audiences that cable networks can only dream of attracting.

"Why buy NBC? We believe that we offer enough value-added and unique benefits that we could make this asset even more valuable than it is currently."

How, exactly?

"Well, ask yourself, What is a network? It's a bunch of stations that get together and amortize the cost of producing top-of-the-line, million-dollar-an-hour programs. And they create copyrights based upon that relationship. That's the basics.

"Now, what's interesting about the economics of a network," he continues, "is that for every *Seinfeld* or *Home Improvement*, there's a whole string of very costly shows that make up the lower part of a network pyramid. This is the most costly part of their operations because they have to keep retooling each year, dumping the shows that don't catch on and producing new shows for the next year. So there's almost no payoff for all the investment they've made into the bottom half of their lineup."

How could Turner get value from those shows that are on the lower portion of the network ladder—the ones that don't become major hits?

"Simple. We have a guaranteed place to run them where the economics make sense—our cable systems. I'll give you an example. There's a show called *Saved by the Bell*. It's a teen sitcom that used to run on Saturday mornings on NBC. As a prime-time show it wouldn't have a chance going up against *Roseanne* and shows like that, which have broader audience appeal. And it didn't do well in syndication because it appealed only to teenagers, and teenagers alone aren't enough of an audience to make the local TV station that's running it competitive.

"So we got it for TBS," he smiles. "Now TBS runs it all across the country and—surprise, surprise!—its 2.5 rating makes it the highest-rated sitcom on cable. [In contrast, the network show *Roseanne* was getting a 17.5 rating at the time Sassa made these remarks.] In a local syndication market, a 2.5 rating is a disaster. But spread over a much larger base, where the costs are much less, a smaller audience can work."

So Hollywood's not dead?

"No," he laughs. "Hollywood's not going to wither away because of the multimedia revolution. We'll see Hollywood get even more powerful and more competitive."

Even when ordinary citizens in Akron, Ohio, begin to broadcast their own camcorder movies on the neighborhood arts and entertainment channel?

He pauses a moment. "Remember the original episode of [the short-lived TV series] *Max Headroom*? What happens is, in this apocalyptic future everybody has their own channel, but nobody can afford to make any real movies, so all the TV shows are boring, produced by people who carry their own little camera and walk around with a little satellite dish.

"My point is, even with the explosion from the grass roots, there's still going to be a need for mass culture, for truly great entertainment that transcends all the little niches and links people together. And even when some guy in Akron, Ohio, comes up with a funny show, it'll just be one amongst the universe of little grass-roots shows out there. How do people find it? How do they know about it? Hollywood is still going to be there to popularize the best that comes up from below and try to make killer copyrights out of them."

Sassa offers one additional and crucial thought on the subject: "We shouldn't forget that, just as there are only so many Monets and so many Picassos, there are only so many filmmakers who can make a *Citizen Kane* or a *Gone With the Wind* that captures the imaginations of tens of millions of people. Not everybody can do that. Really great artistic talent is not a commodity. It's always a scarce resource.

"So yeah, Hollywood's going to have to reinvent itself. But Hollywood as a leading cultural force, as a major industry, and even as a physical place—a watering hole that brings together this critical mass of storytelling talent and resources—that's never going to change."

"Never," of course, is an exceedingly long time, and everyone in the content business would be well served by keeping an open mind about big changes that may occur over the long term. New technology is also empowering other media centers, from London to Shanghai, and 100 years from now, one of these may have emerged as the principal locus of planetary culture. But with that long-term caveat in mind, Scott Sassa's argument is dead-on the money (so to speak).

If new technology merely acted to elevate the content business to a new and more central prominence in economic life, that would surely be exciting enough. But what is all too often missed by economists and industry spokespeople is the fact that the Digital Revolution is also transforming the structure and wealth-creating capacity of the marketplace in which content developers sell their products.

"The hope and the promise of digital technology goes far beyond simply the creation of new products and the launching of new businesses," insists General Magic's Marc Porat. "What's really at stake is the 'genetic material' of the economic system itself." He believes that the emerging new computer and communications technologies—especially the intelligent agent technologies that General

Magic and other companies are developing—could unleash powerful new wealth-creating forces throughout the economy.

Porat has studied the turning points of human economic activity over the ages, and he sees how changes in the way trade and commerce have been organized reflect major technological shifts in the societies in which they have occurred. These changes have led, in turn, to quantum leaps in the dynamics of wealth creation and in living standards.

"Before barter," Porat explains, "each person was constrained by his own limited personal resources and had to learn how to supply all his essential needs. The invention of barter, however, enabled him to trade the value of his intellectual content—the skills and knowledge that he put into making goat cheese, for example—for other goods he needed, like olive oil. Barter enabled people to tap into each other's knowledge and resources, and because of that, society was able to create more total wealth.

"Later, precious metal mining technologies allowed people to substitute gold for the goods themselves, which made the determination of value more efficient. Later still, the creation of paper money and related systems of accounts made it easier to reach into wider markets because you didn't have to lug all that heavy gold around. Finally, the invention of capital stock—shares of ownership in factories and other means of producing goods—helped money to flow where it could be best used to create new productive capacity, expand trade, and increase wealth."

What was the common thread running through these changes? "Abstraction of value was the key," Porat explains. "If I have to carry my goat cheese with me and find you with your olive oil, the market is slow. It's stilted. The transaction cost of finding you and arriving at an exchange value is high. But by abstracting our goods into something called gold—and then paper money and a system of accounts—trade can now move much faster and more broadly across vast distances. And then by abstracting the exchange of goods into the exchange of capital stock—in other words, into the power to produce those goods—we can create entrepreneurial opportunities more quickly and efficiently, which increases our ability to create more social wealth."

At the level of everyday consumption, however, not much has changed. "We're still limited by physical reality," Porat observes.

"We still go to the grocery store in person. We try to be efficient about it by making an effort to determine which stores have the best goods at the best price, or by looking through the paper for discount coupons and sales. But there's only so much we can do."

How does digital technology change that?

"The invention of electronic agents will now allow people to abstract their commercial desires from their physical selves—to create representatives of themselves that go off and do useful things for them in the marketplace, buying and selling goods and services.

"This has never happened before. We have always been firmly rooted in ourselves, except for minor exceptions like the ability to call a travel agent or a stock broker and have that agent do things for us. Until now, only the rich could afford agents. But with digital technology, people will have the ability to create electronics agents at little cost to do things for them."

He offers some examples: "If you want to take your family on vacation, you'll instruct your agent as to when and where you want to go—and how much you want to pay—and it will go around to hundreds of travel agents and airlines until it finds what you want at a cost you can afford. Or in my case, my kids burn through a pair of Nike shoes every six months, so I'd like to buy them on sale if I can. I'll be able to instruct an agent to sit out there in the electronic market, watching for those shoes to go on sale. When it spots a sale, it'll alert me to that fact or even purchase them and order delivery for me if I've told it to do so. The agent never gets bored, never complains. If what you want is in the marketplace, the agent will find it."

A convenience, to be sure, but how does that change the nature of the marketplace?

"Until now, merchandising has always been organized so that the person who has something to sell floods the market with advertising, promotions, coupons, and so on. But now we can turn that upside down. Now we can say to our agent, 'I want a discount coupon for cereal,' or 'I want the best-priced tune-up for my car.' Sellers will see your agent and, noticing that you're an interested buyer, will come to you to try to fill your request.

"This has never been done before," he adds. "There's never been a time in history where the ordinary consumer can put out to the market a request for proposal—an RFP—and have vendors bid on it. Corporations do it. Governments do it. But not consumers."

The technology could have profound effects on the efficiency of the market as a whole. "320 billion supermarket coupons are printed every year, but only about 8 billion of them are redeemed. What if consumers could use electronic agents to find discount coupons for cornflakes and toothpaste and other necessities without having to cut through newspapers? The economies would be tremendous. Merchandisers would not have to suffer the waste and expense of printing and distributing coupons that are redeemed at a two percent rate. And for the citizen with a disposable income after rents and mortgages of $500, the ability to easily obtain coupons that save him or her an extra $50 a month would mean a five percent raise after taxes in their income."

Does this mean retailing is about to be turned upside down—with the seller's market becoming a buyer's market? Not necessarily. What is likely, however, is that digital technology will give consumers more choice and buying power—even if this added leverage is traded off against some loss of privacy. And the compounding effects of a far more efficient buying and selling process could be enormous.

"As digital technology reduces the transaction cost of sellers and buyers finding each other—and of buyers and sellers reaching into wider and more varied markets on a global scale—the entire economy will become vastly more efficient. This will make available a lot more money that can be invested where it will create new businesses, new growth, and new opportunities."

Such changes will surely not come about overnight. "It'll probably take 30 years to understand what it all means," says Porat. "And by 30 years, I mean if we start right now, maybe when our kids grow up they'll know how to really take advantage of this new economy."

PART THREE

Brave New World

· 10 ·

Private Riches, Social Wealth

Over the last nine chapters, we have observed the Digital Revolution as it is unfolding on some of its most hotly contested fronts. We have seen many of the leading Info Highway road warriors up close in combat, and have taken you into their tents to hear their personal visions. We have analyzed their various strategies and tactics for building new Information Age businesses, and evaluated, as best as we can, their chances of success. And throughout, we have explored the critical long-term issues suggested by the clash of forces and of ideas within our field of vision.

But now it is time to leave the smoke and grit of the battlefield, climb a tall tree, and from higher ground, survey the panorama of this epochal struggle. We need to look beyond the battlefield and behold some of the larger social and economic contours of the Digital Revolution in order to understand the ways in which it is transforming the institutions, structures, and consciousness of our society.

As we have indicated at various points throughout this book, *context* has become a particularly precious resource in a world increasingly glutted with information (or should we say "data," for true information is data placed in context). Analyzing and contextualizing raw data into some sort of usable knowledge, filtering out fiction dressed up as fact, synthesizing the best and the most relevant visions from amid the exploding marketplace of ideas, and offering new and innovative points of view—these are responsibilities of those who presume to be information providers.

We have taken that responsibility seriously, knowing that it prevents us from being encyclopedic or from covering every issue from every angle in this book. In this, perhaps, our approach to communicating our point of view has been well suited to the form in which you are now receiving it—not the deconstructed format of multimedia but rather the logical, rational narrative and argument of a printed book.

So now we turn our attention to the challenge of divining meaning out of complex and seemingly chaotic events and processes. As we have pointed out, most digital revolutionaries share a general sense that the roads they are pioneering through cyberspace, the businesses they are building, and the content they are creating will, over time, change the basic fabric of society and contribute to the definition of a new social order. We have signaled our differences with those who believe these changes will either be more extreme, happen more rapidly, or follow straighter trajectories than we believe they will. But there is no disagreement on the essentially revolutionary nature of the forces unleashed by the new technology. And there can be no doubt that the Digital Revolution is going to change the way knowledge is gained and the way wealth is created.

These changes cannot help but alter fundamental aspects of the way life is lived throughout large parts of this planet. Today, the Digital Revolution is still primarily just a set of technological advances, cultural ideas, experiments, ventures, start-ups, and early-stage businesses. However, as the gap closes between today's status quo and the landscape on tomorrow's horizon line, we are drawing closer to the hour of decision over whether this profound technological revolution will develop a social conscience—and if so, what kind.

It is toward a deeper understanding of the long-term consequences of the Digital Revolution—how its promise might be enhanced and some of its perils minimized—that we turn our attention in the following chapters.

To begin, consider for a moment the much-maligned term "Information Highway." While not an accurate description of the communications matrix that digital technology is now engendering, as metaphor it is nonetheless particularly apt at spotlighting the role transportation systems have played in the commerce and culture of many societies. Roman roads, crusaders' routes, the sea lanes in the age of explorers, the railroads, and the interstate highway system— each of these was integral to the creation of wealth in the societies in which they developed.

Road-building is usually divisible into at least two major phases, two component activities, and two differentiated sources of wealth. First comes the period of trailblazing and setting the infrastructure in place. Then, in phase two, the predominant action shifts to the opportunities presented once the roads are open.

Considered at the level of infrastructure, the development of the American interstate highway system is a drama that involves not just the pouring of concrete but also such wide-ranging phenomena as the power of the oil industry and its political lobbies, the role of the Teamsters union, and fears of the Cold War era. Indeed, the cold war–era beliefs of the Eisenhower administration—formed on the battlefields of Europe a few years earlier and influenced by fear of an aggressive Soviet Union in the early 1950s—caused the emerging highway system to be seen as a military necessity, a defense network system for moving tanks and material in the event of war. That, in turn, brought the federal government into the process in a big way and greatly speeded the highway's completion.

The specialist may take a continuing interest in the infrastructure of America's highway system, from how freeway curves are banked to how rush hour congestion can be eased. But for most people, what is interesting about the highway system now is *not* the story of how it was built but what it begat. And that is a tale of the second phase of road-building. In the case of the highways, it encompasses everything from the development of the automobile industry as the central engine of American economic power, to many less obvious downstream implications.

According to David Halberstam, the reigning chronicler of the decade of the 1950s, the great social insight of the McDonald brothers was *not* necessarily that Americans had an enormous appetite for hamburgers. Rather, it was their understanding of the diaspora of mobility created by new highways and new automobiles, the long distances workers were commuting, and the need to get a quick meal on the way.[1]

It was not just the modern fast-food industry that grew up along-side the highway system. From Holiday Inns and the motel industry, to the "mailing of America," to the ascendancy of southern California and, later, the entire Sunbelt, the highway system influenced the demography of American society and the robustness of the long post–World War II economic boom. In an ultimate sense, the by-products of the highway system are today's highly integrated conti-nent-wide American economy, our personal mobility, social fluidity, and common mass culture.

Infrastructure-building can be exciting. The story of American railroads certainly is. From the construction race that led to driving in the final spike connecting the eastern and western lines at Prom-ontory Point, Utah, in 1869, to Indian wars and robber barons, the creation of America's rail infrastructure is the stuff of legends. The building of the interstate highway system was much less adventurous and certainly less glamorous, but it, too, offers great insights into the thinking of its era. For while no infrastructure has the power to dictate the future, it surely conditions it. Assumptions about the future—correct and incorrect, morally uplifting and cynically avari-cious—lie resident in the thought process of infrastructure designers and builders, as well as those who employ them, invest in them, regulate them, and oppose them.

As Stephen B. Goddard points out in his book *Getting There: The Epic Struggle Between Road and Rail in the American Century,* the private automobile was massively subsidized by an American gov-ernment that saw its political interests in breaking up the power of the railroads and imagined—apparently correctly—that cars, high-ways, and suburbs would become an unending prosperity machine. Washington not only paid for building a highway system so that pas-senger cars could compete with railroads as effective transportation, it shackled the freight train business with onerous regulation and left trucking companies virtually unregulated for decades until the railroads had been eviscerated.

As Goddard shows, policy makers winked at the intrigues of the auto industry, including a flagrant and now well-documented con-spiracy by General Motors, Standard Oil, and Firestone Tire & Rub-ber in the 1940s to put big-city trolley lines out of business.[2] Some critics would argue today that the collaboration of government regu-lators with the politically powerful telephone companies at the expense of the cable industry's interests is not unlike that cabal of half a century ago.

On the other side, the positive fruit of corporate involvement in developing enjoyable, easy-to-use, free services on the World Wide Web is analogous to the Ford Motor Company's support in the early part of this century for the development of scenic roadways in order to encourage the art of motoring. Along the romantic Columbia River Gorge, for example, a road was lovingly carved out of the mountainside by stone masons imported for the job from Italy. The highway would wend its way through some of America's most awe-inspiring forests and around the sides of breathtaking waterfalls. In the Columbia Gorge even today—as on the Arroyo Seco in southern California, the Merritt Parkway in Connecticut, and other early highways, the aesthetic that favored scenic, winding roads is still in evidence. By making driving enjoyable and the weekend trip in the car an "event," the early road builders made people want to drive, fueling both the highway construction industry as well as the automotive industry.

And just as Deep Throat once urged reporters Woodward and Bernstein to "follow the money" in order to crack the mystery of the Watergate break-in, those who want to glimpse the future shape of the Information Highway should follow the trail of investments being made by infrastructure builders today. Such a method does not guarantee an accurate picture of tomorrow's highway, but at least it allows us to see what some of those who have the best evidence to go on believe this highway will look like.

Until now, most of the action has been concentrated in phase one of this great game. The focus is on the infrastructure builders—those who are "pouring the concrete" for the roads (telephone, cable, and satellite companies) and on the "vehicle" makers who are designing the "cars" (computers, television sets, telephones, PDAs, set-top boxes, etc.) that will use these roads.

One can have decent vehicles and decent roads, but as General Magic CEO Marc Porat observed in the last chapter, the bottom line for growth and profit is developing exciting destinations to which consumers will want to travel. Without meaningful content and broadly popular applications, the technology can't be scaled up sufficiently to be perfected or deployed profitably. History books record, for example, that the first permanent telegraph line designed for public use (and subsidized by the U.S. government) stood virtually idle for the first 20 years of its existence. People were not familiar with the technology, and they weren't inspired to think of uses for it. Or look at the Internet and the commercial online services. These have been around in one form or another for over 20 years. But it is only since 1993 or so that there's been enough interesting content to begin attracting public interest beyond the narrow community of scientists, engineers, and computer enthusiasts.

Sensing the power of digital technology, many corporations are looking for so-called killer apps (applications). Video-on-demand, home shopping, and games are often cited. But the more likely truth is that there will be no one, two, or even three discrete applications of such scope and popularity that they drive the entire market and justify investments in it.

Rather, in a broadband, digitally switched world, thousands of interesting applications will arise besides the obvious ones. Looking for the killer app of the Info Highway is a bit like looking for the killer app of electricity. Is it lighting? Is it refrigerators? Is it television? Is it computers, copying machines, VCRs, or blow dryers? Thomas Edison was surely a man of great vision. He knew electricity would mean much more than lighting, even though electric lights were the greatest-felt need of his day. He experimented with recorded music and images. But it is safe to say he never imagined 99 percent of what's in the Sharper Image catalog. And there is no indication that he would have even believed that in 1995 there would be a billion-dollar-a-year worldwide market in electric blow dryers.

You can have all the market tests and focus groups you want, but you can't predict with any certitude which services from the coming communicopia people will want to pay for and use. And once the system is in use, you certainly can't predict the innovations that will be developed by those who are exposed to it, particularly the new generation that will grow up using digital technology like water.

What we do know is that the ultimate market size is potentially staggering. Indeed, this may be the biggest marketplace in history. But quantifying it can be tricky, and those who've tried have had mixed results.

In 1992, for example, John Sculley, then CEO of Apple Computer, launched an internal company study to try to envision the next phase of technological development after the personal computer. What he saw was a huge and converging information industry marketplace in which the computer industry would thrive by connecting itself to what were then still considered widely disparate businesses, such as office equipment, telecommunications, consumer electronics, entertainment, publishing, and media. What really induced future shock was when Sculley, with the aid of a Harvard think tank, went out on a limb and forecast that the annual global revenues of this converged information industry marketplace would be $3.5 *trillion* by the year 2000!

Even analysts accustomed to dealing with the computer industry's propensity for hyperbole found *that* figure too alluring to pass up. It soon moved into popular parlance in Silicon Valley, in Hollywood, on Wall Street, and wherever media men and women gathered. In doing so, Sculley's magic number added fuel to the wildfire of hype about the Digital Revolution that was just then beginning to burn across the corporate and media landscapes.

By early 1994, however, Sculley was gone from his post at Apple, the TCI–Bell Atlantic merger had fallen apart, interactive TV trials were failing and flailing, and the roller coaster of hype had peaked and was plunging back to earth precipitously.

One can hang almost any CEO or industry savant on the overly inflated words spoken at the dawn of Info Highway fever in 1992–1993, when it first became evident that digital compression and switching technology could lead to interactive broadband networks about 10 years sooner than had previously been thought. As the *Economist* points out, 1993 was a year in which the Info Highway went from "fantasy to commonplace to cliché," and then to backlash.[3] In the view of industry consultant Richard Shaffer:

> Expectations of the potential market size of the digital electronics business rose to unbelievable heights in 1993, crashed down to almost nothing in early 1994, and have now recovered to reasonably plausible levels. We have gone from talking about a market size in the trillions of dollars, to one in the millions, and back up to one in the hundreds of billions—all in the absence of this business yet producing anything more than a statistically insignificant sliver of real revenues.

The fact that building the Info Highway is a complex task, subject to huge mood swings in the media as well as within public policy-making circles and even within the leading companies involved in the effort, should not be taken to mean that the project is failing.

Yes, cynics can point to the failures of interactive TV trials and the backing away from earlier rollout schedules. Some home shopping projects have fizzled, many online ventures have failed to attract interest, and publishers who have solved the technical problems in repurposing their traditional content into a multimedia environment have not necessarily found a way to make any money doing so. Indeed, if you look behind the emerald curtains of some of the big players in the field, you will find little men with big PR budgets pretending to be great and terrible Wizards of Oz.

(In one of the early tests of interactive television, for example, a consumer's choice of movie came into a communications center as a message on a computer screen accompanied by a ringing alarm bell. The alarm bell cued a high school student on Rollerblades to race to find the right video and load it into a cassette player—hardly the futuristic image we associate with the high-speed digital switching systems of tomorrow's Infobahn.)

But directing all those digitized bits of information to the right places at the right times is no mean feat. For public consumption, some cable and telephone company executives may imply that it's going to be a piece of cake. But that's a bit like Einstein concluding in 1905 that his general theory of relativity would make it easy to develop an atomic bomb, or the Wright Brothers positing after Kitty Hawk that it was only a short hop to the Concorde.

Like most other economic processes, building the Information Highway will be a complex evolution that proceeds in every which way *except* that of a straight, quick line. It is worth remembering that it took almost 70 years to wire half of America for basic telephone service. A similar period elapsed between the time the first real automotive highways were paved and when a fully integrated national highway system was more or less completed. No matter how much the world seems to have speeded up these days, the integration of new technology still takes time.

But given a bit more time and some more sobriety in understanding the constituent elements, Sculley's 1992 forecast may turn out to be more right than it now looks.

When Sculley came up with his $3.5 trillion number, he had engaged in a relatively simple exercise of aggregating the projected worldwide revenues for the year 2000 of significant parts of the following businesses: computer hardware, software, and peripherals; telephone hardware and services, including cellular phones, mobile phones, and pagers; office equipment and consumer electronics devices of all kinds; broadcast and cable television; entertainment, including filmed entertainment, recorded music, video rentals and sales, and games; home shopping and catalog retailing; magazine, newspaper, book, references, and new media publishing; advertising and marketing; information and online transactional services; home educational and self-improvement tools; medical imaging and diagnostics; online and at-home financial and investment services; satellite communications; and perhaps a number of other slices of existing and emerging sectors where digital technology has the possibility of influencing or changing the business.

Although it has become less fashionable to say so than it was in 1993, most of these businesses, which once had little to do with each other, *are* converging—at least to some degree. They are obviously not merging into one single $3.5 trillion market, but they certainly are moving closer together in terms of their markets.

If video games, encyclopedias, human voices, and medical records can all be converted into digitized bits traveling the same networks, then there is going to be at least a pronounced tendency for those in the business of handling this traffic flow, as well as those who create and supply the traffic itself, to be drawn together. The fact that all this content is, electronically speaking, reducible to mere ones and zeros, implies that the right business leaders with the right vision can find the way either to step next door into another sector of the convergence grid or even leap across it to enter businesses that appear far afield.

Alliances, partnerships, new marketing techniques, and cobranding are expanding the ability of a company to reach from any one point on the grid to any other. As MCI's Vinton G. Cerf pointed out in announcing a new service providing consumer Internet connections and an electronic mall with products from Timberland shoes to Aetna insurance, "MCI just turned left—we're not just a telecommunications company anymore."[4]

The convergence grid is not simply limited to leading-edge businesses, however. It will also pull more traditional kinds of businesses into its orbit in the years ahead.

As on-screen and online shopping become more of a reality, for example, the traditional supermarket business will face an imperative to change. Over the short term, supermarkets may be unaffected by the slow percolation and evolution of cyber-shopping. Their main technology challenge may lie in bar-coded checking and inventory management or wider use of electronic payment vehicles. But long term, the heart of the supermarket business will be up for grabs if consumers can order most of their staples and daily necessities from home shopping systems tied in to remote warehouses and trucking systems. The high cost of choice supermarket real estate, coupled with the high overhead of checkers and retail merchandising, could become literally unsustainable in many locations.

The point is that the Digital Revolution will be shaped not just by what John Malone, Ray Smith, Bill Gates, and the other road warriors do with their corporate strategies, but by the decisions of Safeway and the A&P as well.

Consider how the telecommuting trend is moving into everyday life, creating new markets and wreaking havoc with old ones. Already, over 7 million Americans work for their employer from their homes, and 20 million are involved with home-based businesses. The Home Office Association estimates that upward of 40 million were doing some or all of their work from home in 1994. Improved videophone and video conferencing, groupware software, E-mail, high-speed modems, online information resources, and eventually, broadband switched networks, will make it more possible to do many kinds of traditional collaborative office work at home. Advanced telecommunications and online services that might not otherwise be justified by household needs or budgets will enter many homes via business necessity and the tax-deductible home office.

The growing telecommuting trend is already beginning to affect the construction business (more homes built or renovated to create home offices) and even the fashion business (diminished sales volume of formal office work clothes, increased sales of casual sports clothes for comfortable telecommuting).

The home appliance industry is also undergoing change. New devices and services are being researched and developed, including online recipe terminals in the kitchen, remote utility meter-reading, portable wireless touchscreen pads that depict an image of the house and allow the user to set lights, temperature, and security controls room by room. Computer, telephone, and cable companies will compete with utilities, consumer electronics companies, and home security firms for pieces of this business.

The television news business may change as video clipping services and video databases become more important. NBC Cable is already offering a service that allows instant access to televised news reports about companies or news-making speeches by public figures. Bond traders, equity analysts, and corporate communications people are the market: the videotape of the finance minister's face as he says his country has no intention of devaluing its currency can sometimes be more informative than the wire service text. Eventually, these services will ride down the cost curve. The big users over time won't be confined to the "master of the universe" community but will expand to ordinary folks who will be able to access video databases of school plays and sports events as well as the speeches of candidates in community elections.

The selling of automobiles and other consumer durables will also change, thanks to the impending rollout of interactive TV services. Already, car buyers are comparison shopping with remote dealers online. Some customers are getting product information from automotive Web sites where shoppers can compare features in detail and even test virtual versions of color schemes. Moreover, cars themselves will change as they become what futurist Paul Saffo calls "carcoons"—vehicles rich with information appliances from phones and faxes to satellite geopositioning maps.

And don't forget the advertising, marketing, and public relations professions. These will undergo huge makeovers as a result of the media's new ability to target and create one-to-one "relationship" marketing with consumers. Much of the cost of new interactive services will be borne by advertisers and marketers who offer free or reduced-cost access to movies or other fare in order to bring particular customers into their orbit and to position themselves and their messages favorably. Anything sold electronically has the potential to create a more customized database of consumer needs and wants. The more you buy, the more you tell the marketer about yourself, and the easier it will become for some marketers to sell to you.

A good manifesto for the coming digital marketing revolution was contained in a *Harvard Business Review* article by consultants B. Joseph Pine, Don Peppers, and Martha Rogers, who argued that companies seeking to thrive in the future will need to "use technology to become two things: a *mass customizer* that efficiently provides individually customized goods and services, and a *one-to-one marketer* that elicits information from each customer about his or her specific needs and preferences." The correct combination of these qualities creates "a learning relationship—an ongoing connection that becomes smarter as the two interact with each other," collaborating to help smart companies keep their customers "forever." Or at least keep them one step ahead of their competitors, unless, of course, the competition is even smarter.[5]

Still photography may slowly—very slowly—begin to disappear, except as an art form, as digital cameras and photo-processors steadily improve their performance. The photographic empires of Kodak and Fuji are already shifting more into the consumer electronics and office equipment markets with scanners and digital image processing tools of all kinds. Home video cameras, whose output was once confined to playback on home VCRs, will be developing transmission ports for televising images to friends and family members over phone or cable lines.

Telemedicine will be another growing area, giving new meaning to "house calls." Patients will be able to stay at home, yet consult by video conference with doctors and specialists. Today's cumbersome movement of X rays and other paper medical records will be automated and speeded up via network transmission. Many of these services will be provided not by doctors or hospitals but by new service companies attracted to the idea of taking a slice out of the trillion-dollar-a-year health care pie.

Toys, entertainment, and education—everything having to do with children—will be adding interactive dimensions and changing as a result. CD-ROMs have already extended the notion of the pop-up book and brought new levels of creativity, artfulness, and interactivity to the field of children's publishing. Parental attitudes toward television may change when the best quality children's programming, historical movies, documentaries, and personally customized tours of the world's great museums are available all the time and include the opportunity to ask questions and interact with experts. And Dare to Dream, a start-up company, is designing a new kind of "social interface" to the digital world—lovable stuffed animals that act as book-reading, song-singing, game-playing robots, directed wirelessly by digital instructions from videotapes and CD-ROMs.

The debate will continue, of course, about the degree to which computer-based tools ought to be used in classroom learning and about the ideal pedagogical balance between human teachers and teaching machines. But the reality is that the learning experience available from today's best educational software is probably better than that from many poor-quality teachers. Even the hallowed Ivy League halls are not safe from the cost-benefit challenge of interactive education. Arno Penzias, the Nobel Prize winner who heads AT&T's Bell Labs, wonders—with good reason—"Will we get our education in the future from Arthur Andersen or Microsoft instead of Berkeley or Harvard?"

Banks and brokerage firms will go head-to-head with software companies, online services, and mutual fund managers for control of the at-home personal investment and financial services market. Indeed, if the banks aren't careful, Microsoft or another software company could sweep aside traditional retail banking with a powerful home program. The efforts to develop "cybercash" and "E-money" (secure, anonymous settlement mechanisms for buying and selling goods in cyberspace) could turn small companies with computer security expertise into major banking institutions of the future.

All of this only scratches the surface of the changing face of business. Nearly 70 percent of the U.S. economy is tied up in the consumer sector. And digital technology will turn every home computer and TV set into a window facing out onto vast shopping malls. The convenience of built-in, 24-hour points of purchase in the home (not to mention in offices, cars, taxicabs, airplanes, restaurants, and kiosks) will, over time, have dramatic effects on consumption patterns involving hundreds of billions of dollars.

Yet it is always important to remember that while the Digital Revolution makes many new technologies and products possible, the job of creating real-world markets is constrained by the laws of capitalism and as well as those of human nature. New markets are competing with old ones for a finite supply of consumer dollars. And new digital services are reliant on old-fashioned analog humans to understand and embrace them.

Consider this case in point: everyone conversant in Info Highway issues can imagine that one way or another, a broadband network will eventually deliver video-on-demand. Everyone knows this will cannibalize large parts of the video store business over the long run. But right now, today, Blockbuster is still doing very well, thank you. For the next five years—maybe ten—its business in renting out old-fashioned videos will be far more profitable than the efforts of cable and telephone companies trying to deliver movies electronically.

As Frank Biondi, CEO of Blockbuster's parent company, Viacom, points out, "Even ten years from now, our best-case scenario is that only half of American homes will be wired for interactive television with access to a broad film library. The other half will still be going to Blockbuster." And even for the half that has access to video-on-demand, there will be consumers who won't want to pay what the interactive networks will charge them. "So we may get a piece of that market as well," adds Biondi. Then there are Blockbuster's product line extensions (half a billion dollars in video game rentals in 1994) and its growth in booming foreign markets, where it will take much longer for video-on-demand to arrive. "So don't worry about us," concludes Biondi.

Blockbuster, of course, knows full well that it must move eventually toward an electronic delivery model. But through some of its own experiments, it has discovered that the day of reckoning with electronic delivery may be further off than it looks. In 1994, for example, the company launched a venture with IBM to develop a prototype service to create music CDs "on demand" in Blockbuster stores. This kind of in-store shopping-on-demand is thought by many experts to be the way software of all kinds (including printed books) may go. It is an attractive road for merchants because it solves the inventory problem, reduces shipping costs, and streamlines overhead. The technology to do this is largely available, including the ability to customize a personal CD with specific track selections and even customer-specific packaging. But in the Blockbuster case, the company soon found itself in the middle of a war with powerful forces in the recording industry that wanted the experiment stopped. The record companies, it turned out, were not yet ready to cede control of their physical products or overturn their publishing business model.

Meanwhile, at some movie studios, there is suddenly more confidence in taking a small incremental step up the technology ladder to the Digital Video Disk (DVD) as the successor to the video cassette for the next few years, than there is about interactive television.

Economic downturns and fickle public mood swings will also wreak havoc with elegant engineering plans for other new digital services. Just as interactive TV investments were hot in 1993 but turned cold in 1994, we can expect the same thing to happen to today's red-hot world of Internet investment and to whatever follows in its place.

Yet throughout this vast Darwinian struggle, digital technology will continue to evolve. Businesspeople on the front lines understand that there's no turning back the digital tide. "The change from analog to digital is changing every cost curve, every investment curve, and every set of expectations about our business and our competition," declared Ivan Seidenberg in the spring of 1995, shortly after assuming the job as NYNEX's CEO.

"Digital technology will change or render obsolete every product our company makes or sells in the next few years," adds Joe Clayton, the chief of marketing and sales for Thomson Consumer Electronics, which has been in the forefront of the fast-growing market for satellite TV services. "But we don't expect customers will know or care that what they are buying is 'digital.'" Clayton speaks with some authority, for while the cable companies were carrying out limited trials of expanded channel service, wondering if customers wanted video-on-demand and how much they'd be willing to pay, Thomson and its partners moved onto fast-forward. They put 175-channel service into a stunning 900,000 homes in the first nine months of business—with consumers paying $699 a pop for the pizza-size dishes needed to receive the satellite signals.

As new businesses are created and old businesses adapt or die, two underlying processes are at work creating new social wealth. The first of these—one that we call *revenue substitution*—involves a dynamic whereby both new and established companies seek to divert the cash flows of existing businesses. As we have seen, much of the battle between telephone companies and cable television companies is about diverting major chunks of the hundreds of billions of dollars worth of cable TV and telephony revenues from their former owners as new technology and government deregulation open these markets to real competition.

Similarly, over the next few years, CD-ROMs and online services will take some market share from print publishing, electronic home shopping will divert revenue from catalog and retail shopping, World Wide Web marketing will muscle in on traditional advertising and public relations budgets, personal digital assistants may replace some Filofaxes and some real personal assistants, and so forth. The point is that the *entry strategy* for most new competitors is to divert enough revenue from the old way the game was played to get started in building what eventually becomes a new market.

Revenue substitution might at first appear to be nothing but a zero-sum game in the overall picture of total economic output. If the 1995 total U.S. market size for telephone and television services is roughly $380 billion, and the market size in the year 2000 turns out to be basically the same when adjusted for inflation and population growth, then it will look outwardly as if nothing happened. But underneath the surface of those steady-state figures, we can anticipate very significant changes. Companies that now get much of their revenue from television may find their fastest growth in telephone services, and vice-versa. Print publishers may lose money for years with their online experiments but then suddenly develop enough critical mass in the market to turn highly profitable.

As NYNEX's Seidenberg points out, "We're facing absolute shrinkage of our revenues because competitors are able to come into our markets and snatch pieces, but we can't yet go into theirs. We will solve this problem one way or another—by getting the right to enter their markets, by entering totally new markets, and by going abroad." Indeed, the company whose acronym stands for New York and New England already owns nearly 30 percent of the cable and telephone market in some parts of the United Kingdom.

The technologies will change, the investment formulas will change, the packaging and bundling of services will change. New competition will spur innovation and price cutting, so that even if the total market size in a given sector remains the same and consumers are not asked to pay more, they may end up getting much more service. This is what has happened in long-distance telephony, for example, where consumers now pay less per call but make a much higher volume of long-distance calls than ever before. Meanwhile, changes in the underlying technology and new business efficiencies allow the long-distance carriers to make higher profits on lower pricing.

The fact that old markets are cracking open like giant piñatas means that the roster of winners, losers, and ongoing players will change drastically. New companies will arise, existing companies will gain strength, and gargantuan megamergers will consolidate the shape of these industries. Some current competitors will lose, fail, and disappear. Fear will drive many companies to explore this new world and change their culture. Actually believed in many boardrooms at the moment are the overstated warnings of a San Francisco computer magazine: "Get on the Internet. Remember that those who cannot communicate electronically will simply perish, at least businesswise."[6]

Some surprising entrants into the competition will also try to reinvent themselves in order to participate in the digital marketplace. Utility companies, for example, have visions of using their lines into consumer's homes as a "third" pipe for the Information Highway. They would like to turn their mere gas and electric lines into transmission belts for a host of value-added, higher-margin services, just as phone companies are doing. In short, they want in on the content business.

Defense companies, trying to pick up the pieces of their business after the cold war ended, are recognizing that within their storehouses of human engineering capital they have some of the best computer scientists, communications specialists, and software developers in the world. The smartest of the defense companies are shifting considerable resources into the effort to change their culture, tap into their talents, and reemerge as information technology companies instead.

Even the giants who once pioneered the world of ones and zeros, such as IBM, are now trying to reinvent themselves to capture positions in the new desktop-based distributed architectures of the Digital Revolution. Thus, Big Blue was willing to pay more than twice what the stock market believed Lotus was worth, all to get ahold of one key hit product, Lotus Notes, which has the potential to transform the way many kinds of office work are done.

In sum, revenue substitution creates new wealth for society—but it does so indirectly. As new players topple established ones, as market leaders are forced to innovate, new efficiencies and economies of scale are created. These in turn allow capital to flow where it can be productively used to fund new businesses and build new markets. In a process of creative destruction and construction, revenue substitution can be the mother's milk of change and growth.

The more direct path to creating new wealth in society—we call it the *quantum growth leap*—is through the development of entirely new products and services, markets and businesses. Some of these new markets are already growing at prairie fire pace but from such low bases that they don't yet count for much. Yet the law of compounding numbers suggests that businesses enjoying today's double-digit monthly growth rates will reach sizable scale in the not-too-distant future, even assuming that today's 15-percent-per-month growth rate in a field such as Internet communications cools off to a mere 15 percent per year.

The mathematical exercise in which you put a penny on the first square of a chessboard and then double it to two pennies on the next, then double it again to four, eight, sixteen, and so forth is instructive here: By the time you get to the other side of the board your penny has mushroomed into nearly all the money in the world. High compound growth rates over just a single generation allowed Japan, for example, to go from postwar rubble to economic superpower.

The information economy, with its double-digit annual growth rates, is comparable to having a huge "emerging market" within America's borders. Depending on which digital business we are speaking about, growth rates vary generally between three and ten times faster than the rest of the economy—and some, of course, are off the charts entirely. This kind of growth is almost unprecedented in the world's developed economies at the moment. And it is even impressive when compared to the excitement that has been generated about investing in the emerging markets of East Asia and Latin America. Like a real emerging market, the digital sector can absorb huge amounts of investment and convert that investment in a relatively short time to profit. Like a real emerging market, too, the more capital is allocated for the massive infrastructure-building needs, the faster the digital economy can grow.

When you have virgin territory of this type, it is possible for pioneers to lay claim to vast stretches. A single concept successfully implemented or a single acquisition well made, can open up an enormous franchise. Think, for example of Sumner Redstone, who was once merely a movie theater chain owner with an entrepreneurial flair. He took control of Viacom, then bought MTV early on, and now

Viacom is a mooing cash cow capable of swallowing Paramount and becoming the world's second biggest media company. Or take a company like General Instrument, once a relatively dull commodity cable converter maker and now a hot contender to lead the sales of millions upon millions of new juiced-up set-top boxes. Or a Broad-Band Technologies, with a proprietary approach to bringing fiber to the curb. Or an Intuit, which built a whole new market in computerized home finance and may well provide the interface through which millions of Americans will look at their bank accounts and portfolios in the years to come.

However, it is worth remembering that the digital marketplace, just like China or Brazil, may offer higher profit potential than elsewhere, but also higher risk.

Those with capital will make big bets on new markets, and some of them will fail. Remember pen-based computing and the hot little company, Eo, which made tablet computers with heavy support from AT&T? It was a hot company with an interesting technology and major backers, yet it failed.

Remember Chris Whittle's Medical News Network? Doctors could call up the latest scientific studies, get information from pharmaceutical companies, watch the latest TV news report on the problems with a new wonder drug, review medical conference proceedings, or log in to continuing education courses. Whittle and his investors pumped close to $2 million a week into this venture and had installed the system in several thousand medical offices. Drug companies had agreed to advertise, yet it failed.

Or how about MecklerWeb, a much-ballyhooed start-up from Alan Meckler, a man who made his high-tech reputation by organizing conferences on topics like virtual reality and the Internet. He sought to parlay his connections into a high-end service advising big corporations on developing their Web sites and their interactive services. MecklerWeb was announced with great fanfare in October 1994. DEC lent hundreds of thousands of dollars worth of computer equipment to the venture. Other blue-chip backers included computer services giant EDS and advertising behemoth Ogilvy & Mather. But MecklerWeb's server went up into the cloud and then promptly came crashing down. Within two weeks of its launch, MecklerWeb was shut down. No one wanted to pay the excessive costs for a Web design service that, when first contemplated, was unique, but was competing with commodity vendors just a few months later.

Obviously, there are no guarantees. Being digital is not enough. But the successes are going to far outstrip the failures, especially if you know how to pick 'em. The upside of this revolution *is* after all, a kingdom of riches. That's why, in the words of Smith Barney media analyst John Reidy, "everybody's talking to everybody" in Hollywood[7] even though, as screenwriter William Goldman pointed out long ago, the one thing you can always count on about Hollywood is that "nobody knows anything." It's why Strauss Zelnick, who ran a start-up video game company for a while in between stints as an executive at 20th Century Fox and Bertelsmann, declares, "There's no shortage of capital willing to chase almost every harebrained scheme as long as it's called interactive."[8]

The digital gold rush is on, generating a madcap frenzy to stake claims. That's why heretofore conservative communications companies are willing to plop down billions of dollars at auction for PCS licenses, using their arsenals of lawyers, investment bankers, and Nobel Prize–winning "game" theorists to muscle the competition out of the way as they build crazy quilts of spectrum across the continent. "Nobody has any idea of what they're going to do with the license, how they're going to use it, what value it has, if any. But they have to act now," because now is the time the FCC is allowing prospectors to stake their spectrum claims, observes communications consultant Hershel Shoesteck.[9]

It is that chance to stake claims on big chunks of tomorrow's $3.5 trillion market that has turned American CEOs who were once criticized for being short-term oriented into, comparatively speaking, long-term planners. Those making new media investments and acquisitions believe they are gaining footholds in enterprises that will benefit from high compounded growth rates.

Look at this process the way the managers of the Bear Sterns New Age Media Fund do: "In our view, the creation of a fully interactive nationwide communications network could open up *the largest market opportunity in history*, possibly generating several hundred billion dollars in new net GNP growth over the next fifteen years."[10]

Take note: this comment speaks of several hundred billion dollars a year in *new net GNP growth*. Not revenue substitution. Net growth. And this view was expressed at the *end* of 1994, long *after* the early phase of overinflated hype had become passe. The boys at Bear Stearns—and many of their counterparts at financial firms up and down Wall Street—believe that the complex chain reactions set in motion by the Digital Revolution's sweep through business and the marketplace will, in time, yield a quantum leap in the total process of wealth creation. Ahead lies a period of new capital formation so substantial it could renew and reinvigorate the American Dream.

In fact, it is already starting to happen. For a long time, the net effect of investment in computer technology on the U.S. economy was a topic shrouded in a gray fog of academic argument. Although personal computers proliferated in the 1980s and the computer industry became one of the largest sectors of American business activity, some economists argued that the decade's trillion-dollar investment in computer technology was not paying off. They cited statistics showing, for example, that office productivity was about the same at the end of the decade as at the beginning, despite the fact that over 20 million personal computers had been plunked down on the desktops of corporate America. But it became obvious by 1993 that the productivity curve was starting to skew in a positive direction as a result of information technology.

Enough computers had been installed, enough investment in computerizing operations had been made, enough people had developed the appropriate skills, and enough communications and networking capabilities were now baked into the technology to allow significant and observable increases in service sector productivity. In the 1980s, the abysmally low rates of service sector productivity growth were one of the causes of stagnating American living standards. But in the nineties, economist Paul Krugman, one of the world's leading experts on productivity, could declare that computers "are finally being used to eliminate paperwork, back offices are shrinking, and corporate hierarchies are getting flatter." All of this, said Krugman, was finally starting to show up in the macroeconomic patterns of productivity growth.[11]

The information sector of the economy has become increasingly important to the total process of output, value, and wealth creation. This notion can be quantified in various ways. For example, if we assume that business makes rational investment decisions (a dangerous but popular assumption), we could note that ever since 1991, U.S. investment in the basic tools of the information trade—

computers and telecommunications gear—has outpaced capital spending for industrial economy hardware. By 1992, only one year after the two trend lines had crossed for the first time, capital investment in information technology was nearly $25 billion higher than traditional industrial capital investment, and pulling away fast.

Despite the armies of economists gathering and publishing statistics, our systems of accounting, data collection, and analysis are generally based on outdated inputs. They tend to pose yesterday's questions and therefore get less than leading-edge answers back. So we don't yet have good ways to quantify the value of the human capital and knowledge assets inside a company, nor do we have clear methods of calculating the true profit margin on information-driven transactions.

"The old accounting system, which tells us the cost of material and labor, isn't applicable" anymore, declares Edmund Jenkins, the Arthur Andersen partner who has chaired a task force of the American Institute of Certified Public Accountants looking into new accounting procedures to value information-intensive assets properly. Today, the component of cost in many products is a function of the information invested in them, or what Jenkins classes as "R&D, intellectual assets, and services."[12]

Put another way, intellectual capital is "material that has been formalized, captured, and leveraged to produce a higher-valued asset," according to Ernst & Young's Larry Prusak. And the ability of intellectual capital to yield wealth is growing as companies learn to harness it. Betty Zucker, who studies knowledge management at the Swiss-based Gottlieb Duttweiler Foundation, believes that at best, only 20 percent of the intellectual capital inside most business organizations is being tapped or utilized. The real boons to productivity and profitability lie ahead as digital technology, combined with new attitudes and values, allows enterprises to use more of their collective brain. Just imagine the implications for a company if it could go from a 20 percent utilization rate of its intellectual capital to 30 percent, says Zucker.[13]

So let us for a moment stipulate the intuitive understanding shared by many people who have thought about these issues, even if they can't yet be fully quantified: the development of information tools, applications, and content has become the highest value-added sector of large-scale economic activity.

With this digital growth engine fueling the fin de siècle economy, we could begin to see the type of productivity growth for which the U.S. has been starved since 1971, when the post–World War II boom finally burned out. For a quarter century we have been experiencing stagnating or declining productivity, savings, and investment rates. The chance to reverse this spiral is now in our midst. And with it, we have the chance to turn around the falling average living standards that have, in the last 25 years, correlated so closely with public cynicism and the sense of American decline. Ahead, as BellSouth senior financial officer Earle Mauldin puts it simply, could be "the greatest economic boom of all times."[14]

On the road to this great boom, it is worth having a look at where many of these big bucks are stopping. America's wealth has always been highly personal. But the digital era represents an acrobatic leap off this chart. It's definitely not your father's generation of wealth creation out there. The corporatizing and gray flannel suiting of American wealth that took place from the thirties through the seventies is metamorphosing. Now we're headed "back to the future." Ahead lies an era of Digital Revolutionaries whose kindred spirits are the railroad magnates and robber barons, not the traditional Organization Men. Like Cornelius Vanderbilt or William Randolph Hearst, Bill Gates is building the kind of personal mansion no mainstream *Fortune* 500 CEO would dare build.

Because of the new economic forces and structures at work in the Digital Revolution, a highly visible percentage of the new wealth it creates is flowing to individuals, entrepreneurs, and small businesses—or at least businesses that start small. This characteristic carries with it particularly significant influences for the business and social structure that grows up around digital technology. Inventors used to be a bit like starving artists, with many of them going unrecognized in their lifetimes. Today, the search for innovative ideas is so intense that it has become hard to be an innovator and *not* be mightily rewarded.

This is not to say that "small" has become "beautiful" in the way that New Age business seers such as George Gilder pretend. At the end of the day, the lion's share of new digital wealth will be gobbled up by giant corporations. Less innovative than their small entrepreneurial brethren, the giants still pack plenty of clout with their money and political muscle. Gilder sees a landscape of collapsing oligopolies and small innovators rising to the high ground of the future economy. But the reality is that while small companies have more room to maneuver and more chance to grow large, and while some particularly dinosauric behemoth corporations may be crushed under their own slow-moving weight, the successful oligopolies, especially in telephony, cable, and computer hardware and software, are consolidating and growing even more oligopolic. Indeed, consolidations and shakeouts will wend their way through every digital domain.

One of the ways the oligopolies will be successful is by emulating to some degree the entrepreneurialism of their smaller brethren. The smart corporations know that innovation is best nurtured in small, creative surroundings. That frequently means getting outside the box of the corporation. And that's why, no matter how big their in-house budgets, they also rely heavily on other modes for carrying out the R&D necessary to explore new markets: venture capital and mergers and acquisitions.

Through the professionalization of venture capital and the evolution of the thriving M&A business between large and small companies, a well-scripted process now exists for entrepreneurs and technologists to pioneer a business, create a prototype, take the risks, invest the sweat equity, develop a market and a franchise, and then sell all or part of their equity to a big corporation. Such choreography has become second nature to entrepreneurs, financial investors, and strategic investors from the corporate world. A huge army of advisors, consultants, and other intermediaries is at work at this very moment, helping to finance the start-up of the next killer app company or selling a somewhat more mature venture to the right corporate buyer.

Indeed, equity ownership has become the financial equivalent of abundant bandwidth. The twin motivators of money and fame, greed and glory, flow through the system, making almost any technological achievement possible. This is an age when many new millionaires are created every month in the information and entertainment businesses. It is a time when personally taking $10 million out of an equity stake in a successful company is a realistic goal for a start-up entrepreneur with smarts. And when becoming a *billionaire* is not at all out of the question.

One of the interesting features of the Bill Gates phenomenon is that it is not at all just about Bill Gates. He, of course, used the Digital Revolution to become the richest man in America—the postmodern equivalent of a John D. Rockefeller or a J. P. Morgan. But less well known is the fact that Microsoft's success produced an estimated 1,200 millionaires among the company's *employees* who had early stock positions. Gates's less-publicized founding partner, Paul Allen, is also a billionaire, who cashed in his equity and left his day-to-day involvement with the company but not the Digital Revolution. Today Allen uses his abundant financial bandwidth to seed all manner of digital start-ups and acquisitions. His non-Microsoft investments in companies from Egghead Software to Ticketmaster to Storyopolis (a multimedia company aimed at creative products for children) to a $500 million stake in Hollywood's greatest new adventure, DreamWorks, were valued recently at around $5 billion.

Still close to the Microsoft helm is Steve Ballmer, a former classmate of Gates's at Harvard, the company's number-two executive, and also a billionaire. And it isn't just Bill and Paul and Steve, it's Bill's archrival Larry Ellison, the CEO of Oracle, who became worth an estimated $3 billion personally by commercializing the arcane world of relational databases so crucial to all the switching, sorting, and navigating required by the digital age. (And incidentally, when Oracle was on the ropes and Nippon Steel bailed Ellison out with an equity infusion, the giant Japanese steel maker ended up making one of the most profitable investments in its history!)

The lure of personal billions is also making it harder for big corporations to keep their top talent, which in turn serves to provide a continuous stream of new recruits to the world of entrepreneurial equity. Just look at what's happened at AT&T: First, Bob Kavner, who some people believed was in line to be the next CEO, jumped ship in 1994 to become a "player" in Hollywood as a multimedia deal broker with Mike Ovitz's Creative Artists Agency. Then Jerry Stead, who headed up AT&T's $7-billion-a-year computer business, left in 1995 to run Legent, a $500-million-a-year software company that was able to offer him a reported $20 million in stock options that presumably became worth even more when Computer Associates paid a huge premium to acquire Legent. Two weeks later, James L. Barksdale, AT&T's chief of wireless communications, departed. Barksdale had already made a reported $20 million from his shares in McCaw Cellular when AT&T bought out McCaw. But recognizing in the burgeoning Internet market some of the same fundamentals he had seen as a pioneer in cellular telephony, Barksdale joined Jim Clark's Netscape Communications. Clark gave him what was described as a "huge chunk" of the equity in Netscape.

Along the same lines is the story of Howard Stringer, the former president of CBS, who spent the last two years of his long, distinguished career with that network deriding the 500-channel world and the prospects for interactivity. Then, to the surprise of many, he suddenly picked up stakes and jumped to one of the most aggressive projects aimed squarely at promoting the 500-channel, interactive world—the new media company formed by Bell Atlantic, NYNEX, and Pacific Telesis with a little help from superagent Mike Ovitz. According to Stringer, he changed his tune and his horse when he discovered the chance to give the masses the choice of watching "operas, ballets, and things without sex and violence" whenever they want. But all this high-minded talk aside, one need not be too cynical to suggest that the rumored $20 million he was offered to take the job—about ten times his salary as a CBS executive—probably had a lot to do with his change of heart.

The attraction inherent in the possibility of building these spectacular personal fortunes so quickly has a qualitative impact on the shape of business. It promotes risk-taking, fast action, and quick market development. It takes natural leaders and born entrepreneurs out of the gray ranks of the bureaucratic organization and lets them get to work—this year instead of three years from now when the big corporate board might have finally approved their game plan. In other words, it makes the creation of wealth more efficient and more market-driven.

Much of the claims-staking and prospecting we are witnessing on the new corporate landscape is reminiscent of America in the time of the Old West. Cyberspace is a place where there are, as yet, few limits and even less "adult supervision," as it were. This is where you go if you want to think and dream BIG.

As Frederick Jackson Turner argued long ago in his seminal discussion of the "frontier thesis" in American history, the opening up of the West played a particularly powerful and long-lasting role in shaping American capitalism and American democracy as well as our national character and psyche. After the West was won, the conquest of other kinds of frontiers continued to be a potent force in energizing and renewing American life.

Having lacked a collective American frontier to conquer since Kennedy interpreted the space race in that context, the United States now enjoys a new and emerging frontier spirit aimed at cracking through technological barriers and building the businesses of the digital future. For every slacker in Generation X, there is a gung-ho explorer or entrepreneur, ready to ride digital technology to go where no one else has yet gone.

This spirit has broken out of the computer industry and is now spreading across the entire matrix of businesses subsumed by the Digital Revolution, from entertainment to publishing to retailing. In this time when the glow of media celebrity shines so intensely on all phenomena—especially those that impact the future of the media themselves—there is more glory to go around for more people. Dozens and even scores of digital entrepreneurs show up regularly on magazine covers and the evening news. For a point of comparison, one might note that when Metro-Goldwyn-Mayer was formed, it was not generally front-page news outside of Hollywood. But when Spielberg-Katzenberg-Geffen created DreamWorks, it was front-page news around the world.

DreamWorks is also unique in other ways. Never before has a start-up been so heavily capitalized or had so many different kinds of institutions so eager to invest in it on less-than-attractive financial terms. Never before have three entrepreneur-founders had the audacity—and the track record—to justify valuing their combined "intellectual capital" at an astounding *$1.6 billion*. This figure is not only a sign of the times reminding us of the new values the Digital Revolution assigns to traditional businesses. It is also a signal that the game now sports new rules that allow creative people, *as individuals*, to essentially become whole industries unto themselves.

Prodded in part by the desire to gain the glory that comes from going where no one else has gone, today's digerati are a far more diverse and eclectic lot than have ever had the chance to sit atop American business in modern times. One of the best gatherings of this digital tribe is at investment banker Herb Allen's annual retreat at his sumptuous ranch in Sun Valley, Idaho. Look at the group portrait from this shindig, and you've essentially got the "class picture" of the Digital Revolution in America—people like Bill Gates, Barry

Diller, Sumner Redstone, John Malone, Mike Ovitz, Rupert Murdoch, David Geffen, Wayne Huizenga, Scott Sassa, Michael Eisner, Warren Buffet, Jeffrey Katzenberg. For the most part, these are cowboys and gunslingers, dropouts, creative artists, lone wolves, and visionaries. Hardly a one of those gathered is a traditional corporate type. These are people ready to defy convention and write their own rules. They are the "swashbucklers of the Information Age" and the "highwaymen of the Infobahn" according to *Vanity Fair*.

In a period when fashion and entertainment have an increasing impact on business, *Vanity Fair* has as good a feel of the table for the future of wealth and power as anyone else. Add to the roster of Herb Allen's 1994 conclave pals the magazine's own all-star team of powerful digerati—including Ray Smith, Craig McCaw, Barbra Streisand, Oprah Winfrey, Steven Spielberg, Ted Turner, and Ronald Perelman—and you have a cast of characters whose "collective power and influence," according to *Vanity Fair*, "have eclipsed both Wall Street and Washington."[15]

Well, perhaps not quite. But one gets the point.

In trying to define what's going on out there amid such chaotic winds of change, eloquent thinkers about the future such as Michael Rothschild, author of *Bionomics*, have urged those who wish to understand what's coming at us to get away from the imagery of simple Newtonian physics. Instead, we ought to think in terms of the dynamics of the rain forest and the ecosystem, the Network, the hive. Many argue that the Internet is not just a new communications medium, but a new model of social and economic organization.

These insights are valuable, as long as you don't overstate the case. Most of the economic and social world in which we dwell is still pretty much the way it used to be. But the imagery of the rain forest and the Net and the hive can help us understand what's new and developing. Writes Kevin Kelly, executive editor of *Wired* and the author of *Out of Control: The Rise of Neo-Biological Civilization:*

> If 20th century science can be said to have a single icon, it is the Atom. The Atom whirls alone, the epitome of singleness. The Atom stands for power and knowledge and certainty. It conveys the naked power of simplicity.
>
> The iconic reign of the Atom is now passing. The symbol of science for the next century is the dynamic Net. The icon of the Net, in contradis-

tinction to the Atom, has no center. It is a bunch of dots connected to other dots. The Net is the archetype displayed to represent all circuits, all intelligence, all interdependence. The Net conveys the logic of both the computer and nature. In nature, the Net finds form in, for example, the beehive. The hive is unabashedly of many minds, but it decides as a whole when to swarm and where to move. A hive possesses an intelligence that none of its parts does.[16]

That's a taste of the new philosophy that attempts to explain where the Digital Revolution is headed. There's also a more businesslike approach, as in the comments of Time Warner's Walter Isaacson: "The old establishment was a club. The new establishment is a network." Isaacson has a bird's-eye vantage point from which to compare the old and new power elites. He knows the old from years at *Time* and from writing a biography of Henry Kissinger. He knows the new from heading up *Time*'s forays into news-on-demand and other new media. Isaacson concludes that this new power elite, linked by cellular phones, fax machines, and an increasing amount of E-mail traffic, is held together by "a sense of interlocking ventures and relationships that mean that they're inextricably tied with one another because of the deals they've made."[17]

The movement toward the "virtual corporation" has its center in the digital economy, as do a variety of other new approaches to business and new ways to conceptualize business activity. The strategies used to develop and win in new and explosive growth markets will set benchmarks for the business world more broadly. So, too, will the thinking of the individual entrepreneurs who blaze these trails. True to the image of the hive, for example, there is a growing trend toward cross-industry alliances and partnerships. As we saw in Chapters 1 and 3 with General Magic, such partnerships are particularly useful between small companies with new and innovative technologies and big companies with the capital and scale needed to commercialize those technologies.

Partnerships are also being created because of the immense complexity of many of the Information Highway projects. No one company can possibly have all the right skills for designing an Orlando-style Full Service Network. Thus, complex partnership arrangements between a Time Warner, a US West, a Silicon Graphics, and many other hardware suppliers and content providers must be worked out.

The scale of these projects and their potential upside is even bringing former competitors into partnership. As Sony cofounder Akio Morita used to say, his company enjoyed "competitive cooperation" with Philips, the Dutch electronics giant with whom Sony jointly developed the CD format—and with whom Sony now competes fiercely in the marketplace.

Still, strategic partnerships and alliances are not quite the magic wands some would believe. They are difficult to manage, and their ability to distribute risk among a number of players also increases the likelihood of greater total losses from an unprofitable venture than in previous business models. And when combined with certain other trends in business organization—downsizing and outsourcing come to mind—they can easily serve to distance companies from their customers and from direct knowledge of the market through byzantine layers of distribution intermediaries, outsourcing contractors, and co-venture relationships. If your Sony Magic Link goes on the blink, for instance, who do you call? The software provider (General Magic), the hardware manufacturer (Sony), or the network provider (AT&T)?

Nonetheless, there is clearly a new natural selection process at work in the emerging new ecology of business. Forming alliances with competitors, nurturing big company–small company relationships, managing the wealth of "human capital" inside a company, going global—those who are adept at such processes will enjoy a clear advantage. The old way of doing business simply can't manage the complexity—or the cash flow—of the Digital Revolution, and those who cling stubbornly to it are headed for extinction.

Perhaps it is important to qualify this argument once again by noting that we do not believe big corporations are a dying breed. The changes coming are fast in a historical sense but slower than the excitable business press sometimes makes out. Smart, well-managed, visionary companies will have plenty of time to trade their weighty assets of size and scale for whatever they lack. No matter how decentralized, customized, and fragmented American society and business culture become, it will generally be preferable to be big and smart, rather than small and smart. The increasing decentralization and fragmentation of business and markets engendered by new technology only mean that the big and dumb will die a lot faster and the small and smart will be able to seize opportunity more quickly.

The continuing role of the big corporation in shaping the marketplace is well expounded by Dr. Joseph S. Kraemer, a senior executive with EDS Management and Consulting Services, who authored a recent paper advising management decision makers on how to avoid becoming road kill on the Information Highway:

> Conventional wisdom suggests that the advent of the broadband interactive multimedia era constitutes a discontinuity with the past that favors new players and dooms a whole series of established industries and the leading companies within those industries. In the spirit of Jurassic Park, the image is that of the dinosaurs abruptly and completely vanishing. The glib perception is that established industries cannot compete with electronic distribution channels. Their decline is considered inevitable and taken for granted.

> Well-managed established players, however, have a high probability of prospering in the interactive multimedia era. They enjoy certain significant advantages such as a) dominant market position, b) a large and loyal customer base, c) one or more recognized brands, and d) access to capital. These advantages are especially leverageable given that the interactive multimedia era will arrive slowly and take seven or eight years (best case) to establish itself as a mass market.[18]

Quietly continuing his argument with the likes of George Gilder, Kraemer goes on to point out that supposed dinosaurs such as over-the-air broadcasters, traditional telephony companies, and print media empires have plenty of time to adapt to the new conditions. Indeed, with the 1994 revenues of the big three television networks up 9 percent over 1993 (even without baseball) and their cash flows up 19 percent, perhaps these dinosaurs are already adapting. Or perhaps the rumors of their demise had been exaggerated.

Some of the frontier fever that is now afoot will no doubt cool as we settle in for the long, difficult job of commercializing new markets. What's at stake here, however, is not just profits of businesses yet to be built but major opportunities for the U.S. and global economies. We are on the threshold of what economist Paul Romer has called the "unexpected innovation, the new big idea," that can reweave the basic fabric of an entire economy. These new ideas are like recipes that create new value, sustain economic growth, and take it to the next level. Romer, one of the most interesting new economic theorists on the subject of growth, says what the world needs now is not just new ideas for products and services but the next "meta-idea"—the next step up the evolutionary ladder in structuring the intellectual process that underpins wealth creation.

Somewhere in this frenzied frontier of digital activity, that meta-idea may well be present. And *if* we unlock it, *if* we trigger a quantum leap in wealth creation, we may have answers for the otherwise unanswerable questions of our political-economic times. To wit: where will we get the capital to reinvest in the American Dream, how will we balance the budget and still educate and train the growing armies of the disenfranchised, how can developed countries invest in the developing world sufficiently to pull it into the modern world without disinvesting at home?

As many people already sense, and as we shall discuss in more detail in Chapter 12, the Digital Revolution is by no means a royal road to economic utopia. Indeed, the factors for dystopia—for a growing cleavage between digital haves and digital have-nots—are presently in the process of metastasizing. But in the best-case scenario, the wealth generated by the Digital Revolution may afford us an economic climate that will allow us to use the knowledge supposedly inherent in this age to make the right social and political choices, so that we move into the twenty-first century with fewer human casualties than we would otherwise suffer.

▪ 11 ▪

The Global Challenge

Just a few years ago, before the Information Highway ascended to the throne it now occupies as the reigning buzz concept in business circles and on magazine covers, another issue occupied that exalted position: competitiveness.

Under the heading of competitiveness in the late 1980s came a long list of strategic problems that were thought to account for the sense of precipitous decline Americans felt when comparing their economy to foreign rivals, particularly Japan: staggering trade deficits, falling productivity, disappearing savings and investment rates, high cost of capital, poor-quality products, a hollowing out of manufacturing capacity, the self-destructive short-term time horizons of American business, and much more.

Today, however, the very word "competitiveness" has an almost antique ring to it. After all, it's been three or four years since it dominated the talk of American CEOs, presidential candidates, academics, and editorialists. The fear that Japan, Inc. was going to buy up the United States and turn America into a neocolony has largely dissipated, along with concerns about many less extreme scenarios.

Given the economic problems the Japanese have faced since the puncturing of their "Bubble Economy" at the end of 1991, many of those Americans who were once enthusiastic about the Japanese model of capitalism now have their doubts. Even in Japan itself, the private utterances of businessmen and political leaders today reflect a pronounced degree of envy for American-style economic flexibility, creativity, and innovation, especially in the new industries growing up along the Information Highway. As recently as 1992, the American visitor to Tokyo was rarely spared a lecture from one or another elite figure making clear his contempt for an America that was presumed to be locked in a permanent spiral of economic decline. Today, the same people are likely to ask an American visitor politely for suggestions on how Japan might replicate the American experience in cultivating new software and content-driven industries of the future.

Even if the U.S. economy looks better today relative to Japan than it did a few years ago, the key strategic problems looming in the American future have by no means been solved. A deep sense of anxiety and cynicism still pervades much of the American polis. But the national apprehension about the future is no longer necessarily twinned with the fear that Japan or a resurgent German-led European Union will overtake the United States economically. From Wall Street to Main Street Americans tend these days to be more worried about the social and economic problems that afflict us *within* our borders, rather than our ability to withstand the competition from outside them.

The issues associated with the competitiveness debate of the late 1980s and early 1990s have obviously lost some of their centrality and urgency. Arguments about protectionism vs. free trade, the merits of industrial policy, and whether or not manufacturing matters have largely disappeared from the political discourse. Although competitiveness was a focal point of the 1992 U.S. presidential election (with the Ross Perot campaign built four-square upon it, and with Bill Clinton's "It's the economy, stupid" message directly related to it), competitiveness is unlikely to be more than a sideshow issue in 1996.

Yet while it has been pushed under the surface of public attention, the competitiveness agenda has not gone away. Indeed, when we consider the future impact of the Information Highway on the American economy, we would do well to keep the realities of growing global competition in mind.

In the way-cool cosmology of some cyberspace visionaries, those who even talk about national economies and their relative competitiveness are living in an ancient time warp, failing to get with the program of the new global village whose marketplace is purportedly linked seamlessly by computer networks. These visionaries wax ecstatic about the way a trillion dollars a *day* flies electronically through the global currency trading system, compared to a mere trillion dollars a *year* in physically traded goods. We hear tell of how engineering teams in half a dozen countries, linked electronically through computers and video conferences, work around the clock to design the next Ford car, even though most of them have never met in person. We are reminded that wherever you are, from Orlando to Osaka, you can be part of the same Internet newsgroup. And with 12 percent of America's assets now owned by foreigners, you never know when it might turn out that behind an All-American name brand, employees are working for a foreign company. Indeed, it could happen to you! With electrons speeding through national boundaries at will, leaving this kind of cross-border linkage in their wake, the cyber-visionaries tell us there is no such thing anymore as the "American" national interest.

We beg to differ. As real-world futurists, we see, of course, the increasing globalization of national economies and the powerful role digital technology will play in accelerating that process. But we also observe that as of the end of the twentieth century, employment patterns—and unemployment problems—are still overwhelmingly national in scope and still influenced significantly by national political and economic policy. How competitive the national (and regional) economic infrastructure is in the manufacture of tradable goods and the vending of tradable services still says much about where the good jobs will be. Interest rates, while sensitive to global pressures, are still set by central bankers based on their own national agendas. The budget deficits of national governments, notably ours, still determine how much capital is left over for private sector investments. Who owns a business or a factory still matters in terms of where the profits from its operation ultimately come to rest and how they are reinvested.

GDP—Gross *Domestic* Product—still matters. Indeed, the developed world is starved for the kind of quantum leap in real GDP growth that characterized the post–World War II U.S. economy until the early seventies and continued driving the Japanese and German miracle economies right through the roof in the eighties. As we have argued in Chapter 10, the Digital Revolution *is* capable of generating significant new productivity growth. With that possibility comes the logic of the entire virtuous circle of prosperity: increased productivity leading to higher savings rates, higher savings to higher investment, higher investment to still-higher productivity growth. This equation, if sustained for any length of time, leads to a quantum leap in output, with the net result that we could return to the golden age of rapidly rising living standards distributed widely across society.

If that virtuous circle is indeed a possible scenario as a result of the Digital Revolution—and we believe it is—then it behooves Washington to design competitive policies that will ensure we keep as much of that action onshore as possible.

If American government and business interests are fused together coherently and strategically, there will be a greater chance that the United States will keep the long lead it currently enjoys in most technologies and commercial applications of the Digital Revolution. Such fusion will also create the basis for turning the abundance of corporate technological resources into energy for revitalizing the overall economy and delivering higher and better living standards to ordinary citizens.

On the other hand, failure to anticipate the global competition and adapt to its challenges could mean that today's unquestioned American leadership is undermined and even frittered away. Americans know this path all too well, for this is exactly what happened in traditional industries such as automobiles and steel, and even in some new industries like memory chips.

The jobs, skills, and profits the Digital Revolution will generate are now on track to go disproportionately to Americans. But all over the world, competitors have their sights set on changing that outcome. If we aren't careful, they will be successful not just in getting a slice of the pie, which is inevitable, but in getting the critical mass of it that comes with being the leader of a vast new global industry.

Is it hopelessly jingoist and anachronistic to imagine an *American* strategy for cyberspace? Again, we don't think so. Just as dying rust belt towns have a responsibility to figure out how to revitalize their neighborhoods and factories—and some have done remarkably well at it in the last decade—the U.S. government has a responsibility to seize the opportunity before us, turn it to maximum advantage, and try to leverage it into a force for the overall economic and social renewal we so badly need.

Implementing such a strategy, however, will necessitate the development of a "third road" approach to questions about national competitiveness. The road that puts all faith in the marketplace and rejects any role for government is obviously flawed. But just as obviously, those who imagine a comprehensive, micromanaged, government-led competitiveness strategy—à la Japan or Europe—are headed toward a dead end. The third road must take seriously the warnings about government's inadequacies made by those on the first road and come up with a minimalist, experimental set of initiatives focused on supporting and enhancing the efforts of the private sector, not constraining or dictating them. It must seek to open foreign markets, not to close our own.

Competing in the global digital marketplace has a different coloration these days than it did when the agenda was framed in light of traditional industrial products in the 1980s. New complexities have arisen about nationality of corporations, for example. In the classic argument popularized by Robert Reich when he was teaching at the Kennedy school and publishing in the *Harvard Business Review*, the answers to questions about "Who is *us?*" and "Who is *them?*" have blurred. Is Sony really a Japanese company if it has created thousands of high value-added jobs at its factories in the United States? Is Zenith really an American company if it is now partially owned by Korean interests and has moved most of its best production jobs offshore?

These are provocative questions that reflect the changing nature of the global marketplace and shed revelatory light on why smokestack-era protectionism is unworkable. We would be shooting ourselves in the foot if we were to close the American economy to the contributions Japan-based companies might make, just because we don't like our lack of access to their economy. And we would be squandering taxpayer dollars if we were to support "American" companies whose workforces were not even predominantly in the United States.

But to leap from these new wrinkles about the new economy all the way to the conclusion that nationality doesn't matter anymore is entirely unjustified. American living standards are still very much affected by the nationality of corporations and of technology. It very much matters whether American companies make their products in the U.S. or stop at the design stage and then download the designs to be manufactured offshore. In the Digital Revolution, the differences that might result from differing policies on this issue could involve literally millions of jobs. It also very much matters where profits are made, how they are taxed, and to where capital is eventually repatriated and reinvested.

Simply put, no matter how dinosauric it sounds, national economic competitiveness is going to be an issue in cyberspace for a very long time to come. We shall take a look in a moment at just how tough that competition might get for American business.

First, however, the good news. One of the reasons competitiveness has disappeared to such a great extent from the American national agenda is that since 1991 (with the Gulf War as the approximate and symbolic turning point), American business has turned the tables on its competitors. The demonstrable vigor of the domestic U.S. economy, with its rising productivity and increased flexibility, has been the big story in the global economy. This has been especially true by comparison to a Japan that has stumbled as never before in its modern history and a Europe whose economic arteries again seem clotted by the disease of "Eurosclerosis." In the street parlance that has become so popular in business discussions, the Japanese and the other hard-bodied manufacturing economies ate America's lunch for much of the 1980s, but U.S. business has come back and kicked ass through much of the 1990s.

This historic reversal of fortunes, especially between Japan and the United States, is the product of a complex set of factors deeply rooted in the political, cultural, and financial characteristics of the two societies, plus an encyclopedia full of issues about trade policy, currency rates, capital formation, and other matters. But what is most interesting for us here is the set of changes that are taking place in all the developed economies: the relative decline of the manufacturing sector, the expansion of the service sector, and the birth of a new "information sector."

In this new information sector, Americans are far, far ahead of the rest of the world. Unlike traditional manufactured products, where the United States is still at a competitive disadvantage with Japan and the Asian dragons (and unlike traditional services such as fast food, car rentals, or accounting—the market for which is overwhelmingly domestic), the information sector is an area where American goods, services, and know-how are exportable, transferable, and licensable. As the leader in most of the core competencies of digital technology, as well as in the entertainment, information content, and financial services increasingly built around it, the United States economy is currently the best positioned to capture the greatest comparative advantage across this multidimensional checkerboard.

Arguably, the U.S. information economy is growing at rates even higher than the automobile sector of the Japanese economy in the best boom years of the eighties. This fact alone would have widespread impact on the total economic picture. But the U.S. economy leads the world not only in the creation of information hardware and software but in the *application* of information technology *outside* the information sector. From Hollywood movies to car leasing, from mutual funds to making jet aircraft engines, information technology is being used to create new products, new services, new efficiencies. Whole new markets are being spawned, and U.S.–based companies are often the originators. Few foreign companies try anymore to compete with standards set by Microsoft in operating systems, or Oracle in database systems, or America Online and other U.S.–based commercial online services. The Japanese, of course, retain leadership in a number of relevant areas from industrial robotics to consumer electronics. But the pattern and the trend lines have changed markedly in the new and emerging sectors of digital technology.

The global rush is on across Europe, Asia, and Latin America to do digital things the American way. To take but one example, Bertelsmann, the powerful German-based publishing and media empire, undoubtedly has the resources to develop its own online services for Europe. But instead of trying to invent a system from scratch, Bertelsmann chose to invest over $100 million in the comparatively tiny America Online in order to create a partnership that could transfer American know-how in this area to Europe.

Although American manufacturing has improved dramatically in recent years—thanks in no small measure to the better use of information technology in production systems—the Japanese still enjoy a net edge in quality and productivity. This is particularly true in the competition over the key globally traded goods such as automobiles and consumer electronics items. Those factors—plus Japan's continued maintenance of an uneven playing field through its discriminatory trade policies—explain why the United States still suffers a $60 billion annual trade deficit with the Japanese.

While there remains a debate over the importance of trying to maintain vibrant manufacturing industries (and at what cost), hardly any economist can deny that manufacturing as a sector is declining in its overall importance and impact on the U.S. economy. It has now stabilized at about a fifth of the American workforce—and even that number may be overstating the case. In some statistical models, a company like Microsoft is classed as a manufacturing company because it "makes" something that consumers can go into the store and buy in a package. Yet amid all the stresses and strains the "microserf" workforce may be forced to endure, standing on an assembly line lifting heavy digits onto floppy disks and CD-ROMs isn't one of them. (Of course there is a small traditional assembly line manufacturing element to encoding disks, printing manuals, and shrink wrapping boxes, but it is an extremely minimal element of Microsoft's business, or any software business, for that matter.)

In fact, it doesn't even make sense to think of Microsoft as a service company, although that is how the government statistics classify it now. Yes, of course, operating systems and applications software can be thought of as a "service," but it is a very different class of service from hamburger-flipping at McDonald's. With the service sector as it is traditionally defined now comprising over 70 percent of all jobs and output in the United States, it makes no sense to speak of services as an undifferentiated mass.

Many trends are playing out within the service economy, but the key one is the growth of a distinct *information sector* in which businesses are managed very differently than most other areas of the economy. These businesses, in turn, show very different results in terms of value creation, employment patterns, capital structures, dividends (or lack thereof), and competitive practices. The participants in this information sector—whether they do a lot of mass manufacturing as hardware companies, or whether they are small creative software companies—generally have more in common with each other than with traditional manufacturing or service companies. Intel has more in common with Microsoft than it has with General Motors; Microsoft has more in common with Intel than it has with Domino's Pizza.

One of the other chief characteristics of companies across the board in this information sector is that they are playing a powerful role in stimulating American productivity as well as exports. Indeed, one important explanation for the reassertion of undisputed U.S. leadership in the world economy in recent years is the rising importance of the information sector. Productivity growth through the whole of the economy rose faster in 1993–1994 in the United States than in Japan, which had long led the developed world at this benchmark. And developments in the information sector were catalysts in bringing about this change.

Japanese business, with a strong guiding hand from state industrial planners, has focused on the excellence needed to be a great manufacturing nation. The Japanese have structured their economy to maximize their strength in manufacturing (and rigged the competitive rules for added advantage). But while losing chunks of once important manufacturing industries, American talents have shifted up the value chain to the information sector. Its rapid growth, plus its increasingly rich contribution to American exports, more than offsets with internal dynamism the economic losses to Japan and other competitor nations in manufacturing. Meanwhile, the very structures, disciplines, and processes that made Japan the ultimate manufacturing nation, have combined to impose a straitjacket preventing Japanese business from truly excelling in the information industries. Surprisingly, despite Japan's enormous success in many areas of high technology in the eighties and its continued leadership in many kinds of semiconductors, flat panel displays, and all sorts of consumer electronics products, the Digital Revolution has yet to take firm hold there.

It is impossible to draw exact correlations. But it is probable that Japan's long economic nightmare of the first half of the nineties has much to do with the stunted growth of its information sector. Conversely, America's comparative sense of buoyancy in recent years has much to do with the productivity and wealth-creating kicks obtained from our dynamically growing information sector.

Up until now, and probably for the next few years as well, there has been a double happiness factor for the American economy in the new markets that are being created. As soon as new technologies are pioneered and developed in the United States, many of them also become readily exportable. Sometimes the process is simultaneous. And sometimes American companies are able to do abroad what they cannot yet do at home, making foreign markets both opportunities for growth as well as experimental proving grounds.

The export of digital products and services by American companies is moving much faster and at much higher growth rates than the historic curves for the export of physical goods. Time Warner's CEO Gerald Levin sees the future of the United States in the post–cold war world as no longer a military superpower first and foremost but an *information and entertainment superpower*.

This is not wishful thinking. It's happening. Microsoft may be thought of as a quintessentially American company, yet it derives about 40 percent of its revenues from global markets. That is a formula that John Malone, another quintessentially American character in what would seem like the quintessentially American business of cable television, would like to be emulating in a few years' time.

As TCI chief Malone puts it, "We could be talking about America's leading export industry of the twenty-first century here. The United States has supremacy in *both* information and operations software. We're the dominant country in the world in computer software and the dominant country in entertainment software as well. These are clean industries and they're in great demand around the world. They could be the bow of the ship leading a wonderful American economic resurgence in global markets."

Malone argues that digital entrepreneurs are taking advantage of America's unique market size and historical circumstances in the way that Henry Ford once did. At the beginning of the century, only the American market was big enough to allow for cost-effective mass manufacturing of the automobile. Now, at the end of the century, only the American market is big enough to justify developing the next version of Microsoft Windows or making the next *Terminator 2* or *Jurassic Park*. Thus, the United States is evolving as the natural export leader in information and entertainment services.

Proving Malone's point, AT&T and the RBOCs—forbidden by law for most of the first century of their existence from entering global markets—are now busily laying cable and fiber and installing switching centers all over the world. Much of this is for basic telephony. While having hit the growth wall in the United States, telephony is one of the biggest worldwide growth businesses. Countries like China have only 1 telephone line for every 100 citizens; Vietnam has just 0.25, compared to the United States, where there are

56 telephone lines per 100 people. Just bringing those numbers up to modern norms in the emerging markets will be a trillion-dollar growth business over the next 20 years. A staggering 800 million *new* wired telephone lines are expected to be installed worldwide during the next 15 years, and an even more phenomenal 1.3 billion *wireless* phones will be deployed. The total number of communications satellites in use will double, and the total number of computers in use will more than double.

In the world's new markets, though, nobody wants plain old-fashioned twisted pair copper wire. It is cheaper and easier these days to lay fiber from scratch for backbone networks or to utilize coaxial cable, satellites, and cellular technology. Thus, American and other international communications companies are busy building broadband Information Highways in somewhat unlikely places.

"With the aid of foreign investment and foreign technology, we can leap directly onto the Information Highway without having to waste our time going through the primitive stages of developing a communications infrastructure," declares a senior member of China's State Planning Commission. This is not a dream but at least a partial reality in the booming capitals and hot growth regions of what was once called the third world. For the evidence, just look at all those cell phones in use in hotel lobbies, restaurants, and Mercedes zooming by in Beijing, Mexico City, Hong Kong, and Bangkok.

Motorola originally entered the Chinese market to take advantage of low-cost labor. The idea was to make pagers for export. But now the company sells its entire production capacity in the domestic Chinese market—and can't get enough for export. Indeed, China *already* has as many pagers in use as Japan and is closing the gap quickly with the United States. Motorola forecasts that China will overtake the United States as the world's largest market for pagers by 1996, when as many as 22 million units will be in use there.

Of course it isn't all sweetness and light for American companies abroad. Some countries are so hungry for the development kick that comes from new technology that they are perfectly willing to allow Americans unobstructed entry into their market. But others still erect towering protectionist walls and insist on forcing foreigners through a veritable obstacle course of corruption and kickbacks, joint ventures with poorly qualified local partners, and preferential technology transfer arrangements.

To the degree that the Digital Revolution is content driven, it poses both opportunities and new cultural questions abroad. Content providers are in the vanguard of benefiting from the ability to export "bits" instead of physical goods. Once an American movie or TV show is made, it can be distributed in scores of other markets, adding huge amounts of incremental revenue at little expense. The same is true for many other kinds of software, although savvy companies know they have to translate, localize, and build up brand identities unique to each market.

Leading voices among the digerati often tell us that electronic bits know no nationality and respect no border. But the prosaic reality is that policy makers in every country, including the United States, are continuing to make *national* decisions about the flow of *global* information based on their own interests.

Islamic fundamentalist nations, for example, which perform customs checks for blasphemous and pornographic materials at their physical borders, may be somewhat confounded by the challenges of trying to attack blasphemous words or pornographic photos zipping into their society via the Internet's global circuitry. Nevertheless, while new communications technology will surely broaden the freedom of expression experienced in some societies, fundamentalists and authoritarians the world over know how to use computers, too. And when they eventually track down cyber-heretics, a few public whippings, hangings, or lopping off of keyboard hands would probably exert a significant chilling effect on the frequency with which the ALT.HERESY newsgroup is accessed.

Even the most democratic-minded, free market–oriented businesspeople are not above waving the national flag when it suits their strategy. NBC, for example, in the course of carrying out an extremely Machiavellian stratagem aimed at Rupert Murdoch's fast-growing Fox network, launched a high-visibility hue and cry to the FCC in January 1995 over Murdoch's true nationality. The NBC executives alleged that the stations making up Murdoch's network were illegally owned by what was, for all intents and purposes, a foreign corporation, headquartered in Australia and controlled by Australian shareholders, even if Mr. Murdoch himself had taken out American citizenship.

No one at NBC, of course, was seriously afraid of Australian domination of the American media as a cultural or political problem.

Rather, the question was simply one of waving the flag as a tool in fighting the war that is today called business competition. This seemingly burning issue of national policy was summarily dropped by NBC a month later—before the FCC had even ruled on the merits of the case. Behind the scenes, a deal had been struck. Murdoch gave NBC two new cable slots on his wildly successful Star TV satellite, whose footprint covers a billion and a half Asians. NBC denied there was a quid pro quo. But the denial was a bit thin to say the least. Analysts valued Murdoch's gift to NBC at close to a billion dollars—plenty of reason to drop feigned concern about Australian ownership.

In other parts of the world, issues about the nationality of technology are even more culturally sensitive than they are in the U.S. Indeed, some see the Digital Revolution as an American Trojan horse entering their economies and then seeking to dominate their indigenous cultures.

Singapore wants its MTV—but only in a culturally suitable form. (MTV, Star TV, and others attempting to reach Asia's booming markets of young, fashion-conscious consumers, have worked with Asian governments to develop formats that rely on the "cleaner" music videos from the West, interspersing mainly American music with a mix of Asian popular music and culture.)

In Chiapas, the hotbed of political violence in Mexico, revolutionaries keep their sympathizers around the world abreast of their activities via regular Internet postings—much to the dismay of the Mexican government.

China, while soaking up new technology like a sponge, has already had the experience of a human rights movement in 1989 that was said to be the first revolution by fax because of the authorities' inability to censor dissidents' fax communications. Hong Kong entrepreneur and new media enthusiast Jimmy Lai, often in trouble in Beijing for speaking his mind, observes that although Chinese authorities would like to control the media, they can't. "If you can control 90 percent of the media in the future, the 10 percent surviving will be enough to inform everybody."[1] Meanwhile, PC ownership in the PRC is following a Chinese version of Moore's law and doubling every two years. And virtual reality attractions are coming to Tiananmen Square itself.

Indeed, the problem for American business in China is not fundamentally one of autocracy or censorship. The Chinese appear interested in absorbing all kinds of American content. The problem is that they just don't see a compelling need to pay for it.

Based on the ease with which digital bits are duplicated, a huge, sophisticated piracy business has grown up in China and elsewhere in Asia, estimated by computer industry sources as cannibalizing $2 billion worth of sales each year. Versions of American software still in beta test and not yet available commercially in the U.S. are hawked on the streets of Guangzhou and in the back rooms of Hong Kong's glittering shopping malls. The same is true for movies not yet released on video. Brand names and logos are routinely appropriated or plagiarized.

The morality of all this is a grayer area than it appears to Western eyes. The Chinese, after all, don't really subscribe to American beliefs about private property and certainly not about intellectual property. Besides, they say, what royalties did Westerners ever pay for the use of Chinese inventions from gunpowder to paper? Where are the licensing fees for Chinese ceramics stolen by foreign devils centuries ago and now on display in Western museums?

All this highly nationalistic and cross-cultural argument came to a head in 1995 with a high-profile confrontation between U.S. Trade Representative Mickey Kantor and Chinese Foreign Trade Minister Madame Wu. Eventually, they negotiated a largely token agreement to end some of the most egregious acts of piracy, such as government-owned factories churning out cloned American software. But piracy of intellectual property will remain a multibillion-dollar business for years to come, along with debates over the differences in law, culture, and politics it entails.

Unlike the Chinese, the French generally observe all standard conventions on licensing American intellectual property. Europe is a large and thriving market for American entertainment exports. The problem in Europe is the French-led lobby that wants to keep out American software on cultural grounds. The word "culture," while having some validity, is also a code word for protectionist economics.

The French want the Brussels-based officials of the European Union to insure that at least 51 percent of content on Europe's more than 100 television stations and 17,000 movie screens is "made in Europe." Needless to say, American exporters of film and television content are waging a highly politicized struggle against the adoption of such rules. In completely unfettered markets, American entertainment companies could easily get 60, 70, and even 80 percent market shares abroad—and wipe out the indigenous competition, just as the French fear.

The French have been trying for years to protect what remains of their film industry by insisting on guaranteed local European content provisions for broadcasting and other media. But now the fear is afoot in France of an American-dominated Information Highway. Worries *Le Monde* reporter Michel Colonna d'Istria: "What will happen to our collective consciousness" in the face of increasing American and Japanese dominance of new information and entertainment technology? Foreign hardware, he believes, will drive foreign software into the French market, reducing the once profoundly philosophical French to a nation of fast-food-eating, video-game-playing morons. His ultimate scare scenario: a tomorrow in which a Gameboy conceived in Tokyo is played in English by French children wolfing down burgers at a McDonald's in Paris. *Merde!*

The same sentiment is echoed by Gerard Thery, former head of the French state telecom monopoly. He favors a grand European telecommunications consortium modeled on the successful Airbus consortium (which made Europeans serious competitors to Boeing and McDonnell-Douglas in aircraft). This proposed European telecom consortium would wire the continent for new media. But its mission would be cultural as well as commercial, seeking to counter Thery's fear that Europe's "diversified culture with ten different languages" will otherwise disappear because of American and Japanese domination of information technology. Another concerned *citoyen*, Philippe-Olivier Rousseau, points out, "The information society will be based on intelligent terminals, mostly made in Japan and the United States, using high-performance chips, made by Intel or Motorola. As far as software, 85 percent of computers use Windows by Microsoft." France, he says, must find a way to get into the act before it finds Microsoft is dominating its software culture so completely that it's too late for alternatives.[2]

Actually, the French have already contributed more than their share to the development of the Information Highway. Long before the Internet took hold in the United States, the French Minitel system was the first working prototype of an Information Highway, providing telephone numbers, yellow pages–type services, and messaging on demand to people in their homes through the telephone system. It is still one of the largest and best-used consumer information systems in the world, with an installed base of 6.5 million units. But its "videotext" system is now ancient, its bandwidth choked, and its applications too narrow.

Sources at the state-owned computer company Bull believe that if done properly, the French market for "teleservices" could grow from 33 billion francs a year currently to 190 billion francs by 2005.[3]

Will France reach out to American companies to be partners in building a new digital telecom infrastructure? Probably, but it is not clear. As in most developed countries, the hangover of mid-twentieth-century social democratic industrial policies and protectionism for "national champion" companies is still strong. Dealing with the government bureaucrats and state telephone monopoly executives of continental Europe and Japan can be considerably harder for many American companies than dealing with the domestic American regulators about whom they complain so much. Although the rhetoricians of the *Wall Street Journal* liken the FCC's Reed Hundt to a "French bureaucrat," his regulatory operation is transparent, swift, and fair by comparison to that of many of his global counterparts—especially those in Paris.

But no matter. The ineluctable force of the Digital Revolution will open most markets, *eventually*, or condemn their keepers to autarky and even economic ruin. Even the Japanese are getting this message. From their office towers in Tokyo's government bureaucracy district of Kasumigaseki, they have watched the ferocious lead they captured in many areas of advanced technology during the 1980s begin to wash away under the pressure of the digital tsunami from the West.

Japanese officialdom will try as long as possible to keep the telecommunications door open as narrowly as possible. At the Ministry of International Trade and Industry (MITI), inside the Ministry of Posts and Telecommunications (MPT), and particularly among the pinch-yens of the Ministry of Finance (MoF), many bureaucrats hope the feverish excitement about the Information Highway is only another American fashion trend that will run its course before Japan has to emulate it.

A strong desire exists to declare digital technology a kind of American disease. The chain-smoking men in the blue suits, who understood the world so much better when their planning task was to ramp up automobile exports, would be very happy if the world woke up to the twenty-first century to discover that interactive television doesn't work and that consumers don't like traveling the Infobahn. Their premises would thus be vindicated, their society would not have to undergo another wrenching change, and the soft underbelly of the American economy would end up even more ripe for incision by the sharp sword of Japanese manufactured goods. In the meantime, the next best scenario is to maintain 1,001 maddening kinds of protectionism that keep most American digital goods and services out of Japan while Japan's great electronics companies try to catch up.

Yet there are also forward thinkers among Japanese officials who understand that in the postmiracle, postbubble phase of life they are now in, their economy lacks a new engine of growth. Having succeeded at so many transformations and reinventions of their economic structure, they know Japan is now stymied. The bureaucracy is unable to deliver on the stated commitments made by five successive prime ministers to invigorate the consumer sector. The Japanese are unable to get the benefits of competition and open markets. They can't compete fully in making the kind of innovations and creative breakthroughs that are producing new wealth and a sense of dynamism in the American economy.

"In the information revolution, Japan is being left behind other industrialized countries, especially the United States. Such has become the standard notion," inside Japan itself, according to a publication of JETRO, the Japanese government's external trade organization. The report cites some stunning facts. Per capita computer processing power in the United States is four times what it is in Japan. In American offices, there are 42 computers for every 100 office workers; in Japan, only 10. Among desktop PCs in the United States, 66 percent are linked to networks, whereas in Japan only 17 percent are linked. Cable television in the United States reaches roughly 60 million households; in Japan, only about one million. Yet despite the wide chasm suggested by these numbers, the Japanese could change very quickly once a certain critical consensus is established. Indeed, according to the same JETRO report, the Japanese are beginning to be bitten by the Internet bug. The growth rate for new Internet links to computers in Japan in 1995 was about 30 percent higher than during a comparable period in the United States.[4]

By some accounts, Japanese apprehension about falling further behind the United States in the digital race "is rising to the level of panic."[5] Among the many books and articles on this subject pouring into the mainstream of Japanese public attention is one titled *The Threat of the Superhighway: The Danger of Annihilation Facing the Japanese Information Industry.*

Japan's brilliant cadre of MITI technocrats, long the primary architects of the nation's economic planning success, look jealously on the growth of digital technology markets around the world, knowing that they could have—and should have—had a bigger role. But MITI itself remains surprisingly inert, more focused on turf battles with MPT than on new initiatives.

"The two ministries confront each other on everything," declared an article in *Tokyo Business*, which also claimed that Japanese information technology of 1995 is roughly a full decade behind American norms. Innovators are forced to "develop half-baked plans so as not to antagonize either ministry." MPT and MITI have battled over telephony, broadcasting, value-added networks, and even whether the buzzword *joho tsushin* (information communications) must be hyphenated. When MPT launched its Teletopia project, MITI responded with its New Media Community plan. "Local governments maintained impartiality toward both ministries, and the result was a rash of meaningless local projects," with the ministries competing over which ones they would adopt and subsidize.[6]

Those foreign analysts who remain bullish on Japan's long-term prospects keep expecting that the next MITI white paper will unlock the multimedia secret, but so far, there's been little evidence to justify that view. A few MITI-backed initiatives are of interest. One of them is Digital Vision Laboratories, which provides small subsidies and research support to seven big Japanese electronics companies. Rather than trying to go head-to-head with U.S. companies, this effort is deliberately designed to play at the margins, developing Japanese leadership in emerging areas that have no American leader now. A spokesman at one of the participating companies acknowledges that Bill Gates has "the basic operating system" locked up— "so what else do you do?"[7] These digital visionaries will look for other niches, such as computer-television interfaces.

The possibility that the quantum economic kick of the Digital Revolution could be the catalyst Japan needs to get over its restructuring hump is understood and appreciated by at least a small community of senior government officials and businesspeople. Their power, and the attractiveness of their solution, is likely to increase as the Japanese economy continues to flounder and politicians prove unable to succeed with structural reform. As that happens, Japanese business may reach out to American technology as never before.

The Japanese have also been through their own period of deflating Information Highway hype. At several points in the early nineties, government officials, in conjunction with NTT (the former government telephone monopoly that is slowly being privatized), detailed extremely ambitious plans for an all-fiber to-the-home broadband network. Early versions of this plan suggested a completion date in 2015 at a cost of roughly $400 billion. It was as if the Japanese government planned to be the architect of a Time Warner–style full-service network reaching into every single Japanese household.

In early 1995, however, the Ministry of Posts and Telecommunications acknowledged that the plan was too ambitious and involved too many unknowns. As happened with the scaling back of interactive TV projects in the United States, the Japanese now wondered if it wouldn't be a better idea to wait for more of the technology and its applications to develop before committing so massively to it. But government officials and telecom business leaders made clear that they still intended to forge ahead with the Japanese version of the Information Highway. This time, though, there would be a more realistic plan—one that would by 2010 establish a more limited vision of a backbone fiber system. This system could then serve a variety of technologies for interconnection into the home based on cost, application, and market interest.

On the road to that vision, the government has begun to show some signs of life by modest, incremental regulatory steps in areas such as cable television. Japanese business has also started to show more interest in collaborating with technology- and content-rich American partners. Itochu and Toshiba, which are investors in Time Warner's entertainment business and participants in the Full Service Network project, are now including Time Warner in the creation of Titus Communications, a new company that plans to take cable TV and alternative telephony connections into as many as two million Japanese homes in the near future.

The Japanese investment boom in the United States, which had dried up almost completely in 1992–1993, is now beginning to come back in the form of strategic investments in new American technology that can be used to seed the digital market in Japan. One innovative Japanese company, Softbank, surprised many American computer industry savants when it bought out ownership and control of the Comdex trade show, the world's largest computer industry event, for a stunning $800 million. Meanwhile, NTT has invested in small American start-up companies like General Magic and Nextel and formed various kinds of partnerships with the likes of Microsoft and Silicon Graphics. Says NTT President Masashi Kojima, "This is a cultural revolution." Until recently, "making a cooperative research agreement with an American company was never considered. Now it's nothing special." Indeed, he forecasts an important role for "aggressive alliances with strong, innovative companies from overseas."[8]

Adds NTT America's R&D Director, Junichi Kishigami in discussing the growing numbers of Japanese research facilities in the U.S. (over 160 at last count) and the growing wave of trans-Pacific strategic alliances in digital businesses, "Basic concepts like computer operating systems and microprocessors originated in the U.S., and those for the next generation are coming from the U.S. We have to be here."[9]

Neither the unique characteristics of the Japanese economy nor the strains in the U.S.–Japan trade relationship are likely to disappear completely, however, in a blizzard of ones and zeros. Nevertheless, the digital frontier presents one of the best places for both sides to try to create mutually beneficial business partnerships where the latest American technology is traded for market access and capital in Japan.

As Jeffrey E. Garten, the U.S. undersecretary of commerce for international trade, argues, "In the past we were asleep at the switch in sectors where we were ahead but where Japanese firms were gathering momentum. Then, when we woke up, we found that the Japanese had caught up with us, penetrated our market, and shut us out of theirs. With information technology, we want to try to *preempt* problems." In Garten's view that means making this argument to the Japanese:

The U.S. is years ahead of you in most areas of information technology. But we know you plan to spend a trillion dollars to catch up.

We will watch carefully how you do this. We want to avoid the model of the past in which you follow a Japan-first industrial policy that keeps out foreign firms even as you penetrate the markets of others. We therefore expect that in this new sector, where we can do so much together, that your key policies—on intellectual property, deregulation, digital procurement, financing, etc.—do not repeat the Japanese habits of the past. If they do, we will be sounding the alarm everywhere we can and at the earliest possible time to prevent trade problems before they become acute.[10]

Garten's approach is a good one, although there is no guarantee this argument will be a compelling one in Japanese eyes. But Garten alludes to a troubling issue: how do we make sure we don't fall asleep at the switch in the new industries digital technology is making possible? Our lead may be very, very long—but economic history is even longer. The Japanese may well decide to go it alone. They may keep their market closed until they are ready to launch a cascade of highly competitive products. And they may be more successful at coming up with those than we now think.

When John Malone and Bill Gates and Gerald Levin speak so confidently about America as a digital superpower, the facts would appear to be on their side. Digital technology, and especially the software and content associated with it, seem to tap into America's unique proclivity for Yankee ingenuity. Our excellence in these areas derives in part from our special frontier spirit and culture. But correct as Malone, Gates, and Levin may be today, their comments sound disquietingly like those made by the American auto executives of the 1960s. Back then, Detroit executives were so untroubled by the thought of Japanese competition—so convinced that automotive engineering was a uniquely American skill—that they never even bothered to come down from their office towers to look at a Toyota until it was too late.

At a minimum, Americans should be aware that the Digital Revolution is sweeping the world and touching down in many places. Wherever it does, it develops indigenous characteristics and local competitive power. Consider, for example, a brief inventory of signs telling us that new digital competition is afoot throughout the world, and suggesting that American companies have no permanently guaranteed markets:

Mobile telephony is growing extremely fast in Europe and parts of

Asia, making hardware market leaders out of companies like Nokia and Mitsubishi. It's not all Motorola's world anymore. Europe's digital wireless technology is leapfrogging the backbone analog infrastructure for cellular telephony in the United States and is estimated to be as much as 18 months ahead in product development. European deployment of digital wireless is going to "leave the U.S. in the dust," according to a spokesman for US West's European operations—and give Europeans leadership in exporting their digital telephony standard, GSM, to other markets.[11] European efforts to develop "smartcards" to replace wallets and an "electronic purse" for consumer purchases on the Info Highway are also a step ahead of many similar U.S. experiments.

The next 10 years will bring a boom in sales of PCs, modems, and CD-ROM drives that will give much of Europe rough parity with U.S. penetration rates, according to Deborah Monas, an analyst with Kagan World Media in London. She notes that the U.S. could reach 57 percent home-PC penetration by 2003. Britain could catch up to that figure by then. Germany may be even slightly ahead of American norms.

New communications systems in the United Kingdom are more advanced in some respects than in the United States owing to a more liberal regulatory environment. Cable companies such as TCI are already deeply involved in the local British telephone market, and phone companies such as US West and NYNEX are involved in consortia to deliver cable service.

With European social democracy more conscious of the troubling gap between info haves and info have-nots, more conscious state-sponsored efforts are under way to redress this imbalance. The Dutch province of Utrecht, for example, is offering all citizens connections to the Internet for the cost of local phone calls, as well as daylong workshops on using the service that cost just three dollars. One result could be that new businesses and new technology breakthroughs will arise from widespread access to new services.

In Canada, Citytv, the popular "alternative" station in Toronto run by Moses Znaimer, has been experimenting with interactive programming and multimedia for more than 20 years. Even without much of the fancy technology utilized in the interactive TV trials of major telephone and cable companies, Znaimer's band of television-aries has developed workable, exciting, content-rich ways to bring the audience in off the streets to participate in the creation of programming. With the explosion of the direct broadcast satellite TV market, Citytv became the first source of foreign television content to be regularly and continuously available in the U.S. market.

Although the rapid growth in the number of American homes using the new pizza-size Direct Broadcast Satellite dishes is impressive, the experience curve with DBS in Europe, Japan, and parts of Asia is actually much further along. Observes a senior executive with NBC Cable: "Sure, satellite TV is starting to take off in the U.S. But even the optimists don't see more than five million dishes in home use in America by the year 2000. Indonesia, by comparison, could add eight million dishes in the same time frame."

HDTV, although not the market driver for new technology it was imagined to be in the 1980s, is continuing to make progress in European and Japanese labs. When it is finally introduced in the United States, the hardware sets may have American names like RCA (now owned by the French company Thomson) and Magnavox (now owned by the Dutch company Philips), but the parent companies will, for the most part, be European and Asian. Indeed, wherever consumer electronics are involved, the Japanese have not lost their touch. From automobile navigation systems to the digital video disks (DVD), Japanese manufacturing know-how will dominate the marketplace.

Other Asian countries are also excelling at the digital game. The hottest one of the near future is Korea, where the Ministry of Information and Communications has pledged to invest nearly $2 billion to beef up the country's role in multimedia and application software. The new chairman of Samsung has issued a directive to his vast workforce comprising more than 100,000 employees: trade in the company's stodgy, clonish image for one that is state of the art and leading edge. Do it by innovating, as well as by acquisition. Samsung has taken up this spirit with surprising zeal, investing in small U.S. companies, taking a $500 million interest in AST Research (a leading U.S. computer maker), and even at one point considering financing the DreamWorks venture in Hollywood.

After years of low-profile buildup of their high-tech electronics businesses, Korean giants such as Samsung, the LG Group (the former Lucky Goldstar), and Hyundai are now coming on like gangbusters in the global markets. Those three massive companies now control more of the world semiconductor memory business than all of Japan, Inc. does. And the LG Group is now attempting to acquire the last "American" TV manufacturer, Zenith.

Memory chips are a business in which the Japanese beat out the Americans a decade ago. For a long time, Americans argued that the Japanese victory was pyrrhic; that all the Japanese had won was control of a low-growth, low-margin commodity business. Except that the explosion of digital devices means an explosion of computer chip memory will be needed to support it. In fact, some forecasters expect the global memory chip business to quintuple in volume by 2005, reaching a stunning $170 billion in annual sales. "These are really significant markets," says Daniel Klesken, an analyst with Robertson Stephens & Co. in San Francisco—much more significant, in fact, than Americans imagined when they were surrendering the market to Japanese companies a decade ago, and more significant than the Japanese thought as they began to slow their own investment in memory chip plant capacity in the nineties.[12]

With the profits from these growing markets at their backs, the Koreans are diversifying into everything from multimedia hardware and software to entertainment content, although with far more care than the bubble economy–fueled Japanese of the last decade. The Koreans have a sense of mission. They've read the tea leaves of economic Darwinism and its withering competitive heat. They understand they can only grow their businesses profitably by investing *up* the value chain—from components to hardware to software, services, and content. Inevitably, the sectors the Koreans now dominate will be taken over by the Chinese, which means Korea, Inc. needs to jump to the next level before the Chinese catch them.

As Korea's newly prominent role in world technology suggests, the division of labor in creating information products and services is constantly changing. High-speed communication links make it possible to shift data-entry work and laborious computer coding to many sites around the world. "Back offices" are not just moving out of fancy real estate in Manhattan, they are moving to Ireland, Jamaica, China, and the Philippines. Bangalore, a city in India, has become one of the most important centers for software development in the world.

China already has a cadre of 350,000 information technology engineers, whose average salary is only $105 a month. The personal computer market is currently growing at about 30 percent a year.

Through a nexus of native-born Chinese and ethnic Chinese with advanced scientific and engineering skills from abroad, China is developing a high-tech infrastructure that belies the rest of its economic backwardness—making, for example, state-of-the-art gas-plasma displays. A grand national plan under the auspices of the Ministry of Machine Building seeks to create "Information Highways" to tie together Chinese customs operations in major port cities and local tax authorities, as well as to develop a wide network of credit card users and ATM machines, and a business and commerce data exchange system.

In eastern Europe and especially in Russia, the "other half" of the world's top computer scientists has been downsized out of the military-industrial complex and is now toying around with new private sector entrepreneurship schemes, as well as tie-ups with foreign companies. Tetris, one of the most popular video games of all time, came out of a Russian design. It is only a matter of time before the talented computer scientists of the former Soviet republics begin to emerge as important indigenous forces in the development of new technology.

No one, of course, could legitimately expect or even hope that the United States would monopolize the Digital Revolution forever. As the above examples show, the revolution is already spreading far and wide and will continue to do so. As it does, the stakes grow greater. Says Viacom CEO Frank Biondi, "I expect that the growth of foreign markets for U.S. entertainment software over the next 10 years will be even more dramatic than the growth produced by the introduction of new media technology inside the domestic market."

Whether American companies will get the full fruit of their labors in return for having pioneered cyberspace—and whether those rewards will filter through broadly to the American people—are open questions. In considering them, a raft of policy issues come to the forefront. Let us look at just a few of these.

Manufacturing still matters. In the current stage of the Digital Revolution, many of the important products of the future are still in the R&D lab, which is America's area of greatest strength. The problem comes later when products are commercialized and markets grow to encompass mass demand. Historically speaking, that's when the prototype manufacturing operation inside the United States is shut down, and the technology and jobs move overseas where hardware can be manufactured more cost-effectively or to higher quality specifications.

Neither government nor concerned citizens ought to let this happen in the Digital Revolution. Millions of Americans are being downsized out of the middle class, while a teeming underclass threatens the nation's long-term security. Especially against that backdrop, it is imperative that we use any opportunity we have to create manufacturing jobs that can be performed without impossibly high educational levels.

By the end of the century alone, roughly $1 trillion worth of hardware devices, from modems to CD-ROM drives, will be manufactured annually *somewhere* by workers of *some* nationality. With American R&D labs playing the major role in designing these devices, it would be a serious strategic error not to capitalize on this golden opportunity to rebuild the ranks of the employed and productive citizenry in America. As John F. Kennedy once observed, "If men have the talent to invent new machines that put men out of work, they have the talent to put those men back to work."

Taking special measures to ensure that a large part of the manufacturing base for new high-tech products stays at home is not just good social policy, it is good economic policy, and even good competitive business practice. As Jim Clark, the former chairman of Silicon Graphics observed of his experiences with that leading-edge, fast-growing firm: "If we just did the R&D and let others manufacture our workstations offshore, eventually they would learn how to do the R&D themselves and they'd do it better because they would have hands-on experience with the product. Then we'd be lost." Instead of being lost, SGI is a growing contributor to the American economy. In 1995, while downsizing was going on all around it, SGI announced plans to hire three thousand new employees.

Every job can't stay at home. And every company will, quite legitimately, try to take advantage of foreign manufacturing to reduce labor and shipping costs and to get closer to the customer in those marketplaces. But if Washington doesn't take specific policy initiatives to keep digital manufacturing onshore, most of it will move offshore to whatever locale makes good business sense.

In this kind of fluid global environment, where technologies can move so rapidly from one geographical center to another, the United States needs to learn from our trade partners. In recent years, for example, Singapore has specialized in disk drives; Taiwan has become the center for fully assembled PC clones and is now seeking to upgrade its presence in telephone hardware; semiconductor memory chips have come from South Korea.

One of the reasons these Asian economies have been able to develop leadership in various niches of high-tech manufacturing is that their governments have designed tax policies to support that goal, as well as government-sponsored training programs and government-funded science and technology parks. All of these are part of specific, conscious missions to create high-value-added jobs and move national economies up the value chain. Why shouldn't we do the same in this country? Why can't similar policies work to develop opportunity and a sense of the future for our unemployed youth? America's failure to go toe-to-toe with the competition in government-directed economic planning will not, by itself, undermine American corporate leadership in the Digital Revolution. But it could mean the transfer of many of the best jobs abroad.

Open markets and free competition. The U.S. telecommunications market is one of the more open in the world, and it is moving ever faster in that direction. This has undoubtedly contributed to the vibrancy of competition in the U.S. and is reflected in the fact that Americans enjoy the lowest telephone cost structure in the G-7 world. But the reality is that European and Asian-based companies have an easier time penetrating U.S. markets than American companies do in reverse. European companies have been able to buy major interests in U.S. long-distance companies such as Sprint and MCI while American companies have not been able to obtain similar-size equity stakes in some of the key continental European telecom companies.

"I'd rather have 10 percent of the world than 100 percent of New England," observes NYNEX chief Ivan G. Seidenberg. And of course—when you look at the relative market sizes, who wouldn't? But can NYNEX get 10 percent of the world telecom market in an environment where so many countries restrict foreign participation so heavily? Probably not, if some free-trading Republicans have their way. A growing group of true believers in laissez-faire are introducing Congressional legislation that would unilaterally remove all restrictions on foreign ownership of the U.S. telecommunications infrastructure without any commensurate concessions from foreigners.

The Clinton administration, to its credit, has resisted this strategic giveaway of our market-opening leverage. Instead, Clinton and Gore have spoken out in favor of a reciprocal market-opening plan in which the U.S. would open fully only to those countries that have opened *their* markets fully to American companies. But this is an area to watch closely: past U.S. practice on trade issues suggests that Washington, under pressure from American telecommunications companies that desire foreign investment, will wink at the closed market practices of the Germans, French, Japanese, and others, and let companies from those countries in anyway.

The approach to the have-not world. As representatives of the world's seven wealthiest economies met in Brussels for a conclave on global telecommunications policy in 1995, Thabo Mbeki, South Africa's first deputy president, reminded them of two sobering realities. First, he pointed out that there are more telephone lines in Manhattan than in sub-Saharan Africa. Then, he added, half the world's population has never made even a single telephone call.[13]

Amid all the Info Highway enthusiasm, it is often optimistically asserted that digital technology will somehow bring wondrous benefits to the less-developed world. As in America's own increasingly polarized society, the likely reality is probably the opposite. Without global policy intervention, the rich countries of the world, along with the high-growth emerging markets, will use digital technology to get richer. The poorest countries of the world, meanwhile, will fall further behind—although it may now be easier for their miniscule elites and middle classes to make cellular phone calls or check their portfolios in London and New York.

The G-7, the European Union, and the United Nations routinely churn out a lot of pious twaddle about the need to prevent the world from being polarized into info rich and info poor. But well-intentioned words can't stop the trend from unfolding.

No one has an ideal answer to this problem. But two basic approaches are crucial. The first is to understand that technology alone cannot solve the underlying crises these countries face. Rwandans don't really need Internet connections, although do-gooding organizations are trying to introduce them in the hope that better communication with the outside world can guarantee peace. What the poor and dysfunctional countries of the world need is help making their basic agricultural, economic, political, and educational infrastructures functional.

Second, within the context of such initiatives, improved telecommunications has a role to play. The United States can contribute to global economic security—and can also stimulate good business opportunities for American companies—by supporting a large-scale effort to bring low-cost, appropriate-scale communications technology to the have-not world.

But we should be careful of the overly liberal, overly disinterested policies of the past on foreign aid. In the past, we generously dispensed aid with no strings attached to less-developed countries while the Japanese dispensed much less aid but required beneficiaries to use it to buy Japanese products. The result was that when the commercial markets finally took off, the Japanese got a disproportionate share of the business.

The less-developed world, with its huge populations, is eventually going to comprise significant markets for new telecommunications services. American companies ought to be grandfathered into serving these markets as a result of the aid American taxpayers are willing to invest.

The need for a strategic technology policy. It is fashionable these days to believe that government can do no right if it gets anywhere near issues concerning high technology. As we saw in Chapter 2, the expensive, much vaunted Japanese and European projects to develop HDTV as a new kind of television—and as the centerpiece of national competition strategies—failed rather miserably on both counts. America's ad-hocracy and *lack* of policy won the day and opened the door to the Digital Revolution. But Europeans and Asians haven't given up. They are continuing to evolve national technology policies, complete with targeted sectors and industries. Their plans call systematically for upgrading their abilities to compete with dominant American providers of digital products and services.

In the face of what the competition is doing, it would be blindness, if not madness, to avoid developing a competitive technology policy for the United States. We may not be so lucky the next time as we were with HDTV. Even in the case of HDTV, we may yet see the Japanese smile on the way to the bank when it comes time to manufacture the sets in mass quantities around 2005 or 2010. Some estimates show a $40-billion-a-year market for HDTV hardware by the end of the first decade of the next century. Americans may set the new digital standards, but without new technology policies, we will still need Japanese know-how to manufacture them.

The technology policy we propose is not one of micromanagement or heavy European- or Japanese-style interventionism. Rather, what makes sense for the United States is for government to continue to sponsor the kind of basic research that led to the origination of the Internet, as well as to provide seed money for promising technologies that are not readily financed in the private sector. It also makes sense for government to lift some antitrust restrictions and take other special measures in areas where doing so will stimulate collaborative research in the private sector.

We tend to forget how much of our American technological achievements actually have their origins in government-funded programs. We like to think that we don't lean on the crutch of industrial policy in this country—that it is some market-distorting approach used only by Japanese and Europeans. But the fact is that the Pentagon presided over a massive industrial and technological planning process throughout the cold war that was America's functional equivalent of industrial policy. To be sure, it gave us pork-barreled $7,000 toilet seats and $1,200 screwdrivers. But it also gave us the backing for many of the building blocks of the computer revolution and of high technology more generally. Indeed, Defense Department research and spending figured prominently not just in the development of the Internet but in many aspects of the personal computer, database software, satellite and cellular communications, and a host of other areas where the American private sector is today the world leader.

It is important to understand this legacy because Pentagon support for the kind of research done in the past is now drying up. Engineers are being laid off and research labs shuttered as cold war readiness winds down. America's de facto national strategic technology policy is thus withering away, replaced as yet by no other institutional force.

The steamroller seeking to get government out of the technology business led by Republican Speaker of the House Newt Gingrich, has targeted six small government-supported technology programs for elimination. The budget savings will actually be minimal. This is not a deficit-cutting move but an ideological pogrom. It seeks to purge government influence from areas where the recent track record is not at all bad, such as stimulating American abilities to compete with the Japanese in semiconductor equipment manufacturing and flat panel displays.

One of the items on the Republican hit list is funding for the Office of Technology Assessment (OTA), a Washington agency that has issued frequent reports illustrating American competitive strengths and weaknesses in high-technology fields. The Republicans have yet to make a case about why, especially in the Information Age, we wouldn't want to have that very crucial competitive information prepared by an objective government agency. Indeed, tracking what's going on in the development of technology outside our borders is increasingly important. As *Business Week* warned in a recent special issue devoted to the major issues facing twenty-first-century capitalism, "In the digital age, product cycles are measured in months." Technology has never moved so quickly or caused so much uncertainty. Over the next decade, world technology leadership will be up for grabs, with new global challengers emerging everywhere.

> Since mathematics is the foundation of all digital advances, nations well versed in that discipline—including China, India, and the nations of Southeast Asia—could turn their homelands into formidable technology powers . . . Scientists sitting in Taiwan's Hsinchu science park or in Seoul can run the same computational models as their counterparts at MIT or Stanford. One result may be the erosion of America's commanding lead in basic research . . . When so much brainpower is linked together, *there are no permanent birthrights.*[14]

All those warnings are important ones, but not necessarily in the way most people might think about them. The danger is *not* primarily the one widely imagined in the 1980s, when many forecasters sensed a period of techno-nationalism ahead. The problem is *not* that the Japanese (or the Chinese or the Indians) might somehow gain a stranglehood on advanced technology that they could use to exploit America economically and turn the United States into some kind of neocolony. Nor is there much danger the United States will do that to other countries—whatever the French may think.

Yes, some degree of techno-nationalism is in the air just ahead, as well as some big issues about market opening, reciprocity, copyrights, and protection of intellectual property. We will see wrangling about technology and culture, the virtues and vices of government-led technology policies, the propriety of national spy agencies participating in industrial espionage, and the dangers of cyber-terrorists. Certainly we will hear demands from the less-developed countries for America, Japan, and the G-7 to do more to get them onto the global Information Highway and into the knowledge age.

The next time we have a Gulf War, intellectuals around the world will no doubt debate the merits of cutting off Internet links to Baghdad, just as they debated whether CNN should or shouldn't have aired Saddam Hussein's propaganda last time around. Indeed, wars themselves will increasingly be waged "virtually" with information sector weapons, and practically with potent new physical weapons that will, even more than we have seen to date, harness the vicious violence of digital exactitude.

But while all the above are real issues of concern, they will not be the focal points of the policy discussion we need to have over the question of how to maintain U.S. leadership. The cold war *is* over. We no longer need to be motivated to scale economic heights by fear of threats to our national security—although we should pay attention to them. Rather, we need to focus on how to best play the spectacularly good hand the United States economy has been dealt.

Specifically, America has the opportunity before it to unleash the explosive economic growth of the Digital Revolution to solve many of our intractable domestic problems and to refashion the American Dream for the children of the twenty-first century. Or we could end up squandering that opportunity through arrogance, blindness, and lack of planning.

Let us assume there is no single clear-cut ideological answer. But let us seek, from all the complexity of the Net enveloping this issue and all the buzz inside the hive, some new and intelligent collective working assumptions about how best to compete in the terra incognita that lies ahead.

· 12 ·

To Have and Have Not

66 The major advances in civilization are processes that all but wreck the societies in which they occur." So said the great mathematician-philosopher Alfred North Whitehead.

Just look at the history of the Industrial Revolution, the best historical analogy to the rite of passage from one economic era to another that we are now experiencing. Yes, the Industrial Revolution brought wealth, progress, and modernity to the nineteenth-century world. But it also disenfranchised millions of farmers and rural dwellers and filled the cities of Europe with crime, squalor, and disease.

The old feudal order wouldn't get out of industry's way peacefully, while the new working class rose up violently against capitalism's excesses and extremes. Ultimately, the Industrial Revolution left a trail of blood across Europe and North America. First in the American and French revolutions, later in the revolutions of 1848, and eventually in the Paris Commune of 1871, the forces unleashed by the clash of the old feudal order and the new industrial order brought down almost every ancien régime and social institution.

Today, as industrialism fades and the Information Age presents itself, we have much more highly evolved political processes and much stronger safety nets. Or so we like to think. The reality is that

317

the political processes are gridlocked and the safety nets are already tearing.

If the Industrial Revolution sparked extreme tumult and disloca-tion, the fire next time could be even worse. The Luddites, after all, could only smash machines one at a time. They couldn't crash vast computer networks on which all of society had become dependent. And the poor, the hungry, and the disenfranchised depicted by Charles Dickens posed little threat to the rest of established society. For one thing, they didn't have drugs and guns. For another, the old moral order, although tattered, held together better than ours is doing today. Moreover, it was only a brief period of time before the great industrial job machine sucked most of the early-nineteenth-century poor into its upwardly mobile process of middle class creation. The Industrial Revolution could do so because it exchanged the brawn power of the farmer for the brawn power of the factory worker. Wrenching as that change was, it can't compare to the social chal-lenge of shifting from a brawn-driven economy to a brain-driven one.

Well before the Digital Revolution arrived on the scene, the wrecker's ball, packing the punch of an entire generation's worth of accumulated, wrenching changes, was already lurching and swinging violently at the edifices of late-twentieth-century society.

In our time, unprecedented economic wealth has been created, wondrous scientific discoveries made, marvelous technological feats performed. From space travel to bioengineering to the wizardry of computers, telephones, and all that this book is about, many of the wildest dreams of the ancient imagination have been achieved in the last few decades.

Yet the philosopher's paradox persists: the more God-like powers we have appropriated for ourselves, the more confused and complex our world has become. At times it even seems that what we have gained in scientific knowledge we have lost in common sense.

Only yesterday, we had precious little scientific understanding of the cosmos. But we knew perfectly well how to deal effectively with crime and how to run educational systems that taught the basics to all our children. We knew how to structure an economy where the total pot kept growing and the middle class kept widening. And in a nation always long on democracy and individuality, our political institutions somehow managed to maintain a strong overarching com-mitment to the general interest and to the future.

Today, all the prior elements of the equation are standing on their heads. We have tamed most of nature's forces and reordered the laws of physics to suit our needs. We are busy decoding the secret of the human genome; we think we know what happened in the first few seconds after the Big Bang; we now have credible explanations of where, quite literally, the universe is headed. If we ourselves won't soon be able to travel at the speed of light, at least our intelligent agents will.

But in the face of the crime crisis, we have no answers—not even any good ideas. The same is true for the crisis in our public schools, even though we hear every day how crucial education is to jobs and opportunity in the Information Age. We can't reform the health system or the welfare system intelligently. We blithely run up deficits and debts, the size of which would have been declared a national emergency long ago by any prior leadership generation. We know we will face a multitrillion-dollar shortfall in the Social Security and Medicare programs in just a few years, yet we can't bear to do anything about the problem while there's still time.

For all the ubiquity that information is supposed to enjoy in this era, our political process is shrouded in the darkness of dogma, superstition, myth, and lies. Thus politicians who even talk about serious reform of our entitlement system are ignored, while those who attempt to do something about the problem court political suicide by daring to touch the sacred "third rail." The same is true on a multitude of other fronts. Indeed, on telecommunications reform, every member of Congress recites the requisite incantation about deregulation and competition. Yet meaningful legislation does not follow. The Digital Revolution continues to be hamstrung by our fifty-year-old telecommunications laws, while its maximum economic and social benefits are slowly sacrificed on the altar of a Congress gridlocked by the competing claims of special interests and antiquated ideologues.

Throughout most of the last two thousand years (with some notable exceptions), powerful civilizing forces of Progress and Order have worked to curb humanity's ever-present if recessive tendencies toward self-destruction and chaos. Yet in *our* times, these civilizing forces have lost their magnetic hold on human thought and behavior, and are now weakening and even expiring around us. Religion, political structures, social institutions, moral principles—all of these are still with us, but none commands the breadth or depth of allegiance it used to. The Ten Commandments may have worked well for several millennia, but they fail to serve as much of a deterrent to the impulses swirling through the ids of today's society. As a result, society shows signs of unraveling.

For the vast majority of the population in developed economies, neither the brute struggle for survival nor even the quotidian necessity to work exerts the kinds of centripetal force toward cooperative action it did in prior eras. Those at the bottom of the social pyramid can get by relatively easily (or at least with much less personal effort expended on food, shelter, and clothing than would have been required of the poor in previous times). This translates into little compelling need to become educated or to participate in the social disciplines of organized society. Easy as it may be to get by, if you are uneducated and unaccepting of social discipline, you can never get ahead. Thus, a growing underclass is institutionalized, rife with alienation and rage. Its pro-social behaviors are the exception; its anti-social behaviors the rule.

Meanwhile, throughout the middle and even at the top of our society, the struggle for actual physical survival has been replaced with abstracted stresses and strains, ferociously accentuated by the breakdown of the old moral and institutional pillars. All this adds pressure and questions to daily life but not meaning or purpose.

Traditional ethics, morality, community, social responsibility, and social vision are all in decline—with little or nothing to replace their role as conscience and consciousness for modern life. Much of the challenge to the old order can, of course, be innovative and liberating. Moreover, the process of reinvention it connotes is absolutely necessary if we are to develop the new forms of human society most serviceable for the needs of the future. We cannot, after all, return to the idealized nostalgic past, even if we wanted to. But all too often, what fills the vacuum left by the collapse of the old institutional arrangements is not a new morality or a new order or a new social compact—or even any coherent sense that these are in development—but rather, amorality, anarchy, and a naked individualism severed from the balancing force of social responsibility.

Against that backdrop, it is not surprising that while the society continues to churn out great wealth, it is distributing it increasingly unevenly. The middle class, whose nearly constant expansion defined the American economy and the national political framework for most of the twentieth century, is now being downsized—with extremely ugly and uncomfortable long-term consequences.

Not knowing what to believe, cynical about nearly everything, and living in a society where the extremes of individuality and ultrademocracy would horrify Jefferson, we splinter and fragment into narrow, self-centered interest groups. Those claiming the mantle of social responsibility are sometimes no less guilty of promoting the surrealist spectacle of special interest politics than those seeking to ignore society altogether. In New York, lobbyists for the disabled succeeded in blocking installation of badly needed portable public toilet facilities on the grounds that if they weren't wheelchair accessible, no one should be able to use them. In California's Marin County, citizens recently sued to block the spraying of the largest harvest of mosquito young in the state's history after record rainfall. The litigants claimed to be "environmentally sensitive." But when the state offered to move them temporarily, and to provide free masks and air filters, the litigants refused. "I have my rights," said one. Yes, but what about the rights of millions of other citizens who will be affected by the mosquito swarm? Our society has become the first to be paralyzed in the face of a public health threat not from lack of scientific knowledge or equipment, but by absurd extensions of the concept of individual rights.

Primitive emotions are vented everywhere on matters having to do with race, ethnicity, religion, and gender. It isn't yet Bosnia, but it could someday go in that direction. Indeed, among the reporters and the rescue workers grappling with the Oklahoma City tragedy of April 1995, there were several who had been to Bosnia and could not avoid drawing the parallel to that conflict's emotions, imagery, and, of course, senseless, sudden eruptions of violence.

Our political system begins to look like a circus, our financial system like a casino. Increasingly, our consumption-driven economy is a machine not for savings and investment but for squandering our social wealth and, in Neal Postman's memorable phrase, for "amusing ourselves to death."

The stark, if often denied truth is this: our society may still be quite rich, but it is increasingly dysfunctional. It is already disenfranchising large numbers of citizens. It can no longer deliver with any consistency the very items that are almost self-definitional in a modern, advanced economy: a secure, relatively prosperous middle class with the possibility of upward mobility, a social commitment to the goal of equal opportunity, broad public education, public safety, effective government.

What is perhaps most troubling is that there are no answers and no apparent likelihood of getting any. Nowhere is there an inspirational movement or political leader with real answers to today's problems—not in the United States, not in the Western world, and not in the third world. In East Asia there are a series of stunning economic success stories unfolding—and there are some valuable lessons to be learned from those experiences. But even Japan faces its own version of institutional gridlock and its own homegrown (and almost inexplicable) fanaticism and violence as well.

Nowhere is there a body of political, economic, or social thought that offers compelling, definitive alternatives. The most profound social critics raise good questions but have few, if any, answers. The best political leaders and economists have one or two creative ideas, but nothing that could be called a working model for the future.

Enter the Digital Revolution, quite theatrically, at the approximate turn of the millennium—with all the rich symbolism that entails. Vaguely, we begin to see the future on the other side of the divide and hope that, somehow, this new technology can be the catalyst of change. It is full of excitement, promise, and hope—ingredients in short supply in the rest of our social mix these days. The Digital Revolution is like an important character appearing on the stage for the first time in the second act of the play. A torrent of emotional energy has already been unleashed by the other actors. Yet the audience knows that from here forward, this new actor may drive the plot.

The technology, however, is only a tool. For all its bells and whistles—for all it can do remotely, robotically, virtually—it cannot solve social and economic problems in the absence of social and economic policy. Technology cannot by itself cut health care costs, although we are often told it can and will. In fact, the cost of health care in the United States has skyrocketed with the introduction of each new generation of medical technology. Technology cannot balance the budget, although with creative thinking it can be used to improve the efficiency of government and minimize the cost.

Technology may be able to fill some of the holes in the hearts of an alienated world, but it cannot substitute for human contact. A handful of like-minded souls may meet on the Internet and then later F2F (face-to-face); some have even gotten married this way. But while virtual communities have many merits and much positive social value, they will not be a decisive force in overthrowing the rampant alienation and anomie of our times.

Technology is sold to us as promoting efficiency and thus freeing up leisure time. But early evidence about the executive use of new communication tools from fax machines to cellular phones suggests that while these do, indeed, enhance efficiency, they add time pressure, stress, and complexity to many people's lives as the separation between home and work or work and leisure becomes virtually nonexistent.

Technology alone cannot make our streets safe at night. It cannot heal the wounds of abused children or bring romance back to rocky marriages. Nor can it offer much hope for a productive and meaningful future to most of those languishing in the all too real communities we euphemistically call inner cities. Despite all the excitement over technology's multifaceted promise, it will tend—in the absence of enlightened public policy—to serve as a force that accelerates the dangerous polarization, fragmentation, and splintering of our society—which is exactly what it is doing right now.

What technology *can* do, however, is provide an engine of wealth creation capable of carrying forward any vision of social renewal we, as a society, consciously choose to pursue. This is no small matter. In a time when we are already cutting back on areas of spending once deemed essential to the stability and smooth functioning of our system—and when we do not even know how we are going to pay for the retirement of baby boomers in the next century, let alone how we will house the homeless—the linkage between social vision and cost analysis has become close. Indeed, without a plan for how massive social changes will be paid for, all visions and blueprints of the future are academic at best. Technology, with its new efficiencies, new productivities, and new possibilities, holds the key to *that* part of the equation.

Utopia or dystopia? The future tends to unfold along the middle road between extreme forecasts. Our species, while full of hotheads, is decidedly pragmatic on the whole and generally slower than we think to change its course of evolution. Peril is counterbalanced with promise; fear with hope; nightmares with dreams.

Indeed, dreams abound about the good the digital age will bring. To reiterate just a few of these: new personal and corporate fortunes; greater convenience in daily life; enhanced productivity; expanded knowledge and discoveries; an increasing realization of human potential and a deeper sense of meaning and purpose in life; virtual communities bringing back some of the values of old-fashioned neighborhoods; a renaissance of self-expression and creativity; heightened global awareness and interconnectedness; a return to the democracy of the agora through electronic town halls and a chance to cut the bloat of bureaucracy with electronic bulletin boards and interactive tools; work environments that become less alienating; and ultimately, a new economic model that relies on knowledge, information, and creativity to produce high, clean, sustainable growth on a continuous basis.

On the other side of the ledger, though, the nightmare scenarios are as frightening as the dream scenarios are inspiring: dehumanization in the face of so much technology; overdependence on systems and networks vulnerable to hacker and terrorist attack—or "only" to the vagaries of software bugs, power outages, and squirrels chewing up fiber-optic lines; governments and corporations increasingly able to play Big Brother in monitoring home activities; economic anarchy bred by a new order that doesn't respect intellectual property rights and steals usable "bits" at will; a society rendered irrational and illiterate by its infatuation with the image and the soundbite; teledemocracy that turns into Rush Limbaugh–style mob rule; global, generational, and class wars between info-rich and info-poor.

All these primal fears in the face of extraordinary change have varying degrees of validity. But let us look for a moment at the most basic and widely feared nightmare scenario: mass and permanent unemployment, accelerating disenfranchisement of major sections of the population, and a society hewn deeply and irreversibly between those who have and those who have not. This concern is especially valid because we can already see its early signs overlaid on the fragmentation and the polarizing trends ongoing in American life. When comparing people who use computers with those who don't in the *same* jobs, the wage gap is 15 percent and rising fast. To the extent that Internet-type communications represent the seeds of new knowledge and wealth systems, it is important to reiterate the basic truth about Internet demography: the system's active users are overwhelmingly young white well-educated males. (If the Internet were a country club, it would no doubt be facing multiple lawsuits over discrimination.) The 30 percent of American homes that supposedly have computers (many out-of-date or gathering dust in the attic) are almost all concentrated in the most affluent third of the population.

As *Time* magazine recently argued in a special issue devoted to the opportunities and challenges of cyberspace, access to the Info Highway is not going to be a luxury in the future. Rather, it will be part of "the basic ability to function in a democratic society." It may "determine how well people are educated, the kind of job they eventually get, how they are retrained if they lose their job, how much access they have to their government, and how they will learn about the critical issues affecting them and the country."[1]

We often assume in the white heat of the new economy's dynamism that "everyone in America has a phone," but the truth is there are *seven million* American homes without so much as basic telephone service. Given that reality check, it is impossible to believe that America will ever become a nation where "everyone" has computers, intelligent TVs, modems, advanced communications software, online service accounts, and whatever else it will take to access the Info Highway of tomorrow—*and* knows how to use all this hardware and software. It isn't even a plausible utopian science fiction scenario, at least not in our lifetimes.

From the experience we can see thus far, there is no valid reason to believe that the advent of new technology—absent intelligent social and political policy—will narrow the widening polarities in our society. Just the opposite: unless we, as a society, choose otherwise, the Information Highway will only widen the distance between Watts and Beverly Hills.

At the heart of the political-economy of the Digital Revolution lies a troubling, foreboding enigma: we are taking a leap toward a society where the historic correlation between wealth creation and the input of labor power is severed—or at least becomes less highly correlated than it used to be.

Consider an extreme version of the information sector's power to create wealth without labor. A hedge fund manager uses raw information to develop a proprietary analysis about the likely movements of a certain currency. He then uses computer trading technology to accumulate huge positions in this currency. He uses communications technology to monitor his positions and analyze technical details on a moment-by-moment basis. Perhaps this hedge fund manager then uses the media to publicize his strategy—or to convey disinformation—to the markets. Eventually, the markets begin to move in a favorable direction, and again using his computer and communications tools, he sells his positions.

Two billion dollars. One man, with a small team of assistants, may have just made two billion dollars in a few weeks' time for himself and his investors. He needed no physical raw materials. He needed no significant number of employees to carry this off; he needed little in the way of physical facilities. The computer and communications tools he used may be comparatively expensive, or they could actually be no more powerful than the systems his children play with at home. Either way, they are an infinitesimal cost of doing this kind of business and bear scant relation to the way manufacturing machinery is used to create value.

The above, of course, is indeed an extreme scenario. George Soros doesn't stare down the Bank of England every day—and sometimes even *he* gets it wrong. Although information technology allows such huge bets to be made in financial markets, it doesn't guarantee their success. As amply demonstrated by a trio of successive financial collapses in Orange County, California, in Mexico, and at Barings (a result of huge futures gambles), there are big risks involved with the human judgments of those who must manage the computer and trading power in financial markets. Computer power has not only enhanced the productivity for creating wealth, it has also had the perverse effect of increasing the "productivity for making losses," according to Federal Reserve Chairman Alan Greenspan. Commenting on the fact that a single trader in Singapore was able to lose a billion dollars for Barings and thus destroy the two-hundred-year-old firm that had financed the Louisiana Purchase and served as banker to the British monarchy, Greenspan observed, "You couldn't write the [trade] execution slips fast enough 25 years ago to lose as much money as was lost by one individual, aided by terrific technology."[2]

Nevertheless, despite the prominent risk-management problems with derivatives, they have functioned remarkably efficiently considering just how much is at stake. Indeed, it is nothing short of mind-boggling to think that the derivatives business has grown to a size of

$16 trillion annually. This torrential flow of funds—equal to about half the total wealth of the United States and more than twice the size of our nation's total annual output of goods and services—is created, managed, and traded by a statistically insignificant number of people.

In short, we can observe a magnifying trend in which a very small number of people can now create a significant amount of wealth primarily through value-adding information and use of information tools. Let's be clear not to overstate this, as some forecasters of the future do. What is happening is going on *at the margins*. It is not the central economic trend of our time, but it is *becoming* a factor. And although such astronomical people-to-value ratios reveal themselves in pristine form in the financial services business, it is by no means confined there. Something similar, minus some of the decimal places, is happening across a range of businesses and at various scales within the economy. Consider, for example:

The screenwriter who develops the story that spawns a mini-industry as it moves from movie to video game to product licensing.

The software team that produces an applications program saving millions of people tens of millions of hours of repetitive work.

The biotechnologist who clones a new gene that will be the basis of a new medicine.

The Wal-Mart information systems manager who arranges for checkout scanners to do the jobs formerly done by a legion of inventory control and reorder managers.

In all these cases, the bottom line is the same: value and wealth are being created primarily through management and manipulation of the information process, rather than through the traditional inputs of the last economic millennium, such as raw materials, land, labor, machinery, or even capital.

It is not that people are unnecessary to this process. People *are* indeed necessary, but it is their *knowledge*—and their ability to use information tools and to communicate that knowledge in a commercial form—that matters, not the mere headcount. This trend, of course, has enormous positive implications for productivity and wealth creation. To borrow Negroponte's metaphor, very significant values are being created in these cases by knowledgeable, skilled people moving "bits" almost costlessly through the appropriate systems. The old high-cost, labor-intensive model of manufacturing goods based on "atoms" and then transporting and trading all those physical atoms is being obviated, at least in a few high-end businesses.

Of course the creation of physical goods is not about to cease and desist. No matter how much the Net enthusiasts imply that life has become some sort of virtual experience, the prosaic reality is that we continue to live in the real, physical world, subject to its physical laws—and to most of the long-established laws of capitalism.

We may see *some* substitution of "bits" for "atoms" in the next decade. For instance, the day will undoubtedly come when we will no longer go into a video store to rent or buy a video. Instead, we will just have the digital bits that make up that movie downloaded into our system when we want to watch it. We might no longer have a physical newspaper but an electronic touch screen that delivers the news and features we want. Bulky books such as encyclopedias will almost certainly become collector's items. They will be replaced with online services and CD-ROMs. (Already, in 1994, the sale of CD-ROM–based encyclopedias surpassed the sale of print encyclopedias, and the Encyclopedia Britannica was racing for survival to reinvent itself as a Web site.) We might not carry around cash or even a plethora of credit cards but instead maintain a single "E-money" smartcard that would be used for all our purchases.

But by and large, bits will only replace atoms in the process of developing, moving, exchanging, and adding value to information. Ultimately, most bits will have to take atomic, physical form in order to realize their true value in the marketplace. Atoms will continue to be the fundamental building blocks of the economy for a long, long time. Even 50 years from now, we will all still want, buy, and have most of the same physical atom-based goods we have today—from cars to clothes to computers to cappuccino machines—and plenty more besides.

The profound point about economics here is not that the virtual will triumph over the real, because it won't. But several relevant trends are unfolding.

First, because of increased manufacturing efficiencies (and export of manufacturing jobs to more cost-efficient low-wage economies), we will need continuously fewer manufacturing workers in the U.S. economy, *unless, as a matter of social policy, we choose to steer the U.S. economy in a different direction.* While business has congratulated itself on its reengineering and downsizing accomplishments, workers have had little to cheer about. Over three million net manufacturing jobs have disappeared in the last decade alone. Those who continue to have manufacturing jobs have seen real wages and benefits decline, even while their productivity has shot up. And even though American manufacturing workers are grinning and bearing what continues to be a severe squeeze on their living standards, we still continue to see jobs moving to other economies where workers work for far, far less. Over the next century, some manufacturing worker in America may travel along the trail blazed by the disappearing farmer over the last century. We *can* alter that pattern if we wish, but only as a conscious matter of political choice. And that choice can only be sustained over time if we can design a way to maintain a vibrant manufacturing sector that makes economic sense, not just political patronage sense.

Second, what is less well understood is that we will also need fewer service workers. Just in the last half decade, we have witnessed a net shrinkage of 600,000 secretarial jobs and over a million management positions in the United States. The Digital Revolution will further accelerate these trends. Increasingly, the center of economic activity—the place where real value is added, where future "products" and "services" are differentiated, and where the highest profit margins and salaries can be commanded—will be in the information sector. Almost everything else is subject to a high degree of redundancy and job obsolescence.

Finally, across very wide bands of the social and economic spectrum, whether among blue- or white-collar workers, a growing mountain of statistical data shows that workers are sharing a smaller portion of the total benefit pie in the new economy, while top executives are taking more. As Lazard Freres investment banker Steven Rattner points out, the compensation of the typical corporate CEO is today a staggering 150 times greater than that company's average worker, when it was a more reasonable 35 times the average worker's pay as recently as 1974. "In just one year—from 1992 to 1993—the premium for a college graduate appears to have risen by as much as 10 percent . . . The pressure is most acute on young male workers with only a high school education: Between 1973 and 1993, they lost 30 percent of their real incomes . . . Productivity has been rising at a 2 percent rate since 1993—a positive harbinger for average wages. So far, that hasn't helped. Companies have been able to transform those cost savings into higher profits—leading to a sharp drop in labor's share of the economic pie."[3] One such blatant example was an announcement in mid-1995 by IBM that it had ordered a pay cut of up to 36 percent for secretaries who still remained after thousands had lost their jobs in massive rounds of downsizing. The announcement came at the very moment when IBM's stock had rebounded to a two-year record high and the company had just announced it had $10 billion in cash on its balance sheet, record quarterly earnings, and excellent forecasts on future profitability.

But it isn't just IBM. The latest studies from several respected sources confirm that the United States, with the world's most advanced technological economy, has also become the most economically polarized nation in the developed world. The once wide American middle class is thinning out, as the demographic picture of America in recent years has begun to look startlingly like a banana republic. The wealthiest one percent of American households—with assets worth $2.3 million each—now owns a whopping 40 percent of the nation's wealth. In contrast, the richest one percent of the British population owns only 18 percent of the wealth. The top 20 percent of American households, with assets of $180,000 or more, owns nearly all of America's wealth—four-fifths, to be exact. Meanwhile, the lowest-earning 20 percent of American households earn only 5.7 percent of the country's total after-tax income. In Finland, the lowest 20 percent earns twice as much.

Many experts argue—provocatively but ultimately perversely—that these trends are all actually good news stories, showing the vitality of American capitalism in constantly redistributing wealth to those who deserve it, even if that process entails facing up to the downside of Schumpeter's "creative destruction."

Medieval alchemists searched in vain for the philosopher's stone that would turn base metals into gold. They didn't find it, but postmodern man has. For in the new economy, we are discovering a system that converts knowledge into wealth much more directly than before, without the clumsy intermediation of raw materials or labor.

The possibilities here are as stunning as they are endless. But let's not go to the extremes that some prophets of the new economy do. First, inherited wealth and making money the many "old-fashioned ways" remain the preponderant sources of today's great

American and global fortunes. Second, while the new knowledge-based model is already an important material factor in U.S. economic life, it is not yet widespread. And there are reasons why it will be very difficult for it to become truly widespread. A great deal of wealth is being created this way but by shockingly few people. Observes George Bennett, chairman of Symmetrix, a consulting firm, "If 2 percent of the population can grow all the food we need, what if another 2 percent can manufacture all the refrigerators and other things we need?"[4] Eliminating work and labor from the productive process is not necessarily all it's cracked up to be. Certainly, it is no social panacea.

A recent political cartoon by Ted Rall speaks volumes about the problem. It depicts a grid of multiple factories and enterprises, with a caption bubble coming out of each one that says, "Let others hire people. We'll sell them stuff." The main caption on the cartoon is, "AMERICA: WHAT WENT WRONG."

"Making things" is not the be-all and end-all of wealth creation that those still stuck in industrial-era economics would like to believe. But manufacturing still builds a powerful value chain, capable of productively deploying those without the advanced education and skills necessary to enter the ranks of the computer literate. Henry Ford's idea that his factory workers were also the market for his cars, and that the average worker ought to be able to buy the average car, is not a bad or outdated one. Unfortunately, however, it is becoming a disused paradigm. The architects of the new economy have many things figured out, but most of what they have figured out applies to their well-educated, highly skilled colleagues at the top of the demographic pyramid. Generally, they have no answer to the question of what society will do with those who are disenfranchised from opportunity by the new economy, let alone any comment about what the disenfranchised might do to society. Unless those questions are addressed and answered proactively—by business, by government, and by citizens—they may evolve their own answer—one that is destabilizing and dangerous. As James Fallows, a thoughtful commentator on issues of technology and the new economy, including America's long-term competition with Japan, points out:

> While it's arguable from a business school perspective that you can
> maximize return on assets by staying out of capital-intensive manufac-

turing work, things look dramatically different from the perspective of a country's social and political well-being. Within our borders, a lot of different people have to live together. Not just software designers and managers, but also millions of ordinary workers. And if they don't share a common economic interest—if they don't roughly rise and fall together—the society then is polarized. And then we have serious social overhead costs.

We need large-scale production work—and the millions of jobs and broad-based economic benefits that result—in order to have a rising economic tide that truly lifts all boats.

Again, let's try to be clear about the problem of ordinary manufacturing and other non-technical jobs disappearing. This is not an argument about automation rendering everyone unemployed, as was popular years ago and was later proven false. In the 1970s, for example, Congressional committees discussed the possibility of the 22-hour work week becoming the American standard as a result of automation and computers. While a great deal of automation and computerization did, in fact, follow, so too did other economic trends, notably the rush of women into the workforce and the decline and stagnation in real wages that became institutionalized in the 1970s and has continued to this day. The social context is all important in evaluating how future trends will shape up. And what we can see on the horizon is a bifurcation driven by technology and how different people with different skills will relate to it. Many people will be working more hours than ever, but an increasing number of citizens will have no jobs or insecure jobs.

We are not suggesting some sort of virtual fantasy in which labor is no longer needed at all (which, given our apparently genetic imperative to work and be productive, would actually be more of a nightmare than a dream if it could ever be achieved). Rather, what we are observing is only a *tendency* for labor inputs to decouple from total wealth creation somewhat more rapidly than had previously been the case. This tendency is occurring for now only at the *margins* of total output and total employment, which means its consequences are not often fully seen. But as trends compound, the process will be moving closer to center stage.

The shriveling of the manufacturing economy has already contributed to the creation of a permanently unemployed underclass in

America. Now what we are starting to see is a *tendency* toward the shriveling of certain sectors of service workers, such as secretaries, managers, and young entrants into the workforce without specific skills and goals. Most of these people will eventually find jobs in the service/administration economy. The question is, will they find good jobs they can grow with?

Throughout history, societies in transition have faced crises as huge populations have been rendered "surplus" by large-scale economic change. The factories of the Industrial Revolution could not, at first, absorb all the farmers and artisans being thrown off the land and out of work. The hunger, anger, and confusion that ensued ignited riot, rebellion, and revolutions. Study the history of feudal Europe or Japan and you will discover that the improvement of agricultural technology created large pools of surplus labor that were eventually organized into hordes of Crusaders and samurai. In our own time, in both Western Europe as well as North America, we have developed to a high art the vast web of the welfare state.

For all the political talk about welfare cheats, welfare queens, and corruption in these systems, the reality is that most people are on welfare because they lack the skills to participate in the productive opportunities of our societies and because our societies, for the last generation, have generally found it easier to pay for their subsistence than to develop a massive program to create opportunities and meaningful work for them. It is not that it cannot be done. The problem is that we are not doing it. And the Digital Revolution turns up the pressure on this trend.

These trends, of course, are the subject of many differing analyses and much debate. No less an authority on economic trends than the Fed's Alan Greenspan has declared that there's little here to worry about: digital technology will actually serve to bring the poor and the unskilled further into the center of the economic pie and narrow the income gap. According to an account of remarks he made on this topic in 1994, Greenspan believes that "graphics and touch-screens will enable illiterate people to perform functions via computer that have significant economic value."[5] But this misses the point.

Digital technology will undoubtedly reach into everyone's home, school, and work environment. Menial jobs of the future will surely continue to rely on the preconfigured intelligence of networks and systems, just as McDonald's counter personnel press buttons on computers today that avoid the need for them to have to know how to add and subtract or even use a calculator. But the vast bulk of the economic value in such processes lies with those who write the software programs and those who own and invest in the business, not those who marginally brush up against its windows and interfaces. Even those with good education and skills levels are not immune from being marginalized if their education and skills are the wrong kind. That's why Paul Krugman has likened the middle manager of the nineties to the skilled weavers of the Industrial Revolution who were put out of work by the arrival of the power loom.

No wonder Greenspan sees "extraordinarily deep-rooted foreboding" among consumers about the future as we shift from manufactured goods to knowledge-based services. What is surprising is that he would find this foreboding "inexplicable."[6] The people with the sense of foreboding perhaps understand the future better than the economists do.

Currently, only about 20 percent of the U.S. workforce participates meaningfully and directly in the information sector. This 20 percent includes the authors of this book and most of those reading it. We are what Labor Secretary Robert B. Reich has called the "symbolic analysts." Symbolic analysts are people with the education, skills, and/or entrepreneurial talents necessary to get involved with the genetic material of the Digital Revolution and to create, manipulate, understand, and make high-productivity use of "symbols"—the abstracted content of information, finance, entertainment, art, and so forth.

For this 20 percent of the population, the digital age is highly attractive. The transition from analog to digital content creates many new possibilities for symbolic analysts to be far better compensated for their work and to own pieces of equity in large revenue streams of the future. We will enjoy lifestyles, opportunities, and benefits unimaginable in previous generations to anyone without access to inherited wealth.

One of the exciting aspects of the digital age is that a small number of individuals previously excluded from this elite 20 percent of the population, can, under the right circumstances, enter the club at the top quickly and even become powerful figures within it. For example, a number of well-known African-American artists, musicians, filmmakers, and entertainers have been able to capitalize on the potent role of content in the value chain in order to become empire owners and decision makers. Among them are Oprah Winfrey, Bill Cosby, Quincy Jones, and Michael Jordan, to name just a few of the new wealthiest people in America who are no longer just "performers" but equity owners in major businesses.

Ironically, in a period of time that is supposed to value education and knowledge, many of the most successful figures have been college dropouts. The two Steves who founded Apple were the key examples of this in the seventies; Gates and Allen were the example in the eighties, and now in the nineties, among the Spielberg-Geffen-Katzenberg trio that founded the DreamWorks studio, there is not only not a single MBA, two don't even have college degrees.

This inspiring diversity also has its global dimension. Fortunes are being made almost overnight in introducing satellites, cellular phone systems, and cable television to the knowledge-hungry emerging middle classes of the big emerging markets like Mexico, Brazil, Indonesia, and China. The multimillionaires and billionaires arising from this process are generally shrewd entrepreneurs more than they are great intellects or information creators.

But the fact that the new digital order makes it possible, and even easy, for a small number of high-profile college dropouts to realize their dreams—or for a bright Indian villager to become an international software baron—does not mean that the vast majority of the people within the U.S. or other societies can follow such a path. Certainly, we will see more diversity at the top of the pyramid of wealth and power in the era ahead. But an enormous challenge remains to maintain jobs and living standards for those at the wide base of the pyramid—and even for those in the middle.

Peter Drucker has proposed that the proper definition of a knowledge worker is not so much someone who has gained some particular knowledge or skill but someone who has "learned how to learn" and can constantly move to new skills and new challenges. "Knowledge workers will *not* be the majority in the new society," Drucker forecasts. But they will be powerful, for they will be the leading class of this new society, the people who "will give the emerging knowledge society its character, its leadership, and its social profile." As to non-knowledge workers, Drucker suggests that the *central* social challenge of the future will be to find ways to share with them the fruits of rising productivity in the knowledge sector.[7]

We often hear politicians and business leaders proclaim that the Info Highway will create jobs. But this premise may be specious, at least in the early phase of the Digital Revolution we are now experiencing. Indeed, it flies in the face of the apparent evidence.

How many jobs would an Info Highway create if an Information Highway could create jobs? The answer might well be a negative number. The very companies most closely associated with building the Info Highway have been among those shedding jobs in the biggest numbers. IBM announced 85,000 job cuts between 1991 and 1995; AT&T, 83,000; NYNEX, 22,000; Hughes, 21,000; GTE, 17,000; Eastman Kodak, 14,000; BellSouth, 20,000; Xerox, 10,000; Pacific Telesis, 10,000; US West, 9,000. Of the 25 companies that have eliminated the most jobs during the nineties in the United States, 40 percent of them are directly and deeply involved in new digital technology. Another 32 percent are entities affected and influenced by the Information Highway in other ways besides building it. The U.S. Post Office, for example, has reduced its work force by 55,000. The employment outlook there is increasingly bleak as business wakes up to the fact that much of what passes through the post office today can eventually pass through web servers and Internet-type messaging services at much lower prices and instantaneous speeds—and with many new interactive features built in for replying to, indexing, saving, and carrying out transactions.[8]

Of course, job loss numbers are offset by the thousands of jobs created every month in the small and medium-size companies that are developing and employing the new technology. Even so, there is a small net loss of total employment. We now wink at 6 percent unemployment in the United States and call it "full" employment, even after several years of a strong economic recovery. The underclass grows, the ranks of the unemployed proliferate, and the living standards of the middle class stagnate.

It would appear that there is a new kind of macroeconomic Moore's Law showing up: As the rate of new wealth creation fueled by digital technology rises, the number of people required to produce it is decreasing. Not only are fewer people contributing to the productive process, fewer are *capable* of doing so even when the opportunity presents itself. Thus, the Digital Revolution's schizophrenic character: its promise of enormous social riches coexists side by side with the peril of a society cleaving ever more dramatically into haves and have-nots.

For better or worse, government remains the best tool for intervening in this spontaneous economic process and attempting to exercise leadership and choice on behalf of society as a whole. What, then, can government do to minimize or even reverse the increasing polarization trend and thereby maximize the chances for a new American Dream to emerge from the Digital Revolution? Admittedly, there are no clear answers to this and other questions. It's relatively easy to see the changes coming and—depending on one's philosophical or ideological bent—the problems and opportunities these large-scale transformations will bring. It is much, much harder to figure out how to intervene in the process intelligently and attempt to steer such powerful, rapidly moving forces to any specific end without crashing and burning.

Several broad attempts have been made to provide ideas and responses to some of these issues. One of the better such initiatives is the work of the Electronic Frontier Foundation (EFF), seeded by Lotus founder Mitch Kapor. Its chief evangelist is John Perry Barlow, a Wyoming frontiersman who once wrote lyrics for the Greatful Dead. Somewhat countercultural in its origins, EFF is now supported by an array of major communications companies. EFF has stressed a "Jeffersonian" approach to cyberspace. To EFF's leaders, this means arguing for interactive networks to be styled on the "open" rather than the "gatekeeping" model, for networks to be accessible to all on a universal service model, and for broad two-way capabilities to be built in the networks so that citizens not only get access to what's coming down the pipe but can pump their own ideas and content back upstream. For EFF, Jeffersonianism in cyberspace also means an intense focus on freedom of expression, protection of personal privacy from the prying eyes of both corporations and government, and, in general, keeping government from becoming the thought police of the Info Highway.

EFF has become well connected in Washington, particularly within the Clinton administration and among Democratic congressional leaders. Its approach represents one major aspect of the social conscience needed. But after asserting the primacy of the rights and interests of individuals in the future development of cyberspace, EFF has relatively little to say about the real-world problems that lie at the intersection where the Info Highway meets business, economics, and the dystopian society we already see around us. In particular, there is almost nothing in the EFF literature about the problem of shrinking workforces or what to do to promote the economic future of the nonsymbol analysts, other than to guarantee them access to cyberspace.

Whatever the merits of EFF's appeal for a Jeffersonian approach, it serves, if only incidentally, to remind us of the obvious: we no longer live in an agrarian society, and furthermore, there are no Jeffersons among us today. If a new social order is being born out of today's economic and technological changes, we lack the depth of insight that Jefferson and the early Federalists had in imagining the political structures that will be necessary. Indeed, if we examine the proposals of even the most cyber-enthusiastic in both established political parties, we find very little of interest beyond rhetoric, and a lot of noninnovative, old-fashioned policies dressed up to appear relevant to the new age.

The Clinton administration's approach is one of inveterate wonkism. The President and his advisors believe they have the whole future of cyberspace scoped out and that they know exactly what government should be doing on every issue. Attending their high-level hearings and brainstorming sessions, you get no sense that they appreciate the enormity of what is unknown about the digital future or how much those unknowns, as they become known, might redefine intelligent policy.

With Al Gore's interest in the information superhighway as a signature issue apparent from their first days in power, the Clintonites set about developing a comprehensive blueprint for government: the National Information Infrastructure (NII). The NII was a byzantine soup-to-nuts plan. It was designed to address every significant area of public concern—telecommunications reform, access, standards, advanced R&D, privacy, international economic competitiveness, and more.

The concerns addressed by NII were, of course, legitimate, and the effort to establish government leadership in these areas positively motivated. But the entire approach was out of date. It is as if the Clinton people sat down to design another New Deal, only this time for information technology. Every constituency is covered under NII; every grand claim about the supposed benefits of new technology to the economy and the political system is invoked. The original working paper outlining the NII is a wonk's dream writ large. It proposes to reevaluate copyright laws to bring them up to date, eliminate barriers caused by incompatible standards, open up overseas markets, and make government itself a leading-edge technology user. Information technology is depicted as a bit like manna from heaven—the NII calls for it to be used to help solve the health care crisis, to reshape the relationship between the federal government and the states, and to facilitate the crusade to "reinvent government," delivering more service for less cost to citizens.

But neither the original NII documents nor subsequent action by the Clinton administration sheds much light on *how* any of these ambitious goals will be achieved. NII acknowledges that the private sector should play the leading role in building networks and creating applications but wants government somehow to meld all this activity together into a vast public utility with interoperable standards, universal service, and enlightening, virtuous, democratic content flowing through it—a "network of networks" that is "seamless, interactive, and user-driven." Good idea. But how do we get there?

When we descend the mountain of political hype and wonkish jargon contained in Clinton's NII, it turns out that aside from setting up task forces, holding conferences, and supporting some (moderately useful) demonstration projects, very little has been accomplished. On the other hand, where we have seen Clinton administration policies in action, they usually suggested directions that were *not* particularly responsive to the NII goals but rather to a Democratic Party agenda that precedes the Information Age altogether.

For example, the NII held that the private sector should take the lead in the actual construction of Info Highway networks. So why, then, the controversial cable rate crackdown and rollback of February 1994, which lowered cash flows for major cable companies, provided the catalyst for shattering the incipient trend toward cable-telco mergers, and led to a slowdown in private sector Info Highway investment and deployment? The answer from the FCC was technically accurate: the companies were charging too much for cable service according to a narrow reading of the Cable Act. But why choose *that* moment in time to pick on them over a few dollars—most of which have *still* not shown up in lowered cable bills for most consumers? And who says cable television service is such an inalienable democratic right that the government should be involved in micro-managing its price in the first place?

Underlying much of the Clinton administration's sentiment for lower rates is the issue of *access*; or more specifically, the desire to make sure that the poor and disadvantaged will have equal access to whatever Info Highways are built in America. Again, the goal is noble and correct. But very few of the politicians talking about access even begin to understand what it is they want people to have access to. Both the politicians of the left and the right (including Newt Gingrich, as we shall see below) seem to think this is the early 1900s and we are building a nationwide telephone system again. In their simplistic, mechanistic view, they seem to foresee some sort of single wire coming into a home or a school that will provide instant complete access to some totality of world knowledge and information. NII's "network of networks" approach specifically upholds this model.

But it just ain't that way anymore. We're not talking here about a single technology such as telephony but a vast, complex multiplicity of technologies. For a very long time into the future, and maybe forever, there will be lots and lots of systems, many forms of connection to them, and many ways to access and manipulate their diverse information and entertainment content. Some of this content will be important and interesting while much will be trivial and banal. Getting value from cyberspace will be only marginally related to cost and access issues. A much bigger role will be played by knowledge, skill, and culture. Can people use what's available? Will they want to? A recent study showed that in some of America's ghetto communities, the penetration of cable TV in homes is actually higher than it is for telephones. Access is not the problem. If anything, it's harder and more expensive to get cable TV installed than telephone service. What can we learn from the fact that in some lifestyles entertainment is apparently more valued than communication?

The Clintonomic oversimplification of the access issue is replicated in the question of who should own new communication systems. This could be seen when the FCC introduced an affirmative action campaign into the middle of the $10 billion spectrum auction for PCS licenses in 1994–1995. Now under review, the original policy would have allowed individuals and companies with *no* communications industry experience a chance to own big slices of the available spectrum simply because they happened to fall into one of the categories subsumed under the acronym SWMRs (or more conveniently, Swimmers)—small businesses, women, minorities, and rural-based entrepreneurs.

The government was not only going to set aside spectrum for Swimmers to buy. It was then going to discount the price, and better yet, provide most of the financing. Then it was going to allow the winning Swimmers to flip their ownership interests back to corporate America in five years' time. This approach, if ultimately adopted (it remains the subject of legal and legislative conflict), would not re-dress the long-term disadvantage to minorities and women in the communications business. Indeed, it is safe to say that any intelli-gent Swimmer who got into the business with government help would have delightedly exited the business five years later laughing all the way to the bank. The FCC program was, essentially, nothing more than a one-time windfall for a handful of well-positioned Swimmers (many of whom were directly or indirectly backed by large corporate white male urban interests anyway).

Another example of real-world political follies that had nothing to do with the high-minded goals of NII was how the Clinton team han-dled the issues surrounding the "clipper chip" and encryption tech-nology. The initial administration policy (also now under review) was right out of the cold war and J. Edgar Hoover's FBI. Under the guise of fighting crime, the White House wanted a special chip installed in Info Highway devices that would have allowed law enforcement to override encryption codes and tap into private communications at will. This frightened civil libertarians for obvious reasons. But it also frightened the business community and economists who track issues relating to competitiveness. They feared that U.S. high-tech companies could lose the booming business in foreign markets if it became known that buying American meant opening up a country's private business and government communications to easy surveil-lance by the FBI or CIA. (Imagine yourself trying to sell the Chi-nese—or, God save you, the French—this computer with what amounts to a wiretapping device embedded in it. "Oh, and don't worry," you find yourself saying. "The wiretapping capabilities will only be used by American officials to fight the drug lords. Never, scout's honor, will they be used to interfere in the affairs of your

government, your businesses, or your law-abiding private citizens."
Good luck.)

In pursuit of this ill-conceived policy, the Clinton people also
ended up fighting American entrepreneurs such as RSA Data Security, a California company that has developed one of the best software
encryption systems for guaranteeing privacy in communications.
Clinton's national security and law enforcement officialdom has tried
to stop RSA from selling its encryption software in foreign countries,
even though the banned cryptographic algorithms are "widely published and literally being sold on the streets of Moscow," according
to the *New York Times*.[9]

Given these real-world applications of the Clinton-Gore team's
supposed vision of the electronic future, it is not surprising that the
administration's standing in the eyes of high-tech companies and
entrepreneurs has plummeted precipitously.

But are Newt Gingrich and his band of "New Republican" revolutionaries any more in touch with the new realities? Souped-up with
incredible enthusiasm and hyperbolic rhetoric, is Newt's vision of
cyberspace any more workable than the Clinton-Gore version?

Newt advocates a breakup of the federal bureaucracy and increased decentralization of power and decision making. He claims
these steps are critical to advance America's economic interests in
cyberspace, although the causal link between devolving federal
power to the states and pioneering cyberspace is far from clear. But
even assuming you believe there is close linkage between decentralization of power and the spread of social wealth–generating information technology, potholes appear almost as soon as you set off down
the primrose path of decentralization.

The sign saying Decentralization points toward a utopian future
where information technology is used to help local institutions experiment with new approaches to truculent social problems, where business and the nonprofit sector play partnership roles with government
in problem solving, where new kinds of interest groups work together
as part of larger communities, and where teledemocracy allows the
citizenry to be better informed and to participate more actively in all
issues of citizenship.

In fact, however, Newt's decentralization road is leading us not to
the future but back to the past—to the days of states' rights Dixie-
crats and a time when church and state were often fused in practice.

The forces on the new right calling for decentralization want local power, to be sure. But they do not want it to better promote the will of the majority, or to make government more efficient, or to bring the charms of the Internet to the masses. They want it to keep Washington from doing the valuable part of what it has done since the New Deal—leading society in the generally favorable direction of integration, education, women's rights, expanded economic opportunity, and modernization.

This contradiction between past and future came to a symbolic head at the Republican governors conference soon after the November 1994 congressional elections that swept the Republicans into power and Newt Gingrich into his role as Speaker of the House. At this event, Newt had arranged for futurists Alvin and Heidi Toffler to speak, and enthusiastically endorsed their notion of building a "Third Wave," decentralized, information-driven new American economy. But a Southern governor took the floor to argue that he didn't think the Republican election victory that had just occurred was a referendum on all this futuristic stuff about cyberspace and new institutions. Instead, he thought it was a call to return to the old-fashioned American values of the 1950s. Newt was mute, but Heidi Toffler pointedly returned the fire by asking if the governor's vision of the future was one of sending women back to the kitchen and blacks back to segregation.

Then, on his second day as Speaker, Gingrich again raised the banner of the cyber-future when he issued this clarion call to the House Ways and Means Committee: "I would suggest to you and to your staff and to the witnesses you bring in that about every policy we should ask the question, 'Does it accelerate our transition into a Third Wave information age, or does it slow it down?' "

But as Clinton Labor Secretary Robert Reich pointed out, "Ironically, the Speaker's own agenda does not pass this test." According to Reich, success in the Information Age requires diverse and continually evolving skills. Yet Newt Gingrich's Contract with America "says almost nothing about skills or the workforce. Nowhere is there any proposal to help Americans struggling to swim from the Second Wave to the Third . . . Instead, House Republicans are busy cutting the lifelines and puncturing the lifeboats.[10]

For a Speaker who sometimes sounds as if his constituency were located not in Georgia but in cyberspace, Gingrich has made precious few practical proposals relevant to developing new information technology and applications. And those proposals he *has* made reflect little understanding of the issues and challenges before us.

Gingrich's now infamous proposal for government tax credits to allow the poor to buy laptop computers was, as he sheepishly admitted a few days after announcing it, a "dumb idea." Dumb, yes—but also worth dissecting to understand the philosophical approach behind it.

Like Gore and Clinton, Newt is quite savvy about playing the "social concern" chord in America's heartstrings. He certainly understands that there is a potential problem with the less affluent and the poor being denied access to the new technologies he touts as so critical to our economic and social future.

With the laptop scheme, Newt was trying to carve out a quasi private sector spin on the concept of universal access Clinton and Gore had proposed two years before. But instead of government simply mandating access, Gingrich wanted the poor to buy their own equipment from private sector manufacturers, with the government somehow stimulating the process through tax credits rather than direct subsidies. (Had the idea stayed long enough on the table, the media would no doubt have asked Newt why the poor would need new tax credits—unless he was thinking of taking away the earned income credit that already allows most of the poor to avoid paying income tax at all. But never mind.)

We could, and probably should, put Internet connections into schools—although it is doubtful that Newt's Republicans would stand for the content that would wash in as a result. (Newt himself has proven his libertarian bona fides in opposing the Exon bill's effort to curb "indecency" on the Internet, but on this issue he is miles out in front of his Republican cohorts.) We could, and probably should, encourage telephone, cable, and computer companies to provide low-cost Internet connections to communities and help design government, school, and community bulletin boards, home pages, and other interactive information systems.

But "access" in general, while an important concept, is only the first step. Access to what? Which of the many competing services that will evolve ought to be made available at low cost to every citizen? Who will train people to use the system? This is not a telephone that you pick up and dial or a TV set that you turn on and watch. No matter how user-friendly the broadband switched networks of the future will claim to be, they will likely require some degree of thought and skill to access deeply and meaningfully. Otherwise, they will just be used for their entertainment, sports, music, and pornography applications—not exactly the stuff that, even if allowed to thrive uncensored, ought to be the domain of government subsidies according to Newt's more-virtuous-than-thou Republican friends.

More important than the new issue of access to technology, then, is the longstanding one of education and even basic literacy. Pundits among the digerati urge us to believe that electronic technology is giving a new lease on life to words and the logic of written communications. It is said, for example, that one year's worth of Internet traffic represents more words than have ever been published through traditional means in all of human history or that letter-writing *was* disappearing because of the telephone until E-mail came along to revivify the written message. All the most senior figures of the Digital Revolution are still publishing print books and articles to express their views, and the best way to figure out the Internet is to go out and buy one of the hundreds of how-to manuals in printed book form about using it.

The educated and skilled *may* be experiencing some of this renaissance of words. But then again the prose of the Internet leaves much to be desired in terms of the sensibilities of logic, order, and rationality historically associated with the printed word. The word content of multimedia may be great by volume, says Katharine Graham of the *Washington Post*, but not by weight. Although her own company and its subsidiaries are aggressively pursuing online services, CD-ROM publishing, and other new media, she makes no bones about her bottom-line view: "Print must prevail." Business, and the news business in particular, may find astounding applications for interactive multimedia, but at the end of the day, "for all the magic of pictures, sound and simulations, the complex issues confronting us today can only be understood through words . . . People need *words in print* for a democracy to work."[11]

The debate about how interactive media may affect the thought process of society is a fascinating and far-reaching one to which there are no clear answers. But one thing *is* clear. While cyberspace may be filled with words, a growing portion of the American population will not be able to use, understand, or benefit from those words.

Some of these people may be *digitally literate*, in that they feel at home with joysticks and remote controls and are perfectly capable of absorbing the sights and sounds of multimedia entertainment. But if you are not *functionally literate*, your chances of getting a significant piece of the cyberspace pie are slim, even if you have access to it.

As Silicon Valley consultant Marcia Kaplan points out, some pundits glorify the notion of America as a "post-literate" society where the ability to comprehend the complexities of the written word is devalued and where it is believed everything important can be turned into an image. Because we haven't yet grasped that the more positive vision of "our society's future is ineluctably linked to the preservation of the printed word," says Kaplan, we could "revert to a Pre-Renaissance model in which only an elite class—the clergy in that era, the technical specialist in ours—will know how to read and write" effectively.[12]

It is against this backdrop that it is important to view Newt Gingrich's second specific proposal relative to government and cyberspace—namely the Thomas project (an allusion to Thomas Jefferson), a plan to put all the activities of government, including texts of bills and congressional debate, on the Internet. This one is now up and running. But it, too, deserves a closer look.

The idea behind Thomas is that ordinary citizens will be able to download all government information at will and therefore, presumably, be able to participate more fully in the debate over national issues. This idea is not altogether dumb—nor is it new. The basic notion of "putting government online" was already moving forward as a result of the Clinton administration's NII project.

Unfortunately, the whole concept of "putting government online" has little do with actual democracy, let alone the citizen empowerment its promoters suggest. Making vast accumulations of government information accessible online is one thing; actually giving ordinary citizens more incentive and power to participate in government, let alone more actual control over government operations, is quite another. The main effect of the Thomas project will be to further empower the media, the lobbyists of Gucci Gulch, and the inside-the-beltway policy wonks. These are the people who come armed with the computers, high-speed modems, and printers—not to mention the time and the interest—to probe every detail of government activity say, of Clinton's 1,400-page health care plan that failed. (After all, this is their job and they're paid to do it.)

To the extent that the masses use Thomas, it may become another radio call-in show type of forum. Already there is all too much anonymous ranting and irresponsible spleen-venting on the Internet. The right to flame your congressman by E-mail is not likely to improve the quality of democracy.

Some good will probably come eventually from Thomas. But in terms of advancing the American economy's march into cyberspace, far more benefit for the have-nots could be achieved by skills training programs and basic literacy efforts.

In Gingrich's 1984 book, *Window of Opportunity*, the Speaker advocated a variety of U.S. government subsidies and tax credits for new and emerging technologies. These even included a dollop of the very far-out and esoteric, such as "a mirror system in space" that "could provide the light equivalent of many full moons so that there would be no need for nighttime lighting of the highways."[13]

Since galvanizing an extremely conservative social movement and riding it to power, however, Newt has reversed gears and now opposes government seed money for new technology. His supporters are rushing to abolish the supposedly wasteful Office of Technology Assessment (one of the few organizations that warns American business about areas where we may be losing competitiveness). The handful of recent experiments with government-financed technology initiatives are now all under Republican-led funding threat, even though most are puny budget items: flat-panel displays, high-performance computing, new materials, and intelligent highways.

The passion for defunding government initiatives in the technology sector is particularly ironic when it comes from cybercrats like Gingrich. They seem to be wholly unaware that there would be no cyberspace today—and certainly no Internet—without the government-funded, government-directed research of DARPA. This Defense Department agency conceived of, designed, and built the rudiments of the Internet in the 1960s, and then passed the baton in more recent times to the National Science Foundation and other government-funded institutions that collectively nurtured it to the point where it could become today's mass-public phenomenon. The Internet is almost the ideal study in state-sponsored technology policy: government funded the basic research and construction, ordi-

nary citizens made use of the infrastructure to generate thousands of
creative and diverse applications, and the private sector is now adding to this treasure trove, taking over the operations, and commercializing the system. With such a success story at the heart of
cyberspace, why would we want to foreclose the chance to achieve
similar triumphs for innovation and wealth generation in the future?

Finally, there is the matter of the ravenous Republican appetite
for defunding the Public Broadcasting System. It may be that in an
ideal free market the government doesn't belong in the business of
funding television programming. It may also be that PBS has a left-
leaning bias. But the fact is that with a very limited budget PBS has
produced or distributed at least a third and maybe a half of all the
high-quality educational and informational television content we
have in this country. Why would anyone who purports to be both
enthused about the Information Age and worried about the dumbing
and numbing effects of popular culture, as Newt claims he is, be
opposed to supporting PBS?

Like other revolutionaries before him, Newt's appetite, once in
power, for continuing to address difficult questions has begun to
wane. In January 1995, he appeared to be the Speaker from Cyberspace. By June, aside from his disagreement with the Exon approach
to the Internet, cyberspace was hardly even in his vocabulary anymore.

As computer industry savant Esther Dyson observed after an interview with Newt, there is no question that he "gets it" with regard to
cyberspace, but "What does he want to do with what he gets? Do I
want to live in the world he wants to create?"[14]

While claiming he would use his "bully pulpit" to promote the
new cyberspace economy, after "laptops for the poor" and Thomas,
the Gingrich record of practical initiatives comes to a screeching
halt. However, to the extent one is curious to know what this supposed revolutionary thinks about cyberspace, one can look back to
the dizzying contradictions of his prior statements and involvements.

Just before the 1994 election, his think tank, the Progress and
Freedom Foundation, sponsored a series of discussions among lead-
ing futurists and technology experts that led to something called the
Magna Carta for Cyberspace. This Magna Carta is an interesting doc-
ument, although it couldn't be more different from the original one.
The Magna Carta issued by King John at Runnymede in 1215

spelled out with admirable specificity and brevity the rights the king was granting to his noblemen and citizens. This new Magna Carta, however, like everything else having to do with cyberspace, is verbose, complex, elliptical, often self-contradictory, long on questions, and short on answers.

It is ironic, given Newt's current politics—and the prominent role of George Gilder in drafting the document (alongside Alvin Toffler, Esther Dyson, and George Keyworth)—that the Magna Carta advocates a strong, proactive role for government. While stressing the primacy of the private sector, the document declares that the transition from Second Wave to Third Wave will require "a level of government activity not seen since the New Deal."

The Magna Carta outlines five specific areas in need of major government action, including such weighty matters as overhauling the tax code and redefining intellectual property law to promote the growth of the cyber-economy. Yet of these five areas, only one has received any serious attention from the Gingrich-led Congress—the goal of promoting wider competition in telecommunications. And even here the reviews are negative. Rather than any stirring vision of the future cyber-economy, Congress has responded primarily to the power of telecommunications companies and their legions of lobbyists, who are embroiled in a slugfest over control of an existing market that already has $300 billion a year in revenues. With these sums at stake, the campaign contributions are flying fast and furiously into the war chests of politicians willing to defend the conflicting special interests of long-distance companies, RBOCs, cellular phone companies, alternative access providers, cable companies, and broadcast networks. Quite literally, there are more lobbyists working on telecom reform than there are members of Congress.

All over the world, and especially in the United States, it is fashionable to bash government. Thick with the bureaucracy and ossification that has piled up over two centuries of the Industrial Age, governments are among the forces most resistant to change. Compared to business, which is often on the front line of change—forced to compete, adapt, and innovate—government grows fatter and less effective even while its leaders claim to be making it leaner and more effective. Everyone talks about reinventing government, but so far, nobody has done anything about it.

The failures of government help make techno-libertarianism the powerful trend it is today. Many in business say that the only positive thing government can do is get out of the way. And naturally, since government can't lead, "the market should decide" every question.

"The market." It is fashionable to ascribe all-knowing wisdom to it, as if it were some infallible oracle and arbiter of the grand human experiment. To be sure, the market is the arena of mankind's most all-encompassing social endeavor: work, commerce, and wealth creation in today's vocabulary; hunting and gathering back at the beginning of history.

But economics, powerful force that it is, is not the sum total of all human needs and endeavors, nor is the marketplace capable of dealing with many of the questions and challenges faced by our civilization. Human beings invented governments and social institutions for good reason, after all. That reason has a great deal to do with the natural limitations of the market in providing by itself for public good or in mediating the complex conflicts of any society developed enough to have a market.

As it turns out, for all their high costs and political and economic failings, governments remain the only society-wide institutions we possess with sufficient scope and legitimacy to represent the public will (at least to some degree) and to intervene in the flow of history to give it shape and direction. But to make government work at all, businesses and citizens will have to step in and get involved, compelling government institutions to recognize the opportunity at hand and to embrace it with forward-looking policies, not backward ones.

Indeed, if the market is left purely and totally to its own course, we may never realize the true promise of the Digital Revolution and we may never even get the broadband networks into the home that are widely forecast today. As Bellcore's visionary technologist, Robert Lucky, points out, "If government doesn't get involved, the Information Highway will be built, but it will be designed mostly for entertainment, where the known markets are for business. If you want true interactivity and two-way broadband service, government will have to set policies that move the industry in that direction."

The inability of the established political system to offer much innovative thought or policy on the new questions—even with self-styled "revolutionaries" and "outsiders" in power—is a reflection of larger confusion and ambivalence. As a society, we are coming to the end of the Industrial Age tunnel. We can make out the blinding light of the digital future some distance ahead, but we are in a no-man's-land between. Our understanding of the questions we will face is, naturally, only partial, and generally conditioned by the only thing we have to go on—our *past* experiences. We are all trying to model the structures for a new age with brains that were trained and developed in its dying predecessor. Considering that the future itself is only partially visible, is it any surprise that many of the ideas about it are half-baked?

About some major issues, of course, there is enormous consensus, at least superficially. Virtually everyone engaged in the digital debate says they believe that great economic opportunities will be generated by the new technology and that we ought to do whatever we can to maximize that outcome. Most experts further say they believe that the private sector ought to take the lead in constructing the Information Highway. Few are opposed to the principle of introducing more competition into the regulated, monopolized areas of telecommunications—even all the telephone companies swear that they are for greater competition. Most agree, too, that technical standards should evolve from the marketplace, not be dictated by government fiat. Many recognize that there are special social benefits and social dangers associated with the Digital Revolution. If they go that far, they usually go on to the corollary that government ought to play at least some role in attempting to ensure broad access to new communications technology, particularly in schools and other public institutions. Privacy and security are prominent concerns, and almost all commentators want to see a cyberspace that is easy and inexpensive to access, free as well as safe, and culturally uplifting.

The list could go on and on with such statements. They are invoked piously by politicians and business leaders at conferences and in legislative floor debates. But in reality, as we have seen in the practical history of the Clinton administration, all they amount to are platitudes and clichés. The generalities come easily, but on every point, the devil lies lurking in the details.

Take competition for instance. Everyone says they want more competition in telecommunications in order to bring benefits to the consumer. Okay, that part is easy. But now take a look at the questions that flow from that premise.

Why not open up all markets tomorrow to full competition? Well, say some, if we do that then those companies with a monopoly chokehold on their existing markets will leverage that power into domination of new markets. Many contend the RBOCs will do exactly that if given access to the long distance market without first opening up their monopoly control of local telephone service to competition.

Well, so be it, counters the other side, particularly the RBOC lobbyists. There's always winners and losers—that's the nature of the marketplace, after all. Schumpeter, creative destruction and all that . . .

Yes, but, shoots back the skeptic. There are markets and then there are markets, but here we're not talking about any old market. When you talk about telecommunications, you're talking about the warp and woof of our society. Anyway, the RBOCs didn't get their monopoly power by competing in the market, they got it from government in return for agreeing to provide universal access and other public interest benefits. So if government created the unlevel playing field in the first place, doesn't government now have a responsibility not just to get out of the way but to make sure the playing field really is level and competition really happens?

No, say other critics. Every time government tries to micromanage, bureaucracy and inefficiency result. How does that benefit the consumer?

The consumer? If you're so concerned about the consumer, you certainly wouldn't want government to disappear and leave the consumer to the mercies of behemoth corporations who have just been told they no longer have to respect long-standing government policy limiting their prices and profits and regulating their quality and service. Give these companies half a chance and they'll all go rushing after the top business customers and the best neighborhoods—and they'll abandon the rest of America. They'll leave the farms and barrios of America without service.

Hold on—are we sure about that? And even if we are, can't we develop *some* bare-bones regulation that would compel all the competitors to share the cost of maintaining today's universal service standards?

There you go: you say you're for deregulation, but suddenly you find yourself talking about new regulations.

Now that we're delving so deeply into the subject of competition, should telephone companies be allowed to buy cable companies, combine their resources, and bring just "one pipe" into the home?

Some, like the FCC, say no, that would tend to be monopolistic. It would eliminate the consumer benefits that would come from having two competing pipes into the home. But others argue back that if cable companies and telcos have to compete head-to-head for every home, they will squander vast, duplicating resources building two different Information Highways. The consumer will pay much more and get much less service.

By the way, if we are so keen on competition as an operating principle, why should government have any say-so on cable rates and prices? Let private sector companies set their prices as they want, and let the marketplace work its efficiency-inducing magic.

Well, no, say some. Cable television has become a kind of necessity, a regulated public utility of sorts, and it ought to stay that way. If government doesn't set basic cable rates fairly, the John Malones of the world will squeeze every disposable penny out of customers.

Hmmm . . . that's an interesting line of reasoning. Just why is it the public's *right* to get MTV or ESPN or CNN at a low and specified price? Why is the government regulating the price of this business and not the price of cereal or blue jeans or tax preparation services? And why is it that if government policy encourages a "two pipe" approach, the cable companies will continue to be saddled with price regulation, but the telephone companies will be able to bring video services in on an entirely different and potentially much more profitable price structure?

PCS is supposed to be a great new technology capable of bringing all kinds of new benefits to consumers at very low prices. So why did the government auction off the spectrum necessary to provide PCS services at prices that will make it almost impossible to earn a profit on PCS for many years into the future? The spectrum pricing almost guarantees that the technology will be developed very slowly by the entrenched monopolies who won most of the licenses. If you wanted to promote competition, why wouldn't you want to get PCS up and running as fast as possible and have the multitude of new competitors buy the spectrum from the government out of revenues over time? And that's only if you think it's right for those in the PCS world to have to buy spectrum at all when lots of other kinds of telecommunications companies use spectrum for free.

While we're at it, what about foreign companies? If we're so interested in promoting competition and getting more benefit at lower cost to the consumer, why don't we want to let them into the competitive party? Well, because they don't let us into their markets. I see, so this is not *really* about what's best for the consumer, is it?

By the way, why are government regulators so insistent on rate structures that prevent cross-subsidies of one service by another? If we really believe in the wisdom of the market and the leadership of the private sector, why don't we let these guys make their own decisions about what parts of their business they will invest their profits in, what services they will develop, and how those will be priced?

Round and round we go, deeper and deeper into the murky depths of arcane details about the telecommunications business. Nobody can square these circles. No one can come up with a perfectly fair, balanced plan. One interest group's idea of competition turns out to be another's idea of monopoly. No one can know for sure who will grab market share from whom once the games begin.

The truth is that under our old industrial era interest group politics, we cannot readily achieve the competition and deregulation everyone says they desire. We will hem and haw, compromise and chip away, lobby and legislate, hand down court rulings, sue each other like crazy, review bureaucratic filings that run to thousands of pages, and add a patchwork of contradictory state efforts at deregulation to what's happening at the federal level. In short, we will remain gridlocked for years to come, with slow, piecemeal progress taking place at the margins. At the rate we are going, it could take a decade or two to accomplish the deregulation and restructuring of the market that will allow the consumer to get the much-touted benefits.

In the meantime, millions of jobs that might have been created will be on hold. Hundreds of billions of dollars in potential GDP growth will be lost. The highly respected econometric team at the WEFA Group has quantified these losses. According to the WEFA study, if all U.S. communications markets could be fully opened on January 1, 1996, a decade of remarkable growth would be kicked off that would ultimately include the creation of 3.4 million new jobs and $298 billion worth of real GDP growth. Consumers would save $550 billion in communications costs. The net effect of all this would be to increase the average household's net disposable income by $850 a year.[15]

All the WEFA figures are stunning, but that last one is truly impressive. It is more household income growth than is seriously projected from any other source. It is almost twice the size of the tax cuts proposed in 1995—tax cuts supposedly essential to the goal of improving the living standards of American families and stimulating the economy. If these gains were indeed recurring, they would be more than enough to pay for the annual costs of deployment of the most advanced broadband network now under consideration.

"Our findings show that the economic and employment situation in America is significantly worse for every year communications competition is delayed," says WEFA's Mike Raimondi. Indeed, WEFA puts a price tag of $110 billion a year on the overall economic cost of maintaining the status quo.[16]

Perhaps the WEFA statistics are somewhat inflated in the interests of making a point. These costs and benefits are notoriously difficult to quantify accurately. But even if the numbers are only half right, politicians should be leaping out of their seats in Congress to strike down the status quo laws and rules that prevent this kind of job and wealth creation from starting tomorrow.

But they aren't. And that's why one important message of this book is that the American people ought to seize hold of this issue and light a fire under Congress, the White House, and the relevant regulatory agencies to insist on *full deregulation of telecommunications right now.*

But unlike some experts who favor the same goal, we don't believe it can be accomplished by government simply absenting itself from the process. That is a recipe for the re-monopolization of telecommunications by several of the existing special interests. We believe government must have a creative strategy and develop some minimalist, "smart-tech" policies that will maximize competition and at the same time, preserve at least the essential framework of public trust in telecommunications.

While we would favor sweeping away all special-interest roadblocks to full competition—in particular, the local interconnect monopolies of the RBOCs and the Chinese walls between what various kinds of communications companies can do—we believe government must find a way to protect and even expand the public trust aspects of telecommunications, such as the principle of universal access, openness and interoperability of networks, free speech and expression, etc. This doesn't have to be done in the old way—everyone doesn't have to be charged exactly the same amount, for example, regardless of where they live or what the true cost of service is. But everyone should be able to get basic service at reasonably affordable rates.

The FCC should not try to micromanage cable rates and telephone rates as it now does, but neither should it be disbanded as Newt's friends at the Progress and Freedom Foundation and in Congress now propose in their headlong rush to turn government's historic job over to the marketplace. Instead, the FCC should regulate the most essential aspects of the public trust responsibilities of communications companies. All those who would seek to provide competitive telecommunications services would have to demonstrate that they were shouldering their load of that public trust. But this should be done more through guidelines and mission statements that can periodically be reviewed, than through the two-thousand-page FCC filings typical of today's era of micromanagement.

Of course there will be problems. Of course some companies will be losers, and others may become incredibly more powerful in the process. Yes, there will be regions, neighborhoods, and interest groups that might suffer. Freed from the old constraints, we could see the telecom companies engage in some price gouging and poor service standards for a while. But trying to imagine all the problems in advance and put in place a deregulatory framework that also seeks to regulate in advance against imagined problems is the equivalent of blocking a fully competitive environment from ever taking hold.

Instead, the approach ought to be let the competition begin. Later, we'll see what the problems are. The FCC can always threaten to revoke a license if the public trust aspects are abused by a particular company. Congress can always develop specific new legislation to address serious problems or distortions in the marketplace. As with today's social compact that exists in over-the-air broadcasting, no license should be granted in perpetuity. There should be periodic reviews to compare corporate performance to a set of desired goals. If companies are not playing by fair rules and if they are not serving the public adequately, Congress would be empowered to establish penalties or take other measures to rebalance the forces.

But all that discussion should come *after* the decks are swept clean and competition is under way. Let's get the growth kick first and then figure out what to do about the new problems it brings. Indeed, how much re-regulation we might want to introduce a few years down the road will be in large part contingent on seeing whether we get the promised benefits and the expected economic growth.

If would be terrific, of course, to conclude this book with a 10-point program that tied up all the problems raised herein into a nice, neat package. We could then send it all off to Newt Gingrich and give him one hundred days to pass it into law. But that is not possible. Unlike some other pundits, we are compelled by our stance of real-world futurism to make clear that we don't possess any comprehensive, holistic answers to the difficult questions thrown up by the Digital Revolution. And we would urge our readers to mistrust the claims of those who say they do. The answers will have to evolve— through political debate, through experiment, and through experience.

Although we openly acknowledge that we have no full-blown answers, we have some ideas about how to break through the gridlock and start the process in the right direction, just as we have begun to sketch out above on telecommunications reform. We also have some ideas about the *wrong* directions to take. Below, we have elaborated a few possible experiments, a few new ideas, and some overarching points of view we think are highly relevant. This is *not* a program or a blueprint. These are just early-stage ideas and provocations—some appetizers and hors d'oeuvres—for the massive political and social discussion to come.

1. Made in the USA. Develop social and economic incentives to encourage more onshore manufacturing of Info Highway hardware—tax breaks, accelerated depreciation, government-subsidized training programs, etc. Don't be afraid of industrial policy. Instead, embrace it (but call it postindustrial policy). Although content may be king in the value chain, trillions of dollars worth of hardware will be bought and sold on a worldwide basis as global Information Highways are built over the next decade. These devices will be made *somewhere*— and government policy should seek to ensure that the United States keeps a large percentage of those jobs inside our economy for the benefit of our citizens. However, any programs we develop should not be institutionalized in perpetuity. We should carry out stringent cost-benefit analyses and performance reviews on a regular basis. Either this effort proves itself by creating a large number of good jobs or else it should be shut down.

2. The Cyber-Fund (I). Since the cost of telecommunications will be plunging, owing to enhanced competition, the haves in our society will be able to pay a small tax on their telephone and cable bills and scarcely notice it. The proceeds from this tax should *not* go into the general treasury but be reserved for special innovative efforts to provide information access and education to the have-nots. Among such programs might be:

▪ Info vouchers, the digital equivalent of food stamps. These could be used to buy computer or telecommunications hardware and software, pay for online service accounts, etc.

▪ Skills training and retraining programs, emphasizing Information Highway literacy—and basic functional literacy as well.

▪ Partnership funding for schools, libraries, and other community institutions that want to get wired.

3. The Cyber-Fund (II). It may be difficult to raise enough through small taxes to develop all the programs above. Another means would be for the government to seek out philanthropic backing for similar goals. We need a new Andrew Carnegie for the twenty-first century to fund cyber-libraries and Information Highway access and training. A public enterprise should be established for this purpose, one that could attract some of the multibillion-dollar fortunes that have recently been donated to universities.

4. Build up, not down. Take advantage of the current build-down in America's defense infrastructure to convert assets to civilian use in exploring cyberspace. Use closed military bases as skills centers. Transfer defense engineers to Info Highway projects. Open up the technological secrets of the Pentagon to commercial licensing. Expand the mandate of DARPA to continue advanced research that could translate into economic security as well as military security. Outside the defense sector, the federal government should also be involved in continuing to sponsor basic research in digital technology. Government at various levels—including agencies, states, cities, and towns—should support research and demonstration projects that seek to use the technological advances of our times in the solution of social problems.

5. Stick to our guns on market opening. Offer European and Japanese telecommunications companies lots of carrots with regard to their participation in our markets, *but only if* they open theirs demonstrably and fully to our companies.

6. Incentivize social virtue. Government should articulate broad, virtuous public policy goals that the private sector can support, such as developing, distributing, and delivering important educational and informational content and pioneering the rollout of broadband networks in disadvantaged communities and schools. Incentives rather than mandates should be used to encourage the private sector to fulfill these public-service goals. Incentives might include significant tax breaks or the right to bid on large government contracts for communications technology.

7. Putting access in perspective. No fundamental problems of society will be solved by technology alone. Access to technology, while a legitimate concern of government, guarantees little in isolation. In fact, since high value-added use of technology will generally be by the most affluent, the growing social polarization among the educated, the less-educated, and the underclass will tend to get worse. These problems must be addressed by political, cultural, and economic means—we cannot simply hope that access to technology will be a magic bullet.

8. Morality in cyberspace. Government should *not* be in the business of regulating the content of the traffic flowing through cyberspace. However objectionable some content may be to certain parties, government shouldn't—and probably can't—be censor in chief. Private providers of specific online or broadband services should be allowed to set their own ethical and moral standards and systems operation procedures. In the virtual world, just as in the real world, parents still must be moral leaders for their children, paying attention to such issues as what online services their children use and which strangers they are communicating with. The same laws that exist in the real world concerning security, crime, privacy, and knowingly providing pornography to children, just as some examples, need to be applied vigorously to the virtual world.

The future has already arrived; it just isn't evenly distributed. So said William Gibson, the cyberpunk novelist who is to the Information Highway what Jack Kerouac was to the Interstate. This book's journey has been an attempt to reveal what the future will look like, using the part that's already here as the basis for our best guesses.

Diverse trends are shaping tomorrow's realities. The construction of the Information Highway is but one of many seminal experiences of our times. Yet when you look into the deep space of the future, nothing else out there has so much power and potential to revitalize our society and refocus the strength of Yankee ingenuity in productive and virtuous directions.

Americans have always needed and benefited from new frontiers to pioneer. In cyberspace, we have the opportunity to experience anew some of the exhilaration that goes with blazing a trail and opening up virgin territory. Along this electronic frontier—with all its perils and nightmares—we have our last, best chance to rekindle the great American Dream.

APPENDIX A

The Interview Triptych

INTRODUCTION

As much as any three people in America, John Malone, Ray Smith, and Reed Hundt have stood at the stormy center of political and economic controversy during the 1993–1995 period of Information Highway development.

As chairmen, respectively, of the largest U.S. cable TV company, Tele-Communications, Inc.; the most aggressive of the regional Bell companies, Bell Atlantic; and the Federal Communications Commission, each represented (and, indeed, individually personified), the competing values and interests that burst upon the national scene when the largest merger in world business history was being forged . . . and then taken apart. Their differing accounts of what actually happened, as well as their contrasting perspectives on the Information Highway, make for an unusual Rashomon-style portrait of the events and the issues involved in the aborted TCI–Bell Atlantic merger, the subsequent intensification of the cable-telco conflict, and the role of government in this era of great technological and social change.

Among more than one hundred interviews conducted for this book with industry leaders, technology visionaries, and policy experts, these three stand out as particularly enduring expressions of the complex issues surrounding the Digital Revolution that will be debated for years to come. The interviews with Malone and Smith were originally conducted by David Kline and published as cover stories in *Wired* magazine in 1994 and 1995. They were widely discussed and debated in the media, at industry conferences, and on the Internet. The interview with Hundt was originally conducted by Daniel Burstein and was published in *Technology and Media* in 1994.

All three interviews are anchored in particular moments in time, to be sure. But each offers an extraordinarily revealing look at the uncensored thinking and attitudes of three of the most powerful and visible representatives of technological change in America, which is why we have preserved excerpted versions of them here.

THE COWBOY OF CABLE

March 10, 1994. Englewood, Colorado, inside John Malone's offices at TCI headquarters.

DAVID KLINE: **Do you feel that . . .**
JOHN MALONE: Excuse me, I don't know if you've met Ray. [He points to a life-size stuffed gorilla sitting in a chair across from his desk. It is dressed in a vest and tie.]

Is that his name, Ray?
That's [Bell Atlantic CEO] Ray Smith, yeah.

Well, as long as we're on the subject, would you explain finally why the merger with Bell Atlantic crashed?
[He smiles, leans back in his chair.] Most people don't really understand why the deal blew. There were two things: First, their stock was down, and they would have had to give us more than half their company. But number two, they were trying to make a transition from a [conservative company whose] stock was supported by dividend payment to an [aggressive firm whose] stock is supported by earnings growth. Not growth, but *earnings* growth—quarterly earnings growth—which is different.

Now, if you're gonna try and price your company based on earnings, you'll never get credit [on Wall Street] for taking over our $10 billion worth of assets—including our 20 percent of Turner Broadcasting—that don't contribute to short-term earnings. They're going up in value rapidly, but they don't show up on-statement. So they had a real problem paying the price.

But they had to know this when they struck the deal with you in October of '93.
[Shrugs.] They were schizophrenic about it. Half the organization couldn't see past quarterly earnings growth, okay? They couldn't see the value of owning 20 percent of Turner Broadcasting. The other half could. There was a struggle within their company from day one.

And Ray Smith, where was he in all this?
Ray was willing to take that leap of faith all the way. Ray . . . shit,

I got a lot of respect for him. He was absolutely a visionary. It's just his organization wasn't willing to go along. So in the end it was a fundamental problem between two philosophies.

My strategy—and Ray was totally in support of it—is we're gonna own a lot of 20 percents of things, and we're going to put a fair amount of money into it. Those things are going to be leveraged and grow like hell, and we're going to create a lot of shareholder wealth doing that. As for Wall Street, we're just going to have to keep training them to understand the value of [that approach]. I mean, I've been doing it my whole career.

Some analysts believe the phone companies are in the best position to dominate the interactive TV market.

[Malone laughs and shakes his head.]

I take it you don't agree.

It's all posturing . . . more smoke than fire. And I'll tell you why. First, I don't think their culture makes them very competitive, and that's their big vulnerability. Sure, any one RBOC has got as much revenue as the whole cable industry put together. And sure, they're very powerful politically. But they've lived as protected monopolies in a regulated environment all these years and never had to face competition of any kind. Every time the RBOCs have tried to diversify out of their core business, it's been a disaster.

But specifically . . .

Okay, look. All the tests show that the one interactive service the public has a lot of interest in right now is movies on demand. Replacing the video store business with electronics is something that would generate maybe, from our tests, four or five bucks a month of cash flow per cable subscriber.

Now, how much capital can you deploy for that little? If you're already basically there—if you've already got a network in place capable of delivering video, and it's just incremental—you can do it. But if you've only got copper in the home, and you have to build out [a video network] from dollar one, then it's going to be real tough.

So how do these guys get the money to do it? They've either got to cross-subsidize it very heavily out of their existing telephone customers and raise rates—which is going to give their regulators problems—or they've got to raise their debt. But if they do that their debt rating goes down and that's, like, completely verboten for these people. The only other way is to take it out of the shareholders—in other words, cut the dividend—but these guys would rather die than cut the dividend.

[He shrugs.] So when you take a look at all the constraints that an RBOC's balance sheet is really under, you see they've actually got only a limited amount of discretionary capital to work with. They're just not going to be able to do much in the interactive TV business.

Pacific Bell says they're going to spend $16 billion to build the highway in California.

Yeah, we can do California for a small fraction of that and provide the same services, so who's gonna have the low-cost service?

But if what you say is true about their financial constraints, how are they going to come up with $15 billion?

The answer is they won't.

Just to be safe, I think I'll keep an eye on my phone bill. I can't afford that kind of money.

Don't worry. I mean, there's nothing they'd like better than for all this Information Highway stuff go away. All they want is to retain their local phone monopoly, and be able to [go after] the long-distance marketplace.

You're saying the phone companies have no interest in interactive TV?

Let me ask you this: Who started the information superhighway? Who really talked about new technology allowing [interactive two-way information and entertainment services]? We did. It wasn't the telephone companies. I went out on a road show [in 1993], meeting all the RBOC CEOs, and they were all sitting there saying, "Isn't there some way we can avoid conflict?"

What were they afraid of?

Pressure on local telephony rates.

Meaning, if you can one day ship an entire movie down your wire for few bucks, why couldn't you ship a phone call for a few cents?

Right. Once we have the right terminal devices, we certainly would be in a position to provide telephony at substantially lower prices than you're currently being charged. I mean, all of our models say that. So, sure, we can knock the shit out of the cost structure of the whole telephone business.

So they were afraid of you getting into telephony.
Why do you think they started buying up cable companies?

Well, they said it was to get into interactive TV. To build the Info Highway.
No. It was so that they can go on the offense rather than on the defense in telephony. Look, if you could really get the RBOCs to tell the truth, they'd tell you that just the plain old telephony business is huge—I mean, look at their revenues—and that's what they're primarily going after. And the interactive video business is a lucky strike extra, okay. US West's attitude, when we started seeing the penetrations we were [jointly] getting in the U.K. against British TelCom with our [cable] telephone service, I mean they just said, "Jeez, if you project these numbers to the U.S., wow! This is a terrific business."

So, after your Bell Atlantic merger announcement in October of '93, when everyone said the RBOCs and cable companies would jointly build the Information Highway . . .
That was wrong.

But why would the RBOCs buy you out just to prevent you from maybe competing one day? I mean, even you said that you guys are mere pip-squeaks compared to . . .
Right.

[A long pause.] You're suggesting that the RBOCs' real goal here was raiding other RBOCs!
Ri-i-ight.

So the Information Highway was mostly talk?
Absolutely. I mean, there was an element of legitimacy in their talk about multimedia. But their dominant thinking was, We're

gonna take a hit in our local market from [cable-telephony and cellu-
lar] competition, so let's go over and make that up in the other guy's
market. And it's driven by regulatory concerns. In other words,
they're freer in the other guy's market than in their own. For them,
the idea of using cable to get out of their territory and into the other
guy's territory was like opening a second front.

Machiavelli would be proud.

Oh, they fall apart on a few things, but basically they're a club.
By and large, they coordinate. They talk to each other all the time.
What they do is they have a big meeting out on the golf course
somewhere, and they decide who's gonna do what and to whom.

You're serious.

Yes, absolutely. There's no question in my mind. These guys are
very friendly with each other. I'm not saying anything sinister. I'm
not alleging that these guys are engaged in any practice that's even
close to being illegal. I'm just saying that there's an alignment of
interests.

Did Ray Smith stop getting invited to play golf?

I believe he did. I believe that when he did the deal with us, he
became persona non grata. But I think Ray is probably back in the
club again, doing a mea culpa.

Now, it's interesting, there's an increasing divergence in their
ranks. They've poached a little bit on each other in cellular. And a
little bit in yellow pages, but that created a lot of animosity, and it
didn't work anyway. Clearly US West is out of the club since their
deal with Time Warner. Clearly Southwestern Bell [has broken
ranks] with their move into cable in Bell Atlantic's Washington, D.C.
market area.

So when Bell Atlantic was gonna do a TCI deal, that strategic
alignment got disrupted. And now that it's dead they're realigned
again. And [when] Southwestern Bell's deal with Cox [collapsed],
they realigned, too. So even though the club may not be as cozy this
year as it was a couple of years ago—the strains of strategic vari-
ance, you might say—I suspect that with TCI–Bell Atlantic dead
they're a lot closer in philosophy and strategy than they were at least
a few months ago.

Where else do the RBOCs have a community of interests?

I imagine in mid-1993 after the AT&T buyout of McCaw cellular was announced, they got together and said, "Okay, who can afford to take on AT&T right now? Let's see if we can stir up a little trouble, slow that down a little." And they draw straws, and BellSouth says, "Okay, I'll do it. I'll go sue 'em on this McCaw takeover." There's no question the RBOCs hate the idea of AT&T buying McCaw. They hate it.

Wasn't it shortly after the AT&T-McCaw deal was announced that telecom reform legislation really got moving in Congress? Looking back, do you feel that this effort has been weighted in favor of the RBOCs, as opposed to long distance?

Oh, it's very pro-RBOC. It's weighted very heavily. Any one of the RBOCs has 100, 150 full-time lobbyists in Washington. We have one. These are big giant companies, and they've had 120 years to hone their political skills. They have enormous political clout, and when they focus it on the cable industry, they can get the government to tank us. When they used it to go after AT&T and the long-distance market, they [got] the court to delay the McCaw deal. On the other hand, AT&T's no slouch either, and I think the merits here are very much in favor of the AT&T-McCaw deal.

It's interesting. These guys are far and away the most powerful monopoly in the country. And they've been able to hide their monopoly while attacking ours—which is quite an interesting act of political strength, wouldn't you say? To get away with calling *us* a monopoly?!

Be that as it may, the reality is that many people see TCI as some sort of Attila the Hun company.

The reality is we're really very naive politically. We have never spent any money on it. We've never had any focus on it. We've got one guy in Washington and one guy here, worrying about government and public relations for the whole company—all states, all divisions, everything. That's probably quite inadequate, looking at the realities.

And, yeah, we may be crazy, but we're not stupid. We recognize that we've got to do a better job of telling our story to the public and to the politicians. But for me personally that's not the way I want to spend my life. I don't want to spend my life in front of regulators and at cocktail parties with politicians and so on. So I've got to structure the company so that major executives, people in a decision-making role, can represent the company. And I'll be a resource allocator and a fund-raiser and a strategist and things of that nature, and try to spend more of my time on the things I really like to do—like venture capital.

I'd love to have a venture capital organization for the quote, un-quote "information superhighway," where inventors and entrepreneurs with good ideas can come to us and we can invest in them and help them. I've already got a couple dozen things going. What I want to do is formalize the process, 'cause that's what I enjoy.

But yeah, sure, political sophistication, changing the posture of the company, that's important. You have to remember, though, that we [grew up] as pretty much this frontier, cowboy company. We were growing very rapidly, and at the top, we were spending a lot more time on capital formation than we were even on operations, let alone public relations. Our guys did the best they could, but we were growing very rapidly, and it was not a focus of the company.

You've also had the FCC on your back. What effect has the rollback of cable rates had?

I think the cable industry was only temporarily injured by the FCC. I mean, was it bothersome? Well, of course! It's more than bothersome. But for the last three or four years we've been shifting a lot of our assets into the international arena. I mean if you really look at TCI today, two-thirds of our market value is based on nondomestic cable businesses.

We'll also continue [moving] into programming, which the government has a very hard time regulating because of First Ammendment issues. These noxious FCC rules are not going to be able to constrain for very long the economics in entertainment because what's gonna happen is there'll be a shift from basic to à la carte services. If our programming is strong—and [we deploy] digital compression and an explosion of channel capacity—then we'll see a quick recovery of the economic growth rate of the cable industry in entertainment and in interactive video and so on.

So we'll continue to diversify away from the regulated government-attacked core. And meanwhile, we'll continue to slug it out in the trenches in the domestic cable business, recognizing that the government's got to kill a lot of smaller cable operators before they can really hurt us much.

Hopefully, when the blood and the body count start to pile up, we think government will finally realize that they've gone too far. And despite what Mr. Hundt [the FCC Commissioner] says, he's wrong. I think they have gone too far.

Do you feel like the sacrificial lamb here? Like the government just went after the easiest target around? Meaning you, the so-called Darth Vader and all-around bad boy of the cable industry.

I think there were forces in Congress that really wanted to see blood from the cable industry and when, after the first rate rollback, the blood wasn't very visible—and it certainly wasn't uniform—they just decided to come back for a second bite. [Representative] Ed Markey felt like the cable industry had gotten away too easy with the first round of FCC rules. So he put a lot of pressure on Hundt and got him to take another whack.

But I've been around long enough to know that this pendulum will swing back the other way again. It's just reality. I'm not a conspiracy theorist. I don't believe that there's this great big conspiracy between the RBOCs and the politicians and regulators to kill the cable industry. I just don't see that. What I do see is some pretty naive regulators wanting to hand Ed Markey his victory.

In fact—and maybe this is being naive—I wouldn't be at all surprised to see Markey soon become the cable industry's best friend. Those RBOCs are going to be even more powerful now, and people are pretty soon gonna want someone to stand up to them.

I mean, [Senator Howard] Metzenbaum, after we announced the Bell Atlantic deal, he says, "Jesus, John, I always thought you were gonna be the guy who'd take on the RBOCs." [Representative] Jack Brooks, same story: "What the fuck are you doing merging with the RBOCs?" he said to me. And I says, "Jack, they're just so big and they're so powerful, and I'm getting old, and I just can't fight 'em anymore."

Gee, maybe you should lie down or something. [Laughter.] But before you do, let's sketch out a map of the competitive battlefield here.

The first thing you're gonna see is the RBOCs, or at least a lot of the RBOCs, getting together and combining their cellular activities, so that they have a strategy to take on AT&T-McCaw in cellular. That's the first manifestation of circling the wagon.

Which presents the long-distance providers with a rather difficult strategic problem, wouldn't you say?

The only immediate thing they can do is move into local telephony through cellular. So yeah, the long-distance guys have a serious long-term strategic issue here. For several years, I think, they figured that they could maintain some kind of uneasy peace with the RBOCs and maybe just haggle over the access fees and poach a little bit in terms of cellular.

But now the game has changed. I think their perception now is that it's going to be a full-scale war.

Between long distance and the RBOCs?

That's correct. And so now the long-distance guys are very anxious to find allies against the RBOCs. And we in the cable industry represent a kind of strategic leverage, a strategic advantage in this war. So everything, all the alignments, are going to shift.

What you're talking about is an alliance with AT&T.

AT&T or an MCI or a Sprint, yeah. And now that the long-distance guys know that the RBOCs are coming at 'em, I think they'll find it very much in their interests to try and stimulate competition in local telephony. And the cable people are the only people on a cost basis who can provide local telephony besides the RBOCs.

What are your chances of pulling off an arrangement with one of the long-distance companies?

[Smiles.] Excellent.

Are we talking relatively near- or long-term?

Relatively near. Yeah, I mean, as long as we were screwing around with Bell Atlantic it was hard to pursue those discussions. But I've been very busy. I've been to New York and Washington [many] times in [recent months]. And there's a lot of interest from the long-distance guys, so we'll see what evolves. But I do think something very interesting and very powerful is going to evolve.

And the chief advantage for you of an alliance with a long-distance network, say AT&T?

Well, skill in telephony, financial strength, but especially branded services. For us it's the branding that's really important. If it's AT&T cellular or MCI long distance or Sprint video telephony, as long as it's a well-known, branded name that we promote on our network, people will feel like there's real value in the bundle because they recognize the value of each one of the branded components. If I can do a deal with an MCI or an AT&T or a Sprint, then I have stronger brands to play with in telephony than the RBOCs do, and I got all the brands in entertainment, okay.

So that's my strategy. If I can go in with a bundled package with MCI or AT&T or Sprint, and then match that up with, say, an HBO in movies and then a PG&E and Microsoft for home energy management—you know, I can save the homeowner probably enough money on his electric bill to pay for his cable service—if I can do that, then I've got a very powerful package.

That's the race, for bundled services to the home—branded bundled services. And if I can buy it wholesale and sell it retail—bundle it, package it, discount it—then I think I've got an enormous edge.

Okay, now we come to the biggest question of all. You've got your RBOCs over in one corner of the ring, your long distance over in the other, and the cable operators running around the center of the ring attracting lightning from all sides. What I want to know is, Who's building the damn information superhighway?

Us. We're the guys building it. We've got 35 percent of the country done right now.

For a broadband network that can carry . . .

By the end of '94, we'll be 55 percent done. And by the end of '96, we'll be completely done in terms of fiber and coaxed deployment—the terrestrial network that is the superhighway.

With compression capable of carrying . . .

Five hundred channels, interactivity. We'll be done except for the terminals, the set-top box, and whatever we put at the central location to do the server activities, which we're testing with Gates.

And what about switching technology?

Well, for telephony, we're doing it now. If you're talking about switching multimedia traffic, high data-rate traffic, that's ATM switchers. It's a pretty well developed technology. We pretty much know how to do that. We're building Sonnet rings right now with ATM switchers, so that part we know how to do.

So switching for true interactive, two-way multimedia communication is not a big technological hurdle?

No! The only big uncertainties in my opinion are the actual functioning and capacity of the servers, and the capital costs of the in-the-home device—the set-top box. Yeah, the big capital issue is the terminal in the home, 'cause it's the one you gotta make millions off of, right? But we've got a gazillion vendors that are proposing those.

As for the server—the device you're gonna have one per city or one per metropolitan area—it has not been fully invented yet. We're talking about a system that is more complex than anything that's ever been designed, probably by close to an order of magnitude.

Than *anything* that's ever been designed?

Yeah. The combination of the operating system and how it interfaces with all the applications, the services running through it—yeah you're talking about more instructions than any integrated system that's ever been designed for anything.

I mean, shit. The whole system for the space program is small compared to this. The hardware's easy. It's the software that's tough, and it's important that it be open—that the protocols be open, the architecture be open and interactive—so that the whole industry will be able to develop applications right from the get-go.

So that's what we're testing with Gates. The servers. We've got four vendors basically—Gates, Silicon Graphics, Oracle, and IBM—that are all proposing server systems.

Gates, huh?

We're going initially with Bill, in terms of testing, but we're not committing to him on deployment. But so far Bill's proposal is far and away the best from a financial perspective that we've seen.

And the concern from people like [former Silicon Graphics chairman] Jim Clark?

That he's locked out?

That doing a server deal with Gates means he'll squeeze his control in at the head end of the network. Lock you in or lock everyone else out. That sort of thing.

[Laughs.] I see. The big concern is, Is Bill Gates a bigger monopolist than I am? And if I get together with him, is that going to be the worst thing that ever happened in history? Yeah, that is the concern that has been expressed to me by a lot of people in the software industry. Everybody in the business is warning us about how not to get suckered.

To me, it really comes down to, if you decide to use Bill's stuff, what kind of a deal do you get? If Bill wants to deploy he's going to have to be aware of the concerns about his reputation, and he is.

And our deal with Bill, which we haven't disclosed publicly, is essentially if we pick him we have a preset maximum price. It's nonexclusive, and he's free to market it to anybody else he wants. And we have a "most-favored nations" deal, which just basically says if he sells it to anybody else for less, then we get the lower price, too. Basically we spec it, he builds it, and then we use it if it's the best deal. If he doesn't give us the best deal, we don't have to use it and we get price protection and most favored rates, so it's very open. It's purely a vendor-customer relationship.

According to Clark, in 1993 you almost struck a deal with SGI, until Gates got wind of it and, in Clark's words, "raised his skirt" to you. What was the problem with SGI?

A house divided.

Clark said yes, but [CEO Edward] McCracken said no?

[Shrugs.] We're still very interested in Silicon Graphics being involved. It's a wide-open field right now, and anybody with skills in this area is certainly invited to come in and demonstrate their wares. But what we want is the most cost-effective server structure, from a software and a hardware point of view, aimed at full deployment by '96.

So it's not the eighties anymore, and you're not IBM?

No, I think if Bill wins, he's gonna win because he's gonna have the best product.

Tell me about the set-top boxes.

Our deployment scheme is, if you're a customer and you want it, you're gonna finance out of incremental charges the capital required to put it in your home.

Do you have a ballpark estimate of that yet?

We're hoping that the whole megillah, the cost to do everything, you're looking at maybe 500 bucks a home, and that's incremental. Now an addressable analog [set-top box] is right now 150 bucks. A digital box that does everything should be about 500 bucks.

Which will be amortized, right?

Yeah, we'd finance it. If we think it's got a life of five years, then it's a hundred bucks a year. We're talking about, what, seven bucks a month? And you're already paying us three or four bucks a month for the old box, so for this new device it's another three bucks a month. But now you can have an expansion of channels and movies-on-demand. You can have video telephony and multimedia services. You can have load control. You can play Sega games. You can have digital music. You can have high-definition TV. You can have wireless telephony in your home.

So we're really not talking about backbreaking economics here. And when you pay that extra amount you're gonna get certain services free as part of that. You'll probably get a navigator for free. And I think we can easily finance it against the growth in the revenues. The servers—if Bill is right in his projections of capital costs—are not gonna be that burdensome. So I don't see any big impediments for us rolling this thing out and having a true, full-service network out there by the end of '96, available to most homes.

Once it's built, where will the big entrepeneurial opportunities be in the network?

In programming, a special kind of programming. It's got to really add value to all the content that'll be out there. It'll need strong branding. If you're talking about news, I as the subscriber have to ask, Whose editorial service do I want? I can't possibly stay informed of everything that I'm interested in, so why don't I subscribe to the Kline and Burstein Editorial Service. You'll ask me one time what I'm interested in, and from that point on I'll have a customized news service that hits the things I'm interested in.

To me, we're gonna go very much into a customized world. It's not one-size-fits-all. These technologies are gonna allow us to make television very personal. That's the really exciting area.

Individuality will be emphasized. That's what I mean by an electronic community. Your own perspectives, your own individuality, will be amplified by your ability to reach sources that are of interest to you.

And the whole interactive home shopping business is also going to be tremendous, explosive. That's why General Magic's "agent" thing is exactly right. You send your smart agent out to look for a stereo, and it'll research *Consumer Reports*, give you feedback, find the best deal it can.

Okay, one last question: if you say you'll have the network deployed by the end of '96, doesn't that suggest that you never really needed the Bell Atlantic merger?

Only politically. We have enough internally generated capital to build it ourselves. All the deal did was commit us to a very accelerated capital deployment. I mean, year one in our draft contract they were kicking in an extra billion dollars to our capital program, so we were gonna take our capital program for '94 from $1.1 to $2.1 billion. Which really meant we were going to be able to move full deployment from '96 up to '95. We were looking at getting most of the terrestrial job done by the end of '95, which we were all quite excited about. So were the vendors.

But that's not possible now. We're back on our original '96 deployment schedule. And I believe we're gonna get there.

God and the FCC willing?

Yeah, well if it helps, I'll make a commitment to [the vice president], okay? Listen Al, I know you haven't asked for it, but we'll make a commitment to complete the job by the end of '96. All we need is a little help . . . you know, *shoot Hundt!* Don't let him do any more damage, know what I'm saying?

For the record, maybe you should say you're kidding.
Not about getting the highway up by the end of '96.

THE TITAN OF TELEPHONY

John Malone's uncensored view of the collapse of his $33 billion merger with Bell Atlantic Corporation—not to mention his audacious jest about shooting the chair of the Federal Communications Commission—ignited a good deal of controversy in 1994. A few months later, David Kline sought out the view from the opposing corner of the gladiator arena. Clearly the most enterprising and farsighted of the telco leaders, Bell Atlantic CEO Ray Smith was the first to start construction on a broadband network, the first to win federal approval to offer commercial video dial-tone service, the first to win court permission to develop the company's own video content, and the first to begin shifting his once stodgy utility to an entrepreneurial footing.

Smith enjoys poking fun at his old monopolist image as much as anyone. When Kline arrived for the interview, Smith had the following displayed on a white board in his office: (1) Buy AT&T, (2) Sell Pennsylvania, (3) Retire, (4) Work for IBM (depose Gerstner), (5) Cancel subscriptions to all magazines and newspapers.

DAVID KLINE: **So, what's the plan? Are you going to buy AT&T or sell Pennsylvania?**
RAY SMITH: No, don't use that. I put that up just to amuse you. All we need is to have a rumor going around that we're going to sell Pennsylvania . . .

I can imagine. I mean, even John Malone said that compared to you . . . by the way, I presume you read my *Wired* interview with him?
Of course.

Well, he said compared to you he's just a pipsqueak. He said you telco guys are the real monopolists.
Yeah, in my career I've come to know a number of humble, one-shoe-over-the-other billionaires.

So you're not a monopolist, and you have no near-term plans to sell Pennsylvania?

Absolutely not.

I see.

We're gonna sell West Virginia.

[Laughter.] Well, now that we've got that settled, can we talk about the aborted merger with TCI? Because people still want to know what *really* happened the day that the biggest deal in American history crashed and burned.

You know what amazes me? There were only four people in the room that day, but there are at least 20 different versions of what happened. It's like *Rashomon*.

Well, Malone said the merger was aborted because you couldn't get your board of directors to go along—that they were skittish about changing from a regulated utility into a high-growth company.

No, that's absolutely not true. The whole board was in favor of it. There wasn't a single voice against it.

But let me tell you what *is* true. What really was going on was a struggle in the shareholder base. We have a million shareholders, and they are basically high-yield oriented. We froze the dividend, and it frightened the life out of our shareholders. And our stock, which leaped up for a while on the promise of the merger, well it dropped as the yield-oriented shareholders sort of pealed away.

And so the struggle was really in the investment community. It was not a debate on our board about whether to change into a high-growth company versus a low-growth company. My cash-flow growth is faster than John's!

Now, I'm not trying to say we didn't have cultural differences, in terms of TCI being more entrepreneurial and all. But the issue was, how do we get the cash out of our company to complete the deal without scaring off our shareholders? Because if you cut the dividend too much, then the shareholders leave and the stock drops so low that you can no longer do the deal.

But you knew you faced that problem going in.

I knew it going in. I knew it'd be a struggle that we'd have to handle with some sensitivity. Unfortunately, it sort of became public. At one point John was quoted saying we'd have to cut the dividend in the future, and the stock dropped five points.

Why'd he say that?

[Shrugs.] He thought that was what we had to do. John was just being honest. But to say it like that is like lighting a match in a gas-filled room.

Not that you aren't going to tell shareholders the truth. You are. It's just that we were trying to find [less onerous] ways of making the deal work financially. Why announce something like that before you know for sure?

You see, John's approach to this issue was like his regulatory approach. He didn't say, "Shoot the shareholders"—don't quote me on that—but he was saying let's just go cut the dividend. John, being the road warrior you pictured him being [in *Wired*], just wanted to get it over with. But that's not how you deal with regulation, and that is not how you deal with a large shareholder base.

I'm more of a builder. An architect. I like to do things one brick at a time. My view is align and conquer.

So what finally killed the deal?

John's cash flow went down. Remember, when we set the deal, John's cash flow was at $200 a subscriber and we agreed to pay him about 11.75 times cash flow. But there was a cash-flow test. If his cash flow went down, as it did [after the FCC cable-rate rollbacks of February 1994], then I would give him fewer shares of my stock, which had a fixed price of $64 in the deal.

Now, by February, because of the declining cash flow, the value of TCI stock was by then dropping close to $20 or $21, okay? Well, I was willing to pay something like $25 per share. But John still had it in his head that it was a $35 stock. That's just too big a difference.

In the final meeting, we kept trying to figure out some way to make it work. John said, "If I take this [reduced] number of shares, I'll never get my major shareholders to accept it. And there's no way you can give me the number of shares I need. You'd be paying 14 times cash flow." And I said, "You're right."

Finally, he said, "Well, we can't just sit around here forever."

And I said, "Yeah, let's look at the press release and get this over with."

What's your strongest memory of that last meeting?

[A long pause.] I guess it's the last words he said as we separated. He said, "Nice try, my friend."

You guys really like each other.

We do. We're both old techies, you know, and we get along very well. John and I were just on a panel together, and we were standing at the urinals talking about things. Barry Diller comes in and stands between us. And Barry says, "C'mon, you seem like such good friends. Just split the difference."

[Laughter.] Okay, but seriously, what does the failure of the merger tell us about the strategic planning capabilities of big companies like yours? One day you're spinning together these huge deals, and the next day you're taking them apart and going about your business?

Actually, I think it's positive. It shows that although we had a good strategic idea in trying to merge with TCI, when the conditions changed, as they did, then we were willing to pull back. You don't just stick to a deal out of sheer, cussed egotism when it's no longer good for the shareholders. Cutting mergers is a hard thing to do.

And you know what? If I could get the same deal today that I agreed to a year ago, I'd sign it right now. Right this minute.

What if Malone reads this and calls you up and says, "Okay, Ray, you're on!"

I'd take it. Exactly as I signed it a year ago.

Gee, my finder's fee on a deal like this could be worth $50 million! Well, in any event, many now say the collapse of the merger shows that the Info Highway is way overhyped. What do you think?

There was a lot of hype before the merger. The media was full of it. But for all the hype, there was also a lot of naysaying.

Still, I do think the merger announcement moved things forward. The moment that hit, there was no way that anyone could say that it all was just hype, or that the whole notion of [the Information Highway] was silly. The naysayers were just swept away.

You mean, the naysayers in your company?

Not so much in our company. Remember, we were the first [of the regional Bell companies] to see it coming. We very consciously set out to prepare for in 1990 when we filed the court case to change the Cable Act of 1984 [which barred telephone companies from providing video services].

And you know, when we launched that court case, we offered it to all of the other telephone companies, including GTE. None of them saw any need to get into the video industry.

And the merger changed that?

It really began to change when we won the case [in 1993]. Before that, there was not one single procurement by the other Bell companies concerning video. There was not any support of ADSL, which is video over copper. There were no hybrid fiber-coax discussions whatsoever among the other phone companies.

Now, I happen to know there were battles within at least four of the [seven] Bell companies over whether or not video was practical. You know, a lot of discussion along the lines of, "We'll never be able to make it pay; we can't do it," that type of thing. They were in the "yes—but" phase.

Once the court case was won, that was the end of "yes—but." They all called and said, "We want to get into this."

But even then, there still wasn't sufficient critical mass in most of the telephone industry to actually take practical steps forward on video.

But the day after the TCI merger announcement, there was. Suddenly, video became a necessity. The top decks of all the Bell companies knew that, at the very least, they'd have to get into the video business because cable was going to get into the telephone business.

It was like the merger announcement came down and—wham!— everything became very, very clear. There was no argument any more. It wasn't whether we should do it, but *how* we should do it.

In fact, the announcement changed the picture so much that the merger itself became less necessary for us. Because, don't forget, one of the motivations for the merger was to get enough scale to bring equipment costs down. But when all these other companies suddenly jumped in after the TCI deal with their own infrastructure investments, obviously costs were going to come down anyway.

So while many debunkers, especially in the media, point to the collapse of the merger as proof that all this is hype, in fact the evidence shows it concretely moved things forward. It was like a demonstration atomic bomb. Of course, then it became not only conventional wisdom but conventional wisdom times two. We were in hyperspace, and we were all going to have talking television sets by the end of 1994.

And Time Warner's Full Service Network in Orlando was going to be up and running *early* '94, remember?

Yeah, they were saying they had solved all the technical problems. Well, sure, they solved the technical problems. But the set-top was $11,000! Okay, so now it's $3,000. Big deal. I mean, the issue is, can you do it at a price that people can afford, so it can actually be deployed in the real world?

Anyway, the merger announcement served its purpose. It was a kick-start that moved things forward.

What do you think about the conventional wisdom that says the telcos will probably lose 30 percent of their market share to cable-provided telephony services, while cable could lose 30 percent of its video business to the telcos? I mean, cable executives say that's fine with them, because their 30 percent is going to look a lot sweeter than your 30 percent?

Oh, for Christ's sake! C'mon, this notion that cable companies are going to get 30 percent of the $100 billion telephone business, whereas we'll only get 30 percent of cable's $20 billion business-that's ridiculous.

I mean, c'mon guys. Bell Atlantic is not one business but 13 different businesses, most of them not subject to any real competition from the cable industry.

We get a billion dollars of our revenues from the federal government. You're saying cable's going to take the federal government—the 25-year-contract with the Pentagon that we have—that they're going to take that away? It doesn't make any sense. Cable companies aren't going to touch that.

Or look at yellow pages. If the cable companies offer local telephone services, is that going to affect our yellow pages business? And are they going to compete for our lifeline services?

Oh, I'm sure they're dying to get their hands on that!

Right, we're quivering in our boots waiting to see a cable company come into New Jersey and offer a local phone service for $6.50. So the more you look at it, the more the percentage of our revenues that are really subject to cable competition keeps shrinking. Of our $13 billion in total revenues, only $4 billion of that—the consumer business—is really subject to competition from cable companies.

Now, the cable companies in our territory also have about $4 billion in revenues. But while we cover 100 percent of their customers, they only cover 60 to 70 percent of our customers [the percentage of telephone-using homes that subscribe to cable TV service.] So actually there is only about $3 billion they can try to get their hands on.

But how successful are they likely to be? Consider the fact that Philadelphia, for example, is served by maybe 10 or 11 cable companies. Even inside the city proper there are 4 different cable companies. Four different ones!

Now you're telling me a consumer is going to subscribe with a cable-phone service that serves only one section of the city? That's going to be a pretty hard sale.

And what about power? Remember, when the power's out so's your cable phone!

So, this 30 percent versus 30 percent . . .

It's wrong. It won't be dollar-for-dollar. It'll be ten-to-one in our favor. I would say that by the year 2000, we'll have 50 percent of the cable TV business—no doubt about it, which is why some cable companies are in a panic.

Meanwhile, the cable companies will not have even three percent of telephony revenues in their best market. Not in their very, very best market. It's just not going to happen.

But isn't your real concern here not so much that cable companies will take a big chunk of your total revenues, but that they'll cherry-pick your most profitable businesses, like your $3 billion-plus local access services?

We've already got competition there. No, cable is not where our real competition will come from. The competition's going to come from AT&T and from wireless, not from cable companies reequipping their ancient and crappy systems.

Yeah, but now TCI and two other cable firms have hooked up with Sprint to bid on wireless PCS spectrum.

Bidding is one thing. Building a truly robust and competitive service is another.

Well, *your* wireless business has certainly gotten more robust lately. By combining with NYNEX, AirTouch, and US West, you've now got the biggest wireless footprint in the country. But what about the failure of your talks with MCI? Doesn't that leave you without the sort of national brand-name you'll need to compete with AT&T or even Sprint-TCI?

For us, the mot important thing, far and away, was the footprint, not the brand name. We estimate we need a footprint that covers somewhere around 150 million potential customers to give us the scale to compete with AT&T.

As for the brand, we can create it. It'll cost money, and it won't be as quick as if we had MCI with us. But we can create a national brand that's up in the 60 percent range within a year in terms of recognition, maybe up to 85 percent in two years.

So have you given up, then, on MCI?

[A pause.] MCI needs a wireless strategy. They have got to be connected with a company that has a wireless presence. As for what may or may not happen, that certainly isn't going to be talked about today.

Okay, you've laid out some of your competitive advantages over the cable industry. But you've also got some disadvantages, don't you? For instance, whereas cable firms have already laid their coax—which is 80 percent of the cost of building the network—don't you still have this massive construction job in front of you?

We've been equipping our network for years now.

But I'm talking about laying coax, especially that "last mile" to the home. Look what happened to Pactel in Milpitas, California. When city officials there saw that PacTel planned to dig up 60 miles of city streets and disrupt businesses for months—just to lay coax to one thousand homes, mind you—they refused to grant construction permits. And that's just one

city. So how easy is it going to be for the phone companies to go into thousands of towns and cities nationwide and get similar permits?

Well, I think [Milpitas] was an anomaly. We know how to build so you hardly even know we're there. As you know, we have a construction permit for Dover [Township, New Jersey, the site of Bell Atlantic's first interactive trial]. If you polled the people in Dover and asked, "What cataclysmic thing is going on here?" they wouldn't know what it was.

Maybe what happened [in Milpitas] was an overreaction by the city council or something of that sort. In any case, we know how to build in a way that would satisfy any community. It can be done with care, delicacy, and with a little bit of explanation. In Morris County [New Jersey], in fact, people are virtually cheering . . . it's like the Persian Gulf War or something and everyone's waving Bell Atlantic flags saying, "Please come! Please come!"

And cheering, no less?

Sure, because they see us as finally bringing decent cable TV service. We've had people calling us, asking how soon they can sign up for our cable service.

I mean, look. I'm in Montgomery County [Maryland]. Just this week, my cable TV service has been out for three days. Fortunately it wasn't out on Monday when the Steelers were on *Monday Night Football*, but it went out Tuesday, and today's Friday! We get terrible cable service, really lousy service. And everybody says so.

Yeah, but what's going to happen to your service as you make Bell Atlantic leaner and meaner and more competitive?

What do you mean?

Look what's happening with US West. It's been reengineering, laying off workers, and cutting costs in order to become more competitive with the cable companies. And guess what? Colorado regulators have now charged them with major violations of state service guidelines because their customer service has gone down the tubes.

Well, they may have gone over some line, but there's no . . . look, just because US West has a couple of problems, that doesn't compare to virtually every cable company in the country being considered the worst service provider in the community. I mean, I don't remember my telephone ever going out of service.

We've got good service and I don't see that changing. We've got such a competitive advantage over cable because of our service reputation that we'll get 15 percent of video market share just by putting out our shingle. I mean, we don't have to do absolutely anything for that because of the cable companies' terrible service.

Well, the fact that the Bells have collectively cut more than 80,000 jobs in the past year does point up an interesting contradiction: people say the Info Highway will create jobs, yet in order to compete in building it, the telcos have become the biggest job destroyers in America.

Like you said, it has to do with competition, which is coming into our business. We've already [streamlined], but we still have a way to go—and so do the other RBOCs—to meet the ultimate competition. So that's what you're talking about. That's the downward pressure on the workforce.

But we think that after these downsizings are done—and when the market beings to develop fully in 1996—you're going to see a lot of hiring going on. The building of the superhighway will act as an upward pressure on the workforce. There'll be a great expansion in order to build all these new interactive services.

So we see a short-term need to get our costs down. Long term, we're going to be a much bigger company in 10 years.

Well, you certainly sound like you're ready and willing to take on all competitors. So why do you think Senator Hollings, Congressman Markey, and Consumer Federation of America, and even Vice President Gore all put the blame for killing the 1994 telecom bill—which would have opened communications markets to greater competition—squarely on the regional phone companies?

I don't think that's fair at all. I think the Senate just ran out of time.

But wasn't that because some of the telcos just wouldn't compromise on certain of the bill's provisions regarding the opening of their markets to competition? Whereas your company and other Bells were much more willing to work out a compromise?

Yeah, I think that's pretty accurate. We certainly were more willing to move forward with that bill and negotiate some of our differences in conference. Some of the other companies felt that it was too dangerous to do so.

Ultimately, does it matter whether there's wholesale telecom reform package passed into law? You seem to be moving anyway to build out your network, develop programming, etc.

I think it does matter. We've got to get these barriers down. We've got to get into full competition in our business and in long distance. You know, we obviously are already in the cable business.

So that side of it isn't important to us. But we've got to open everything up in order to expand the market. This balkanization we've got now is causing dislocations in pricing and so on that are unnecessary. The market won't expand the way we want it to unless we have full and open competition in all areas.

Okay, let's talk about what precisely this network is going to look like. You mentioned earlier that you saw yourself as a builder, an architect, rather than a John Malone–style road warrior. So what's your blueprint for the network?

It's going to be built differently in every town. That's the part that hasn't been captured yet, the unspoken story. The way it's been reported to date is that we are all going to put out hybrid fiber-coax and connect it to a so-and-so with a micronet. Like there's a grand plan.

Of course that's ridiculous. It's that old manufacturing model, like you create one automobile design and then make a hundred million cars that all look the same. But that's never how things of this sort get deployed.

Here's how it's going to be built. There are five different technologies that we'll use to provide video services in competition with cable companies. The first will be the fiber-to-the-curb, which is the approach taken by companies like Broadband Technologies. This is what we're going to do in Dover [Township, New Jersey].

What's today's ballpark cost per home?

Probably about $900, including the drops into the home but not including the cost of the servers and set-tops. And once you start to see that kind of technology being ordered in larger volumes, we'll get down well below that number.

For fiber all the way?

Fiber all the way to curbside, with two lines going out to between 20 and 30 homes. One line will be coax and carry video, the other is twisted pair for voice. Clearly, that's the preferred architecture. It's switched, digital, fully interactive, and you get a tremendous reduction in maintenance expense and an improvement in service. So that's one way.

Number two is hybrid fiber-coax, where we run fiber to a neighborhood hub and then coax from there to a few hundred homes. In some locations this will be the preferred solution, especially where the interactivity is not expected to be as robust or where the demographics of certain areas demand lower costs.

Today's price for that?

Maybe a couple of hundred less than for fiber to the curb, but we're not even so sure about that anymore. These estimates are based on certain assumptions about early rollout volumes, rather than full-blown nationwide deployment.

The third approach is ADSL. When you see what we're doing with it, you'll see that it's not an interim technology—at least not in the sense that it's second-best or doesn't work well. It has excellent quality. You can do the virtual VCR over it. You can fast forward and back, and you can have a whole batch of channels. It's server-based. It's digital.

But it is interim in the sense of being a transition technology, right?

Yeah, transition. That's a much better way to say it. It's a market entry kind of thing. It doesn't require conditioning the whole plant. It doesn't require big switchers or anything like that. It's modular. You go in house by house, and if people want it, you just stick in a circuit pack. When you get enough people in the neighborhood who want interactive services, then you bring fiber to them. Pull out the [ADSL] circuit packs and bring them out to a more remote area. They're reusable hundreds of times, so it's an interim technology that will be with us 40 years.

Then what's limiting about ADSL compared to fiber?

The cost is higher per house.

But isn't the level of interactivity different?

Oh, there's a big difference between that and full fiber to the home. A big, big difference. It doesn't give you infinite channels and infinite interactivity, but it does give you video-on-demand and home shopping. And it gives you excellent picture quality and good production values and our Stargazer user interface.

What about live broadcasts, live sports?

Well, as currently deployed, no. It's 1.5 megabits per second. But future versions of ADSL will carry 6 megabits a second. That gives you live broadcasts. It'll give you everything except the gee-whiz levels of interactivity.

Okay, then the fourth approach is wireless cable. Twenty-eight gigahertz is working, and it's great. And remember you're talking about antennas that are paste-on-the-window size. You paste it on and put in your telephone jack, and you now have two-way video. Of course, it's not applicable to every location and every terrain.

And DBS, satellite, is the fifth approach. And these will all be integrated, so if you're the customer you can say, "Yes, I'd like your telephone service and your wireless cable TV service," or, "Give me ADSL service," or whatever. It'll depend on your location, how far the engineering and construction of the network in your area has developed, etc.

Do you think that eventually there'll be one, most common architecture?

Yes, there will be. But I can't predict whether it'll be fiber-to-the-curb or fiber-to-the-node plus coax. But probably those two will be the most common.

But who knows? In three or four years, if wireless cable takes off . . . remember, the capacity of that is 28 gigahertz. That's huge. If you can get that to work well—and be interactive, too, which we have high hopes for—then it has the capacity for as many channels as you want. If that develops, we won't have to build out all the other things.

But by whatever combination of means, we will deliver broadband services to all of our customers within the next ten years. We'll deploy it in each location and each market differently, depending on the economics. But we will deliver it to all of our customers.

Why deliver it through the TV, by the way? Some pundits predict that by the year 2000 the PC will be the dominant interactive appliance in the home.

I say that that's not going to be the case. I think they're missing the whole point, because you're going to have intelligence in the home. The intelligence, of course, could be a set-top or a PC. In fact, the PCs that will come out in the next few years will be able to act as a set-top, once they figure out what the interactive set-top will look like. And all it'll take is a wire from the one to the other to make that intelligence energize the tube.

But you're not going to watch television on a little monitor. You're going to watch it on a big, big set. That's what you'll use when you want entertainment. You'll use the PC and keyboard when text is more important.

So you're going to have both in many houses. But even in the year 2000, you'll still have 75 percent or more of the population that doesn't have a sufficiently intelligent PC to handle the kind of interactive services that we'll be able to offer over television sets.

The other thing to keep in mind is, the real diffusion rate of PCs into the home is not progressing the way people say it is. They talk about the number of PCs shipped each year, and there are a lot of them. But many of them are seconds and replacements. What percentage of the homes in Pittsburgh today, for instance, do you think have a 486 PC in their residence?

Based on estimates of total PC penetration of around 30 percent of American homes, I don't know—5 to 10 percent?

That might be my guess, too. Don't forget, when they call and ask, "Do you have a PC?", many people will say yes. But what they've got is some old Amiga or 286 or something.

It's also a demand question. More people want entertainment, basically. You've got to start with entertainment—entertainment-on-demand, time-shifted sports, and time-shifted news. And people will be able to get all that without having to put a $2,000 PC in the house.

So basically it's the Willie Sutton factor?
Exactly. Why TV? Because that's where the people are.

Ameritech recently announced that it expects to see 20 percent of its revenues coming from content by the year 2000. Do you have similar goals for your joint programming venture with NYNEX, PacTel, and Creative Artists Agency in Hollywood?
How can I answer that? I mean, everything's up in the air. Cellular revenues are growing by 40 to 45 percent a year. Cellular subscribership is up by maybe 60 percent. There'll be new competitors in every field. So there's no way I can answer that question.

All right, before we end, could I conduct a little free-association thing with you? Kind of a Rorschach test, you might say. You game?
Uh, okay.

All right, here's the first one: Bill Gates?
Jane Seymour.

Pardon me?
Jane Seymour.

I'm sorry, I don't . . .
I saw a movie last night with Jane Seymour in it. She's been on my mind. She's intelligent and beautiful . . .

[Laughs.] I see. Now, everything's not going to come up Jane Seymour is it?
No, sorry . . . go ahead.

Okay . . . Bill Gates?
Many more billions to make.

AT&T?
Competitor.

The Internet?
Unruly wave of the future.

Electronic Frontier Foundation?
[Pause.] One of many.

Government regulation?
Barriers coming down.

And your worst business nightmare?
Government regulation.

Equal access?
All for it. It's in our interests.

That's interesting. Because you and the other Bells have been accused of redlining—of concentrating your rollout efforts on more upscale and whiter communities.
I think it's an absolute red herring. Lord knows where it comes from. Have you looked at our 214s?

Yes, and truthfully, as far as I can tell the demographics in your proposed service areas show not only higher minority representation than in your region as a whole, but higher than the country as a whole, too.
That's right. So the only thing I can think of is that because the very first location that we requested was in [Dover Township] New Jersey, somebody may have looked at that one town and said, "Aha! Redlining!"

Has the anti-redlining coalition since retracted its charge?
Retraction? Of course not. Never in the history of any coalition has *that* happened!

Is Bell Atlantic really prepared to shed its regulated monopoly ways and compete in this uncharted new world?
I'm not sure anyone is able to fully appreciate how powerfully the openness of these new networks is going to affect business and lifestyles. All I can say is we'll do our best to meet the challenges as they come.

I know what they say about the old Bellhead mentality—and it's true! I remember the old days in the sixties when we had a rule for everything, including the correct way to hold a pencil. We even had a written rule that said, "Before you go to a meeting, always go to the bathroom, even if you don't have to."

Well, those days are gone, at least here at Bell Atlantic. It's become clear that all the old givens—like "monopolies are forever"—no longer apply. Which is why we've been working very, very hard for over five years now to transform ourselves.

The world's changing, and we intend to manage that change. It's really that simple.

THE GOVERNMENT REGULATOR

June 30, 1994. Washington, D.C. Chairman Reed Hundt's office in the antiquated Federal Communications Commission headquarters. You can barely hear Hundt's voice above the buzzing of the electric fan in the sweltering office.

DANIEL BURSTEIN: **You've taken office at a time when one can construct feast or famine economic growth scenarios based on whether government does the right thing or the wrong thing vis-à-vis new and emerging communications technologies.**

One view holds that the greatest economic growth kick will be obtained if you do what many high-tech executives in Silicon Valley and elsewhere would like you to do—move government out of the picture entirely. Why can't you just declare your regulatory role over and let the marketplace "work its magic"?

REED HUNDT: Our role at the FCC in this period is to promote marketplace competition and to make sure that competition flourishes in communications markets. It may well be that we will get to the point where competition works well enough so that government can consciously diminish its role—and play no greater a role than it does, say, vis-à-vis Silicon Valley industries, which are viciously competitive. But that remains to be seen.

The situation we have inherited is one in which there is very little competition in almost every area of the market. Competition means choice. How many choices do you have for local telephone service? One? How many for cable TV service? One? How many choices do you have for long-distance telephone service? A few—in most places, anyway, it's at least more than one now.

Our job is to make sure there is competition where there isn't any and that there will be competition where there might not be. This is a classic role for government in the United States. For one-hundred-plus years, under the Sherman Act and the Clayton Act, government has tried to break up price-fixing, break up monopolies, and get choice to consumers. This is a perfectly legitimate role for government.

One could argue that all that effort to create competition doesn't really work in these huge, capital-intensive industries. Take long-distance telephony. It's not as if any entrepreneur who has a better idea can go start a long-distance phone company.

Think of yourself as a consumer of long-distance telephone service. Have you ever switched from one company to another? Almost everyone has. That's because at some point, some competitor came along and offered a better deal than the service you previously subscribed to. Why were they able to offer a better deal? Maybe they were quicker to get fiber optics installed in your region than the other guy. Or maybe they were willing to make less money on their capital. Or maybe they had a different capital structure so they could afford to underprice the other fellow.

All these reasons are issues to which the consumer can be indifferent. Yet it's all to the consumer's benefit. From a policy making perspective, when you see price competition and value competition going on in the marketplace—and the companies are all thriving—you don't have to worry too much. A rough cut tells you as much as you want to know: competition is benefiting the consumer and the economy and certainly not killing the companies.

Where would you place the importance of ensuring that there is a competitive marketplace in communications, as compared with all the other social issues?

There are a lot of social problems that communications can help deal with. Communications can be a force for education. Communications can be a way of tying a whole society together. In a society where everybody can call everybody else, you have a stronger social fabric. Communications can be a tool of foreign policy. It can be used to help open overseas markets to American sellers. In fact, communications technology can help sell American products. L.L. Bean, for example, is doing a booming business in Mexico, because customers there can now dial 1-800 whatever and order L.L. Bean products. In fact, 800 calls are now a very substantial percentage of all AT&T's long-distance traffic. So communications can be a tremendous force for commercial enterprise.

Competition doesn't diminish your ability to manage social problems, it gives you more ways to resolve them.

Can you be more specific?

Let's say you live in a remote area. As a social goal, I want to be sure you have good telephone service. Well, there are two ways I can do this.

In one scenario, I can let AT&T run the whole bulk service, and I can say to AT&T: please make sure you connect Mr. Remote to the network. While the real cost of connecting him might be 30 bucks a month, only charge him 15 because that's all he can afford to pay and let somebody else pay more to subsidize your extra cost. This is how the world was until recently—and still is in some parts of the country.

Now, in that same model with AT&T running everything, along comes a new technology: cellular. Here's what AT&T proposed, I guess back almost 20 years ago—and this is a true story. Cellular, they said, might be a good idea, might be a bad idea; it's very hard to figure out. They said, "FCC, give us 40 megahertz and an exclusive license. We'll try it out—but our estimates are that there will only be 900,000 cellular users by the end of the century."

But the commission said, "Well, we're not so sure. You might be right, you might be wrong. We'll create 50 megahertz and we'll divide it into two licenses of 25 megahertz each—it's almost what you're saying, AT&T, but not quite."

Now, of course AT&T was broken up while this debate was going on and on through the seventies and early eighties. So the commission ultimately gave one of those licenses to each of the regional Bell operating companies. It was an outgrowth of the same original AT&T proposal and the commission's response. But that's the way the duopoly was created in cellular. This duopoly, of course, has not been very price competitive, not very value competitive. If you've ever had a dropped cellular call for which you had to pay, you know that they are not competing on quality in a big-time way.

But this duopoly earned enough money for the industry to enable them to build out a whole system. That's a big plus—it is now a ubiquitous service. It's also a system where there are now 17 million subscribers, instead of the 900,000 that AT&T forecast. And we still have a long way to go to the end of the century.

What AT&T wouldn't have accomplished, this duopoly, to a greater degree, has accomplished. It has built a universal system and it has gotten prices down so that in many parts of the country, it is cheaper to install cellular service than to maintain the wired plant. I'm talking about the more remote parts of the country.

And PCS?

Now we have the next generation of cellular: PCS. It's a slightly different technology that allows the units to be lighter, cheaper, more easily carried around. The service has a lower cost structure overall than traditional cellular.

We've now allocated 120 megahertz of spectrum, and we're going to slice it like a loaf of bread, so that you can buy the thickness that you want. Participants in our auction will be permitted to get a slice that's 10 or 20 or 30 or 40 megahertz. Then they butter it any way they want. That's the basic approach.

Our goal is to let competition among PCS providers and the incumbent cellular companies drive that price on an average per-minute basis down even further. We've been told by people like McKinsey that we can look toward the end of the century for cellular prices, on an average bill basis, to have declined by 50 percent from what they are now in real dollars.

So if you're Mr. Remote America, I am making a still cheaper version of communications available to you. How? Because I've let competitors seek cost-efficient technology, I've encouraged them to drive the price down, I've made the problem of connecting you to the network easier to solve because I'm getting the benefits of competition.

This is just one small example. But I could give you the same kind of examples about video or about almost any technology.

Looking more closely at PCS, how are you getting prepared for the upcoming deluge of interest? While I was waiting to see you, I saw people coming in off the street asking for auction documents as if this was the neighborhood convenience store selling lottery tickets.

Well, there's no question that there's going to be a lot of interest. The OMB has an estimate that says there will be something like $10 billion paid for everything when the whole PCS auction process is over. Consultants tell us that we can anticipate total bids—total dollars offered on the table from all bidders as the auction proceeds—to aggregate at 10 to 20 times that.

In other words, you're presiding over an auction that will see more total capital offered in bids than the entire process of privatizing Eastern Europe and Russia to date.
Well, that may be true. But it's just one of the things we do here.

With PCS you are starting fresh. You aren't inheriting policy from the old FCC, you're making your own.
Well, we are inheriting two existing cellular companies in every market, who have a going-in incumbent's advantage. The downside for them is that, in most cases, they're using analog, not digital technology, and their usable spectrum is in a different place on the total RF spectrum than what PCS will be utilizing. That said, I guess all things considered it's better to be an incumbent.

My point is that we are not inheriting a completely blank slate. But we did get 120 megahertz made available by Congress, and Congress said we could auction it. By far this is the best way to award it. First, because the public gets something for its property and second, the property goes to the person who most values it, which is exactly what you want if you're trying to get businesses started.

The decision we made here in our final week of consideration was to commit absolutely to selling the spectrum in a way that would encourage competition. This is the most dramatic step to introduce competition into a telecommunications market on day one that any country has ever taken.

Everywhere else, people typically start with a monopoly and maybe they break it up into two pieces. Maybe they allow a second provider, that has a real struggle getting market share, and finally, over a long period of time, you end up with two, or at the most three providers.

Here, from day one, we're starting with competition. When you have competition, you have unpredictable and unforeseeable effects. I believe that one of those effects is that the economy will grow faster than otherwise because business will grow faster than otherwise. Job creation will be maximized. Prices will be lower than under any other model.

But another effect is that there will be some people who start these PCS businesses and turn out not to be successful. It's always that way with genuine competition, and we would have to anticipate that will be the case here as well.

Previously, with respect to almost all communications technologies in almost all countries, getting the license practically guaranteed your commercial success. Here, with PCS, getting the license is just a chance to compete, with absolutely *no* guarantee of success.

On the FCC's plan to make special efforts to award licenses to companies controlled by minorities and women, you have said that is not really an affirmative action program in the traditional sense. What's the difference?

Right, what I said was this is a case of affirmative *opportunity*, but the *action* is up to the people who want to take it. That's a concept that I hope will detonate and that people will realize it quickly, because something very unusual is happening here. We're not selling monopoly rights to run businesses in perpetuity. We *are* selling a chance to compete.

Communications should not be an aberrational area where there is no competition. It should be like any other sector. We should trust in competition and the benefits of a competitive marketplace.

But what about the negative side of competition?

People are going to have trouble with this. One question that is sure to be raised: is there a risk of national security, having communications facilities subject to the ups and downs of competitive marketplace pressures? Other people are going to wonder if the social goals of communications can be accomplished with such competition going on. These are reasonable questions.

I may be wrong, but I am very clear about my answer: yes, we can accomplish all these diverse goals—but to do so will require change.

For example, I have recently been instrumental in reconstituting the Network Reliability Council, and we're just getting started with meetings. For the first time it will include not just wired telephone companies but wireless. This council is chaired by Dick Notebaert, chairman of Ameritech. And Dick is saying to its members: "You all want to be in the communications business. You all want to deliver voice. Then you should join in the obligation to make sure that the network—even if it is now going to be a patchwork of networks—is reliable in the event of national disaster or threats to national security." This is a dialogue that has to be had.

Okay, so what's the answer to that one?

Well, if your answer is yes—because that's the way we treated NYNEX when it had 100 percent of the market, then this is an example of a new issue that you will have to deal with. The new entrants will have to carry their fair share of the need to have backup systems in the event of an emergency.

When you look at these new questions, complicated as they are, I think you and I can see that they *do* have solutions. They don't have to wait for new technological breakthroughs or for some genius to arrive. Reasonable people can sit in a room and bang out answers to these questions.

The average person is still against the breakup of AT&T. They don't see it as something that lowered their phone bill and brought them new services—they see it as the cause of a lot of consumer headache.

Well, I'm not sure people are still against it. But when you travel around the country, I'll grant you that you don't find a lot of ordinary people enthusiastically saying it was definitely a great idea. They're kind of indifferent to it at this point. I think that's true for communications issues in general. People are not necessarily attuned to the connection between competition policy issues on the one hand and benefits to the consumer on the other.

But this is changing. There's been such a deluge of data—the term "Information Highway" has entered the public discussion. I was on Larry King recently, and he turned to me and said, "Information Highway—I don't know what that is, but I'm interested." People are becoming aware that the communications revolution is the most important economic development in our country, in so many different ways.

We are probably shifting from being a service economy to becoming an information economy. That is to say we've stabilized our manufacturing base at about a fifth of our work force. It's been around there for a fairly long time. I don't think it's going to go down and it certainly isn't going to go up much. It's become accepted that the majority of the workforce is in the service sector. In the eighties, Walter Mondale was running for president criticizing Ronald Reagan's policies for creating low-wage service jobs. But in the communications revolution we see breathtaking, transformational developments that are leading to the creation of many high-quality, high-wage jobs.

Let's look at the case for which you are probably best known and most criticized: the cable industry rate rollback earlier this year. Walk me through what you did from your perspective.

The Cable Act says that basic and enhanced basic should be charged at reasonable levels. To simplify it, a fair reading of the act is that Congress meant that the prices charged for those services should be similar to what would be charged if there were competition.

What we did was look at the statistical evidence on the prices for basic and enhanced basic in the areas where there is competition and compared it to prices in the areas where there is not. In 99 percent of cable markets there's no competition; in 1 percent there is. And if you look at this evidence, you see that the answer is that a 17 percent reduction takes you from the prices where there is no competition to the prices where there is. That's what the evidence shows, and that's what we called for.

The next question is, after that reduction is accomplished and in an apples-to-apples comparison you have a 17 percent reduction on average nationwide, what if the cable operator doesn't want to sell you the same old apples? What if he wants to sell you an apple and an orange? What if he wants to sell you more channels? That is a reasonable thing for an operator to want to do—and a reasonable thing for a consumer to want to buy.

Step back a minute and consider an analogy: When you take your grocery cart through the grocery store, you like to be able to pick off the shelf the products you like. If I told you this was a store where the clerk says, "Oh, your cart has appeared. Today you are buying milk, eggs, sardines, mustard, and ketchup," you might say, "Gee, I don't really like sardines. The rest is okay, but I don't want the sardines. Do I have a choice?" And the clerk says, "No, not in this store."

That is basic cable or enhanced basic. The cable operator doesn't say to you, what do you want in your package? The cable operator says, "You like the milk and eggs, which, for you, happens to be ESPN and USA network, then you get to have these other free products—the X, Y, and Z channels—and you have no choice."

The question is, should the Cable Act be interpreted to permit the cable operator to force you to buy extra channels as part of basic, or should they be required to freeze the offer the way it was in 1992 and add channels only by choice of the consumer on an à la carte basis?

This is the fork in the road of policy. And it's the exact same fork in the road that the businessman faces.

If you talk to different cable operators, they will tell you, "I've already put an awful lot in that consumer's grocery cart—33 channels that they have to take—and I don't want to try to put any more in. Anything else now is extra, à la carte."

Now, if you talk to a different cable operator, he might say, "I think I can squeeze some more into that consumer's cart. In fact, I'm positive I can make them buy the sardines. They're not going to complain about it and it's not going to add that much in price."

The cable operators are splitting now on that issue. They are facing the same choice we are in making policy. And we don't know the outcome yet.

But back to the more controversial hub of the issue. Did you anticipate that the February rate rollback would be—fairly or unfairly—perceived as an attack on the cable industry at a time when the captains of the cable industry were claiming that they most needed higher cash flows?

Well, people in the cable industry told me before our decision that any reduction in rates would hurt their cash flow and that they should be entitled to that full cash flow because they were going to spend the money to increase capacity and build the Information Highway. They said that all along.

Is there any economic benefit to be obtained by allowing a monopolist to charge whatever that monopolist wants for the products in the grocery cart? Generally speaking in our country, economists say that you should not endure the prospect of a monopolist charging whatever he wants. It's bad for the economy, bad for the consumer, and it means there's less economic growth and less jobs. The burden is on the monopolists to tell you why they are the exception to the rule.

If the monopolists tell you they want to charge monopoly rents in one area in order to have the cash flow to invest in *something else*—well, that's an argument that has been rejected in this country for a long time. Certainly, we didn't let AT&T do it when AT&T was a monopoly.

Curiously, the cable industry is constantly telling us that we have to be vigilant against the telephone industry, to make sure they are not allowed to overcharge their customers. And when we ask them why, they say, "because they'll use the money to invest in video programming." Well, here at the FCC we believe that what's sauce for the goose ought to be sauce for the gander. Neither the telephone industry nor the cable industry ought to be able to extract unreasonable monopoly rents in order to invest in other businesses.

Speaking of the cable-telco love-and-war relationship, how much of all the cable industry hype we hear about the Information Highway is, in your opinion, just a fig leaf for the cable industry's desire to get into where the real money is—the telephone business?

Well, I hope they intend to get into the telephone business. And I hope they deliver more channels and more video programming. No consumer should be against the entry of cable companies into the telephone business, nor the expansion of video programming choices. More channels means more capacity and more opportunity for cable companies to move into the phone business. Bits are bits—they can deliver voice, video, or data. I have nothing against cable companies developing all these businesses.

The real question is should they invest in capacity increases, based on the likely returns on those investments, or alternatively, should their investment come from monopoly profits they can extract from the sale of some other product.

It's no secret where you stand.

Well, I've been reading all the discussion in the press about these issues. I haven't seen a single economist opt in favor of the second of those two alternatives. What I have noted with interest is people pointing out that cable rate regulation may serve to focus cable operators *more* on the need to add capacity to deliver the interactive services that constitute the heart of the Information Highway. If that's true, it's because cable rate regulation is shrinking the monopoly profits available from basic cable and encouraging operators to look at how they can offer services that are not regulated.

If that happens, just don't tell me it was an unintended consequence of our policy.

Moving to the issue of content, do you see an increased role for policy makers in separating content from conduit or otherwise regulating the relationship between content and conduit?

I think it's important to share one key perception between us. And that is this: there is a special deal between the public and broadcasters, a social contract with broadcasters.

You mean traditional, over-the-air broadcasters.

Right. The traditional broadcasters are granted a license to broadcast on the basis that they will provide certain social benefits that the public deserves and expects. The number-one benefit is that they provide free, over-the-air television to the public. I don't know how you quantify that benefit, but if you compare it to what people have to pay to get cable, you know that it's a little north of $20 billion a year. So it is a good deal for the public. But it is also a pretty good deal for broadcasters. You won't hear any broadcaster say they don't like this deal.

The question before us is how can and should this social compact be restated for the next generation. One issue is whether broadcasters are giving the public all the benefits they deserve. For example, children's TV. Should broadcasters be required to deliver more and better children's television? Should we insist that broadcasters be more mindful of the needs of children and hold off on broadcasting certain kinds of material until, hopefully, the children have gone to bed?

However, with respect to most of the rest of the content issue or the social dimension of the new communications revolution, it's just not a subject for us.

What happens when Jesse Helms figures out what kind of sexually explicit content is traveling through the Internet and then realizes that some taxpayer money has been used to build, establish, and run the Internet?

That's an interesting point. I must say I don't know enough about the economics of the Internet. I think there was taxpayer money used originally as seed money, but I don't think there's very much public funding for it right now. Most of the Internet's growth, and the great body of traffic, it seems to me, is obviously coming from the private sector utilization, and customers paying to get access.

The question that you raise is probably more problematic with regard to the coaxial cable network, which is privately funded and not subject to the same social compact as traditional broadcasting. As channel capacity expands, a lot of things will be available over coaxial cable that will cause a lot of Americans to scratch their heads. Certainly, there will be a lot of things that will require parental discretion.

So you don't anticipate being called in to regulate the Internet and its content?

I would find that unlikely. Not speaking of the FCC but of government more generally, we don't try to regulate the content of telecommunications, although, of course, we have the authority to prevent, for example, the fraudulent use of the telephone network. To the degree that there are concerns about *illegal* activity taking place in any system, government has the means to prosecute and enforce the law.

But if you put that aside and say that's not what you're really talking about in terms of issues about content—then I would say to you that when you and I talk on the telephone, there's nobody suggesting that there ought to be a censor or monitor of that, with the exception that law enforcement ought to be able to obtain a warrant where necessary to intercept a call. But the fundamental paradigm is that a telephone call is a private matter. I don't see any reason why that paradigm wouldn't apply to the Internet as well.

APPENDIX B

Twenty-First Century Salon

May 1, 1994
Stars Restaurant
San Francisco, California

PARTICIPANTS

Alvin Toffler
Futurist and Author

Jeffrey Berg
International Creative Management

Larry Ellison
Oracle Corporation

Marc Porat
General Magic, Inc.

Denise Caruso
New Media Analyst

Paul Saffo
Institute for the Future

Denise Luria, Ph.D.
Psychologist

Michael Rothschild
Economist, The Bionomics Institute

HOSTS

Daniel Burstein and David Kline

PURPOSE

To stimulate ideas, concerns, and visions not necessarily obvious
in the public discourse surrounding the Digital Revolution

Burstein: Let's start with the assumption that the Information Highway is being built upon the landscape of a society that is increasingly, and dangerously, dysfunctional. To what degree do any of you believe that the Digital Revolution is going to be an overwhelmingly positive force—contributing to the solution of major social problems—versus a polarizing force that exacerbates the disparity between haves and have-nots, and creates new and more-profoundly troubling social dilemmas?

Ellison: Why do you say this is an increasingly dysfunctional society? I mean, there are tribal wars going on in Rwanda. And look at Ireland. Now *that's* dysfunctional.

Kline: Well, we've got millions of unemployed and unemployable people who are basically cut off from playing any meaningful or productive role in society. We've got crime, urban decay, a school system on the brink of collapse . . .

Ellison: How do you feel about the steam engine? Was that a terrible thing? Look at all the people that had to leave the farm because of steam engines. It was awful.

Because of tractors, people were displaced. We forget that it wasn't that long ago that the vast majority of our population was on the farm, gainfully employed and feeding the population. And then this horrible thing happened: industrialization, and this caused incredible human suffering. I mean, read *Grapes of Wrath*.

Whenever there's change, whenever you go through a technology transition, there's incredible pain as society reorients itself. But I'm not sure what conclusions you can make from that.

Generally I think the new technology will dramatically improve communication, increase specialization, and increase total wealth. But in doing so it's going to thoroughly reorient society and cause layoffs and dislocations. There'll be terrible human suffering to go along with this transition.

Toffler: If you're asking about dysfunction, I think we have to look outside the technological field and ask ourselves if we really believe that this is some kind of revolution—in other words, it isn't just an incremental change, but something big is really happening. This helps us explain why the United States in particular, but other countries as well, are seeing simultaneous institutional crises. Crisis in the education system, crisis in the urban systems, crisis in the family system, crisis in all of the subsystems that make an industrial society operate.

All of these institutions were designed for industrialism, for smokestack society, and now they're collapsing under the weight of increased diversity, heterogeneity, complexity, and speed. So that's why we have not just unemployment, which *is* going to get far worse, but also a near vaccum of institutional innovation.

We've become very skilled at technological innovation. We can accelerate that very, very well. But how many people are thinking about what a new political system would look like for the twenty-first century? Or what any new institutions would look like? Very few. Or if they are, there's certainly no critical mass of them. So what we have are a lot of very smart people functioning on the technological side and the corporate side, and not much going on the social side of the equation.

Remember, what we're doing is on a scale much larger than the Industrial Revolution. It is global. It is happening at incredible rates of speed, and it is very, very hard to really get our hands around.

So it's hardly a surprise that there's dysfunction and that there's dislocation in society. The question is (A) Who should be doing something about that—Who has responsibility? And (B) What should they do?

Caruso: I've never seen any indication that technology comes down either on the positive or the negative side of the equation. Technology is a magnifying glass for conditions that already exist. Therefore, it's going to be both, of course, because it always is.

I think that probably various groups in society will be able to use technology in their own way. Certainly if you start talking about the government's Clipper technologies, and criminals getting their hands on powerful encryption tools, that certainly is one way to look at a negative side of powerful technology.

On the other hand, one of the reasons that I got really interested in this field in the first place is because of the incredible interactive education applications I saw in Apple's multimedia lab. If those applications were coming over my TV set or the TV sets of any number of millions of people in the world, it'd be a great positive force in society.

Saffo: My worst nightmare and also my fondest hope is the same thing. We're going to get what we wish for. I agree with Denise. The technology is profoundly neutral. It's the cultural response that determines how it's used. The problem isn't technology. The problem and the opportunity is culture.

Toffler: There are two things I want to say. One is about education and people teaching people. I just wanted to make a side comment, that the single most important piece of learning that went on in the United States—say, between the mid seventies and the present— was where tens of millions of people learned how to use PCs. And nobody went to school to do that, or very few. It was the proverbial, pimply 16-year-old at Radio Shack who got that started. So there are social learning processes that take place that have nothing to do with the institutions formally created to carry them out.

That takes me to the second point. Which is that these social learning processes may not be so different today from the past. I'm always struck by the wonderful case of the Lunar Society. It's just a wonderful story.

In 1765, a group of what were regarded as provincial yokels began meeting once a month in Birmingham in England. They met on the night of the full moon because it was safer to walk home after the meeting in the light of the moon.

Burstein: You're not implying that unsafe streets have been with us for a long time. [Laughter.]

Toffler: They've been around for a while, yes. Anyway, they met once a month from 1765 to 1805. They never wrote a report. They never arrived at a consensus statement of any kind. The people in London called them "lunatics" because of "lunar," and they happened to include Priestley, [steam engine inventor] James Watt, [poet and naturalist] Erasmus Darwin, Ben Franklin (when he was over there), and many other entrepreneurs and scientists. And they became the guiding spirits of the Industrial Revolution.

But they were coming really out of left field. I mean, what would you expect coming out of Birmingham when the Royal Society was in London? And I think that's a wonderful story, and it makes me wonder, you know, if something is also stirring out there today.

Caruso: I would put to you that at this point in time, we are seeing actual, real job loss because of technology. Take the person who answers the switchboard at the catalog shopping company. Voice mail technology makes it possible to put that person who answers that phone out of work.

So what happens to that person? What does the person do? Without retraining, maybe this person answers the phone at some other place, but everybody's getting voice mail. So let's assume this is one job lost forever. And that there are going to be many people of that skill level—high school graduates, maybe a couple years of college—and there is not going to be a lot of work out there for them.

Toffler: Can I take that for a minute? Because I think the politics of this question are going to change very radically, and here's why.

I suspect you know my wife and I use a shorthand—the "Second Wave," or industrial society; and the "Third Wave," or what we are creating now. Okay, in a Second Wave economy, if you get a million people unemployed, you can go in there—we learned this from the Great Depression—and you can lower interest rates, you can futz with the taxes, you can use some macroeconomics like deficit spending. What you can do is stimulate the economy. You then produce a million new jobs. Those million laid-off workers take the million new jobs, and you've solved your problem.

But now you get a million people unemployed, and you do all those things—you lower the interest rate, you stimulate the economy—and even if you create 10 million jobs, those people can't do them!

So the problem of unemployment goes from quantitative to qualitative. Now, the Clinton administration's answer is "retraining." But by the time you've got somebody retrained, the skill-set that is required has changed again. Moreover, it isn't just people without skills who are unemployed. We've got rocket scientists walking the streets.

So it isn't skills versus no skills. It's appropriate skills versus inappropriate skills. My sense is that we're going to see a lot of middle-class people like those rocket scientists displaced for periods of their lives. At a certain time everybody's going to experience some unemployment, and that will change the politics of unemployment because it's no longer them. It's also us.

Then the question is what policy . . .

Rothschild: Policy has to drive technology transfer. In other words, if you have a displaced worker from Martin Marietta who was working on the space program, and he could be redeployed into transportation, someone's going to have to give that message to policy makers on a national level.

Toffler: The market will give that message. But, of course, if you leave things entirely to the market, you're going to have a lot of pain and misery that is perhaps unnecessary. If you don't leave it to the market—if you give a national [policy] signal—well, if the signal's correct then it's great. If the signal's wrong, the problems are only amplified.

Porat: The question that was posed is really about winners and losers, and how they might react socially and economically. To get the question right, I think you need to get the metaphor right, so I'm going to propose a metaphor: think of technology as the Big Wheel of society, down at the level of what Karl Marx called the material conditions of society.

The Big Wheel is changing because we've learned how to tap deep stuff. The Industrial Revolution is a perfect example of a Big Wheel changing. We harnessed energy and did something with it through the mediation of technologies which we had to invent. But now we're harnessing a different kind of energy—information—which we're tapping and mediating through a different kind of technology—the information machine, the communication machine.

Now when the Big Wheel changes, a smaller wheel reacts. The Big Wheel moves and has all the energy, which slides all the little wheels around—our institutions, like education and government, for instance, and our culture. And they scramble as best they can to adjust.

What we're asking is, Do we understand the Big Wheel such that we can anticipate the impact of its shifting? Because when the Big Wheel makes a shift, Schumpeter comes alive and says, "There will be destruction!" Whether it's institutional or cultural or at the material level of jobs, there will be destruction.

We always try to avoid Schumpeter's Fate, which is creative destruction. But to me the whole effort is specious because it's just very hard to anticipate what changes will take place. I think that at net, people will get thrown out of jobs. But in one sense that's irrelevant. If we build the Information Highway, which will stimulate the economy, it won't matter how many people are needed or not needed to mix the concrete. Because wonderful new opportunities are going to plunk themselves down on the highway. That's where the jobs are, not in mixing concrete.

Rothschild: The metaphor that was used by Marc is caught up with all the imagery of the steam engine, the Industrial Age. You know, the *engines of growth*, and *job-making machine*. We've got to *shift gears* here. With all due respect, when we start talking about *wheels* we keep *driving* ourselves back to a set of solutions. We limit our vision in understanding what's ahead.

Saffo: This conversation is *off the tracks*. [Laughter.]

Rothschild: That language was appropriate if we were still in the machine age, but that ended in the summer of 1971 when the microprocessor was invented. There's a very new kind of age [emerging] now. And it's very much a self-organizing, spontaneous process. I'm not sure we can direct it.

Porat: Well, education is not my field, but maybe that's one of the few areas where we really can anticipate and shape what's coming— informal education more so than formal. Education in the family, education in the workplace. You know, the training director is usually the first person to get laid off in any recession. Nobody cares about them. We don't even have one in our company and probably won't for years.

Schools systems? A joke. Parochial education? Not much better. Because in a world in which the only thing that matters is your ability to deal with information and communication, it becomes the forerunner of whether you're going to succeed or fail as an individual or as a company. But we're not teaching people in any sense of the word how to deal with information and communication. We just don't teach it. It's not in the curriculum.

Saffo: For those of you who don't know Marc well, he's in the category of, quote, "I'm not real good at pool, but I like to play for money," unquote. [Laughter.]

Porat: The point is, just to finish, that a child emerges into a world and understands that there are losers and there are winners. In 1869, they probably checked their biceps and did some fine motor-skill movements to see if they were going to be successful. Now what are they doing? They're saying, "Hey, I can make it. I can play a video game. I can program my VCR. I can use my PC. I'm okay. I'm cool." You don't teach them; you don't force them. You just leave the stuff sprinkled around, and like little mice, they'll sort of move to where the cheese is.

Caruso: If they can. If they can.

Porat: If they don't, they're lost. I would submit to you they'll be lost in our society in 10 years.

Burstein: Tell us more about the new winners and losers.

Porat: There will be two sets of winners: The first are people who are providing the tools and technologies. The enabling technologies. That's one set of winners.

The other set of winners are people who grab it and make intelligent use of it. This is where the information haves and have-nots begin to distinguish themselves. People who jump on board and begin to use these tools in commercial ways that are more and more interesting will succeed. Out of that mix of people will emerge the Sears and Roebucks and the Sam Waltons.

Those guys broke the paradigm of their day. They were laughed at. I can imagine Sears and Roebuck being greeted with howls of derision when they said, "Stores? I don't think so. I think people want to buy out of a catalog book." You know, howls! And then eventually, of course, they lost their own ascendancy because of Schumpeter's Fate. Sears and Roebuck died. And then Sam Walton came along.

I think that in this new environment someone will come along who will say, "Give me the tools. Get out of my way. I know what to do." And they're the other set of winners.

Kline: What about the losers? What about the very large number of people who have neither the skills nor the economic means to be a part of this whole process?

Toffler: You know, when the telephone came along—and there are people in this room who would probably know the history better than I—when the telephone came along it was immediately assumed that only rich people needed it. The idea was nobody would ever use it except the rich and maybe some companies.

So the argument about info rich and poor overlooks one important aspect or possibility. Which is that it would be in the interests of the rich to have the poor on the Info Highway. That's why access will be universalized. If, in fact, you're a company and you want to have as many possible customers to send your deliveries to—as many outlets as possible—then you want everyone to have access. So it is therefore in everybody's interest to get everybody as much as possible into the system.

Porat: Can I build on that? I clearly agree with you because supply constantly tries to find demand and demand tries to find supply. In the real world that we're familiar with today—the mechanical world—we jump in a car, we go to the shopping mall. We enter a well-understood "user interface," which is called a parking lot. We get out. We walk up and down the aisles. We find merchandise. We shop, and we buy.

And it is absolutely in the capitalist interest to make shopping widely available to everyone, irrespective of social class or race and so on. And that's what we do—we have built roads that lead everywhere.

Now, the analogy, pushing it forward, is still that supply wants to find demand. Your theme is completely correct. You want to make sure that the most ubiquitous forms of symbolic interaction, which are the telephone and the television, become important sources of demand, commercial demand, expressing itself in the form of "I want." I want goods. I want services. I want entertainment. And if you don't provide that to everybody—information poor, rich, and in between—you are really a bad businessman because you've just disenfranchised your market. If you're in the mass-market business, that is.

Toffler: But that raises a whole other fundamental question about the mass market. One of the arguments that we have been making for years is that industrialism produced a mass-market system.

The assumption was the more technology you have, the more massified it was going to be, that everything was going to become bigger, more regimented, more totalitarian, more bureaucratic, etcetera. If you read Huxley, you read Orwell, you read all the science fiction, and all the sociology—it was a linear projection moving toward more massification.

But what's happening now is actually the reverse of that. The society's becoming more heterogeneous, and we're not only demassifying and customizing production, we're also demassifying markets.

Rothschild: What you're really alluding to is an atomized society, and I'm wondering what that means for political structures. As you said, governments and institutions are predicated upon economic need, and that need has now shifted. So what does the American interest vis-à-vis corporate interest mean, when corporate interests today are global and not national?

Michael Porter wrote a book, *The Competitive Advantage of Nations*, that shows how certain countries help industries succeed in specific markets because it's in the national interest. I'm wondering whether that's going to be true anymore.

My question is, if the corporation and the institution don't have the same vested interest anymore—if the telecommunications companies lay off thousands of workers because they need a [leaner and] smarter structure—then who is going to bear the social cost of that dispossessed worker?

Just today, in the *New York Times*, there are three articles on dispossessed workers—in the tobacco industry, in the automobile industry, and in the phone companies.

Kline: And three more in the *San Francisco Chronicle* today.

Porat: The answer is still the same in an atomistic society. Look, I'm me—the individual, the demand side—and I want. I don't feel necessarily like I'm a part of any mass, but I want to find goods, services, and entertainment that appeal to me.

You, the supply side, portray yourself to the marketplace as being come-one, come-all. Your customers may view themselves as individuals, but you need them all. And for that reason you need to have access to everyone. Therefore, you cannot deal with elitist or partial solutions. You can't deal with a system that says, "If you're [rich], or have a PC, and it's in color, and you have a high-speed modem and it's got Intel inside, then it's okay."

Capitalism will crush that kind of thinking. If you have any content where supply is looking for demand, you'd better prepare your business to [handle] the greatest number of different kinds of communities coming to you. You do not want exclusion.

To me, that speaks to the natural capitalist instinct, which always asks, "Where is demand?" You want 17 ways to get into absolutely everyone's home.

Caruso: But that doesn't speak to what we started this whole conversation with, which is that there will be a growing unemployed class of people who don't have the money to buy his stuff. Which completely eliminates your argument that the forces of capitalism will make this technology available to everyone without the need for regulation.

Porat: I don't understand what you just said. Ninety-seven percent of U.S. households today have a television set. One can construct a view, where there's x-trillion dollars of final demand, companies wanting to sell the household something, who say, "I'm sitting here on trillions of dollars of final demand. Everyone has a TV set. Now, if I can only find some way of equipping that TV set—or the wireless or wireline channels that go into the TV set—so I can find demand, boy, am I willing to subsidize that."

Caruso: Let's talk about how that happens, how you subsidize demand in an increasingly rich-and-poor world. My point is that I don't think it's so simplistic.

Porat: There's a big sea change, in my view, in the way supply will find demand in the next 20 years. Huge. Today it's a push model, where you set up everything to push. The advertiser pushes. The purpose of television is to package audiences and put them before advertisers. The purpose of the shopping mall is to aggregate potential shoppers for the seller. It's a push, push, push, push model.

It'll turn into a pull model, where the individual—and I agree with you completely on this point—sits there and says, "What have you got out there?" And merchants have to get themselves into a framework of pulling.

Toffler: Here's how it works. You turn on your screen and you say, "I'm in the market for a camera . . . how many of you out there make cameras for [less than] a certain price?" The supplier says, "What kind of camera do you want?" And you say, "I want blah, blah camera. Show me the models . . . oh, and I want an electronic auction." So whoever offers the best price for the same equipment, you'll do business with. So the pull model . . . it destandardizes prices.

Porat: You send out your "electronic agents" to find the best sources of supply, right? The problem with that model—and by the way, it's a completely correct model, except it doesn't go far enough—is no self-respecting merchant will ever want to participate in a market where they know . . . I mean, merchants *live* off imperfect information.

Porat: Neoclassical economics [teaches] that perfect information creates perfect markets. But the last thing a merchant wants is perfect information.

Toffler: That is the way the world worked prior to industrialism. Standard prices—a nickel for a Coke—was an invention of the Industrial Age. It went with standardization technology. We're going to change all that now . . . and merchants will have to live with it.

Caruso: But how does all of that subsidize programming on interactive TV?

Porat: Each of the 13 manufacturers of cameras has an autonomous choice they can make. Which is, if I'm the merchant and you inquire what cameras I have in stock and what I recommend to you, I'll reward you. I'll give you "frequent [networking] coupons."

Or maybe I'll pump in a few dollars . . . it could take the form of, say, Proposition 1: I'll give you first run movies with advertising every 12 minutes for free. That's today's model.

Or Proposition 2 is I'll give you the movie that you want for $5 with no commercials. Or Proposition 3 is, tell me what infomercials you're interested in. Ah, you're interested in cameras. Fine. I promise to break your movie three times during the course of 100 minutes with infomercials on cameras. And you can have that movie for a dollar because the merchant has paid for it.

Burstein: In working on our book, I've spent a lot of time in Orlando with the Time Warner Full Service Network, and this is exactly their approach. They've off-loaded the cost entirely from the consumer to the infomercial provider—the info merchant—and they've said, "'We're going to have a grocery delivery service, and if you order staples off your screen, we're going to get 1 percent of your grocery bill, which will allow us to fund movies. And if you sit down and will watch a Lexus commercial, we'll print out on your printer a special

$50 coupon if you come in and take the test drive—and we'll give you three free movies besides."

Berg: I'm interested in how these structures are going to finance themselves, because finally that's the market in which I live. I'm basically brokering intellectual property in the form of music or publishing or programmed entertainment. We're also finding that the catalogs are being repurposed for new usages every generation.

The best analogy is to look back 15 years ago, when we had LPs. The LPs would be [transferred onto] cassette, and then later it was CD. Mini CDs will be micro CDs, and maybe there'll even be an implant in the brain one day. [Laughter.]

But that's why I was interested in what Marc had to say about the fact that the carriers themselves, which have excessive cash flow even in a regulated environment, will act as consumer credit organizations the same way GM has affinity deals with credit card firms. And whether it's free miles or free gas or free cards or a free lunch, I think what you're going to find is in this market—which will be a deregulated market—there will be a lot of give-aways. There will be premiums. There will be added value that comes through marketing strategies that the consumer has never seen before.

I mean, you may be going to *Lethal Weapon 4* and at the same time get a coupon to buy a program or a CD or get some free credit on your mileage. What I see emerging is an interwoven economy. I see goods and services really being traded in a barter fashion.

Ellison: Advertising will become vastly more efficient.

Caruso: Is this the good news or the bad news?

Ellison: I think it's great news. Now, I don't like commercials on Clinique and Lancôme because I don't wear makeup except on weekends. [Laughter.]

Oh, good, good . . . I can see you wondering, "Where do you go on weekends?"

But anyway, why do commercials work? Commercials work because people don't have a lot of information about the products they're buying. They're information hungry, and they use it to make decisions about buying products. I don't mind watching commercials on products that I'm interested in.

Caruso: Do you really use TV commercials for information on buying products? Be honest.

Ellison: Except for the news, I don't watch television. So I think I'm a bad example. And they don't advertise the products I'm interested in. I'm in a funny segment of the market, but if you tailored ads for me, you bet I would use commercials.

Caruso: But how is what we're talking about here—commercials and push-pull and information—how does that subsidize the production of entertainment?

Ellison: Suddenly Mercedes can reach their markets and Hyundai can reach their markets because they know who's watching the TV. But then the privacy issue becomes fascinating. And this is a personal choice, but I'm willing to surrender my privacy to get the right information. We give up tons of our privacy to get certain things. Denise, I will not loan you a dime unless I know everything about your payment history. You want to be private? Okay, but you can't get a credit card. You can't rent an apartment in this town because you have no credit history. You can't do anything without giving up your privacy. The question is how much.

Berg: Now the privacy issue—this social contract that we enter into with finance companies—I believe we've already given that up. There's an intelligent agent called TRW, which knows more about each of us than we would ever want anyone to know—our buying habits, our travel habits, what our net worth is.

Ellison: We have a very knee-jerk reaction to privacy. Some people think privacy is very important. And you can't go any deeper in discussing the issue than that.

Caruso: Oh, that's not true, Larry. That's simply not true.

Toffler: One of the functions of government historically has been to act as an accelerator to certain things that are necessary for the system. If you talk about the enterprise in the early Industrial Age, government did a lot of things which were preconditions of the development of Industrial Capitalism—whether it was providing an education system or whether it was digging canals.

So the same thing is possible here. If there are going to be these big pockets of unemployed and uneducated people, then these pockets can have [negative] macroeconomic consequences for the system.

So the question I would raise is, Is there a way in which that also can be treated as a market? That is, the government says "Yes, we want to make sure that x-population has y, and we'll pay somebody to do that. We'll buy information vouchers to do that."

Porat: Could you explain your information voucher?

Toffler: Well, the back door to the social market, which is far more acceptable to the conservatives than the front door, is vouchers. Vouchers for education, if they're big enough, are a pretty good idea. But you could also have vouchers for housing or even vouchers for socially useful technology and information services. I mean, the GI Bill was a voucher, the best social legislation we had in the last 50 years. Government can play a positive role.

Burstein: Most of the businesspeople you talk to wish the government would get the hell out of their business. But the government isn't going to get out of their business. The government is here to stay. It isn't going to implode before the Digital Revolution comes. So what is the appropriate role for government?

Porat: We have not yet mentioned the Bible. Remember the Bible? There's a place called Babylon. There's a tower in that place, and my one concern, the only concern I have, about the future of what we're all trying to do is that people, left to their natural devices, build a Tower of Babel. Especially businesspeople, who like to bully and do not want a level playing ground. Every good businessman is looking for every unfair advantage to kill the other person gracefully, you know, in the shadows.

[To Ellison.] That's what you probably do every day. That's what all of us do.

Now, this is especially true in a world where the essence of all this new technology is really about communication. The chances that this technology, left to its own devices, will compile into something that is not a Tower of Babel is very low. And the reason is because there are natural forces, competitive capitalistic forces at work, that crack standards. The powerful guy will make his stuff nonstandard, so the less powerful guy will not have even the hind tit to suck on and will die of starvation.

When you're talking about building software, boy is that easy to do! Really easy to do. I see it every day in my own job. So, the question is, if we anticipate a Tower of Babel, which will fracture the spontaneous community that we're fond of and the commercial community that we're so fond of also, how do we keep the Tower of Babel from emerging?

There are two canonical solutions. One is, you say government's job is to make sure the Tower of Babel doesn't happen, so we can at least all speak the same language. This is notoriously unsuccessful. It just leads to dinners in dreary places like Geneva where people come up with standards for how to build the tower, which everyone disobeys anyway behind the shadows as soon as they possibly can.

The other approach is de facto standards, which is sort of the Nike strategy—"Just do it." And the problem with the Nike strategy is that there's always a Reebok to try and mess up your standards. You know, for every Oracle there's a Sybase; for every Microsoft there's a General Magic.

So there's no good solution yet because both canonical solutions are flawed in certain respects.

Rothschild: We cannot know a priori which standard would be best in terms of serviceability, etc. Indeed, there will probably be a multiplicity of standards, depending upon bandwidth and use, that will provide a spectrum of specialized economic alternatives to people.
So it's very much an iterative, trail-and-error process as we move forward and try to figure out what works best in each situation. There's no special body that can dictate in advance what the alternatives should be.

Toffler: It seems to me that with respect to standards you can say everybody in this network must speak Bulgarian—must speak the same language—or you can say, "I don't care what language you speak because we have adapters." It seems to me that's a far better and more flexible response than saying everybody has to speak Bulgarian.

Caruso: Let's segue over to something that was really interesting to me. I spoke at the American Society of Magazine Editors conference last weekend, and we were talking about the Information Age and how it's going to impact newsrooms. And we talked about how, when you think about going into a career in journalism, you think about being Woodward or Bernstein, or being the city editor or something. But the truth is that so much of journalism now has become filtering. You can consider at some point maybe some sort of artificial intelligence is going to allow you to have an intelligent filter. It's not next week or next month. So what you're going to have are information factory workers, people who have to synthesize, pull together, touch a piece of information just long enough to send it to the next place that it has to go. I don't see that as any different from driving a rivet on the car. . . .

Ellison: Denise, do you think a high school student is going to tell me what information I'm going to receive? Do you think a high school graduate's going to basically control what I read and see?

Caruso: Well, I think it depends on the business. I was talking about in my business, which is an information-filtering business.

Ellison: I don't have any intermediaries between me and my information, nor will I allow it. That is a most dangerous notion.

Caruso: I find it very hard to believe that you don't have any intermediary between you and your information.

Ellison: I have people, you know, stopping human beings in front of my office. But anyone can send me electronic mail, and no one reads it but me. I get much more information electronically than I do face-to-face. I remember Corporal Wickham in *Catch 22*. He was the guy who mimeographed orders for the European theater of operations in World War II, and if he didn't like Eisenhower's orders he would change them. He was the most powerful person in the European theater. I just don't think that this high school student is going to get between me and my information.

Saffo: You talk about having no intermediaries, but you actually have more intermediaries than ever. What you've done is eliminated the small cadre of corporate intermediaries so that you can get directly to the outside—but even there, all [information] is still intermediated.

Ellison: Well, if you mean that the only true reality is that which you can take in directly through your senses, then I agree with you. Right now we have incredible intermediators in our life. They're the anchors and bureau chiefs of ABC, NBC, and CBS, who decide what in the world happened, and if it's not on TV it didn't happen. I spoke at the Museum of Radio and Television in New York a while ago. And I was complaining that a hundred thousand people were getting killed in Rwanda. This is the last hundred thousand, not the recent hundred thousand. But no one knows about it because they decided not to cover it.

Still, despite that, I still have many more windows onto the world than I had before. I'm not willing to give that up.

Burstein: Larry's unique in not allowing people to get in the way of his information flow. Most people, even in his position, are not making that choice. For the rest of us, I have a question about the use of intelligent agents and other information-filtering systems— specifically, are the people who are programming these functions knowledgeable enough to understand my needs? I think Larry is saying that no one else is knowledgeable enough about his needs.

Porat: You just asked a question, Are the people who program infor-mation-access systems knowledgeable enough about you to be able to do a good job? It's like asking, Are the people who are providing the bricks and mortar able to know what you as the builder of a house or a shopping mall want?

Completely wrong. In the world we're talking about, our job is to give you the tools to express your own emotions and your own per ceptions, your own sense of reality. It may be flawed, it may be profound, it may be trivial, it may be illegal. But that's not our con-cern. Our job is to propagate tools as widely as possible so people can jump in and navigate, cruise around, and find what they want for themselves. It's up to them. Their values will determine what they do with the access tools that we give them.

The whole concept of intelligent agents that General Magic is working on aims at creating a set of capabilities where people can impose their feelings and their personalities on this incoherent mass of very hostile stuff called the digital domain.

You see, people will run away from anything that damages their self-esteem—and the digital world we're all talking about so fluidly here is like razor blades on most people's self-esteem. Pipes and servers and all that—it makes you feel utterly stupid and inade-quate. Most people hate it. They don't want to touch it. They don't want to go near it, and yet at the same time they'd like to be part of this world of infinite possibility.

So that's a huge disconnect. And the real value added will be finding a way of cushioning people—who are analog creatures and very impulsive and irrational—from the hostility of the digital world that they want to get into.

Ellison: Let me take a contrary view. I don't think people have trouble learning how to drive cars. Driving a car is very difficult, but there's a real value in learning how to drive a car. You get some return on that investment. The reason people don't set those stupid clocks on their VCRs is, who cares? What's the return? People don't learn to use computers because [until now] there hasn't been much return.

But I think people will learn how to use digital technology on the Information Highway because there'll be real value in it. Once we have real services out there, they'll say, "Gee, I'm interested in that. Don't stop now. Tell me more." And people will learn how to push a few buttons, which is much easier than driving a car and much safer, once they can get some return.

Kline: Push a few buttons? You are absolutely *not* talking about to-day's PCs!

Porat: Right. You can drive a car without reading the user manual. What we've got to do here—and let's be kind on ourselves because the PC is only 14 years old—is make our stuff as easy to use. So that the "razor bladeness" of it has been smoothed out and anyone can jump in one these vehicles and just cruise and have a wonderful time going to Larry's servers and getting hold of your content and having a blast.

Remember that burst of liberation we all felt the first time we got into a car and had the personal power to go anywhere? I submit it required three preconditions then, just as the Info Highway requires three now.

Number one, you need a great vehicle. One you can jump into and drive easily. These will be easy-to-use computers, intelligent TVs, personal communicators, and so on. Second, the roads have to be reasonably good. The digital networks we're building have to be pretty easy to navigate around on.

And third and most important, you need an interesting place to go. At the end of the day, the vehicle and the road are merely the means to satisfy the impulse, the liberating impulse to go somewhere. But *where* you want to go is the most important thing.

Burstein: Speaking of roads and vehicles, should we care whether cable companies or telephone companies become the dominant network providers into the home? And should we care whether Intel and computer companies drive the technology onto a box loosely called a PC that becomes the primary Info Highway vehicle of the masses, versus the efforts to drive it into a TV set or set-top box and have that be the main vehicle? Do these questions matter?

Toffler: To me it doesn't matter. I may be mistaken, but I don't give a damn what corporation merges with what other corporation or who provides what network that connects to what device as long as people are not constrained from going where they want to go.

Caruso: But that's exactly why how you snap together the pieces of the network—and who can control the network—is so [important]. Because there are very different paradigms. There are very different ways that different industries look at how you grant access to consumers and to people like publishers and artists and other content providers.

So it matters a lot. What matters is that the network be snapped together so as to allow anyone who wants access to it access to it. And the method of access has to be prescribed just by nature of the fact that we're living in a physical universe.

Saffo: If you think it doesn't matter, just look at your watches—those of you who have analog watches. Clocks run clockwise. They don't run counter clockwise. It matters because of the influence the players have on standards.

Personally, I have to confess that when it comes to the telcos versus the cable companies, I feel a lot like Henry Kissinger did about the Arab-Israeli War when someone asked who he would like to see win. And Kissinger said, "You know, it would be nice if both sides lost." But that said . . .

Caruso: Which is not too far-fetched a scenario in this situation, either.

Ellison: The idea of Bell Atlantic going into programming is as sensible as Union Pacific going into automobile manufacturing just because they move so much of the auto industry's freight around the country.

I mean, we have a hard time doing well in businesses we know a lot about. We just barely do that. For us to go into some other business wouldn't be a good idea to me. Same thing with the phone company.

Berg: In dealing with the regional Bells, the wireless operators, the cable companies, who by nature are carriers—they're channel guys, not programming guys—I've seen how the vocabulary of intellectual property itself is completely alien to these people. They're going to, in essence, have to retrain themselves.

I think the rudest awakening in store for carriers is going to be how they begin to program in a world in which they have not participated in the past. That's true whether that's electronic publishing, entertainment, or information or education.

Ellison: I think the phone companies will win. I mean, there's no doubt. This is a silly question. There are many phone companies that could buy all the cable companies on the planet if they wanted to.

Kline: Yeah, but the phone companies generally have no expertise in developing and marketing entertainment, whereas the bigger cable companies have at least some experience in this area.

Burstein: Okay, let's go around the table and speak to the question of so-called "killer apps." What, in your opinion, might become really significant as a new kind of application and a potentially large market?

Berg: Box office receipts in North America last year were $4.3 billion. Catalog sales in the United States last year? Fifty-eight billion dollars. I think home shopping, video catalogs, is a huge app. The other huge app is personal communications. It is people talking to other people electronically in all forms, whether it's video mail or store-and-forward electronic mail, video conferencing—all the different forms of electronic communication. Those, I think, are the two overwhelming apps.

I think the entertainment networks believe that multi-user games are also going to be a big market. But if you had to pick two, I think home shopping and communication are the overwhelming apps.

Toffler: I think I'm pretty much lined up where you are, Jeff. I think home shopping is going to prove to be a fundamental economic change in the country and indeed even in our trade relationships.

Another big application will be in the area of character morphology, where images are transposed out of the frame and reintroduced with new characters. In other words, I want to see *Gone with the Wind*, but I want to see Whoopi Goldberg play Scarlet O'Hara.

Kline: And for parents, an expanded *Consumer Reports*–type service online that basically does it for you: Which school? Which summer camp? Things like that.

Caruso: I think that movies-on-demand and home shopping will be less the "killer apps" than expected, at least in the way they're being thought about today. And I think that fully switched video telephony would drive this technology way down into a whole lot of homes that wouldn't even consider it at this point.

Saffo: I would second what Denise said. Movies-on-demand is a "killer app" without question but in an utterly unintended way. We already have killer apps out there now—they're applications that prove absolutely lethal to the companies that came up with them.

Maybe this isn't an information revolution. It's a community revolution. The outcome 20 years from now may be a new kind of tele-community. And all the apps will just be an excuse for people connecting with people, mediated by machines. To me that's the fundamental desire fueling this. It's not video games or anything else.

Burstein: Marc, aside from personal communications, do you have any "killer apps?"

Porat: A human being's social experience is focused on interpersonal relationships. And we will continue to grab every technology at our disposal and play with it in our relationships, whether they're formal relationships or love relationships or friendship relationships. Video-on-demand, electronic mail—we'll experiment with all of it to see how it works in the dimension called interpersonal relationship.

To me, a second "killer app" in the future is just allowing people to convert an emotion called "I want"—which is usually incoherent, irrational, impulsive, and incomplete—into something that hops through an interface into a digital environment where something can be done with it. While it's just an emotion it's useless. When it turns into zeros and ones, hey, you can send it out and find what you want.

You want to know how to get to this restaurant? Well, someone has set themselves up a grassroots map company somewhere with a server and says, "Here's [the directions]!" You want to save some money on buying something? Here's some coupons!

So the killer app is, "I want." If you chase that through, it turns today's economics—certainly retail-level economics—on its head.

Burstein: Let's go around the table again. Which company not represented here is doing the most interesting things? And conversely, who do you think is riding for a giant fall?

Saffo: If Marc weren't here I would mention General Magic, but since he's here I actually think the place to look is not companies. It's individuals. It's innovation the way it's always occurred—people with crazy ideas, shoestring budgets, and not a lot of adult supervision trying to make it happen; and for the most part it's not happening inside corporations.

Caruso: I think I would have to second that. The most interesting thing that I've seen is . . . there's a person working on an entertainment project in Los Angeles that, the more I hear about it, the more my mind gets blown. It is completely and fundamentally different from anything that you can think of today in terms of entertainment. My point is that the tools are becoming inexpensive enough now that it's moving out of the priesthood and into the hands of people who don't think of computers in the same way that we have traditionally thought of computers over the last ten years.

Kline: What about Microsoft? Is it heading for a fall?

Caruso: I would never answer that question. That would be a foolish question to answer for a book that's going to come out a year from now.

Kline: Is that your best opinion?

Ellison: I think those who have the most to lose . . . I mean, even monopolies granted by the queen eventually erode. Microsoft and

Intel are very unusual creations of the single worst business mistake in the history of enterprise on earth. I mean, IBM became the first distributor and marketer of the Microsoft-Intel PC, which they mistakenly put their label on. This is what, a 70-billion-dollar error in IBM's accounting?

Now, as we go into the next generation, where these enormously profitable companies are faced with innovating and growing their business beyond where they are, I think that's going to be very difficult—because, again, just to hold on to what they have is going to be difficult.

Caruso: Isn't it difficult for you, too?

Ellison: I'd argue that, first of all, we don't have anywhere near the market share of a Microsoft or Intel. Also, until now, little machines have been riding the microprocessor curve, and PCs are a thousand times faster and a thousand times more cost efficient than when they were first introduced in 1981. But that's not true of large computers.

As we go to the next generation . . . maybe this is our chance. As big machines become incredibly cheap—and I've teased Bill about the fact that the problem with PCs is that they're just too expensive and too difficult to use—huge digital content libraries become more and more important. I think we have a tremendous business opportunity right now in servers.

Saffo: Concerning Microsoft, I should relate Ted Nelson's famous quote about DOS—that all power corrupts, and obsolete power corrupts obsoletely.

Porat: The world I'm looking for in the reasonably near future doesn't have much to do with Microsoft or Intel. I see a world where there are lots and lots of tools where people can take very simple, prepackaged software and set themselves up in business—an electronic merchant of goods and services or entertainment, or as a spontaneous member of an electronic community.

When that begins to happen is when we know that the information is finally beginning to be interesting.

Berg: I think the big winner in part of this will be the owner of rights and catalogs and libraries. One of the peculiar ironies of the entertainment market right now is that you have all of these studios that are financially wrecked, but yet in the sale of rights the companies do well. In other words, movies can perform poorly over a three or four-year period, and that studio can sell it and be worth five billion dollars more than it was two years ago because the library has such significant value. It's an annuity, a renewable source.

Saffo: The notion of repurposing is one of those very slippery ideas that really amounts to nothing more than a high-speed intellectual strip mining of a dying old medium in an attempt to get the new thing up to speed.

Berg: What will you say about home video?

Porat: Paul's not saying strip mining's unprofitable.

Saffo: Yeah, you can make money strip mining, but the place where the old properties have value—as Paramount and *Star Trek* showed —is to create new properties based on the character identification.

Ellison: If all media die, when do books go?

Saffo: No, no . . . That's not what I was saying. Older properties have value without a doubt. But the process of putting them into a new medium takes all the subtleness and sophistication that the very best content people can muster. It's not a question of just moving it across.

Caruso: The point about archives is that you have to look at how much, let's say, of the Paramount film library does anybody care to see again. You know, you can try to assign a value to a big blob of stuff because it happens to be there, but there's probably a pretty narrow percentage of it that actually people would want to buy again in a different medium.

Rothschild: Isn't it fair to assume that, despite the fact that these content libraries are a huge reservoir of value, the cost of actually producing new content has collapsed? And that the rate at which the reservoir of new information grows will dwarf the value of old material?

Berg: The value of past library rights is real tricky because what you find when you look at a profit and loss statement of a major studio is that the largest contributor towards operating income comes from syndication and television rights. So it's not so much that some old movie is going to go out on video. Rather it's that as the global television market expands, where all of a sudden you have new networks being created in South America and Southeast Asia and Europe, the competitive dynamics behind the price-option model on these old shows has doubled and trebled in value. And that's where the hidden value is for the libraries.

Caruso: I completely agree, but that's not new media.

Berg: No, it's not new media, but it's a new avenue of exploitation. I think what you're talking about—where you just transfer an old title onto a new application—you're right. I don't think there's a tremendous value behind that, but I would also say that the spin-off possibilities for existing franchises is significant.

Burstein: Okay, I'd like to ask one final question. What's the biggest *unseen* issue, the biggest undiscussed issue that may explode in our faces in the next few years?

Toffler: I think when anything can be digitally simulated and manipulated, the biggest issue will be just what can you believe and what can you not believe? The big issue will be new technologies that affect credibility, trust, and perception, and their use both commercially and militarily.

Saffo: Do you think that well-known branded information sources, like ABC and CNN and AP news, will have greater credibility then?

Toffler: In the end, no. I don't think so.

Caruso: Not unless they can protect that information.

Toffler: What's going to happen is we're going to see morphs and clones of CNN for sale.

Ellison: What percentage of people didn't believe that the moon landing happened? That it was a simulation? A huge percentage, 20 percent of the people.

Saffo: We're entering an age of myth-information. Not misinformation, but myth-information.

Toffler: We'll have to learn to mistrust them all.

Saffo: I'm somewhat optimistic. I think we'll adapt to that. To me, the big surprise is going to be artificial life. What we're really doing is creating an electronic ecology, an electronic landscape that will be inhabited by humans, by agents, but also by electronic life forms that will increasingly exhibit the qualities we might call intelligent. I'm less worried about figuring out what's real than about determining what's intelligent. Coping with that is going to be the big surprise of the next two decades.

Luria: Something I hear about in psychology circles concerns kids in adolescence who hook up on the computer for interpersonal relationships. It's a great way to [communicate], as you were all describing. But then they hook up with somebody who's disturbed, who is totally pulling that wool over their eyes—a young "woman" who's really a guy, for instance.

It's anonymous, and they're preying on children, who don't have the skills to deal with it. So they're crushed, and psychologically it really has a very bad effect on them. There's no one policing that.

Kline: And it's worse than the usual attempts at deception because it's taking place without at least the real-life ability to read faces and body language.

Porat: For me, I've been worried about EMPS for a while— electromagnetic pulses that could disable the whole technology network. And this is really about a deeper fear that I have. We've abstracted ourselves so much from not only our natural state but our civilized state. What if the systems break down?

It could be from any number of reasons: it could be technical breakdowns; it could be terrorists, or it could simply be, as Al suggests, a breakdown in trust. Once you lift all these technological tools away from us—and by now we're habituated to them—what do we do? How do people live?

It's like those *National Geographic* photos of the women who put rings on their neck and elongate them as a sign of maturity or something. And it turns out that if they then commit adultery or some other violation those rings are removed. Because their necks have completely lost the muscular ability to stay rigid, they suffocate and they die.

So the darkest side of what we're all doing is the possibility of losing our technological crutches. And then you get chaos and all the other manifestations of anarchy.

Saffo: These are all tough issues. I think we should remember that everything's been going to hell for as long as we've had good historic records. But we also know that measured against the greater sweep of things, in general life has gotten steadily better.

So there are sound historical reasons to be short-term pessimists and long-term optimists.

NOTES

INTRODUCTION: THE UTOPIA PARADOX

1. George Gilder, "Washington's Bogeyman," *Forbes ASAP*, 6 June 1994.
2. Louis Rossetto, "Why Wired," *Wired*, premier issue, January 1993.
3. *Ibid*.
4. John Huey, "Waking Up to the New Economy," *Fortune*, 27 June 1994.
5. Thomas A. Stewart, "The Information Age in Charts," *Fortune*, 4 April 1994.
6. Robert Friedel, "The History of the Zipper," *Invention & Technology*, summer 1994.
7. Nathan Rosenberg, "Inventions: Their Unfathomable Future," *New York Times*, 7 August 1994.
8. Robert C. Post, "The Frailties and Beauties of Technological Creativity," interview with John Staudenmaier, *Invention & Technology*, spring 1993.
9. *Ibid*.
10. Karl Marx, *The Poverty of Philosophy* (Chicago: Kerr and Company, 1910).

CHAPTER 1: THE FOG OF WAR

1. John Markoff, "General Magic's Shares Soar on First Day," *New York Times*, 11 February 1995.
2. *Ibid*.
3. From a 1993 study by Robert Half International.
4. Steven Levy, *Insanely Great: The Life and Times of Macintosh, the Computer That Changed Everything* (New York: Viking Press, 1994).
5. John Seabrook, "E-Mail From Bill," *New Yorker*, 10 January 1994.
6. See *Wired* magazine, July 1994, and Appendix A of this book for the full transcript of John Malone's interview.
7. Lewis H. Lapham, "Robber Barons Redux," *Harper's*, January 1994.
8. Jennet Conant, "Hardwired," *Esquire*, June 1993.
9. Ken Auletta, "John Malone: Flying Solo," *New Yorker*, 7 February 1994.
10. Johnnie L. Roberts and Laura Landro, "King of Cable," *Wall Street Journal*, 27 September 1993.
11. Randall Smith and Laura Landro, "Viacom Stock Keeps Falling," *Wall Street Journal*, 22 September 1993.
12. Ron Martinez, "Shape Shifter," *Wired*, April 1995.

CHAPTER 2: ACCIDENTAL GENESIS

1. "The World at War," *Economist*, 4 August 1990.
2. Hearing before the Subcommittee on Telecommunications and Finance, 8 October 1987.

3. Bob Davis, "FCC to Grant Owner of Every Station Another License Free," *Wall Street Journal*, 18 March 1992.

4. "Super Television: The Stakes in High-Definition TV," *Business Week*, 30 January 1989.

5. Bob Davis, "High-Definition TV, Once a Capital Idea, Wanes in Washington," *Wall Street Journal*, 6 June 1990.

6. "Screened Out," *Economist*, 24 September 1994.

CHAPTER 3: THE RABBIT IN THE HAT

1. A version of this story was first told by Bruce Tognazzini, head of the user interface department at Apple Computer, in his book, *Tog on Interface*.

2. Susan Mitchell, "Technophobes and Technophiles," *American Demographics*, February 1994.

3. The Yankee Group, "General Magic: The First True Communicator," *Wireless/Mobile Communications*, February 1994.

4. Forrester Research, Inc., "PDAs: Time Will Tell," October 1994.

5. Betty J. Lyter and Greg L. Mischou, "New Media Directions: Investors' Guide to Personal Communicators," 30 March 1994.

6. Gina Smith, "Dear Bill, It's About Bob," *San Francisco Examiner*, 15 January 1995.

7. Joshua Quittner, "Ho, Ho, Ho, Crash!" *Time*, 9 January 1995.

CHAPTER 4: THE INTERNET RECONSIDERED

1. *HotWired*'s address on the World Wide Web is http://hotwired.com.

2. Featured in the 6 January 1995 edition of *HotWired*.

3. Figures have been updated to reflect survey results as of July 1995.

4. Rosalind Resnick, "As the Internet Moves Beyond Text, Business Opportunities Grow Richer," *Miami Herald*, 19 December 1994.

5. Estimated worldwide totals of the readership of these newsgroups for June 1995 were obtained from the Usenet newsgroup NEWS.LISTS.

6. Robert Rossney, "Usenet Poses New Freedom of Speech Questions," *San Francisco Chronicle*, 12 January 1995.

7. Amy Cortese, "Warding Off the Cyberspace Invaders," *Business Week*, 13 March 1995.

8. Neil Munro, "New Info-War Doctrine Poses Risks, Gains," *Washington Technology*, 22 December 1994.

9. *Ibid*.

10. Donna Hoffman and Thomas Novak, "The Challenges of Electronic Commerce," *Hotwired*, 9 January 1995. (Also available on the Web at http://colette.ogsm.vanderbilt.edu.)

11. Lorraine Sileo, Chris Elwell, and Peter Krasilovsky, "Economics of Online Publishing," a report by SIMBA Information, Inc., March 1995.

12. *Ibid*.

13. Fran Maier, "Cyberspace: Where the Women Aren't," *San Francisco Examiner*, 19 February 1995.

14. David Plotnikoff, "Why Women Are Online Outsiders," *San Jose Mercury News*, 24 July 1994.

15. Sileo, Elwell, and Krasilovsky, *op.cit.*

16. *Ibid.*

17. *Ibid.*

18. Peter H. Lewis, "The Boom for On-Line Services," *New York Times*, 12 July 1994.

19. Gene DeRose, "How Far Can Online Services Go?" *Red Herring*, April-May 1994.

20. Peter Lewis, "Microsoft's Next Move Is On Line," *New York Times*, 13 January 1995.

21. Timothy O'Brien, "BankAmerica, NationsBank Buy H&R Block's Meca Software Unit," *Wall Street Journal*, 11 May 1995.

22. Peter H. Lewis, "U.S. Begins Privatizing Internet's Operations," *New York Times*, 22 October 1994.

CHAPTER 5: MONSTER EXPERIMENT

1. Mark Landler, "Now, Time Warner Is a Phone Company," *Business Week*, 21 November 1994.

2. Ken Auletta, "The Magic Box," *New Yorker*, 11 April 1994.

3. *Interactive Video News*, 8 July 1994.

4. Kevin Goldman, "Industry Receives a Fresh Alarm About the Coming Interactive Age," *Wall Street Journal*, 2 February 1995.

5. John Markoff, "From Apple's Chairman, Potshots at the PC Vision," *New York Times*, 1 December 1994.

6. Janice Maloney, "A Time of Trials," *Technology & Media*, September 1994.

7. *Business Wire*, 22 March 1995.

8. John P. Alexander et al., "Interactive Broadband Networks," *WPTC*, July 1994.

9. Eben Shapiro, "Time Warner's Orlando Test to Start—Finally," *Wall Street Journal*, 7 December 1994.

CHAPTER 6: REACH OUT AND CRUSH SOMEONE

1. The Electronic Frontier Foundation, *Toward a New Public Interest Communications Policy Agenda for the Information Age: A Framework for Discussion*, 1 June 1993.

2. George Gilder, "Washington's Bogeymen," *Forbes ASAP*, 6 June 1994.

3. *Ibid.*

4. John Brooks, *Telephone: The First Hundred Years* (New York: Harper & Row, 1975), pp. 121–137.

5. *Ibid.*

6. Alvin Toffler, *The Adaptive Corporation* (New York: McGraw-Hill, 1985), p. 140.

7. Based on a June 1994 Dean Witter Reynolds estimate of 1994 revenues of $13.6 billion, 87 percent of which are derived from local telephone operations in Pennsylvania, New Jersey, Maryland, Virginia, West Virginia, Delaware, and Washington, D.C.

8. John P. Alexander et al., "Interactive Broadband Networks," *WPTC*, July 1994.

9. *Los Angeles Times*, 28 June 1994.

10. Edmund L. Andrews, "From Sibling Rivalry to Civil War," *New York Times*, 28 November 1993.

11. Jorgen Wouters, "Who Will Pay? You Will!" *Washington Technology*, 15 September 1994.

12. *Washington Telecom Week*, 30 June 1994.

13. Paul C. O'Brien, "The Information Superhighway: How Much Is Hype, How Much Is Real?", a speech delivered before the New England Broadcasters Association, 5 May 1994.

14. Andrews, *op. cit.*

15. Mark Landler, Ronald Grover, and Kathy Robello, "Cable's Bright Picture Fades to Gray," *Business Week*, 30 May 1994.

16. Gilder, *op. cit.*

17. *Ibid.*

18. Landler, Grover, and Robello, *op. cit.*

19. David Bank and Mark Johnson, "Cities Pave Way for Superhighway Problem Solving," *San Jose Mercury News*, 11 July 1994.

20. David Bank and Mike Antonucci, "Pac Bell Plans to Offer Cable TV in South Bay," *San Jose Mercury News*, 5 May 1994.

21. Gilder, *op. cit.*

22. John J. Keller, "They'll Spend Lots but Lots Less Than They Say," *Wall Street Journal*, 18 May 1994.

23. *Ibid.*

24. Kathryn Jones, "Bell Atlantic Joins a Cutting Trend," *New York Times*, 16 August 1994.

25. *Business Wire*, 1 March 1995.

26. Wouters, *op. cit.*

27. Bart Ziegler, Robert D. Hof, and Lois Therrien, "Dial R for Risk," *Business Week*, 1 November 1993.

28. Gilder, *op. cit.*

29. From the Associated Press, 1 August 1994.

30. Edmund L. Andrews, "Phone-Bill Lobbyists Wear Out Welcome," *New York Times*, 20 March 1995.

31. From a panel discussion at the Bear Stearns Media and Communications Conference in New York, 27–28 October 1993.

32. Richard Turner and Bart Ziegler, "Disney to Form Video Venture with Baby Bells," *Wall Street Journal*, 9 August 1994; and from 31 October 1994 joint press release issued by Bell Atlantic, NYNEX, and Pacific Telesis.

33. Turner and Ziegler, *op. cit.*

CHAPTER 7: THE GAMES PEOPLE PLAY

1. Statistics cited by Douglas Glen, formerly of Sega of America, in a speech at the annual Bear Stearns Media and Communications Conference, 27–28 October 1993.

2. "Videogames: Serious Fun," *Fortune*, 27 December 1993.

3. Merrill Goozner, "Nintendo Leads but Others Gain," *San Francisco Examiner*, 19 June 1994.

4. John C. Dvorak, "Game Machines: Trend or Fiasco?", *PC*, 9 November 1993.

5. "Home Video Gaming and Electronic Entertainment Through 1999: An Industry Discussion," *Infotainment World, Inc.*, Vol. 2, April 1994.

6. Dvorak, *op. cit.*

7. Jim Carlton, "3DO Faces Revolt by Game Developers Over Fee to Cut Manufacturers' Losses," *Wall Street Journal*, 24 October, 1994.

8. *Ibid.*

9. Ralph T. King, Jr., "3DO Faces Struggle to Keep Video Player Alive," *Wall Street Journal*, 19 May 1994; and John Markoff, "Video-Game Maker Switching to PC Hardware," *New York Times*, 25 August 1994.

10. Glen, Bear Stearns speech.

11. Laura Evenson, "Video Game Makers Target Girls," *San Francisco Chronicle*, 27 June 1994.

12. Adam Grosser, "Connectivity—The Future of Interactive Electronic Entertainment," *Red Herring*, December 1994.

13. Keith E. Benjamin, "Supremacy in Siliwood," *Red Herring*, December 1994; Mike Langberg, "How PC Is Used at Home: Fun First, Work Fourth," *San Jose Mercury News*, 14 July 1994; and Don Clark, "Multimedia's Hype Hides Virtual Reality: An Industry Shakeout," *Wall Street Journal*, 1 March 1995.

14. Peter Jerram, "CD-ROM Titles," *NewMedia*, June 1994.

15. Reuters, "Market Triples for CD-ROMs," *New York Times*, 23 March 1995.

16. Robert Gelman, "For Multimedia, the Future Is Now," *San Francisco Examiner*, 25 December 1994.

17. Reuters, *op. cit.*

18. Janice Maloney, "The Billion-Dollar CD-ROM Business: An Industry on the Brink—But of What?", *Technology & Media*, 16 May 1994.

19. Don Clark, "CD-ROMs Will Stay Hot, Study Says, but Many Buyers Just Don't Use Them," *Wall Street Journal*, 4 August 1994.

20. Lou Dolinar, "Glitches in 'Lion King' CD-ROM?", *Newsday*, 2 January 1995.

21. Maloney, *op. cit.*

22. Gelman, *op. cit.*

23. Jim Carlton, "CD-ROMS: Buggy, Boring, Slow, Frustrating," *Wall Street Journal*, 6 July 1994.

24. Clark, *op. cit.*

25. Don Clark, "Multimedia's Hype Hides Virtual Reality: An Industry Shakeout," *Wall Street Journal*, 1 March 1995.

26. *Ibid.*

27. Michele Matassa Flores, *Seattle Times*, 23 March 1995.

28. Owen Edwards, "Interview With Rick Smolan," *Forbes*, 5 December 1994.

29. Gelman, *op. cit.*

CHAPTER 8: SMART TV OR A PC IN DRAG?

1. Photo illustration by Lance Jack, accompanying an article by Tom Foremski, "Homes Are Prime PC Frontier," *San Francisco Examiner*, 19 June 1994.

2. John Markoff, "Toys Now, Computers Tomorrow?" *New York Times*, 20 April 1994.

3. "Ed McCracken: An Interview with Eric Nee," *Upside*, August 1994.

4. From an interview in *Red Herring*, May–June 1994.

5. *Ibid.*

6. George Gilder, "Life After Television, Updated," *Forbes ASAP*, 28 February 1994.

7. "When Is a TV Not a TV? When It's a Computer," *Warren Publishing*, 11 July 1994.

8. David Kirkpatrick, "Intel Goes for Broke," *Fortune*, 16 May 1994.

9. Catherine Arnst, Paul M. Eng, Richard Brandt, and Peter Burrows, "The Information Appliance: Will the PC Become the All-Purpose Tool for the Digital Age?", *Business Week*, 22 November 1993.

10. Richard A. Shaffer, *ComputerLetter*, 9 August 1993.

11. Gilder, *op. cit.*

12. Ira Sager and Robert Hof, "If It Computes, It's Gonna Sell," *Business Week*, 9 January 1995.

13. Markoff, *op. cit.*; Shaffer, *op. cit.*; and Michael J. Mandel et al. "The Entertainment Economy," *Business Week*, 14 March 1994.

14. Jeff Pelline, "America's Love Affair with PCs Heating Up," *San Francisco Chronicle*, 6 January 1995; and John Markoff, "Digital Devices Draw Consumers," *New York Times*, 7 January 1995. Statistics cited by each author are slightly different but in general agreement.

15. Bart Ziegler, "Share of Homes with PCs Swells to 31% in Survey," *Wall Street Journal*, 6 February 1995.

16. Gilder, *op. cit.*

17. Jonathan Marshall, "Spectre of Costly Gridlock on the Internet," *San Francisco Chronicle*, 24 August 1994.

18. Julie Pitta, "New Hope for Computer Illiterates," *Forbes*, 16 January 1995.

19. David Churbuck, "Help! My PC Won't Work!" *Forbes*, 13 March 1995.

20. Gilder, *op. cit.*

21. Laura Evenson, "Microsoft Charts Future Course," *San Francisco Chronicle*, 27 April 1994.

22. *Ibid.*

23. Denise Caruso and Janice Maloney, "The Many Arms of Microsoft," *Technology & Media*, July 1994.

24. Brent Schlender, "What Bill Gates Really Wants," *Fortune*, 16 January 1995.

25. Caruso and Maloney, *op. cit.*

26. Laurie Flynn, "Now, Microsoft Wants to Gather Information," *New York Times*, 27 July 1994.

27. James Fallows, "Networking," *Atlantic*, July 1994.

28. Stephen Jacobs, *Wired*, July 1994.

29. Schlender, *op. cit.*

30. Don Clark and Viveca Novak, "Microsoft Competitors Belatedly Seek to Derail Its Settlement with Justice," *Wall Street Journal*, 11 January 1995.

31. *Ibid.*

32. *Ibid.*

33. John Seabrook, "E-Mail From Bill," *New Yorker*, 10 January 1994.

34. *Ibid.*

CHAPTER 9: AN INTERESTING PLACE TO GO

1. *Wired*, January 1995.

2. Charlie Haddad, "Ted Turner Assesses His Investment in Movie Industry," *Atlanta Journal and Constitution*, 1 December 1994.

3. *Ibid.*

4. John Dempsey, "Turner Sees Tough Times for Cable Operators," *Daily Variety*, 30 November 1994.

5. Charlie Haddad, "Telephone, Cable, Computer Firms Fight for Attention," *Atlanta Journal and Constitution*, 2 December 1994.

6. Michael J. Mandel, et al., "The Entertainment Economy," *Business Week*, 14 March 1994; and Kathy Rebello and Paul Eng, "Digital Pioneers: Blazing a Trail on the Interactive Frontier," *Business Week*, 2 May 1994.

7. Gerri Hirshey, "Gambling Nation," *New York Times Magazine*, 17 July 1994.

8. Bart Ziegler, "Interactive Options May Be Unwanted Survey Indicates," *Wall Street Journal*, 5 October 1994.

9. Bart Ziegler, "Surveyed Consumers Want Interactive, But Won't Boost Cable-TV Bills for It," *Wall Street Journal*, 29 November 1994.

10. From a joint study by Malarkey-Taylor Associates (MTA) and Economic and Management Consultants International (EMCI), reported in *Interactive Video News*, 8 July 1994.

11. Jon Van, "Interactive Overload: When It Comes to TV, Most People Just Want to Watch," *Chicago Tribune*, 24 July 1994.

12. Jeffrey A. Trachtenberg, "Interactive Movies: Hot Medium or Smell-O-Vision, Part Three?" *Wall Street Journal*, 16 January 1995.

13. From the press packet of the Luxor Hotel, Las Vegas.

14. Reuter, "Interactive TV Must Go Beyond Entertainment," 30 November 1994.

CHAPTER 10: PRIVATE RICHES, SOCIAL WEALTH

1. David Halberstam, *The Fifties* (New York: Villard Books, 1993).

2. Stephen B. Goddard, *Getting There: The Epic Struggle Between Road and Rail in the American Century* (New York: Basic Books, 1994).

3. "Feeling for the Future," *The Economist*, 12 February 1994.

4. Jared Sandberg, "MCI to Offer Internet Access, Electronic Shopping," *Wall Street Journal*, 27 March 1995.

5. B. Joseph Pine II, Don Peppers, and Martha Rogers, "Do You Want to Keep Your Customers Forever?" *Harvard Business Review*, March-April 1995.

6. Bay Area Computer Currents, 17–31 May 1994.

7. Bill Carter, "Media Giants Jockey for Position as Fight for Networks Heats Up," *New York Times*, 12 September 1994.

8. Lisa Gubernick and Nikhil Hutheesing, "Sillywood," *Forbes*, 9 May 1994.

9. Marc Levinson, "It's Raining Phones," *Newsweek*, 7 November 1994.

10. Cliff Friedman, "New Age Media II," a report by Bear Stearns, December 1994.

11. Paul R. Krugman, "Plugging in to Productivity," *U.S. News and World Report*, 15 February 1993.

12. Thomas A. Stewart, "Your Company's Most Valuable Asset: Intellectual Capital," *Fortune*, 3 October 1994.

13. *Ibid.*

14. Ernest Holsendolph, "BellSouth in a Race Full of Risk and Reward," *Atlanta Journal and Constitution*, 14 October 1994.

15. Elise O'Shaughnessy, "The New Establishment: Power. Influence. Vision," *Vanity Fair*, 1994.

16. Kevin Kelly, *Out of Control: The Rise of Neo-Biological Civilization* (Reading, MA: Addison-Wesley, 1994). Quote excerpted and condensed.

17. O'Shaughnessy, *op. cit.*

18. Kraemer, *op. cit.*

CHAPTER 11: THE GLOBAL CHALLENGE

1. Tim W. Ferguson, "From Street Hawking to Karl Popper," *Wall Street Journal*, 19 July 1994.

2. Marcel Michelson, "Information Highway Risk to Europe's Culture, France Says," Reuters, 9 December 1994.

3. *Ibid.*

4. Toru Maegawa, "Is Japan Left Behind in the Information Revolution?" *Inside/Outside Japan*, November 1994.

5. Edward W. Desmond, "Playing Catch Up in the Cyber Race," *Time*, 6 March 1995.

6. Ken Yamanashi, "Petty Infighting at MPT and MITI Put Japan in Slow Lane," *Tokyo Business*, February 1995.

7. Andrew Pollack, "Japan Pushing Information Software," *New York Times*, 16 January 1995.

8. Izumi Aizu, "Not Problems, Opportunities," interview with Masashi Kojima, *Wired*, December 1994.

9. Takashi Masuko, "Software Firms See Future in Alliances with U.S. Start-Ups," *Nikkei Weekly*, 9 January 1995.

10. Jeffrey E. Garten, speech before the Center on Japanese Economy and Business, Columbia Business School, 2 December 1994.

11. Gail Edmondson, "Wireless Terriers," *Business Week*, 23 May 1994.

12. David P. Hamilton and Steve Glain, "Koreans Move to Grab Memory Chip Market from the Japanese," *Wall Street Journal*, 14 March 1995.

13. Nathaniel C. Nash, "Group of 7 Defines Policies About Telecommunications," *New York Times*, 27 February 1995.

14. Neil Gross, "In the Digital Derby, There's No Inside Lane," *Business Week*, 21st Century Capitalism special issue, 1994.

CHAPTER 12: TO HAVE AND HAVE NOT

1. Suneel Ratan, "A New Divide Between Haves and Have-Nots," *Time*, special issue on cyberspace, spring, 1995.

2. Saul Hansell, "Regulators Seek Lesson in Barings," *New York Times*, 6 March 1995.

3. Steven Rattner, "GOP Ignores Income Inequality," *Wall Street Journal*, 23 May 1995.

4. Thomas A. Stewart, "Welcome to the Revolution," *Fortune*, 13 December 1993.

5. "Greenspan Says Technology May Narrow Income Gap," *Wall Street Journal*, 8 April 1994.

6. *Ibid.*

7. Peter Drucker, "The Age of Social Transformation," *Atlantic Monthly*, November 1994.

8. Data on job eliminations from *Business Week*, 9 May 1994.

9. Steven Levy, "Battle of the Clipper Chip," *New York Times Magazine*, 12 June 1994.

10. Robert B. Reich, "Drowning in the Second Wave," *New York Times*, 2 April 1995.

11. Katharine Graham, keynote speech at the Bear Stearns New Age Media conference, 27 October 1993.

12. Marcia Kaplan, "Illiteracy a Looming Crisis in the Information Age," *San Francisco Examiner*, 7 May 1995.

13. Robert Wright, "The $4 Million Mind," *New Republic*, 23 January 1995.

14. Esther Dyson, "Friend and Foe," *Wired*, August 1995.

15. Summary of WEFA study on the cost of delaying competition in telecommunications, PR Newswire, 1 March 1995.

16. *Ibid.*

ACKNOWLEDGMENTS

All books are journeys, but few as intense as this three-year-long odyssey through fascinating, uncharted, and sometimes totally unexpected lands. A great many people have been there to help us along the way, sharing their thinking, brainstorming with us about the future, explaining technological architectures and business issues we didn't understand, and helping with the immensity of logistical details that accumulate in a project such as this one.

The CEOs, technological visionaries, policy makers, thinkers, and other pressed and harried senior statesmen among the digerati who gave so generously of their time to this project deserve very special thanks. Some people were there for us time and again to help us conceptualize an issue. Others weighed in perhaps only on a single illuminating fact or stunning anecdote. All of these contributions are part of the mosaic of this book.

Among those individuals we would like to recognize in particular are: John Malone, Ray Smith, Reed Hundt, Gerald Levin, Marc Porat (and the rest of his team of general magicians including Bill Atkinson, Andy Hertzfeld, Joanna Hoffman, David Leffler, and Leanne Clement), Larry Ellison, Jeff Berg, Scott Sassa, Paul Saffo, Alvin and Heidi Toffler, Bob Kavner, Akio Morita, Mickey Schulhof, Olaf Olafsson, Esther Dyson, Richard Saul Wurman, Donna Hoffman, Matt Kursh, Denise Caruso, Richard Shaffer, Dale Kutnick, Jim Clark, Michael Rothschild, Jim Chiddix, Tom Feige, Hal Wolf, Tom Morrow, Jaron Lanier, Nat Goldhaber, Lucie Fjeldstad, Bob Carberry, Trip Hawkins, Paul Romer, Matt Miller, Brock Meeks, Elie Noam, Michael Dertouzos, Kay Nishi, Alan Kay, John Perry Barlow, John Sculley, Nicholas Negroponte, Wisse Dekker, Piet Bogels, David Londoner, James Fallows, Scott Kurnit, Don Peppers, Mark Lieberman, Filippo Maria Pandolfi, Dan Burton, Gary Reback, Strauss Zelnick, and Al Gore.

Our thanks, of course, to our editor at Dutton, Matthew Carnicelli, and the many people there who have made this book's timely publication possible, especially Marvin Brown, who was there when we needed him most. This book would not be a book without the profound support of our agent, Perry Knowlton, and of Dave Barbor, Kiyoshi Asano, and many other agents and publishers in Europe and Asia who have helped make this truly a global book.

We developed our ideas and understanding of many of the issues explored in this book through writing articles for *Wired* magazine, and for its electronic cousin, HotWired. Both have been enormously supportive and stimulating to our vision. We would like to extend special thanks to Lou Rossetto, Jane Metcalfe, Kevin Kelly, John Battelle, Chip Bayers, Martha Baer, June Cohen, John Plunkett, Barbara Kuhr, Mark Fraunfelder, and Constance Hale.

As consultants, we have worked with a number of companies in the new media and technology fields to develop their positioning and strategy and to help them find investors and financing. These experiences have been enormously helpful to us in understanding the real-world implications for business and the economy of many of the new technologies and media we have written about. Most especially we wish to thank Chuck Hirsch, Jeff Jani, and Ned Menninger of Dare to Dream, whose extraordinary company we worked with through their lightning development from the idea stage to acquisition by Microsoft.

Appreciation and thanks also to Jane Anderson, Makoto Asano, Graham Boynton, Craig Buck, Hilda Chazanovitz, Ralph Collado, Arne de Keijzer, Tess DeLeon, Akio Etori, Kathy Franco, Jay Grossman, Fred Hills, Paul Jones, Rachel Klayman, Shawn Layden, Jeanette Lerman, Susan Maday, Yoshihiro Mita, Walter Murphy, Joan O'Connor, Kei Sakaguchi, Kelly Scott, and Doug Solomon for their logistical support, ideas, coaching, contacts, and enthusiasm. Deserving of special mention are Michael Silverman, our ace transcriptionist (we'll get better audio recordings next time, Michael, we promise), and Myrna Liebers and Paul White, the best researchers and fact-checkers on the planet (sorry, we don't give out their phone numbers).

A number of companies also provided information services and leading-edge products for us to test. We wish to thank Okidata, Caere, Individual Inc., General Magic, 3DO, Atman Computer, the Learning Company, Rosalind Resnick's Interactive Publishing Alert, DSP Solutions, Hayes Microcomputer Products, and Micro Logic Corporation.

Personal Acknowledgments/Dan Burstein

A deep debt of gratitude is owed to Peter G. Peterson and all my colleagues at The Blackstone Group. Pete has been my ultimate mentor in everything having to do with Wall Street, finance and investment, the inner thinking of CEOs, public policy, and much else. One couldn't ask for more sagacious advice than Pete's in trying to struggle through any complex question or problem. As a firm, The Blackstone Group has been extremely supportive of my long engagement with this project and has provided me with the best possible environment for trying to combine the daunting responsibilities of dual careers as a writer and as an investment banker. Especially with regard to my colleagues at Blackstone, but with all the other people acknowledged in these pages as well, I stress the usual authorial caveat: I thank them for their invaluable advice and support; however, as the views expressed here are entirely those of the authors, readers must hold them harmless from any sins in fact, analysis, or judgment we may have made.

Martin Edelston, president of Boardroom Inc., has given me a powerful platform to expound the views in this book—and ideas on many subjects—in the monthly newsletter *Privileged Information*, and has been an important friend and advisor on the substance of the book as well as the marketing of the ideas herein.

David Kline was the ideal collaborator for this project: friend, partner, pioneer of the wired world, master of narrative; originator of many of the breakthrough ideas and powerful insights into all the issues of technology, business, economics, and society that form the context and the essence of this book; the best possible person with whom to review or argue about the meaning of an interview, a business or technology development, or a news story. This is a thoroughly collaborative book in which we have endeavored to speak with one voice, but readers should know that many of the most compelling ideas are David's, as were many of the most spectacular feats of research and analysis. Ultimately, a book like this takes not just intellect, analysis, and polished prose. At a certain stage, it becomes more the product of sheer guts and endurance then the casual reader might suppose. David is probably the only person on the planet with whom I could have worked so long and arduously on such a constantly changing subject from 3,000 physical miles away and still A) produced a seamless jointly written book and B) remained friends. On to the next project.

Julie O'Connor, my wife, muse, complete partner in life, advisor of first and last resort on all my ideas and decisions, made this book possible in the deepest of ways. Through four books, each seemingly more complicated, ambitious, and life-enveloping than the one before, she has provided all the emotional support and nourishment I could ever need. Her love is the magical force that allows me to rise to all challenges, take on all comers, and ultimately, to succeed. Unbelievably, we have now traveled a quarter century together, from hitch-hiking across the one-lane highways of the Sahara to the virtual highways of cyberspace—and so much in between. To live with Julie is to be reminded every day of life's essential forces that make surface changes in technology seem trivial by comparison: the warmth of heart, the depth of soul, the passion of romance. There is nothing wrong with meeting on the Internet—and more couples certainly will. But I hope they all also have the chance sometime in their lives that I have had to fall in love and be in love, face-to-face, forever.

My son David Burstein was a big part of this book. Researching and writing throughout his key developmental years, I found rich material for my own understanding of the future in his interactions with computers, CD-ROMs, and all kinds of educational and entertainment software. If you want reassurance that the young will immediately adapt to that which the rest of us find complex and challenging, you need to know that children like David have already imagined and understood services like video-on-demand, time-shifting, video conference calling, and home electronic shopping. David's question is not "What are these things?" or "What would be their use?"—but rather "Why don't we have them right now?" It is so obvious to David that you ought to be able to select any Disney movie you want to see, when you want to see it, with the click of a mouse from a window on the Disney channel, that he has moved on to more ambitious projects. As evidence, I offer the following conversation from when he was five:

David: There should be a food phone. Like when you're talking to someone on the phone and they tell you they're hungry, you should be able to send a piece of cheese or a cookie through the phone to the person on the other end.

Dan: Hmmm. I'm not sure whether anyone's working on that yet. Maybe you can do it with nanotechnology. That's the next big thing. Maybe in the future I'll be able to say, "That's my son: David Burstein, inventor of the food phone."

Finally, my parents, Dorothy and Leon Burstein. This is my first book that neither of them will be able to read, but their lives continue to give meaning and inspiration to my own, quite literally, every day.

David Kline/Personal Acknowledgments

This is surely not the place to expound on the twists and turns of one's own life journey—I would not, in any event, risk jinxing what I hope will be a long continuation of that journey by attempting to do so here. But truth in advertising requiries that I point out that without Dan Burstein, I would neither be writing these words nor, indeed, probably have much worth saying at all. It was his influence that helped to translate any insights I may have had into genuinely thoughtful analysis. It was his unflagging confidence in the ultimate value of this joint effort that enabled me to keep hammering away at a subject so obstinately resistant to intelligent commentary as "the future." It was his surefooted balance in the face of my sleep-deprived 3:00 A.M. ravings about PCs and TVs and CD-ROMs that is responsible for much of the wisdom contained in this book. And it was his faith and generosity that inspired me to tap inner resources I truthfully was not sure I had. Dan has been a friend for many years, but I now find myself unable to come up with words that adequately express his importance to me or to this book.

There are many, many other people to whom I also owe a special debt of gratitude. Among these are Ruth Rankin, who kept the bonds from breaking; Marion Rose, who for some reason finds my quirks of personality oddly appealing; Francisco "Cisco" Garcia, who is living proof that nothing is impossible; Janice Prager, whose face and inspired wit can still launch a thousand ships; Charlotte Schmidt-Luders, who blessed me with her advice to quit Hollywood and start using my brains again instead; my brother Larry, who saved my butt (and this book) more times than I care to remember by fixing my !#X/& computer; Ralph Silver, who knows a story when he sees one; Anita Kline, my former wife and the most wonderful partner in parenting one could ever hope for; and Nola Kurtz, my mentor in facing the challenges of the heart ever since I was "a punk" (as she used to call me) in high school. I wish she were still here to be proud of me.

Special mention also is due to two of *Wired*'s best mentioned above: John Battelle, managing editor, who is worth far more than whatever he is being paid, and Martha Baer, a terrific editor whose own gifted prose the world will soon discover in her first novel, *As Francesca*. Thanks also to Mike Godwin of the Electronic Frontier Foundation, who stands for the truth—a rare trait in this overly relativist age—and to Donna Hoffman, whose blazing intelligence meant more to me than is possible to describe here, and whose brilliant efforts with her husband and colleague Tom Novak to make "Internet commerce" into something other than an oxymoron can be seen on the World Wide Web at:

http://www2000.ogsm.vanderbilt.edu.

I might not have completed this book were it not for the love and support of Andrea Werboff, whose rare expertise in the real dynamics of consumer marketing runs the gamut from Kibbles and Bits to bits and bytes. Thanks for your patience, your passion, your prowess, and your pasta.

Finally, I want to tell you about my son, Daniel, whose passionate all-boy intensity for life is matched only by the softness of his heart. During these past three years, he never once complained about a work schedule that sometimes left him with less of my time than we both wished. And during these same three years, I have seen him grow from a kid into a teenager without ever losing his sense of inner balance or his empathy for others. I would like to think that his mother and I are responsible for this, but in truth he has taught me more about faith and devotion, and about courage and perservence in the face of adversity, than I have taught him. I try to emulate him as best I can.

INDEX

The typeface used in this book is a version of Bodoni, based on the fonts cut by the Italian printer Giambattista Bodoni (1740–1813) at the turn of the nineteenth century. Early in his career his work was conventional (though he was always forward-looking and was an admirer of the work of John Baskerville), but as a product of his time, Bodoni believed that type design ought to be rational. Late in life he produced the revolutionary fonts named for him, the first of the so-called "moderns," characterized by high contrast between thin and thick strokes and "unbracketed" (untapered), thin, right-angled serifs. For the first time, type left behind both the chisel and the quill, so *modern* is an appropriate term: Once typography was free of its roots in engraving and calligraphy (and despite the disapproval of the likes of William Morris), an explosion of variation in letter forms started, one that has continued ever since.